BOOKS ON COMPUTER SYSTEMS AND TELECOMMUNICATIONS

Video training courses are available on the subjects of these books in the James Martin ADVANCED TECHNOLOGY LIBRARY from Deltak Inc., East/West Technological Center, 1751 West Diehl Road, Naperville, Ill. 60566 (Tel: 312-369-3000).

Books On Interactive Systems	Books On Distributed Processing	Books On Teleprocessing	Books On Telecommunications
VIDEOTEX	PRINCIPLES OF DISTRIBUTED PROCESSING	INTRODUCTION TO TELEPROCESSING	TELEMATIC SOCIETY
DESIGN OF MAN-COMPUTER DIALOGUES	COMPUTER NETWORKS AND DISTRIBUTED PROCESSING	INTRODUCTION TO COMPUTER NETWORKS	TELECOMMUNICATIONS AND THE COMPUTER (second edition)
PROGRAMMING REAL-TIME COMPUTER SYSTEMS	DESIGN AND STRATEGY FOR DISTRIBUTED PROCESSING	TELEPROCESSING NETWORK ORGANIZATION	COMMUNICATIONS SATELLITE SYSTEMS
DESIGN OF REAL-TIME COMPUTER SYSTEMS	DISTRIBUTED FILE AND DATA-BASE DESIGN	SYSTEMS ANALYSIS FOR DATA TRANSMISSION	FUTURE DEVELOPMENTS IN TELECOMMUNICATIONS (second edition)

VSAM

A James Martin **BOOK**

VSAM

Access Method Services and Programming Techniques

JAMES MARTIN

with

Joe Leben / Jim Arnold

The ARBEN Group, Inc.

PRENTICE-HALL, INC. Englewood Cliffs, New Jersey 07632

Library of Congress Cataloging-in-Publication Data

MARTIN, JAMES (date)
VSAM: access method services and programming techniques.

Includes index.
1. Virtual computer systems. I. Leben, Joe.
II. Arnold, Jim. III. ARBEN Group. IV. Title.
QA76.9.V5M37 1987 005.4'3 86-22567
ISBN 0-13-944174-3

Editorial/production supervision: *Kathryn Gollin Marshak*
Jacket design: *Bruce Kenselaar*
Manufacturing buyer: *S. Gordon Osbourne*

VSAM: Access Method Services and Programming Techniques
James Martin, with Joe Leben and Jim Arnold

Printed in the United States of America

10 9 8 7 6 5 4 3 2 1

ISBN 0-13-944174-3 025

PRENTICE-HALL INTERNATIONAL (UK) LIMITED, *London*
PRENTICE-HALL OF AUSTRALIA PTY. LIMITED, *Sydney*
PRENTICE-HALL CANADA INC., *Toronto*
PRENTICE-HALL HISPANOAMERICANA, S.A., *Mexico*
PRENTICE-HALL OF INDIA PRIVATE LIMITED, *New Delhi*
PRENTICE-HALL OF JAPAN, INC., *Tokyo*
PRENTICE-HALL OF SOUTHEAST ASIA PTE. LTD., *Singapore*
EDITORA PRENTICE-HALL DO BRASIL, LTDA., *Rio de Janeiro*

FOR KATIE
Her own book at last

CONTENTS

PART II ACCESS METHOD SERVICES (AMS)

PREFACE

Data management software has made much progress since the first primitive *Input Output Control Systems* (IOCS) were written for the 14xx and 70xx computing systems that were marketed by IBM in the 1950s and early 1960s. A giant step in the automation of data management came in the mid-1960s with the first release of OS/360 for the early System/360s. With OS/360 and its later incarnations, the first real attempts were made in the IBM world at providing data independence at the application program level. The application programmer no longer needed to be concerned with the physical nature of the I/O devices with which the program would work. A great many highly flexible data management access methods were provided with OS/360 that greatly simplified the job of accessing data files.

VSAM represents an evolutionary step in the improvement of the data management access methods that were initially shipped with OS/360. VSAM was first introduced in the 1970s as part of the OS/VS1 and OS/VS2 operating systems for the early System/370s. VSAM is a general-purpose, high-performance access method that is designed to support a wide range of data processing applications. VSAM provides, under a single umbrella, sequential, indexed, and direct access to data stored on direct access storage devices. It runs under the control of all of IBM's most current operating system versions, including VSE, VS1, MVS, MVS/SP, and MVS/XA, and data files can be transferred easily from one operating system environment to another.

It is important for a number of reasons that data processing technical staff members be well acquainted with VSAM. First, VSAM provides better performance than the older access methods that it was designed to replace, including the *indexed sequential access method* (ISAM), the *basic direct access method* (BDAM), and their VSE equivalents. Second, VSAM is the underlying data management access method that most high-performance database management systems for IBM equipment use for low-level access to data records. In order to optimize the functions of today's database management system software, a thorough understanding of VSAM is required. Third, many of the latest versions of IBM's operating system subsystems support only VSAM for certain types of file access. In many of today's environments, VSAM is no longer an option.

Many of the concepts surrounding VSAM are straightforward and need not be mysterious. However, the VSAM software is highly complex, and its documentation is contained in a large number of IBM reference documents that form a stack well over a foot high. The purpose of this volume is to give as complete a picture of VSAM as is possible without overwhelming the reader with detail. The only prerequisite is an understanding of programming concepts and some familiarity with one or more of the operating system environments that support VSAM. The book is oriented mainly towards application programmers and provides detailed programming examples in COBOL, PL/I, and Assembler Language. However, system programmers and data administrators will also find this book useful; many VSAM facilities that can only be accessed in Assembler Language are examined, and the book can be used by the advanced practitioner as a handy reference guide to the most commonly used features and facilities of VSAM. To be of help to the advanced reader, we also make frequent mention of where more detailed coverage of advanced topics can be found in the IBM reference manuals.

The authors would like to express their appreciation to Michelle Pomorski of The ARBEN Group, Inc. for her help in the editing of this manuscript. We would also like to thank Richard Derer, an independent data processing consultant in the Chicago area, for his assistance in preparing the programming examples in the PL/I chapters.

James Martin
Joe Leben
Jim Arnold

VSAM

PART I VSAM DATA SET ORGANIZATION

1 VSAM DATA SET STRUCTURE

The *Virtual Storage Access Method* (VSAM) provides unique, highly efficient facilities for processing files stored on direct access storage devices. In this chapter, we introduce the various types of VSAM data sets and examine their structures.

Conventional non-VSAM access methods generally support only one type of data set organization. VSAM supports three different data set organizations, each of which has unique features and capabilities. Descriptions of the three types of VSAM data sets follow:

- **KSDS.** With a *key-sequenced data set* (KSDS) a record is identified for access by specifying its *key value*. A key is an imbedded field that is used to uniquely identify a particular record. A KSDS has many similarities to data sets created using the indexed-sequential access method (ISAM).
- **ESDS.** With an *entry-sequenced data set* (ESDS) a record is identified for access by specifying its physical byte location of the record's first byte relative to the beginning of the data set. A KSDS corresponds most closely to data sets created using the basic sequential access method (BSAM) or the queued sequential access method (QSAM).
- **RRDS.** With a *relative record data set* (RRDS) a record is identified for access by specifying its record number relative to the first record in the data set. An RRDS has many features in common with data sets managed by the basic direct access method (BDAM).

VSAM DATA SET STRUCTURE

A VSAM data set is often called a *cluster*. A KSDS cluster consists of two components: an *index* component and a *data* component; an ESDS or an RRDS consists of a data component only. The VSAM KSDS facility provides the widest range of features and capabilities, and KSDS clusters are more widely used than either ESDS or RRDS clusters. Therefore, the bulk of this book focuses on the use of key-sequenced data sets. Differences between KSDS, ESDS, and RRDS clusters, however, are highlighted and explained.

KSDS Structure

As mentioned, a KSDS has both an index component and a data component (see Fig. 1.1). Each record in the data component of a KSDS cluster contains a key field, which is of the same size and is stored in the same relative location in each record; the programmer or system designer chooses the size of the key field and its location within the record. Examples of possible key fields are account number, employee number, and part number. The records in a key-sequenced data set, which can be fixed or variable in length, are maintained in logical sequence according to their key field values. An important characteristic of a key field is that each record stored in the data component of a KSDS cluster must have a *unique* key value. The index component of a KSDS cluster maintains a list of key values with pointers into the data component. VSAM uses the index component of the cluster to locate records stored in the data component. Records in a KSDS can be accessed sequentially, in order by key value, or directly, by supplying the key value of the desired record.

ESDS Structure

An ESDS cluster consists of a data component only, and can contain fixed-length or variable-length records. Records are stored in an ESDS in the order in which they are entered into the data set, thus the term *entry-sequenced*. Each record in an ESDS is referenced by its *relative byte address* (RBA). For example, the ESDS in Fig. 1.2 stores fixed-length 100-byte records. The relative byte address of the first record in the data set is 0, the RBA of the second record is

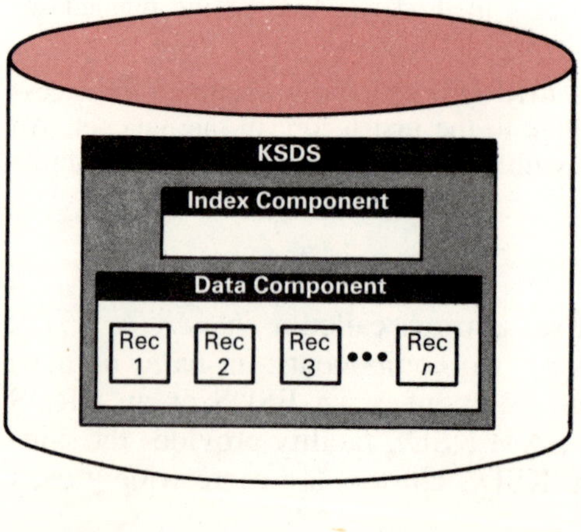

Figure 1.1 KSDS structure.

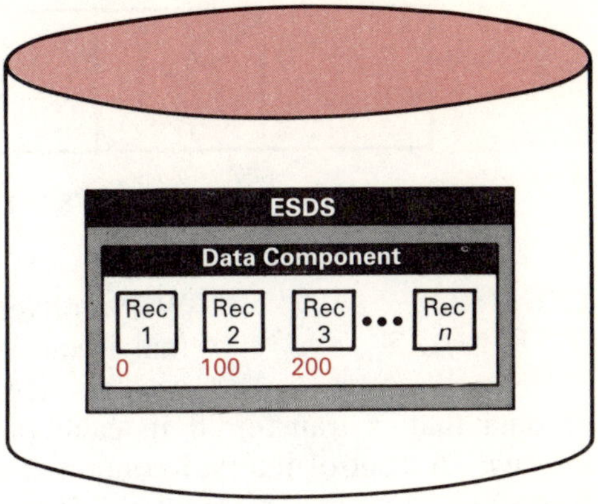

Figure 1.2 ESDS structure.

100, the RBA of the third record is 200, and so on. Records in an ESDS can be accessed sequentially, in order by RBA value, or directly, by supplying the RBA of the desired record.

RRDS Structure

An RRDS cluster consists of a data component alone, which must contain fixed-length records. Each RRDS record can be thought of as being contained in a fixed-length *slot,* and each record is addressed by the relative record number of the slot in which it is stored. In the RRDS shown in Fig. 1.3, the relative record number of the first record in the data set is 0, the relative record number of the second record is 1, and so on. Records in an RRDS can be accessed sequentially, in relative record number order, or directly, by supplying the relative record number of the desired record.

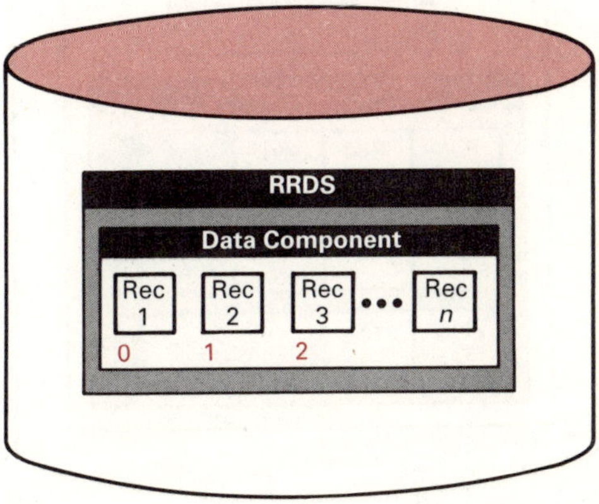

Figure 1.3 RRDS structure.

Figure 1.4 VSAM control interval format.

CONTROL INTERVALS

With conventional access methods, the unit of data that is moved between virtual storage and direct access storage is called a *block*. With VSAM, the unit of data that is transferred in each physical I/O operation is called a *control interval*. A control interval contains *records, control information,* and possibly *free space*. Figure 1.4 shows the logical structure of a control interval.

When a VSAM data set is loaded, control intervals are created and records are written into them as required. With KSDS clusters, the entire control interval is ordinarily not filled when records are initially loaded. Some space is normally left available in the form of free space for KSDS expansion. This is shown in Fig. 1.5. With ESDS clusters, each control interval is filled before records are written into the next control interval in sequence (see Fig. 1.6). With RRDS clusters, control intervals are filled with fixed-length slots, each containing either an active record or a dummy record (see Fig. 1.7). Slots containing dummy records are available for use when new records are added to the data set.

When creating a new KSDS, the programmer or system designer decides

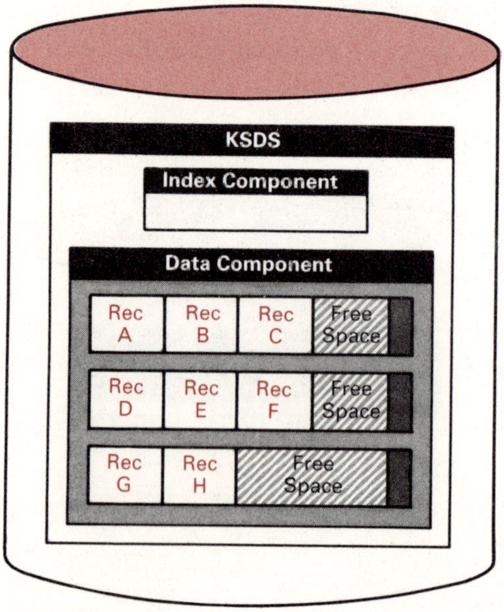

Figure 1.5 KSDS control interval use.

Figure 1.6 ESDS control interval use.

what percentage of each control interval will be set aside as free space. The percentage chosen normally depends on the data set's expected volatility. Too much free space wastes direct access space; too little free space may result in maintenance inefficiencies. It is possible to vary the free space percentage in different parts of the data component of a KSDS cluster. This capability is useful if it is expected that there will be more new records added in some parts of the data set than in others.

In addition to records and possibly free space, each control interval also contains control information. The control information stored in each control interval consists of one or more *record descriptor fields* (RDFs) and a *control interval descriptor field* (CIDF). Each RDF describes the attributes of one or

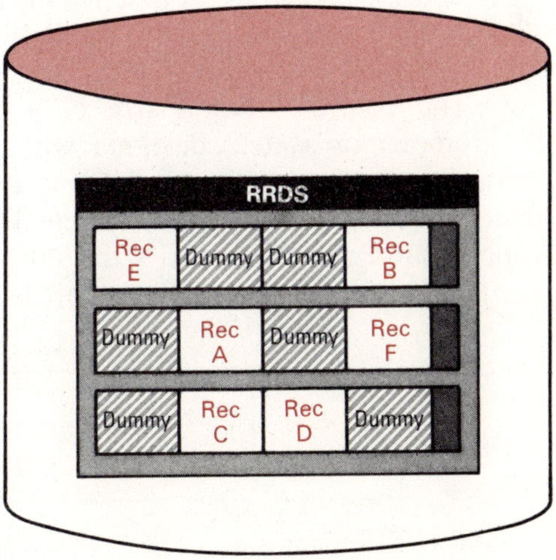

Figure 1.7 RRDS control interval use.

Figure 1.8 Control interval format with fixed-length records.

more records stored in the control interval. The CIDF stores information about the control interval as a whole, including the amount of free space remaining in the control interval. Each control interval has a single CIDF, whether or not it contains free space; the number of RDFs stored in a control interval depends on whether the control interval contains fixed-length records, variable-length records, or a combination of both.

- **Fixed-Length Records.** A control interval that contains fixed-length records has two RDFs, regardless of the number of records stored in the control interval. Fig. 1.8 shows the format of a control interval that contains fixed-length records. The first RDF contains the record length. The second RDF contains the number of records currently stored in the control interval.
- **Variable-Length Records.** A control interval that contains variable-length records has one RDF for each record stored in the control interval; each RDF contains the length of its corresponding record. Figure 1.9 shows the format of a control interval that contains three variable-length records. The RDFs are maintained in reverse order. For example, the first RDF gives the length of the last record in the control interval.
- **Fixed-Length and Variable-Length Records.** A control interval that contains a combination of fixed-length and variable-length records has two RDFs for each set of fixed-length records and one RDF for each variable-length record, as shown in Fig. 1.10. RDF 7 corresponds to record 7 and RDF 6 to record 6. The next two RDFs describe the three fixed-length records 3 through 5. RDF 2 corresponds to record 2 and RDF 1 to record 1.

The control interval size of a VSAM data set can be specified by the programmer or system designer when the data set is created; however, all the control intervals in a given VSAM data set are of the same size. If a control interval size is not specified when the data set is created, VSAM chooses an appropriate control interval size. When calculating an optimum control interval size, VSAM considers the type of device used, the average record length, and

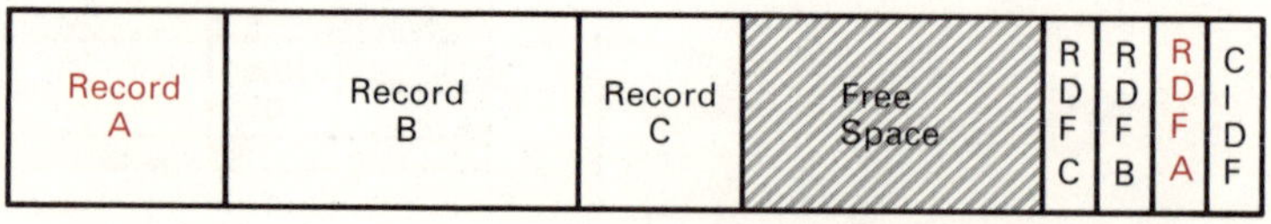

Figure 1.9 Control interval format with variable-length records.

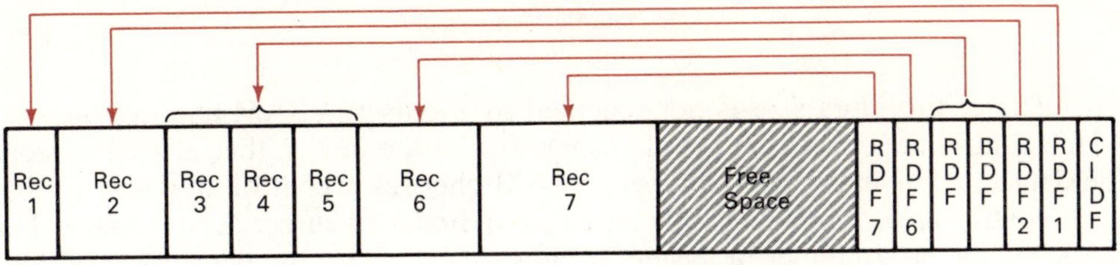

Figure 1.10 Fixed-length and variable-length records.

the amount of virtual storage space available for buffers. Ordinarily, a control interval size is chosen so that several records fit in each control interval. However, there are applications that require unusually large logical records, and in these cases *spanned records* can be used, each of which is stored in as many control intervals as are required.

CONTROL AREAS

Control intervals are grouped together into *control areas*. As a VSAM data set is loaded, control areas are created and control intervals are written into them. With ESDS and RRDS clusters, control areas are filled with control intervals that contain records, as required. With KSDS clusters, some of the control intervals in each control area consist entirely of free space that can be used for data set expansion. Figure 1.11 shows a control area for a KSDS that contains three control intervals. Each of the first two control intervals contains records, free space, and control information. The third control interval contains only free space and control information.

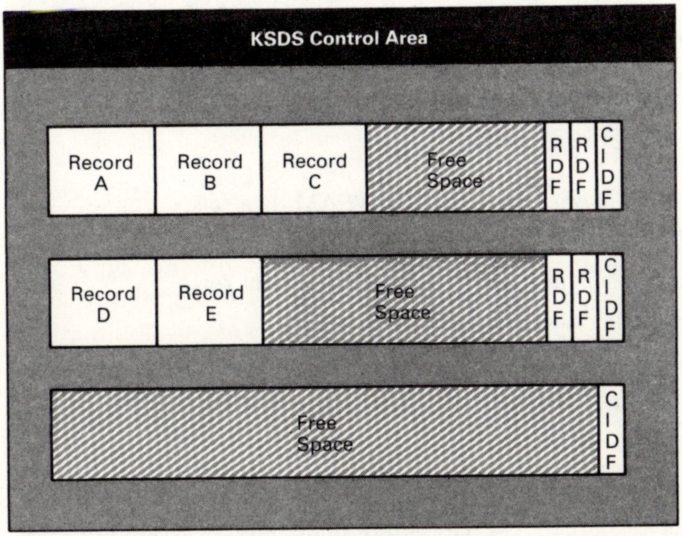

Figure 1.11 KSDS control area.

The control area size is not specified by the user; VSAM chooses the size of the control area based on the characteristics of the device that is used to store the data set. For many device types, VSAM chooses a control area size so that each control area completely fills an entire cylinder of direct access space. For a KSDS, the programmer or system designer can specify the percentage of control intervals within each control area that should be initially set aside as free space. As with the control interval free space determination, the percentage chosen depends on the data set's expected volatility.

CATALOGS

When a conventional non-VSAM data set is created, the user has a choice of whether or not to create an entry in a *catalog* for the data set. The catalog keeps track of the unit and volume on which the data set resides and can be used for later retrieval of the data set. With VSAM data sets, the use of a catalog for keeping track of unit and volume information, as well as other data set attributes, is not optional; all VSAM objects have catalog entries associated with them. Two types of VSAM catalogs are currently in use. In addition, older non-VSAM catalogs can also be used to keep track of non-VSAM data sets. Box 1.1 introduces the three types of catalogs that are used to keep track of information about data sets; all three catalog types can be combined in the same computing system if desired. Additional information about the two VSAM catalog facilities is presented in Chapter 8.

ACCESS METHOD SERVICES

Supplied with VSAM is a general-purpose utility program called *Access Method Services* (AMS). AMS can be used to perform a wide range of functions to support VSAM data sets and their applications. The chapters in Part II of this book examine this powerful utility program in detail. The functions that AMS can be used to perform include:

- Defining, altering, and deleting VSAM data sets.
- Listing and maintaining VSAM catalog entries.
- Loading, copying, and printing VSAM data sets.
- Constructing alternate indexes.
- Recovering from various types of error situations.
- Moving data sets from one operating system to another.

VSAM INDEXES

As we mentioned earlier, a KSDS cluster consists of a data component, which is made up of control intervals containing records, free space, and control information, and an index com-

BOX 1.1 Catalog options

- **OS CVOLs.** OS CVOLs (short for operating system control volumes) are typically used on systems that do not use VSAM. They keep track of unit and volume information only for non-VSAM data sets. Today OS CVOLs are largely obsolete.
- **VSAM Catalogs.** VSAM catalogs are used to keep track of the attributes and locations of VSAM data sets. VSAM catalogs can also be used to maintain unit and volume information for non-VSAM data sets and can be used in place of OS CVOLs for many purposes.
- **Integrated Catalog Facility (ICF) Catalogs.** ICF catalogs provide high-performance replacements for both OS CVOLs and VSAM catalogs. ICF catalogs are used to maintain information about both VSAM and non-VSAM data sets.

All of the functions of OS CVOLs and VSAM catalogs are provided by ICF catalogs; in addition, some additional facilities are provided by ICF catalogs. Most of this book applies equally to VSAM catalogs and to ICF catalogs; however, differences between the two are discussed where necessary. The functions performed by OS CVOLs are beyond the scope of this book.

ponent, which is used to locate records in the data component. The remainder of this chapter focuses on the structure and functions of KSDS indexes.

Figure 1.12 shows how an index relates to the control intervals and control areas that make up the data component of a KSDS. The lowest component of the index is called the *sequence set*. There is one *record* in the sequence set for each control area in the data component of the KSDS. There is one *entry* in a sequence set record for each control interval within that sequence set record's corresponding control area. The records in each control interval are maintained in physical sequence by key value, and the sequence set entries maintain the logical sequence of the control intervals within each control area. Notice that the control intervals in a control area are not necessarily in physical sequence according to the key values of the records contained in them.

The index of a KSDS that contains more than one control area has an *index set* in addition to a sequence set. There is an entry in the index set for each sequence set record. (Thus, there is an index set entry for each control area in the data component of the KSDS.) In many cases, the index set entries are

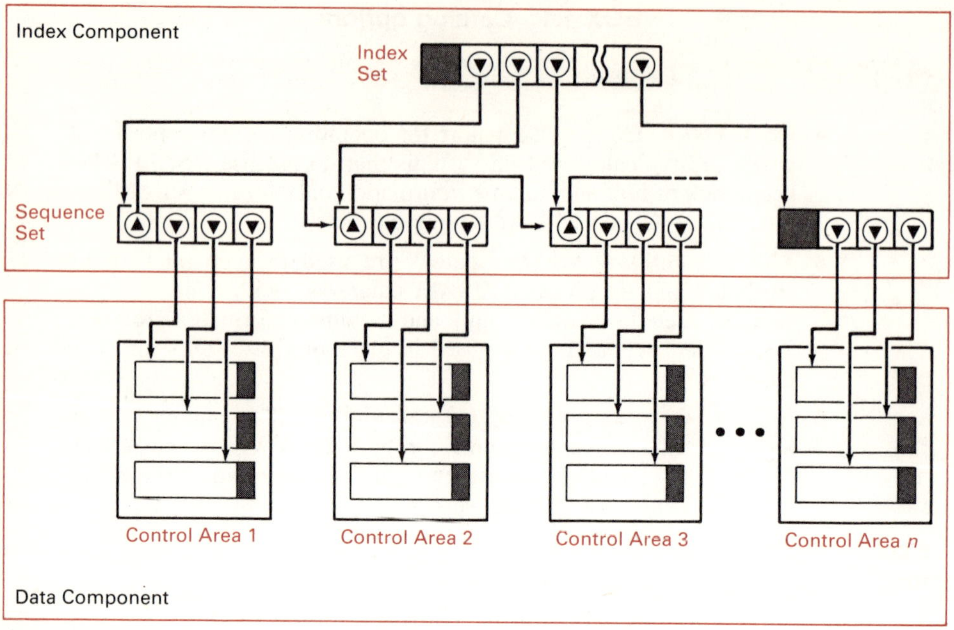

Figure 1.12 KSDS index.

contained in a single record, and the index consists of only the two levels shown in Fig. 1.12. An extremely large KSDS may require multiple index set records to contain all the pointers to sequence set records. In this case, additional levels of index set records are created as required so that the highest level of index set is always contained in a single record. It is important to keep in perspective that KSDS control areas are quite large and may contain thousands of records. A KSDS would have to be very large to require two levels of index set records and would have to contain literally millions of records before three levels of index set records would normally be required.

THE SEQUENCE SET

As mentioned above, each control area in the data set has a corresponding sequence set record, and each sequence set record is stored in a control interval in the index component of the KSDS. Each control interval in the index component of the data set stores a single index record. Figure 1.13 shows the structure of a sequence set record. It consists of four areas, as follows:

- **Header.** The header contains control information for the sequence set record, including a pointer to the next sequence set record.

Figure 1.13 Sequence set record format.

- **Free Space Entries.** A free space entry points to each control interval in the control area that contains only free space.
- **Unused space.** This space is used to expand either the free space entries portion or the index entries portion of the sequence set record.
- **Index Entries.** This portion of the sequence set record contains entries that point to each control interval in the control area that contains records. Each of these sequence set entries contains the key value of the record with the highest key value in the control interval and a pointer to the beginning of that control interval in the control area.

The control area described by the sequence set record in Fig. 1.14 contains three control intervals, one of which consists entirely of free space. The key values

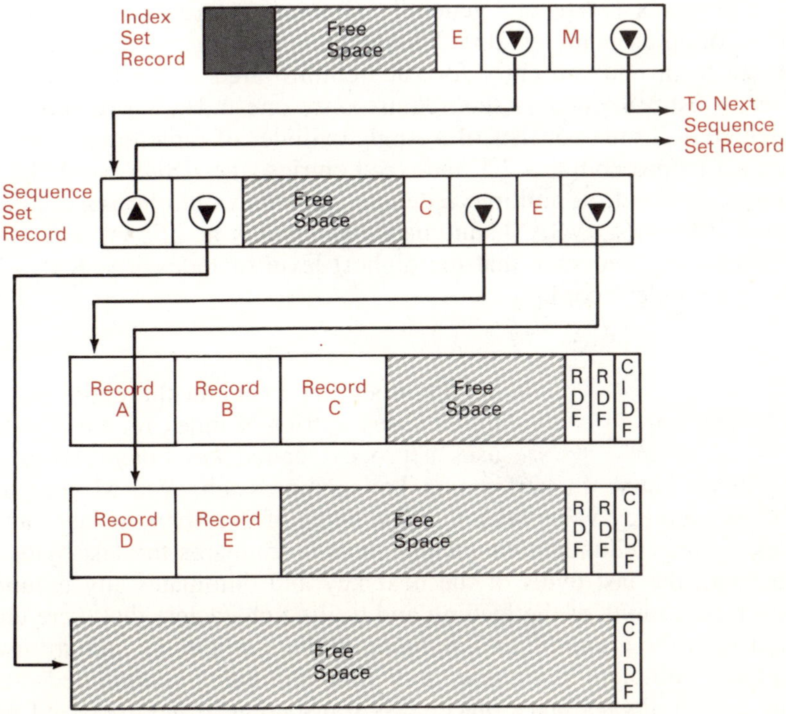

Figure 1.14 KSDS index entries.

of the three records in the first control interval are *A, B,* and *C;* the key values of the two records in the second control interval are *D* and *E*. The header in the sequence set record contains a pointer to the next sequence set record in the sequence set. VSAM uses this lateral pointer when the records of the KSDS are processed sequentially. An entry in the free space portion of the sequence set record contains a pointer to the third control interval, which consists entirely of free space. The first index entry contains the value *C* and a pointer to the location of the first control interval in the control area. The value *C* is the key value of the record with the highest key value in the first control interval. The second index entry contains the value *E* and a pointer to the second control interval.

THE INDEX SET

An index set record contains one entry for each sequence set record (also shown in Fig. 1.14). An index set record has the same format as a sequence set record. Each index entry in an index set record contains a key value and points to a control interval that contains a lower-level index record rather than to a control interval in the data component of the KSDS. In this example, there is only one index set record, so the lateral pointer contains binary zeros. There are no control areas in this data set that contain only free space, so there are no free space entries.

The index set record generally contains a large number of sequence set entries, often as many as 200. VSAM creates as many index set records as are required to provide an entry for each control area in the KSDS. As mentioned earlier, most VSAM data sets require only one index set record. For example, if each control area consists of a single cylinder of direct access space, and each index set record contains 200 index set entries, the KSDS would have to exceed 200 cylinders before multiple index set records would be required. As we have already discussed, VSAM automatically creates additional levels of index set records as required such that the highest level of index in a KSDS always consists of a single record.

KEY COMPRESSION

VSAM does not maintain the entire key of a record in the index entries of index records. Instead, VSAM uses a process called *key compression* as it creates each index entry. In performing key compression, VSAM compares the first bytes of each key value with the first bytes of the previous key value and eliminates leading redundant characters. It also compares the last bytes of each key value with the last bytes of the next key and eliminates any redundant trailing characters. Counts of the leading and trailing characters that were eliminated are stored with the compressed key value in the index entry and are used to reconstruct the complete key value each time the index is searched. Although key compression always takes place, it is transparent to the user, and we will show key values in their entirety in all index examples in this book.

ALTERNATE INDEXES

All KSDS clusters have an index component that is created and maintained automatically by VSAM. This index is often called the *prime index*. In addition to the prime index, the programmer or system designer can create alternate indexes that use fields other than the primary key to index the data component of the KSDS in different ways. An alternate index can also be used to index the records in an ESDS, which does not have a prime index. Chapter 9 discusses the use of alternate indexes with KSDS and ESDS clusters.

BOX 1.2 Index performance options

- **Index Set in Virtual Storage.** The user can make enough buffer space available for index set records so that all index set records can be brought entirely into virtual storage when the KSDS is opened.
- **Index Control Interval Size.** The user can define the index control interval size so that an index control interval completely fills a control area. This minimizes the number of levels that are required in the index set.
- **Index and Data on Separate Volumes.** The index component of the KSDS and the data component can be stored on separate volumes to minimize access mechanism movement in switching back and forth between the index and the data component of the KSDS. This option also allows the index component of the KSDS to be placed on a faster device than the data component.
- **Index Entry Replication.** Index entries can be *replicated*. When the index entries are replicated, they are duplicated as many times as necessary to completely fill up the direct access track on which they are stored. This reduces the rotational delay that occurs in waiting for an index record to come around to the read/write head of the direct access device.
- **Imbedded Sequence Set.** The sequence set records can be *imbedded* in the control areas that make up the data component of the KSDS. When this option is chosen, VSAM puts the sequence set records for each control area on the first track of its corresponding control area and also replicates them around that track. With *imbedded* sequence set records, index entries and their corresponding control intervals are normally located on the same cylinder, thus reducing access mechanism movement.

INDEX PERFORMANCE OPTIONS

VSAM allows the programmer or system designer to choose a number of performance options to increase processing efficiency. Box 1.2 describes the five options available for increasing performance. Many of the performance options require additional virtual storage space to achieve their performance objectives.

2 PROCESSING VSAM DATA SETS

Now that we have examined the major characteristics of VSAM data sets, this chapter discusses the types of processing that application programs can specify for VSAM data sets and shows how VSAM handles the I/O requests that application programs make. We begin with key-sequenced data sets, then discuss entry-sequenced data sets, and conclude by examining relative record data sets.

A major difference between VSAM data sets and non-VSAM data sets is in how new data sets are created. VSAM data sets are created, or *defined,* using a DEFINE command that is processed by the *Access Method Services* (AMS) utility program; non-VSAM data sets are ordinarily created and then optionally cataloged using operating system job management facilities. Also, VSAM data sets are *always* cataloged. Information about the attributes of an individual VSAM data set is stored in the data set's catalog entry, and records can be loaded into a VSAM data set only after its catalog entry has been created and space has been allocated to the data set.

Application programs process VSAM data sets by issuing I/O requests using statements in a high-level language, such as COBOL or PL/I, or by invoking Assembler Language macros. Box 2.1 briefly introduces the types of I/O requests that programs make. Next we will describe in more detail how records are processed in each of the three types of VSAM data sets: KSDS, ESDS, and RRDS clusters. We will begin with key-sequenced data sets.

KSDS PROCESSING

The records in a KSDS can be accessed either sequentially, in ascending or descending sequence by key value, or directly, by supplying the key value of the desired record. A program can combine sequential and direct I/O requests in any desired manner. The following sections examine the types of access that a program has to KSDS records and describe the processing that VSAM performs in executing KSDS I/O requests.

BOX 2.1 VSAM I/O requests

- **Record Retrieval.** A program retrieves a record from a VSAM data set by issuing a READ statement in COBOL or PL/I or a GET macro in Assembler Language. In processing a retrieval request, VSAM reads the entire control interval that contains the record into a virtual storage buffer. VSAM then makes the appropriate record in that control interval available to the application program either by moving the record to a work area or by placing the address of the record in a register.
- **Record Updating.** A program normally updates a record by first retrieving it. The program then makes any desired changes to the retrieved record and issues a REWRITE statement in COBOL or PL/I or a PUT macro in Assembler Language. At an appropriate time, VSAM then writes the entire affected control interval back into its control area on the direct access storage device.
- **Record Deletion.** A program deletes a KSDS or RRDS record by issuing a DELETE statement in COBOL or PL/I or a DELETE macro in Assembler Language. For a KSDS, the space occupied by a deleted record is made part of the free space pool in the control interval. For an RRDS, a deleted record is converted to a dummy record into which another new record can later be placed. An ESDS record can be logically deleted by using a REWRITE or PUT to update the record by storing the hexadecimal value ''FF'' in its first byte.
- **Record Addition.** A program adds a new record to a VSAM data set by issuing a WRITE statement in COBOL or PL/I or a PUT macro in Assembler Language. New KSDS records are placed in logical sequence according to their key values, new ESDS records can be added only to the end of the data set, and new RRDS records replace existing dummy records.

KSDS LOADING

Any type of VSAM data set can be loaded using either the AMS utility program or a user-written application program. KSDS records typically are loaded sequentially by presenting them to the load program (or AMS) in order by key value. VSAM begins by dynamically obtaining a control area from the space allocated to the data set when it was defined. It then begins loading records into control intervals in that control area. VSAM allocates additional control areas, as required, until the data set has been completely loaded. Figure 2.1 shows a completed control area.

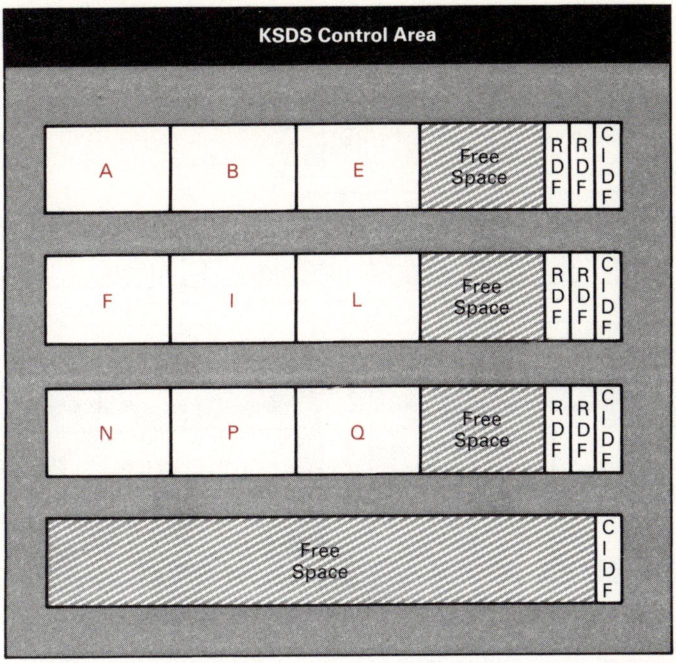

Figure 2.1 KSDS control area.

Since the data set in Fig. 2.1 stores fixed-length records, only two RDFs are needed in each control interval to describe them. A CIDF, which describes the size and location of the free space within the control interval, is also created and formatted for each control interval. In this example, we are assuming the data set was defined so that 25 percent of each control interval initially will contain free space and that 25 percent of the control intervals in each control area initially will consist entirely of free space.

As records are loaded into the KSDS, VSAM automatically creates all required index entries. The sequence set entry for each control interval contains the key value of the record with the highest key value in that control interval and a direct RBA pointer to the beginning of that control interval. All the sequence set entries for each control area are written into one sequence set record, and an index set record is constructed that has an entry for each control area in the data set. For very large data sets, additional levels of index set records are created as required. Figure 2.2 shows the complete index structure for our sample data set, which is contained completely in two control areas. Keep in mind that in actual practice control intervals normally contain many more records and control areas contain many more control intervals than are shown in our simple example.

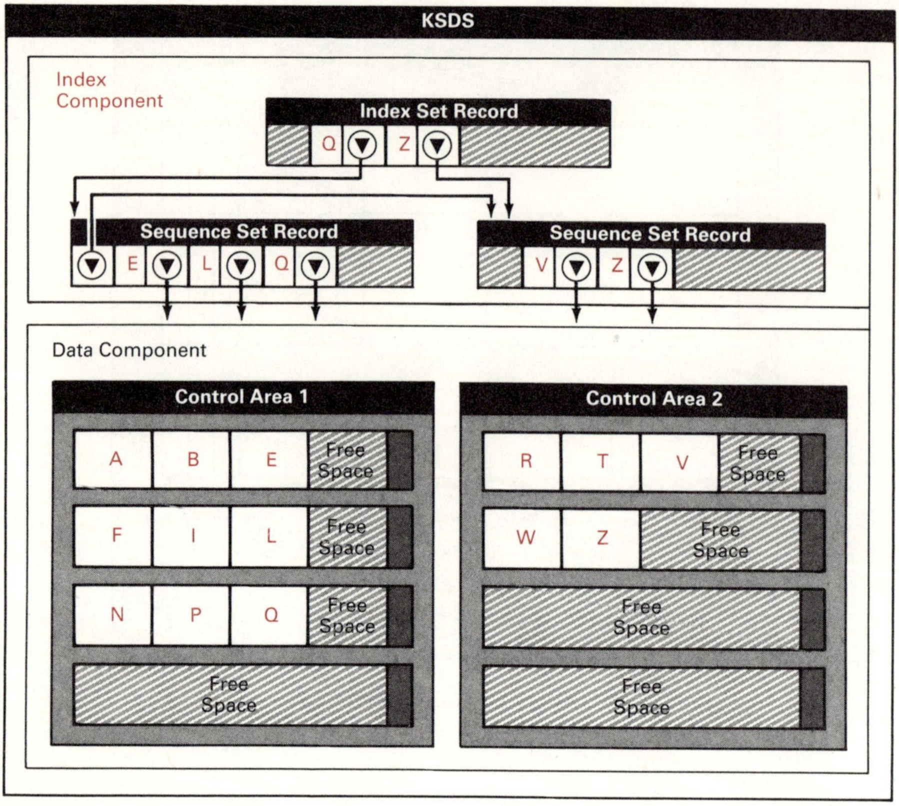

Figure 2.2 Completed KSDS cluster.

KSDS RETRIEVAL

Once a KSDS has been loaded, the records that have been stored in it can be accessed either sequentially or directly. To access the records sequentially, the program issues a series of READ statements or GET macros, and VSAM presents the records to the program in order by key value. The program can request that records be retrieved either in ascending or descending sequence. When retrieving records sequentially, a program can specify the starting point for a series of sequential retrieval requests; sequential retrieval does not have to begin with the record having the lowest key value. VSAM uses the sequence set records in the KSDS index to ensure that records are presented to the application program in key value sequence.

An application program can alternatively retrieve KSDS records directly. In order to perform a direct KSDS retrieval, the application program executes a READ statement or GET macro that passes VSAM the key value of the desired record. VSAM then reads the entire control interval into virtual storage, extracts the requested record, and makes it available to the application program. Figure 2.3 illustrates the processing that VSAM performs in satisfying a direct retrieval request. VSAM begins at the top of the index set and locates the first index entry whose key value is greater than or equal to the key value of the requested record. VSAM then follows the pointer in the index entry down to the sequence set record for the control area that contains the record. It then searches that sequence set record for the first index entry whose key value is greater than or equal to the key value of the record being retrieved. This index entry points to a specific control interval in the data component of the KSDS, and VSAM reads this control interval into virtual storage. It then uses the information in the control interval's RDFs to search sequentially through the records in the control interval to locate the logical record that has the requested key value. This record is then moved to the appropriate work area, or the record's virtual storage address is placed into a register.

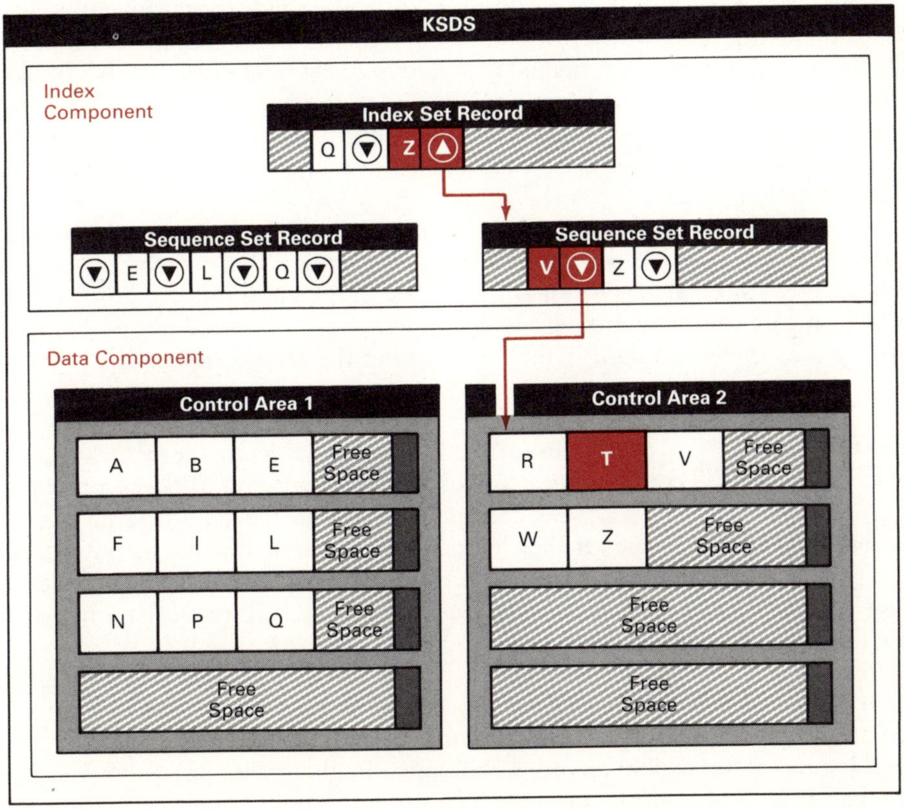

Figure 2.3 KSDS index search.

KSDS UPDATING

As with retrieval, a KSDS can be updated either sequentially or directly. After a KSDS record has been sequentially retrieved, it can be updated if desired by issuing a REWRITE statement or PUT macro. Any field in the record, with the exception of the key field, can be changed in this manner. Records can also be deleted while sequentially processing the data set by issuing ERASE statements or macros. A new record can also be added at any time by building an image of the new record in a work area and then issuing a WRITE statement or PUT macro. This causes VSAM to insert the new record between two existing records. VSAM uses the key value of the record and the sequence set records in the KSDS index to locate the control interval in which the record belongs. It then inserts the record in the proper place.

Direct updates and deletes can also be performed on KSDS records. To update or delete a record directly in an Assembler Language program, the record must first be directly retrieved, indicating in the GET request that the record may later be updated or deleted. In COBOL and PL/I, records can be updated or deleted directly whether or not the record was previously retrieved; the compiler supplies the code to perform the required retrieval. VSAM automatically updates the index after each update or delete request. Records can also be added to the data set directly by issuing a WRITE statement or PUT macro. VSAM searches the index to determine in which control interval the new record logically belongs. VSAM then inserts the record in that control interval and updates the index as required.

If not enough free space is available in the selected control interval to handle a record insertion or a record update operation that increases the size of a record, VSAM creates additional free space in the appropriate control interval. VSAM creates this new free space by performing a *control interval split* and possibly a *control area split* before performing the record insertion.

CONTROL INTERVAL SPLITS

When space is not available in the selected control interval for an update operation, VSAM obtains one of the control intervals in the control area that consists entirely of free space. It then writes into this new control interval approximately half of the records in the control interval to which the new record is being added. VSAM then processes the WRITE or PUT request normally, and adds the new record to the appropriate control interval.

Figure 2.4 shows the structure of one of the control areas of a KSDS into which a new record is being added. In processing a request to add record *K* to the data set, VSAM first performs an index search to locate the control area and control interval in which record *K* belongs. In this case, the record logically belongs in the first control interval. Since there is not enough free space available in that control interval, VSAM performs a control interval split to create more available free space. Figure 2.5 shows what the control area looks like

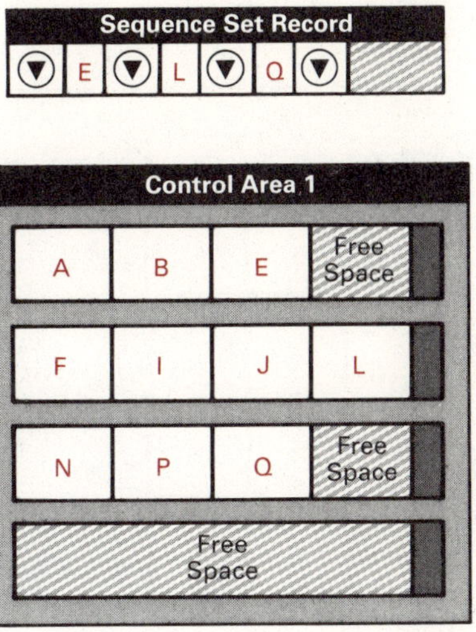

Figure 2.4 Control area contents.

after the control interval split takes place. The fourth control interval, which consisted entirely of free space, now contains approximately half of the records from the first control interval. After the control interval split, VSAM inserts the record in its logical sequence. Notice that the record being added now belongs with the records in the fourth control interval. VSAM inserts the record, updates the control information in the control interval, and then updates all appropriate index entries to reflect the new status of the control area. Figure 2.6 shows the status of the control area and the index records after record *K* has been inserted in its proper place.

Notice that after a control interval split occurs, the records in each control

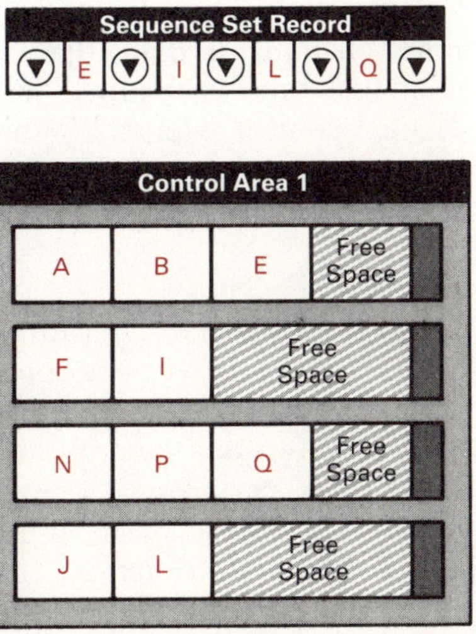

Figure 2.5 Control interval split.

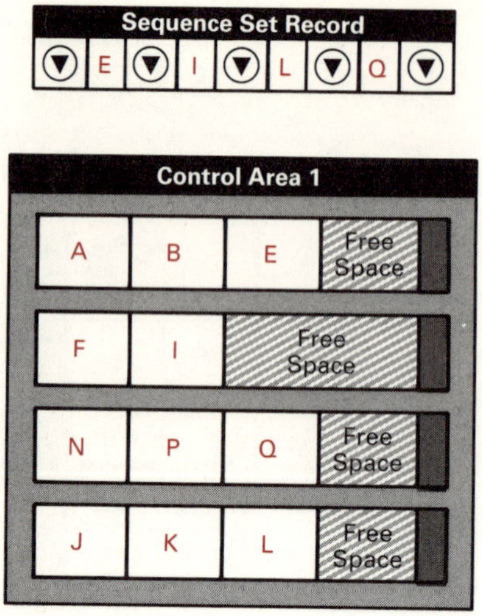

Figure 2.6 New control interval contents.

interval remain in physical sequence; however, the control intervals within the control area may no longer be in order according to the key values of the records they contain. The sequence set record maintains the *logical order* of all the control intervals in a KSDS. When KSDS records are retrieved sequentially, VSAM uses the sequence set records to retrieve the control intervals in the proper logical sequence. The program is not aware of the fact that the logical sequence of records does not necessarily correspond to the physical sequence of control intervals.

A control interval split takes somewhat more processing time than the overflow record chaining techniques used by conventional indexed-sequential access methods. The advantage of the control interval split method over conventional chaining is that after the control interval split has been performed, no additional time is required later to directly retrieve any of the records in the affected control intervals. When chaining techniques are used to add new records, additional processing time is required to walk through the chains in retrieving overflow records.

CONTROL AREA SPLITS

In some cases, there will be no available free space control intervals in the appropriate control area when a control interval split is required. When this occurs, VSAM performs a control area split in order to create new free space control intervals. In performing a control area split, VSAM first creates a new control area from available space. It then writes into the new control area approximately half of the control intervals from the control area into which the new record is being added. VSAM then performs the required control interval split and adds the new record to the appropriate control interval. Figure 2.7 illustrates a control area split.

ESDS PROCESSING

The records in an ESDS can be accessed either sequentially, in the physical order in which they were written into the data set, or directly, by supplying the relative byte address (RBA) of the desired record. A program can combine sequential and direct I/O requests in the same program. The following sections describe the types of access that a program has to ESDS records and the processing that VSAM performs in executing ESDS I/O requests.

ESDS LOADING

Records must be loaded into an ESDS in physical sequence, and VSAM fills each control interval with as many records as will fit. There is no provision for distributed free space in an ESDS, and there is no index. If a record is too large to fit in the remaining space at the end of a control interval, VSAM writes the record into the next control interval in sequence (see Fig. 2.8). Any leftover space at the end of each control interval becomes free space, and is described by the CIDF in the control interval. However, because an ESDS supports only limited updating functions, this free space is not available for later use.

ESDS RETRIEVAL

ESDS records can be retrieved sequentially, using READ statements or GET macros, in the same manner as for KSDS records. VSAM presents the records to the program in the sequence in which they are stored in the data set. It is also possible to access records sequentially in descending order, starting with any record whose RBA is known. An ESDS also provides very efficient direct access to records. However, in order to retrieve an ESDS record directly, its relative byte address must be known and passed to VSAM as part of the retrieval request. Programs use a variety of methods for determining the RBA values of desired records. For example, the RBAs of records that may later need to be retrieved can be recorded as they are loaded into the ESDS and stored in a table or in a cross-reference file. However, if records will later need to be retrieved based on the values of symbolic keys stored in the records themselves, the data set probably should not be organized as an ESDS. KSDS and RRDS clusters are better suited to access based on symbolic keys.

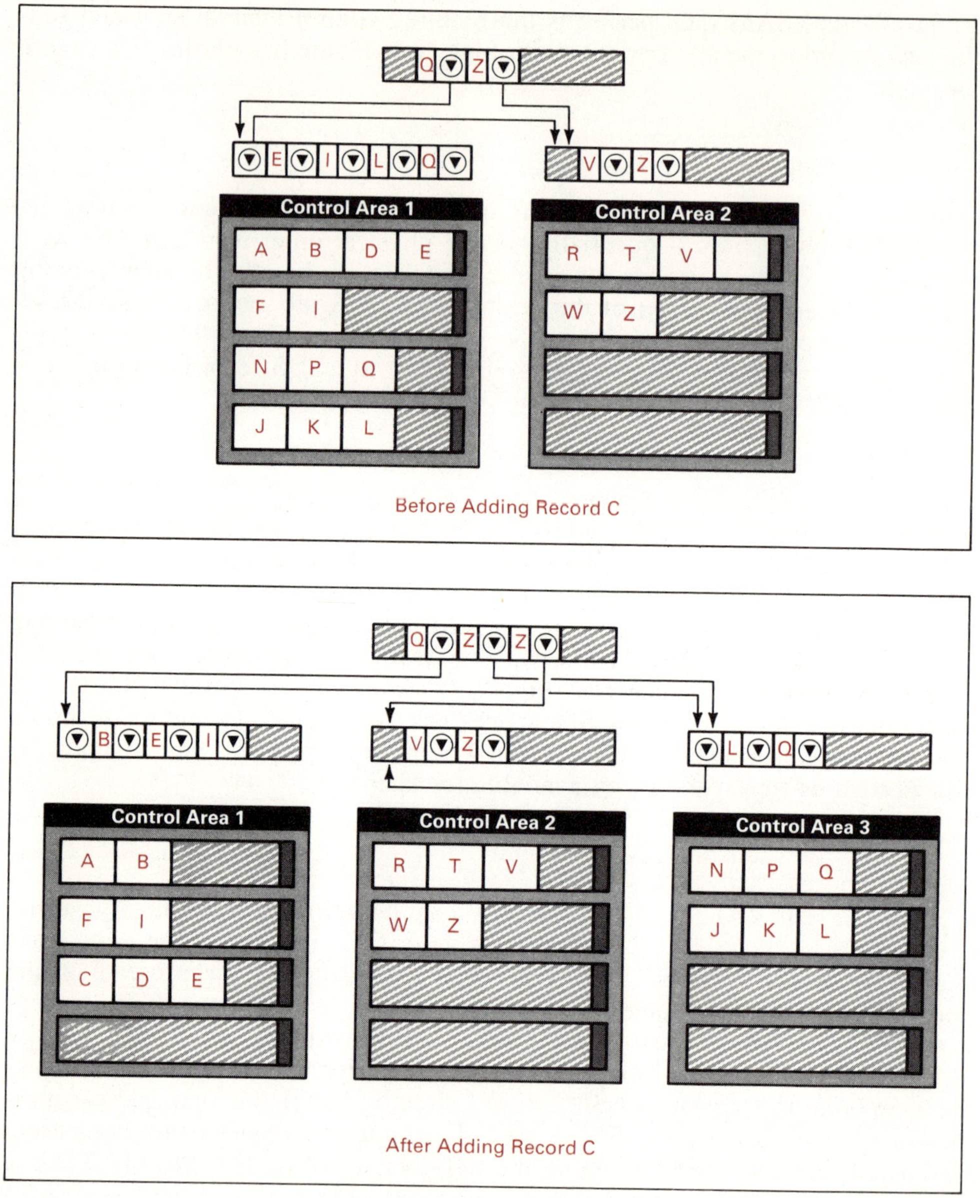

Figure 2.7 Control area split.

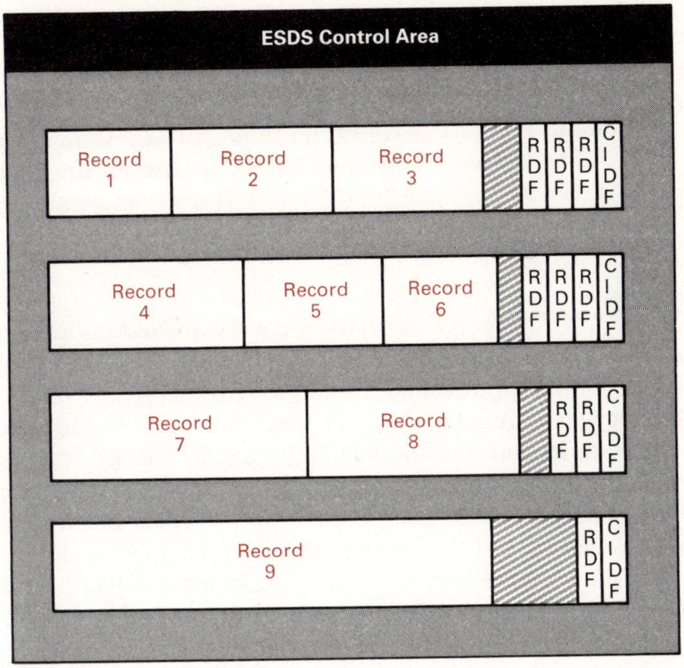

Figure 2.8 ESDS control area.

ESDS UPDATING

ESDS records can be updated while processing the ESDS either sequentially or directly. After an ESDS record has been sequentially retrieved, it can be updated if desired by issuing a REWRITE statement or PUT macro. New records cannot be deleted from an ESDS physically, and ERASE statements or macros are invalid for an ESDS. However an ESDS record can be deleted logically by updating it so the first byte of the record contains the hexadecimal value "FF." Most programs that process ESDS records interpret a record as deleted if it has hexadecimal "FF" in its first byte. New records can be sequentially added only to the end of an ESDS; new records cannot be inserted between two existing records. Direct updates and deletes can also be performed on ESDS records. To update or delete a record directly in Assembler Language, the record must first be directly retrieved indicating an intent to update. In COBOL and PL/I, ESDS records can be updated or deleted directly whether or not the record was previously retrieved.

RRDS PROCESSING

An RRDS is most often used in conjunction with a *randomizing*, or *hashing*, routine that transforms a symbolic key value stored in each record into a relative record number. The records in an RRDS can be accessed either sequentially, in the physical order in which they are stored in the data set, or directly, by supplying the relative record number of the slot that contains the desired record. A program can combine sequential and direct I/O requests in any desired manner. The following sections describe the types of access that a program has to RRDS records and the processing that VSAM performs in executing RRDS I/O requests.

RRDS LOADING

Although it is more common to load an RRDS directly, an RRDS can be loaded either sequentially or directly. A direct RRDS load program views an RRDS as if all of its control intervals initially contain preformatted fixed-length records of the size requested when the data set was defined. (Variable-length records are not allowed for an RRDS.) Records are loaded into the RRDS by using WRITE statements or PUT macros that specify the relative record number of the slot into which the record is to be placed. VSAM locates the desired slot, verifies that the slot does not contain an active record, and then writes the record into that slot.

Figure 2.9 shows the structure of an RRDS after it has been loaded. Just as with an ESDS, any free space that exists at the end of each control interval

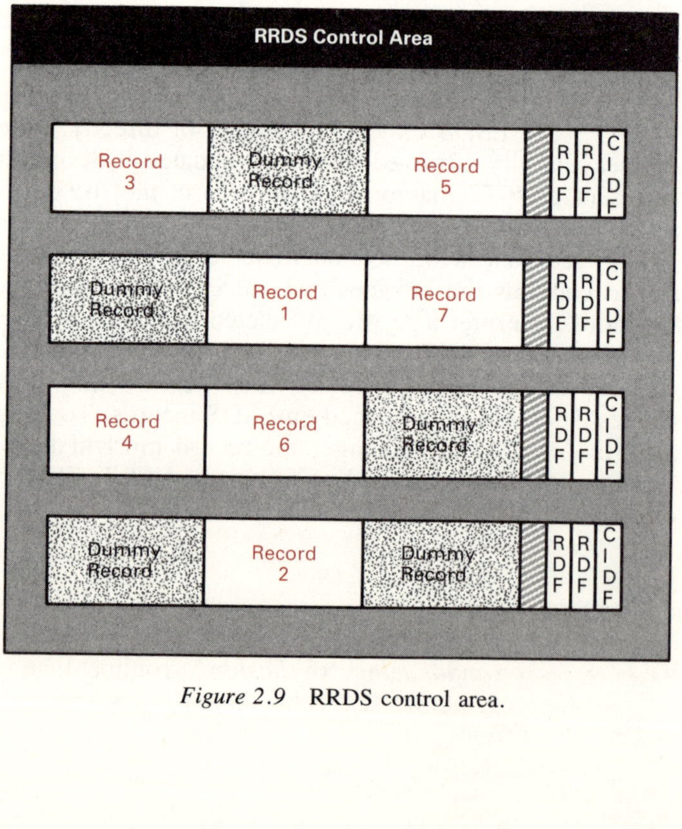

Figure 2.9 RRDS control area.

cannot be reused. However, there may be available space in an RRDS after the load process has been completed. This available space takes the form of dummy records into which no active record has yet been loaded. Generally, more space is allocated to an RRDS than is required to handle the initial loading; the extra space is used both for later expansion and to reduce the number of *synonyms* that occur.

SYNONYMS

In most applications, the load program uses a randomizing routine to transform a symbolic key in the record into a relative record number. The randomizing routine usually causes the records to be scattered at random throughout the data set as the RRDS is loaded. In most applications, situations will occur in which the randomizing routine attempts to place a record into a slot that already contains an active record. Such a record is known as a synonym. An application that uses an RRDS in conjunction with a randomizing routine must make provisions for handling synonyms. Often a chaining technique is used in which the record is written into an available slot and the two records are chained together using a pointer. Randomizing routines and techniques for handling synonyms are discussed in Appendix B.

An RRDS can also be loaded sequentially. However, if the RRDS is used in conjunction with a randomizing routine, it is sometimes difficult to get the records sorted into relative record number sequence. When RRDS records are sequentially loaded, records must be presented to the load program in relative record number sequence, and must include any dummy records that the data set should initially contain.

RRDS RETRIEVAL

Records can be retrieved from an RRDS either sequentially or directly. In processing sequential retrieval requests, VSAM presents the records to the program in order by relative record number. It is important to note that in most cases, relative record number sequence is not the same as the sequence of any symbolic keys that the RRDS records may contain. For this reason, sequential retrieval of RRDS records is generally of limited use. A program retrieves an RRDS record directly by issuing a retrieval request that specifies the relative record number of the desired record. If the program needs to retrieve an RRDS record based on the value of a symbolic key, the program must use some technique for transforming the symbolic key value into a relative record number before issuing the retrieval request. After the retrieval, the program must then verify that the symbolic key value of the retrieved record is correct. If the symbolic key values do not match, the retrieved record is a synonym, and a procedure defined in the program for handling synonyms must be executed.

RRDS UPDATING

RRDS records can be updated while processing the RRDS either sequentially or directly. After an RRDS record has been sequentially retrieved it can be updated if desired by issuing a REWRITE statement or PUT macro. Records can also be deleted while sequentially processing the data set by issuing ERASE statements or macros. VSAM performs the deletion by converting the specified record into a dummy record, which becomes immediately available for later use. New records can be added to an RRDS only by converting a dummy record to an active record. New records cannot be inserted between two existing records. Direct updates, deletes, and record additions can also be performed on RRDS records. To directly update or delete a record in Assembler Language, the record must first be directly retrieved indicating an intent to update. In COBOL and PL/I, ESDS records can be updated or deleted directly whether or not the record was previously retrieved. A new record is added to an RRDS by executing a WRITE statement or PUT macro that specifies the relative record number of the slot into which the new record is to be placed. The WRITE or PUT fails if the slot already contains an active record. This generally indicates a synonym, and the appropriate synonym processing routine is then executed.

CONTROL INTERVAL PROCESSING

In addition to using the techniques discussed above for accessing the logical records in a VSAM data set, Assembler Language techniques can be used to access the control intervals themselves. Control interval access applies to all three types of VSAM data sets and is generally used only by system programmers for special-purpose applications. Control interval access to VSAM objects is beyond the scope of this book. The IBM VSAM reference manuals for your operating system version and catalog facility can be consulted for more information on such advanced VSAM techniques as control interval access.

Now that we have concluded our presentation of VSAM data set organization, the chapters in Part II of the book discuss the Access Method Services utility program that is used to define VSAM data sets and perform various maintenance and utility functions on them.

PART II ACCESS METHOD SERVICES

3 USING ACCESS METHOD SERVICES

In this chapter, we discuss AMS JCL requirements and present the syntax rules that govern the coding of AMS commands. We will use various AMS commands to illustrate AMS concepts. For the most part, the parameters that we include in these examples are self-explanatory; however, keep in mind that it is not our purpose in this chapter to teach the meaning of these parameters. The detailed descriptions of AMS parameters are presented in the chapters that follow. We will begin by looking at a simple AMS job step that issues a DEFINE command that creates a new VSAM KSDS cluster named EMPLOYEE.KSDS on the direct access volume whose serial number is DSK001.

```
//EXAMPLE     JOB   ...
//STEP1       EXEC  PGM=IDCAMS
//SYSPRINT    DD    SYSOUT=A
//SYSIN       DD    *
   DEFINE CLUSTER (NAME        (EMPLOYEE.KSDS)           -
                   VOLUMES     (DSK001)                  -
                   KEYS        (0  4)                    -
                   CYLINDERS   (10 1)                    -
                   RECORDSIZE  (26 26)                   -
                   FREESPACE   (25 25))
```

We will use the above job step to begin analyzing the JCL requirements of AMS and describing the syntax of the commands that control AMS processing.

AMS JCL

Notice in the above example that the JCL is similar to the JCL used by most utility programs. AMS requires a SYSPRINT DD statement to produce a listing. This DD statement generally uses the SYSOUT parameter, but the listing can be directed to any desired sequential output data set. The only other required DD statement is SYSIN, which describes a sequential data set that contains AMS commands. All of our examples use an inline data set for this purpose, but any desired sequential input source can be identified on the SYSIN DD statement. Additional DD statements can be included in an AMS job step, depending on the function being performed. Additional DD statements generally can have any desired name and are referenced by AMS command parameters. For example, the following job step includes a DD statement to allocate the volume on which the new VSAM cluster is being created. The inclusion of this type of DD statement ensures that the required volume is mounted at the time that the DEFINE command is executed.

```
//EXAMPLE     JOB  ...
//STEP1       EXEC PGM=IDCAMS
//SYSPRINT    DD   SYSOUT=A
//VSAMDD      DD   UNIT=3380,VOL=SER=DSK001,DISP=OLD
//SYSIN       DD   *
  DEFINE CLUSTER (NAME        (EMPLOYEE.KSDS)        -
                 VOLUMES      (DSK001)               -
                 FILE         (VSAMDD)               -
                 KEYS         (0  4)                 -
                 CYLINDERS    (10  1)                -
                 RECORDSIZE   (26  26)               -
                 FREESPACE    (25  25))
```

Notice that in the above example, the name coded in the FILE parameter of the DEFINE command matches the name of the DD statement in the JCL. The above type of DD statement is used when a specific volume must be allocated and when no specific data set is identified. This is common when an AMS command describes the data set.

In other cases, the AMS JCL must identify a specific data set rather than the volume as a whole. For example, the following AMS job step issues the PRINT command to display the contents of an existing cluster named EMPLOYEE.KSDS:

```
//PRINT      EXEC  PGM=IDCAMS
//SYSPRINT   DD    SYSOUT=A
//INPUT      DD    DSN=EMPLOYEE.KSDS,DISP=OLD
//SYSIN      DD    *
  PRINT      INFILE (INPUT)
```

The above type of DD statement is used to refer to an already existing VSAM data set that has an entry stored in a VSAM or ICF catalog.

In some cases, an AMS step must refer to a new VSAM data set with a DD statement that includes UNIT and VOLUME information. When UNIT and VOLUME are specified in the JCL, the catalog is not searched, and job management has no way of knowing that the data set is a VSAM data set. When UNIT and VOLUME are specified in the JCL, the AMP-'AMORG' parameter must be included in the JCL to identify the data set as a VSAM data set. The following job step issues the DEFINE and REPRO commands to create a new KSDS cluster and to copy the contents of the EMPLOYEE.KSDS cluster into it:

```
//COPY       EXEC  PGM=IDCAMS
//SYSPRINT   DD    SYSOUT=A
//INPUT      DD    DSN=EMPLOYEE.KSDS,DISP=OLD
//OUTPUT     DD    DSN=EMPLOYEE.BACKUP,DISP=OLD,
//           UNIT=3380,VOL=SER=DSK002,AMP='AMORG'
//SYSIN      DD    *
  DEFINE     CLUSTER                                          -
               (NAME        (EMPLOYEE.BACKUP)                 -
                VOLUMES     (DSK002)                          -
                KEYS        (0  4)                            -
                CYLINDERS   (10 1)                            -
                RECORDSIZE  (26 26)                           -
                FREESPACE   (25 25))

  REPRO      INFILE    (INPUT)                                -
             OUTFILE   (OUTPUT)
```

Box 3.1 summarizes the three types of DD statements discussed; these will handle most of the JCL requirements that are encountered in setting up AMS job steps. The specific AMS examples that are presented in the coming chapters show additional examples of how JCL is used in conjunction with the AMS utility.

AMS COMMAND SYNTAX

The syntax that is used in coding AMS commands is somewhat different (unfortunately) than the syntax that is used with JCL and the syntax that is used with other utility programs. In these days of easy-to-use computers that support free-

BOX 3.1 Volume and data set allocation DD statements

- **Volume Allocation.** Use this type of DD statement to allocate a specific volume:

```
//VSAMDD   DD   UNIT=3380,VOL=SER=DSK001,DISP=OLD
```

- **Cataloged Data Set Allocation.** Use this type of DD statement to allocate an existing VSAM data set using the catalog:

```
//INPUT    DD   DSN=EMPLOYEE.KSDS,DISP=OLD
```

- **Specifying Unit and Volume.** Use this type of DD statement to allocate a data set for which unit and volume information must be specified in the DD statement:

```
//OUTPUT   DD   DSN=EMPLOYEE.KSDS,DISP=OLD,
//              UNIT=3380,VOL=SER=DSK001,AMP='AMORG'
```

BOX 3.2 AMS command coding rules

- **Statement Margins.** The default values for AMS command statement margins are positions 2 and 72.
- **Statement Continuation.** AMS command statements are continued from one record to the next by following the last parameter in a record with a hyphen (-). A value can be continued by immediately following it with a plus sign (+).
- **Comments.** A comment can consist of any text that begins with the /* characters and ends with the */ characters.
- **Blank Lines.** Blank lines can be used at any point before, interspersed with, or after AMS commands.
- **Positional Parameters.** Positional parameters are not optional and must precede all keyword parameters.
- **Keyword Parameters.** Keyword parameters can stand alone or they may have an associated set of values or a subparameter list enclosed in parentheses.
- **Separator Characters.** Parameters, subparameters, and values are separated from one another by spaces, commas, or comments.

form command syntax, AMS syntax seems somewhat arcane. However, the syntax is really quite simple, if somewhat unforgiving. Box 3.2 introduces AMS coding rules.

STATEMENT MARGINS

AMS commands are coded between preset margins, which are set up initially at positions 2 and 72 of the input records for batch jobs. (The default margins can be changed, as discussed in Chapter 7.) This means that AMS ordinarily will interpret anything in positions 2 through 72 (including positions 2 and 72) of the input records as command keywords and parameters. Within the margins, commands are relatively free form. That is, generally spaces can be introduced between keywords and parameters without altering the meaning of the command. The following two equivalent commands show how spaces and extra command lines can be used to help improve the readability of the command:

```
DEFINE CLUSTER (NAME (EMPLOYEE.BACKUP) KEYS (0 4)-
VOLUMES (DSK002) CYLINDERS (10 1) RECORDSIZE (26 26)-
FREESPACE (25 25))
```

```
DEFINE      CLUSTER                                              -
              (NAME          (EMPLOYEE.BACKUP)                   -
               VOLUMES       (DSK002)                            -
               KEYS          (0   4)                             -
               CYLINDERS     (10  1)                             -
               RECORDSIZE    (26  26)                            -
               FREESPACE     (25  25))
```

STATEMENT CONTINUATION

As shown above, AMS commands can be spread out over any desired number of separate lines. When continuing a command from one line to the next, the last parameter (or part of a parameter) on a line must be followed by a hyphen (-) at or before the right margin. The continuation hyphens can be entered anywhere following the final parameter on a line. In the examples in this book, we generally line them up close to the right margin, but this is not a requirement. A specific value within a parameter can also be continued from one line to the next (although this may cause readability problems) by using the plus sign (+). The following example shows how the DSK002 volume serial number from the above example can be split and continued from one line to the next:

```
DEFINE      CLUSTER                                              -
              (NAME          (EMPLOYEE.BACKUP)                   -
               VOLUMES       (DSK+
                              002)                               -
               KEYS          (0   4)                             -
               CYLINDERS     (10  1)                             -
               RECORDSIZE    (26  26)                            -
               FREESPACE     (25  25))
```

COMMENTS AND BLANK LINES

Comments and blank lines can appear at any point either embedded in a command or interspersed between commands. The beginning of a comment is identified by the /* characters and the end of a comment is delimited by the */ characters. The following example illustrates the use of comments and blank lines:

```
/* THE FOLLOWING COMMAND DEFINES EMPLOYEE.BACKUP */

DEFINE      CLUSTER                                              -
              (NAME          (EMPLOYEE.BACKUP)                   -
                                                                 -
               /* VOLUME IS DSK002 */                            -
                                                                 -
               VOLUMES       (DSK002)                            -
               KEYS          (0   4)                             -
               CYLINDERS     (10  1)                             -
               RECORDSIZE    (26  26)                            -
               FREESPACE     (25  25))

/* THE FOLLOWING COMMAND CREATES THE BACKUP COPY */

REPRO          INFILE      (INPUT)                               -
               OUTFILE     (OUTPUT)
```

Notice in the above example that comments and blank lines that are coded before, between, or after AMS commands do not require continuation characters; however, comments and blank lines that are imbedded in a command must include the continuation hyphen.

COMMAND PARAMETERS

AMS parameters are either of the positional or the keyword variety. The following DELETE command includes a positional parameter:

```
DELETE EMPLOYEE.KSDS
```

When an AMS command has one or more positional parameters, they must be coded before any keyword parameters, and they are never optional.

A keyword parameter consists of a keyword, having a specific meaning to AMS, that may or may not have one or more values or subparameters associated with it. Parameter values and subparameters are enclosed in parentheses. The following DELETE command uses a positional parameter to define the name of the object being deleted, a keyword parameter to specify that the object should be deleted whether or not its expiration date has been exceeded, and a keyword parameter with a value enclosed in parentheses to identify the name of the catalog in which the object's catalog entry is stored:

```
DELETE EMPLOYEE.KSDS                                          -
       PURGE                                                  -
       CATALOG (EMPCATLG)
```

SUBPARAMETERS

Some commands, such as DEFINE, have multiple parameters, each of which can have subparameter strings that are sometimes quite long. With these commands, it can sometimes be difficult to make sure that pairs of parentheses are balanced properly. The following DEFINE command uses three major parameters to define a KSDS cluster:

```
DEFINE CLUSTER (NAME        (EMPLOYEE.KSDS.CLUSTER)           -
                KEYS        (0  4)                            -
                RECORDSIZE  (26 26))                          -
                                                              -
       DATA    (NAME        (EMPLOYEE.KSDS.DATA)              -
                VOLUMES     (DSK001)                          -
                CYLINDERS   (10 1)                            -
                FREESPACE   (25 25))                          -
                                                              -
       INDEX   (NAME        (EMPLOYEE.KSDS.INDEX)             -
                VOLUMES     (DSK002)                          -
                CYLINDERS   (1  1)                            -
                FREESPACE   (30 30))
```

The above DEFINE command includes three parameters—CLUSTER, DATA, and INDEX—each of which has several subparameters. Notice that the first character following the keywords CLUSTER, DATA, and INDEX is a left parenthesis, indicating that subparameters follow. Each subparameter of the CLUSTER, DATA, and INDEX parameters is a keyword subparameter that has one or more values associated with it. The subparameter values associated with each subparameter keyword are also enclosed in parentheses. Notice that the final subparameter of each major parameter ends with two parentheses; the first one ends the final subparameter and the second one ends the major parameter.

To make the enclosing parentheses that begin and end a long subparameter string more conspicuous, many installations encourage that they be coded on separate lines. The following DEFINE command is equivalent to the one above:

```
DEFINE CLUSTER (                                                  -
                NAME        (EMPLOYEE.KSDS.CLUSTER)               -
                KEYS        (0  4)                                -
                RECORDSIZE  (26 26)                               -
               )                                                  -
                                                                  -
        DATA   (                                                  -
                NAME        (EMPLOYEE.KSDS.DATA)                  -
                VOLUMES     (DSK001)                              -
                CYLINDERS   (10 1)                                -
                FREESPACE   (25 25)                               -
               )                                                  -
                                                                  -
        INDEX  (                                                  -
                NAME        (EMPLOYEE.KSDS.INDEX)                 -
                VOLUMES     (DSK002)                              -
                CYLINDERS   (1  1)                                -
                FREESPACE   (30 30)                               -
               )
```

Parameter and subparameter values normally are separated from one another by any number of spaces. However, a comma or a comment can be used alternatively as a separator if desired. For example, the following command is equivalent to the two previous ones:

```
DEFINE CLUSTER (NAME        (EMPLOYEE.KSDS.CLUSTER)               -
                KEYS        (0,4)                                 -
                RECORDSIZE  (26,26))                              -
                                                                  -
        DATA   (NAME        (EMPLOYEE.KSDS.DATA)                  -
                VOLUMES     (DSK001)                              -
                CYLINDERS   (10,1)                                -
                FREESPACE   (25,25))                              -
                                                                  -
        INDEX  (NAME        (EMPLOYEE.KSDS.INDEX)                 -
                VOLUMES     (DSK002)                              -
                CYLINDERS   (1,1)                                 -
                FREESPACE   (30/*30% FREE SPACE*/30))
```

Also, a parenthesis itself counts as a separate character, so blanks need not precede or follow parentheses, as in the following example:

```
DEFINE  CLUSTER(NAME(EMPLOYEE.KSDS.CLUSTER)KEYS(0 4)          -
          RECORDSIZE(26 26))                                  -
        DATA(NAME(EMPLOYEE.KSDS.DATA)VOLUMES(DSK001)          -
          CYLINDERS(10 1)FREESPACE (25 25))                   -
        INDEX(NAME(EMPLOYEE.KSDS.INDEX)VOLUMES(DSK002)        -
          CYLINDERS (1 1)FREESPACE (30 30))
```

SYNTAX DIAGRAMS

This book presents many syntax diagrams that are adapted from the information found in the various IBM AMS reference manuals. Box 3.3 shows an example of the syntax diagram for the DEFINE command, which we discuss in detail in Chapter 4. Box 3.4 summarizes the conventions that are used in the parameter syntax diagrams that are included in this book.

BOX 3.3 DEFINE CLUSTER syntax chart

```
DEFINE  CLUSTER
          (NAME(entryname)
            {CYLINDERS(primary[ secondary])|
              RECORDS(primary[ secondary])|
              TRACKS(primary[ secondary])}
           VOLUMES(volser[ volser...])

            [ATTEMPTS(number|2)]
            [AUTHORIZATION(entrypoint[ string])]
            [BUFFERSPACE(size)]
            [CODE(code)]
            [CONTROLINTERVALSIZE(size)]
            [CONTROLPW(password)]
            [DESTAGEWAIT|NODESTAGEWAIT]
            [ERASE|NOERASE]
            [EXCEPTIONEXIT(entrypoint)]
            [FILE(ddname)]
            [FREESPACE(CI-percent[ CA-percent]|0 0)]
            [IMBED|NOIMBED]
            [INDEXED|NONINDEXED|NUMBERED]
            [KEYRANGES((lowkey highkey)[ (lowkey highkey)...])]
            [KEYS(length offset|64 0)]
            [MASTERPW(password)]
            [MODEL(entryname[/password][ catname[/password]])]
            [ORDERED|UNORDERED]
            [OWNER(ownerid)]
            [READPW(password)]
            [RECORDSIZE(average maximum)]
            [REPLICATE|NOREPLICATE]
            [REUSE|NOREUSE]
            [SHAREOPTIONS(crossregion[ crosssystem]|1 3)]
            [SPANNED|NONSPANNED]
            [SPEED|RECOVERY]
```

BOX 3.3 *(Continued)*

```
[STAGE|BIND|CYLINDERFAULT]
[TO(date)|FOR(days)]
[UPDATEPW|password)]
[WRITECHECK|NOWRITECHECK])
```

Optional parameter for VSAM catalogs only

```
[UNIQUE|SUBALLOCATION]
```

Optional parameter for ICF catalogs only

```
[RECATALOG|NORECATALOG]
```

BOX 3.4 AMS command syntax diagrams

- **Abbreviations.** Abbreviations for commands are indicated by boldface type that is somewhat larger than the type used for characters in a keyword that need not be entered.
- **Optional Parameters.** Parameters or subparameters that are optional are enclosed by square brackets ([]).
- **Choices.** Two mutually exclusive alternatives are separated by a vertical line (¦). A list of choices enclosed in braces ({}) indicates that one of the items *must* be coded; a list of choices enclosed in square brackets ([]) indicates all of the choices are optional.
- **Values.** Values that are supplied by the user are represented by words in lowercase that are also underlined; the parameter description indicates what type of value can be substituted.
- **Defaults.** Default values are printed in uppercase and are underlined.
- **Multiple Entries.** An elipsis (. . .) indicates that the preceding entry can be repeated as many times as desired. The parameter description indicates the maximum number of entries that can be included.

4 DEFINING VSAM CLUSTERS

The AMS DEFINE command can be used to create a number of different types of VSAM objects, including clusters, alternate indexes, and user catalogs. In this chapter, we discuss the use of the DEFINE command in creating VSAM clusters. The DEFINE command has a great many parameters and subparameters that can be used to define the attributes of a VSAM data set. We begin this chapter by looking at the general format of the DEFINE CLUSTER command. We then describe the most commonly used DEFINE CLUSTER subparameters.

THE DEFINE CLUSTER COMMAND

In order to create a new VSAM data set, an AMS job step is run that issues the DEFINE CLUSTER command. The syntax of the DEFINE CLUSTER command and descriptions of its major parameters are shown in Box 4.1. (The syntax of each AMS command is described in a similar box as each new command is introduced. For ease of reference, these command syntax descriptions are collected and repeated in Appendix E.) As shown in Box 4.1, up to four main parameters can be included when defining a cluster; each major parameter can include a subparameter list enclosed in parentheses. As with all AMS commands, a DEFINE command can occupy as many lines as required. In most cases, subparameters are coded following the CLUSTER parameter to define attributes for the data set as a whole. In defining a KSDS, the DATA and INDEX parameters can also be coded with subparameters that define different attributes for the data and index components of the KSDS. The DATA and INDEX parameters are not used when defining an ESDS or an RRDS, since these types of clusters do not have index components. The CATALOG parameter is optional for all VSAM data set types and can be used to supply the name, and optionally the password, of a user catalog into which VSAM should place the catalog entry for the cluster being defined. User catalogs are discussed in Chapter 8.

BOX 4.1 The DEFINE CLUSTER command

```
DEFINE   CLUSTER  (subparameter  [subparameter] ... [subparameter])
         [DATA    (subparameter  [subparameter] ... [subparameter])]
         [INDEX   (subparameter  [subparameter] ... [subparameter])]
         [CATALOG (catname[/password])]
```

CLUSTER The subparameters included in the required CLUSTER (CL) subparameter list assign attributes to the cluster as a whole.

DATA The subparameters included in the optional DATA subparameter list assign attributes to the data component of the cluster. (KSDS clusters only.)

INDEX The subparamcters included in the optional INDEX subparameter list assign attributes to the index component of the cluster. (KSDS clusters only.)

CATALOG The optional CATALOG (CAT) parameter specifies the name and optional password of the catalog into which the catalog entries associated with the cluster are to be placed.

Box 4.2 lists and gives brief descriptions of the various subparameters that can be coded following the CLUSTER keyword in a DEFINE command. After we discuss the most commonly used DEFINE CLUSTER subparameters, we will see how to use the DATA and INDEX parameters to assign different attributes to the data and index components of a KSDS.

Notice that the NAME, space allocation, and VOLUMES (VOL) subparameters are not enclosed in square brackets, indicating that they are required subparameters for DEFINE CLUSTER. (However, even the VOLUMES and space allocation subparameters are optional when the MODEL subparameter is used to copy attributes from some other catalog entry.) The three space allocation subparameters—CYLINDERS (CYL), RECORDS (REC), and TRACK (TRK)—are enclosed in braces, and so we must select one of these three options in allocating space. All the remaining CLUSTER subparameters are enclosed in square brackets, indicating that they are all optional; we can choose any of these to supply additional information about the data set.

DEFINING A KSDS

The following simple AMS step executes a DEFINE command that creates a KSDS cluster named EMPLOYEE.KSDS on the volume whose serial number is DSK001:

```
DEFINE CLUSTER                                                    -
        (NAME          (EMPLOYEE.KSDS)                            -
         VOLUMES       (DSK001)                                   -
         RECORDSIZE    (26 26)                                    -
         CYLINDERS     (5  1)                                     -
         FREESPACE     (25 30)                                    -
         KEYS          (0  4)                                     -
         INDEXED)
```

We will next discuss the most commonly used DEFINE CLUSTER subparameters.

NAMING THE CLUSTER

NAME is used to assign a unique name to the cluster being defined. The following NAME subparameter assigns the name EMPLOYEE.KSDS to a new cluster.

```
NAME (EMPLOYEE.KSDS)
```

Although any standard 1- to 44-character name can be assigned in place of entryname, it is important to follow current installation standards when naming a data set. This is to avoid selecting a name that may already have been assigned to an existing cluster.

CHOOSING A VOLUME

VOLUME (VOL) is used to specify one or more volume serial numbers to identify the volumes on which VSAM can assign space for the cluster. If a conventional VSAM catalog is being used, and the UNIQUE subparameter is not included, the specified volume must already contain one or more VSAM data spaces. If an ICF catalog is being used, any volume can be used; VSAM data spaces are not used with ICF catalogs. The following example lists the serial numbers of two volumes on which VSAM can assign space to the cluster.

```
VOLUMES (DSK001 DSK002)
```

REQUESTING SPACE

One of the three available space allocation subparameters must be coded to indicate the size of the new cluster. The following subparameters illustrate the three space allocation options:

- **CYL (5 1)** This example uses CYLINDERS to request a primary allocation of 5 cylinders and a secondary allocation of 1 cylinder.
- **TRK (80 20)** This example uses TRACKS to request an initial allocation of 80 tracks and a secondary allocation of 20 tracks.

BOX 4.2 DEFINE CLUSTER subparameters

```
DEFINE  CLUSTER
          (NAME(entryname)
            {CYLINDERS(primary[ secondary])|
              RECORDS(primary[ secondary])|
              TRACKS(primary[ secondary])}
            VOLUMES(volser[ volser...])

            [ATTEMPTS(number|2)]
            [AUTHORIZATION(entrypoint[ string])]
            [BUFFERSPACE(size)]
            [CODE(code)]
            [CONTROLINTERVALSIZE(size)]
            [CONTROLPW(password)]
            [DESTAGEWAIT|NODESTAGEWAIT]
            [ERASE|NOERASE]
            [EXCEPTIONEXIT(entrypoint)]
            [FILE(ddname)]
            [FREESPACE(CI-percent[ CA-percent]|0 0)]
            [IMBED|NOIMBED]
            [INDEXED|NONINDEXED|NUMBERED]
            [KEYRANGES((lowkey highkey)[ (lowkey highkey)...])]
            [KEYS(length offset|64 0)]
            [MASTERPW(password)]
            [MODEL(entryname[/password][ catname[/password]])]
            [ORDERED|UNORDERED]
            [OWNER(ownerid)]
            [READPW(password)]
            [RECORDSIZE(average maximum)]
            [REPLICATE|NOREPLICATE]
            [REUSE|NOREUSE]
            [SHAREOPTIONS(crossregion[ crosssystem]|1 3)]
            [SPANNED|NONSPANNED]
            [SPEED|RECOVERY]
            [STAGE|BIND|CYLINDERFAULT]
            [TO(date)|FOR(days)]
            [UPDATEPW|password)]
            [WRITECHECK|NOWRITECHECK])
```

Optional parameter for VSAM catalogs only

```
[UNIQUE|SUBALLOCATION]
```

Optional parameter for ICF catalogs only

```
[RECATALOG|NORECATALOG]
```

NAME

The NAME subparameter specifies the name of the cluster being defined.

CYLINDERS ¦ RECORDS ¦ TRACKS

The CYLINDERS (CYL), RECORDS (REC), and TRACKS (TRK) subparameters allocate space for the cluster.

VOLUMES	The VOLUMES (VOL) subparameter lists the serial numbers of the volume or volumes on which space for the cluster is to be allocated.
ATTEMPTS	The ATTEMPTS (ATT) subparameter specifies the maximum number of times the operator can enter a password in gaining access to the cluster.
AUTHORIZATION	The AUTHORIZATION (AUTH) subparameter specifies information about a security verification routine to be used in conjunction with this cluster.
BUFFERSPACE	The BUFFERSPACE (BUFSP or BUFSPC) subparameter specifies the minimum amount of space that VSAM should provide for I/O buffers when processing this cluster.
CODE	The CODE subparameter specifies a code name to be used in password prompting messages when a program attempts to gain access to this cluster without supplying a password.
CONTROLINTERVALSIZE	The CONTROLINTERVALSIZE (CISZ or CNVSZ) subparameter specifies the size of the control interval to be used for this cluster.
CONTROLPW	The CONTROLPW (CTLPW) subparameter assigns a control password to the cluster.
DESTAGEWAIT ¦ <u>NODESTAGEWAIT</u>	The DESTAGEWAIT (DSTGW) and <u>NODESTAGEWAIT</u> (<u>NDSTGW</u>) subparameters are used only in conjunction with a Mass Storage System.
ERASE ¦ <u>NOERASE</u>	The ERASE (ERAS) and <u>NOERASE</u> (<u>NERAS</u>) subparameters specify whether or not VSAM should physically erase the cluster by overwriting it with binary zeros when its catalog entry is deleted.

(Continued)

BOX 4.2 *(Continued)*

EXCEPTIONEXIT	The EXCEPTIONEXIT (EEXIT) subparameter specifies the name of a routine to be executed when an I/O error occurs while processing the cluster.
FILE	The FILE subparameter identifies the DD statement in the AMS job step that defines UNIT and VOLUME information for the cluster.
FREESPACE	The FREESPACE (FSPC) subparameter specifics the percentage of free space that should be allocated in each control interval and each control area when the cluster is loaded and when control interval and control area splits occur. (KSDS clusters only.)
IMBED ¦ NOIMBED	The IMBED (IMBD) and NOIMBED (NIMBD) subparameters specify whether or not VSAM should write the sequence set records as many times as they will fit on the first track of each control area. (KSDS clusters only.)
INDEXED	The INDEXED (IXD) subparameter (the default) specifies that a KSDS cluster is being defined.
NONINDEXED	The NONINDEXED (NIXD) subparameter specifies that an ESDS cluster is being defined.
NUMBERED	The NUMBERED (NUMD) subparameter specifies that an RRDS cluster is being defined.
KEYRANGES	The KEYRANGES (KRNG) subparameter specifies that a KSDS cluster is to be divided into separate areas called key ranges, some of which can be placed on separate volumes. (KSDS clusters only.)

BOX 4.2 *(Continued)*

KEYS	The KEYS subparameter is used to specify the length and the location in the record of the cluster's prime key. (KSDS clusters only.)
MASTERPW	The MASTERPW (MRPW) subparameter assigns a master password to the cluster.
MODEL	The MODEL subparameter specifies the name of an existing cluster to be used as a model in defining this path.
ORDERED ¦ UNORDERED	The ORDERED (ORD) and UNORDERED (UNORD) subparameters specify whether or not VSAM should use the volumes in the order in which they are coded in the VOLUMES parameter.
OWNER	The OWNER subparameter identifies the owner of the cluster.
READPW	The READPW (RDPW) subparameter assigns a read password to the cluster.
RECORDSIZE	The RECORDSIZE (RECSZ) subparameter specifies the average and maximum length of the records to be stored in the data component of the cluster.
REPLICATE ¦ NOREPLICATE	The REPLICATE (REPL) and NOREPLICATE (NREPL) subparameters specify whether or not VSAM should write sequence set records as many times as they will fit on a track. (KSDS clusters only.)
REUSE ¦ NOREUSE	The REUSE (RUS) and NOREUSE (NRUS) subparameters specify whether or not VSAM can reset the cluster's high-used RBA to zero to make the cluster appear empty when opened.

(Continued)

SHAREOPTIONS	The SHAREOPTIONS (SHR) subparameter specifies how the cluster can be shared between concurrently executing tasks.
SPANNED ¦ NONSPANNED	The SPANNED (SPND) and NONSPANNED (NSPND) subparameters specify whether records are allowed to span across control interval boundaries. (KSDS and ESDS clusters only.)
SPEED ¦ RECOVERY	The SPEED and RECOVERY (RCVY) subparameters specify whether or not VSAM should preformat the space allocated to the data set as part of the define process.
STAGE ¦ BIND ¦ CYLINDERFAULT	The STAGE, BIND, and CYLINDERFAULT (CYLF) subparameters are used only in conjunction with a Mass Storage System.
TO ¦ FOR	The TO and FOR subparameters assign an expiration date to the cluster.
UPDATEPW	The UPDATEPW (UPDPW) subparameter assigns an update password to the cluster.
WRITECHECK ¦ NOWRITECHECK	The WRITECHECK (WCK) and NOWRITECHECK (NWCK) subparameters specify whether VSAM should perform write check verification when writing data into the cluster.
UNIQUE ¦ SUBALLOCATION	The UNIQUE (UNQ) and SUBALLOCATION (SUBAL) subparameters specify whether or not VSAM should assign the cluster to its own unique data space. (VSAM catalogs only; not valid for ICF catalogs.)
RECATALOG ¦ NORECATALOG	The RECATALOG (RCTLG) and NORECATALOG (NRCTLOG) subparameters specify whether or not an entry already exists in the VVDS on the primary volume. (ICF catalogs only; not valid for VSAM catalogs.)

- **REC (50000 2000)** This example uses RECORDS to request an initial allocation large enough to hold 50,000 records and a secondary allocation large enough to hold 2000 records.

The primary quantity specifies the amount of space that is initially allocated to the cluster. The secondary quantity is the amount of space that is added to the cluster each time the data set fills up and must be extended. The number of times that additional space can be added to the data set depends on a number of factors and can be as high as 123 times. Specific information on the details of space allocation can be found in the *Access Method Services Reference* manual for your operating system version and catalog facility.

Although any of the three space allocation subparameters can be used to define the size of a cluster, the RECORDS option is preferable in most cases because it provides a device-independent method of requesting space. When the RECORDS option is used, VSAM examines the attributes of the allocated device in determining the number of cylinders or tracks of space to allocate to the cluster. When the CYLINDERS or TRACKS method is used, the number of records that can be stored in the allocated space depends on the number of tracks that make up each cylinder and the track capacity of the device.

ALLOCATING BUFFER SPACE

BUFFERSPACE (BUFSP or BUFSPC) is used to specify the minimum amount of buffer space required to process the data set. The value coded in the BUFFERSPACE subparameter affects the control interval size. VSAM ordinarily chooses a control interval size so that two control intervals and one index record will fit in the specified amount of buffer space. If BUFFERSPACE is specified in the DEFINE command for the cluster, the value specified can later be overridden at execution time by using a JCL parameter.

CONTROL INTERVAL SIZE

In most cases, the CONTROLINTERVALSIZE subparameter should be omitted; this allows VSAM to choose the most efficient control interval size for the data set. However, in some situations, the CONTROLINTERVALSIZE (CISZ or CNVSZ) subparameter is used to explicitly define the control interval size. A control interval can range from 512 to 32,768 bytes in size. If the size is between 512 and 8192 bytes, a multiple of 512 should be specified. If it is between 8192 and 32,768 bytes, a multiple of 2048 should be specified. If the size specified is not a multiple of the appropriate value, VSAM rounds the size *up* to the next appropriate multiple. If a different size is specified for the index component of a KSDS, the specified size must be 512, 1024, 2048, or 4096.

PHYSICAL ERASING

ERASE (ERAS) or NOERASE (NERAS) specify whether or not VSAM should physically erase the data set when it is deleted. Specifying ERASE causes VSAM to overwrite the data set with binary zeros when it is deleted and then free up the space for use by others. Specifying NOERASE (the default) causes VSAM to simply free up the space without first overwriting the data set's records. The ERASE option is useful when deleting a security-protected data set in order to ensure that no one can use specialized utility programs to later access the deleted data set's contents.

FREE SPACE

The FREESPACE (FSPC) subparameter applies only to KSDS clusters and is used to specify the percentage of free space to set aside in each control interval and in each control area. The FREESPACE percentage applies when records initially are loaded into the data set and when control interval and control area splits occur. In the following example, we are requesting that 25 percent of each control interval should be set aside as free space and that 33 percent of the control intervals in each control area should be left empty. If FREESPACE is not coded, VSAM assumes that no free space is needed, and all control intervals are filled as completely as possible when records are loaded into the data set.

```
FREESPACE (25 33)
```

KSDS, ESDS, OR RRDS

INDEXED (IXD), or NONINDEXED (NIXD), and NUMBERED (NUMD) are used to specify the type of data set being defined INDEXED specifies a key-sequenced data set, NONINDEXED specifies an entry-sequenced data set, and NUMBERED specifies a relative record data set.

INDEX SUBPARAMETERS

We discuss three subparameters that are used to supply information about the index component that is associated with a KSDS. These are the KEYS subparameter, the KEYRANGES subparameter, the IMBED and NOIMBED subparameters, and the REPLICATE and NOREPLICATE subparameters. Since indexes are used only with KSDS clusters, these subparameters are not used when defining an ESDS or an RRDS.

The KEYS Subparameter

KEYS is used to specify the length and position of the key within each record. The following example specifies that the keys are 10 characters long, and begin in position 52 of each record (position 0 is considered to be the first byte in the logical record).

```
KEYS (10 52)
```

If KEYS is not coded, VSAM assumes that the key begins in position 0 and is 64 positions in length. Although the KEYS subparameter is not required, it is almost always coded for a KSDS; the default values are not often useful.

The KEYRANGES Subparameters

The KEYRANGES subparameters can be used with the VOLUMES subparameter for a large KSDS that spans two or more volumes. Each KEYRANGES subparameter specifies a range of key values that defines a set of records to be kept together on a volume. If the number of KEYRANGES subparameters is the same as the number of volumes in the VOLUMES subparameter list, each set of records is placed on one of the specified volumes. If there are fewer KEYRANGES than volumes, some of the volumes remain empty and are used for overflow when control area splits occur. If there are more KEYRANGES subparameters than there are volumes, the extra sets of records are placed on the last specified volume. There can be gaps between the specified key ranges; however, when there are gaps, VSAM will not allow records whose key values fall within the gaps to be loaded into the data set.

The ORDERED subparameter can be coded along with KEYRANGES if there is a one-to-one correspondence between KEYRANGES and volumes. When ORDERED is coded, the set of records defined by the first KEYRANGES subparameter will be placed on the first volume in the VOLUME subparameter list, the set of records defined by the second KEYRANGES subparameter will be placed on the second specified volume, and so on. If ORDERED is coded and there is not a one-to-one correspondence between the number of KEYRANGES subparameters and the number of specified volumes, processing of the DEFINE command is terminated with an error message. The following is an example of a DEFINE command that specifies three ranges of key values and three volumes. The ORDERED option is used to ensure that the records are loaded in the order in which the volumes are specified.

```
DEFINE CLUSTER                                         -
        (NAME      (BIG.DATA.SET)                      -
         RECORDS   (1000000,10000)                     -
         VOLUMES   (CSP001 CSP002 CSP003)              -
         KEYRANGES ( (A H) (I P) (R Z) )               -
         ORDERED)
```

In the above example, records whose key values begin with the letters A through H are placed on volume CSP001, records whose keys begin with letters I through P are placed on volume CSP002, and records whose keys begin with the letters R through Z are placed on volume CSP003. Records whose keys begin with the letter Q or any nonalphabetic character will not be allowed to be loaded into the data set.

The REPLICATE and IMBED Subparameters

REPLICATE (REPL) and NOREPLICATE (NREPL) are used to specify whether or not VSAM should write each index record on a track as many times as it will fit. IMBED (IMBD) and NOIMBED (NIMBD) specify whether or not the sequence set records are to be imbedded with the data in the data component of the cluster. When the sequence set is imbedded in the data component, VSAM writes each sequence set record on the first track of its associated control area. The IMBED option automatically implies the REPLICATE option. Without imbedding, the sequence set records are kept in the index component with other index records. The use of REPLICATE and IMBED are performance options that can be used to increase the performance of the data set at the expense of an increase in storage requirements.

COPYING ATTRIBUTES

The MODEL subparameter is used to copy data set attributes from the catalog entry of some other cluster. When MODEL is used, the NAME subparameter is the only other subparameter that is required in the DEFINE CLUSTER command; VSAM can obtain all other data set attributes from the catalog entry specified in the MODEL subparameter. Additional subparameters, however, can be coded on the DEFINE command if desired. When additional subparameters are supplied, they override the values copied from the data set identified in the MODEL subparameter. The following DEFINE CLUSTER command copies data set attributes from a cluster named EXISTING.DATA.SET.

```
DEFINE CLUSTER                                    -
        (NAME     (NEW.DATA.SET)                  -
         MODEL    (EXISTING.DATA.SET)             -
         RECORDS  (1000000,10000))
```

In the above example, all attributes associated with the data set named EXISTING.DATA.SET are assigned to the data set named NEW.DATA.SET, with the exception of space allocation information. Space allocation information is taken from the RECORDS subparameter.

SPECIFYING RECORD SIZE

RECORDSIZE (RECSZ) is used to specify the size of the logical records in the data set. In the RECORDSIZE subparameter, both an *average* record size and a *maximum* record size must be specified. Two examples of RECORD-

SIZE subparameters follow that show how fixed-length and variable-length records can be specified:

- **RECSZ (120 120)** The average and maximum lengths are the same, so this example specifies *fixed-length* records that are 120 bytes in length.
- **RECSZ (120 180)** The average and maximum lengths are different, so this example specifies *variable-length* records whose average record length is 120 bytes and whose maximum record length is 180 bytes.

If the RECORDSIZE subparameter is omitted, VSAM supplies default values for both average record size and maximum record size. If the SPANNED subparameter is not included, the VSAM default is fixed-length records with an average and maximum size of 4089 bytes; for spanned records, the VSAM default is variable-length records with an average record size of 4086 bytes and a maximum size of 32,600 bytes.

REUSABLE DATA SETS

In a cluster's catalog entry, VSAM maintains a pointer to the end of the last data record stored in the cluster. The pointer consists of the relative byte address (RBA) of the last byte in the cluster that is currently occupied by a record. This relative byte address is called the cluster's *high-used RBA*. VSAM uses the high-used RBA to find the end of the data set quickly, which is particularly useful when records are being sequentially added to the data set. When the high-used RBA field contains zero, VSAM assumes the data set is empty.

The REUSE (RUS) subparameter defines a *reusable data set*. When a reusable data set is opened, its high-used RBA pointer can be set to zero, even though the data set currently contains records. This makes the data set appear to be a newly defined, empty data set. Chapter 19 discusses Assembler Language techniques for resetting the high-used RBA pointer. Reusable data sets typically are used as work data sets that are loaded with a new set of records each time the data set is opened for output. The NOREUSE (NRUS) subparameter (the default if neither REUSE nor NOREUSE is specified) is used to define a non-reusable data set. The high-used RBA pointer for a non-reusable data set cannot be reset to zero when the data set is opened.

DATA SET SHARING

Two values (a crossregion value and a crosssystem value) can be coded in a SHAREOPTIONS (SHR) subparameter to specify the manner in which the data set can be shared among multiple tasks that are executing concurrently. The crossregion value specifies the level of sharing that can take place between concurrent tasks executing *in the same computing system*. The crosssystem value specifies the level of sharing that can take place between concurrent tasks executing *in separate, interconnected computing systems*. The numbers 1, 2, 3, or 4 can be specified for the crossregion value; only the numbers 3 or 4 can be specified for the crosssystem value. Box 4.3 gives descriptions of the four allowable share option values.

If the SHAREOPTIONS subparameter is omitted, the data set cannot be shared among multiple concurrent tasks; the first task to request the data set is given exclusive control of it. If SHAREOPTIONS is specified, with no crossregion or crosssystem values, the crossregion value defaults to 1 and the crosssystem value defaults to 3. In order for sharing to be allowed, the DISP parameter of SHR must also be specified in the DD statement for the data set. Programming techniques for controlling data set sharing are discussed in Chapter 23.

SPANNED RECORDS

In most applications, records are small enough so that a large number of records fit in a single control interval. However, VSAM allows applications to use very large records that may be even larger than the control intervals in which they are stored. When applications require access to very large records, spanned

BOX 4.3 Share option values

```
[SHAREOPTIONS(crossregion[ crosssystem]|1 3)]
```

- **Share Option 1.** Any number of users can share the data set if all users are only reading the data set; only one user at a time can access the data set for updating.
- **Share Option 2.** Any number of users can share the data set for reading, and at the same time a single user can also access the data set for updating.
- **Share Option 3.** Any number of users can share the data set for reading and also for updating. Share Option 3 is normally used when the applications that access the data set have their own controls for maintaining data integrity; VSAM makes no attempt to ensure data integrity when this share option is specified.
- **Share Option 4.** Any number of users can share the data set for reading and for updating, and VSAM provides some assistance to applications in maintaining data integrity. With this share option, applications must use the ENQ and DEQ functions to control data integrity, Share Option 4 is not valid for ESDS clusters.

records can be specified by including the SPANNED (SPND) subparameter. Specifying SPANNED records allows VSAM to choose a control interval size that is smaller than the maximum record size. Spanned records can be used with KSDS or ESDS clusters; they are not valid for RRDS clusters.

Including the SPANNED subparameter does not guarantee that all records will span control intervals. It is possible that the control interval size that is chosen for the data set may be large enough to contain many, or even all, of the records in the data set. However, when SPANNED is specified, each record starts at the beginning of a new control interval, even though there may be space available in the previous control interval. So specifying SPANNED for small records may cause wasted space in each control interval.

PREFORMATTING SPACE

The SPEED or RECOVERY (RCVY) subparameters are used to specify whether or not VSAM should preformat the space allocated to the data set as part of the DEFINE process. Specifying RECOVERY (the default) causes VSAM to preformat the space by filling all of the allocated space with records that contain end-of-file markers. When SPEED is specified, VSAM does not preformat the space, and the initial contents of the allocated area are unpredictable.

When RECOVERY is specified and the separate preformatting step is performed, the process of defining and then loading the data set may take longer than when SPEED is specified. However, when RECOVERY is specified, the preformatted end-of-file markers allow VSAM to determine the last record that was successfully loaded if a failure should occur during the load process. This allows VSAM to resume the load from the failure point. If SPEED is specified and the load process fails, the absence of preformatted end-of-file markers in the data set prevents VSAM from determining the last record that was successfully loaded, and the load ordinarily must be rerun from the beginning. Use RECOVERY if it is important to be able to resume the load process from the failure point. Normally, this is important only with very large data sets. Use SPEED if there is no serious disadvantage to resuming the load process from the beginning if a failure should occur during the load.

SPECIFYING A RETENTION PERIOD

TO and FOR are used to specify how long the data set should be kept before it becomes a candidate for deletion. The TO subparameter is used to request that the data set is to be kept until some specified date (in YYDDD format). With the following TO subparameter the data set remains valid until January 10, 1999.

```
TO (99010)
```

The FOR subparameter is used to request that the data set is to be kept for a certain number of days after the current date. With the following TO subparameter, the data set will be kept for 1830 days:

```
FOR (1830)
```

When the TO and FOR subparameters are omitted, the expiration date is the current date, and the data set becomes a candidate for immediate deletion. The maximum number of days that can be specified in the FOR subparameter is 1831. If a value of between 1831 and 9999 is coded, the expiration date is set at 99365.

REQUESTING WRITE VERIFICATION

WRITECHECK (WCK) and NOWRITECHECK (NWCK) are used to specify whether or not VSAM should perform a write check verification after each write operation. In performing a write check operation, the direct access device automatically performs a read operation after each write, thus verifying that the write executed correctly. Processing each write request takes longer when write checks are performed, but the extra processing time may be justified for certain critical applications.

ADDITIONAL CLUSTER SUBPARAMETERS

The CLUSTER subparameters described above are those that are used for most applications. There are additional subparameters that may be included for certain types of specialized applications. Box 4.2 provides brief descriptions of these. Since IBM may add additional subparameters from time to time, the *Access Method Services Reference* manual for your operating system version and catalog facility should be regarded as the final authority concerning the parameters and subparameters that can be coded on AMS commands.

DATA AND INDEX COMPONENTS

The DEFINE CLUSTER subparameters, and possibly a CATALOG parameter, are all those that are required for defining an ESDS or an RRDS cluster. ESDS and RRDS clusters consist of only a data component. A KSDS, on the other hand, consists of a data component and an index component. DEFINE CLUSTER subparameters apply to both the index and the data components of a KSDS cluster. In some cases, however, it is desirable to be able to assign different attributes to the data and index components. For example, it may be necessary, for performance reasons, to place the data and index components on separate volumes. To assign different attributes to the data and index components, DEFINE DATA and DEFINE INDEX subparameter lists can be coded in addition to, or instead of, a DEFINE CLUSTER subparameter list.

Most of the subparameters we have discussed can be coded following the CLUSTER, DATA, and INDEX parameters. When a subparameter is included in the CLUSTER subparameter list, its associated attribute is assigned to both the data and index components of the cluster. When a subparameter is included in the DATA subparameter list, its associated attribute is assigned only to the data component of the cluster. Similarly, when a subparameter is included in the INDEX subparameter list, its associated attribute is assigned only to the index component of the cluster. If a particular subparameter is included in both the CLUSTER list and either the DATA or INDEX list, the CLUSTER subparameter takes precedence, and the DATA or INDEX subparameter is ignored. An exception to this rule is the NAME subparameter. The cluster as a whole can be assigned a name, and both the data and index components can be assigned individual names as well. The following DEFINE command uses the CLUSTER, DATA, and INDEX parameters to define a KSDS cluster:

```
DEFINE CLUSTER (NAME        (VSAM.MASTER.CLUSTER)        -
                KEYS        (10 52)                      -
                CYLINDERS   (10 1)                       -
                RECORDSIZE  (200 200)                    -
                FREESPACE   (40 40))                     -
        DATA   (NAME        (VSAM.MASTER.DATA)           -
                VOLUMES     (DSK001))                    -
        INDEX  (NAME        (VSAM.MASTER.INDEX)          -
                VOLUMES     (DSK002))
```

In the above example, the KEYS, CYLINDERS, RECORDSIZE, and FREESPACE subparameters following the CLUSTER parameter assign attributes to the cluster as a whole. In addition, the NAME and VOLUMES subparameters following DATA and INDEX are used to assign individual names to the data and index components of the cluster and to assign different volumes for the data and index components of the cluster.

Not all subparameters can be coded at every level. For example, the IMBED subparameter can be coded only at the cluster level or the index level; it cannot be coded at the data level because it does not affect the data component of the cluster. Box 4.4 lists those subparameters that can be coded in the DATA and INDEX subparameter lists when defining a cluster.

DEFINING ESDS AND RRDS CLUSTERS

Most of the subparameters described in this chapter apply equally to KSDS, ESDS, and RRDS clusters. The descriptions of the individual subparameters pointed out those that apply only to KSDS clusters. In general, those subparameters that are used to define the characteristics of an index apply only to KSDS clusters. This is because ESDS and RRDS clusters consist only of data components and do not have indexes associated with them. ESDS and RRDS clusters are defined using only a DEFINE CLUSTER subpa-

BOX 4.4 DEFINE DATA and INDEX subparameters

```
DEFINE    [DATA
             ([ATTEMPTS(number)]
             [AUTHORIZATION(entrypoint[ string])]
             [BUFFERSPACE(size)]
             [CODE(code)]
             [CONTROLINTERVALSIZE(size)]
             [CONTROLPW(password)]
             [CYLINDERS(primary[ secondary]) |
        RECORDS(primary[ secondary]) |
        TRACKS(primary[ secondary])]
       [DESTAGEWAIT|NODESTAGEWAIT]
       [ERASE|NOERASE]
       [EXCEPTIONEXIT(entrypoint)]
       [FILE(ddname)]
       [FREESPACE(CI-percent [CA-percent])]
       [KEYRANGES((lowkey highkey)[ (lowkey highkey)...])]
       [KEYS(length offset)]
       [MASTERPW(password)]
       [MODEL(entryname[/password][ catname[/password]])]
       [NAME (entryname)]
       [ORDERED|UNORDERED]
       [OWNER(ownerid)]
       [READPW(password)]
       [RECORDSIZE(average maximum)]
       [REUSE|NOREUSE]
       [SHAREOPTIONS(crossregion[ crosssystem])]
       [SPANNED|NONSPANNED]
       [SPEED|RECOVERY]
       [STAGE|BIND|CYLINDERFAULT]
       [UPDATEPW|password)]
       [VOLUMES(volser[ volser...])]
       [WRITECHECK|NOWRITECHECK])]
```

Optional subparameter for VSAM catalogs only

```
          [UNIQUE|SUBALLOCATION]
```

```
DEFINE    [INDEX
          ([ATTEMPTS(number)]
          [AUTHORIZATION(entrypoint[ string])]
          [CODE(code)]
          [CONTROLINTERVALSIZE(size)]
          [CONTROLPW(password)]
          [CYLINDERS(primary[ secondary]) |
            RECORDS(primary[ secondary]) |
            TRACKS(primary[ secondary])]
          [DESTAGEWAIT|NODESTAGEWAIT]
          [EXCEPTIONEXIT(entrypoint)]
          [FILE(ddname)]
          [IMBED|[NOIMBED]
          [MASTERPW(password)]
          [MODEL(entryname[/password][ catname[/password]])]
          [NAME(entryname]
          [ORDERED|UNORDERED]
          [OWNER(ownerid)]
```

BOX 4.4 *(Continued)*

```
[READPW(password)]
[REPLICATE|NOREPLICATE]
[REUSE|NOREUSE]
[SHAREOPTIONS(crossregion[ crosssystem]))]
[STAGE|BIND|CYLINDERFAULT]
[UPDATEPW|password)]
[VOLUMES(volser[ volser...]))]
[WRITECHECK|NOWRITECHECK]))]
```

Optional subparameter for VSAM catalogs only

```
[UNIQUE|SUBALLOCATION]
```

rameter list; the DEFINE DATA and DEFINE INDEX subparameter lists are used only when defining KSDS clusters. Since INDEXED is the default if no data set type subparameter is coded, a KSDS is defined if the data set type subparameter is omitted.

An entry-sequenced data set is defined by including the NONINDEXED subparameter in the CLUSTER subparameter list. The following DEFINE command creates an ESDS that stores variable-length records:

```
DEFINE CLUSTER                                              -
         (NAME        (EMPLOYEE.ESDS)                       -
          VOLUMES     (DSK001)                              -
          RECORDSIZE  (50 200)                              -
          CYLINDERS   (5  1)                                -
          NONINDEXED)
```

A relative record data set is defined by including the NUMBERED subparameter in the DEFINE CLUSTER subparameter list. The following DEFINE command creates an RRDS cluster that consists of 1000 slots, each of which are 100 bytes in length:

```
DEFINE CLUSTER                                              -
         (NAME        (EMPLOYEE.ESDS)                       -
          VOLUMES     (DSK001)                              -
          RECORDSIZE  (100 100)                             -
          RECORDS     (1000)
          NUMBERED)
```

5 LOADING VSAM DATA SETS

AMS provides a REPRO command that can be used to load records into a VSAM data set. We begin this chapter by showing how to use the REPRO command to copy data from a sequential input source and load a VSAM data set. In this chapter, we introduce most REPRO command parameters, but we will concentrate only on those that are used in loading clusters. Chapter 11 discusses how the REPRO command can also be used to make backup copies of clusters, alternate indexes, and catalogs. After describing REPRO, we examine reusable data sets and discuss procedures for recovering from a load operation that has failed. We conclude this chapter by discussing the ALTER command, which is used to change the attributes of an existing VSAM data set.

THE REPRO COMMAND

The REPRO command has fewer parameters than the DEFINE command; its partial syntax and descriptions of its major parameters are shown in Box 5.1. A number of parameters concerning the use of the *Programmed Cryptographic Facility* and the *Cryptographic Unit Support* have been omitted, since the use of these facilities is beyond the scope of this book. As shown in Box 5.1, at least two parameters must be supplied, specifying the input file to be read and the output VSAM cluster to be loaded. The input data set can be identified using either the INDATASET or INFILE parameter; the output data set can be specified using either the OUTDATASET or OUTFILE parameter. The following job step issues a REPRO command that includes the INFILE and OUTFILE parameters:

```
//COPY       EXEC   PGM=IDCAMS
//SYSPRINT   DD     SYSOUT=A
//ISAMFILE   DD     DSN=ISAM.INPUT,DISP=OLD,DCB=DSORG=IS
//VSAMFILE   DD     DSN=EMPLOYEE.KSDS,DISP=OLD
//SYSIN      DD     *
  REPRO      INFILE  (ISAMFILE)                              -
             OUTFILE (VSAMFILE)
```

BOX 5.1 The REPRO command

```
REPRO   {INFILE(ddname[/password] [ ENVIRONMENT(DUMMY)])|
           INDATASET(entryname[/password] [ ENVIRONMENT(DUMMY)])}
        {OUTFILE(ddname[/password])|
           OUTDATASET(entryname[/password])}

        [FROMKEY(key)|FROMADDRESS(address)|
           FROMNUMBER(number)|SKIP(count)]
        [REPLACE|NOREPLACE]
        [REUSE|NOREUSE]
        [TOKEY(key)|TOADDRESS(address)|
           TONUMBER(number)|COUNT(count)]
```

Optional parameters for ICF catalogs only

```
        [ENTRIES(entryname[/password]
          [entryname[/password]...])|
          LEVEL(level)]
        [FILE(ddname)]
        [MERGECAT|NOMERGECAT]
```

INFILE The INFILE (IFILE) parameter specifies the name of the DD statement that describes the input object.

ENVIRONMENT The ENVIRONMENT (DUMMY) or ENV (DUM) parameter is used only when the input object is an ISAM data set and specifies that dummy records are to be copied along with active records.

INDATASET The INDATASET (IDS) parameter specifies the name of the input object.

OUTFILE The OUTFILE (OFILE) parameter specifies the name of the DD statement that describes the output object.

OUTDATASET The OUTDATASET (ODS) parameter specifies the name of the output object.

FROMKEY The FROMKEY (FKEY) parameter specifies the full or generic key value that defines the starting point of the copy operation. (KSDS clusters, alternate indexes, and ISAM data sets only.)

FROMADDRESS The FROMADDRESS (FADDR) parameter specifies the RBA value that defines the starting point of the copy operation. (KSDS and ESDS clusters only.)

FROMNUMBER	The FROMNUMBER (FNUM) parameter specifies the relative record number that defines the starting point of the copy operation. (RRDS clusters only.)
SKIP	The SKIP parameter specifies the number of records to skip before copying records.
REPLACE ¦ NOREPLACE	The REPLACE (REP) and NOREPLACE (NREP) parameters specify whether VSAM is to replace records in the output data set with matching records in the input data set.
REUSE ¦ NOREUSE	The REUSE (RUS) and NOREUSE (NRUS) parameters specify whether or not VSAM should open the output data set as a reusable data set.
TOKEY	The TOKEY parameter specifies the full or generic key value that defines the ending point of the copy operation. (KSDS clusters, alternate indexes, and ISAM data sets only.)
TOADDRESS	The TOADDRESS (TADDR) parameter specifies the RBA value that defines the ending point of the copy operation. (KSDS and ESDS clusters only.)
TONUMBER	The TONUMBER (TNUM) parameter specifies the relative record number that defines the ending point of the copy operation. (RRDS clusters only.)
COUNT	The COUNT parameter specifies the number of records to include in the copy operation.
ENTRIES	The ENTRIES (ENT) parameter is valid only when the MERGECAT option is in effect and specifies the names of the objects in the input catalog to be merged. (ICF catalogs only; not valid for VSAM catalogs.)
LEVEL	The LEVEL (LVL) parameter specifies the low-level qualifiers that identify the names of the objects to be merged. (ICF catalogs only; not valid for VSAM catalogs.)
FILE	The FILE parameter specifies the name of the DD statement that describes the volumes that contain the VVDSs to be updated. (ICF catalogs only; not valid for VSAM catalogs.)

(Continued)

BOX 5.1 *(Continued)*

MERGECAT NOMERGE- CAT	The MERGECAT (MRGC) and NOMERGECAT (NOMRGC) parameters are valid only when copying ICF catalogs and specify whether or not VSAM should merge the entries in the input catalog with the entries already in the output catalog. (ICF catalogs only; not valid for VSAM catalogs.)

Notice that in the preceding job step, the INFILE and OUTFILE parameters each name a DD statement in the JCL to further identify the data sets to be processed.

LOADING DUMMY RECORDS

The ENVIRONMENT (DUMMY) subparameter is sometimes used when the input file is contained in an ISAM data set. This subparameter causes AMS to copy *all* records from the input ISAM data set, including *dummy records* that are marked for deletion. A dummy ISAM record is one that contains the hexadecimal value "FF" in its first byte. The following REPRO command contains an ENVIRONMENT(DUMMY) subparameter:

```
REPRO   INFILE  (ISAMFILE ENVIRONMENT (DUMMY))
        OUTFILE (VSAMFILE)
```

DYNAMIC ALLOCATION

The OUTDATASET (ODS) and INDATASET (IDS) parameters provide an alternative method to OUTFILE and INFILE for identifying the input and output data sets when either or both data sets are VSAM clusters. When the OUTDATASET parameter is used, no DD statement is required in the AMS JCL to identify the data set to be loaded. AMS dynamically allocates the specified data set. The following AMS job step loads a VSAM data set using the ODS parameter to identify the output data set:

```
//COPY       EXEC   PGM=IDCAMS
//SYSPRINT   DD     SYSOUT=A
//ISAMFILE   DD     DSN=ISAM.INPUT,DISP=OLD,DCB=DSORG=IS
//SYSIN      DD     *
  REPRO      INFILE (ISAMFILE)                           -
             ODS    (EMPLOYEE.KSDS)
```

If the input data set is a VSAM cluster instead of a sequential or ISAM data set, the input data set can be identified in a similar manner. The following AMS job step uses the ODS parameter to identify the data set being loaded and the INDATASET (IDS) parameter to identify the input VSAM data set:

```
//COPY        EXEC  PGM=IDCAMS
//SYSPRINT    DD    SYSOUT=A
//SYSIN       DD    *
  REPRO       INDATASET  (VSAM.INPUT)
              OUTDATASET (VSAM.OUTPUT)
```

A restriction in the use of the INDATASET and OUTDATASET parameters is that the data sets they identify must be mounted and available to the operating system at the time the AMS job step executes. One way to ensure this is to identify only data sets that reside on permanently resident or reserved volumes. Another way is to include one or more DD statements in the JCL that allocates the volumes that contain the required data sets. This is illustrated in the following example:

```
//COPY        EXEC  PGM=IDCAMS
//SYSPRINT    DD    SYSOUT=A
//INPUT       UNIT=3380,VOL=SER=DSK001,DISP=OLD
//OUTPUT      UNIT=3380,VOL=SER=DSK002,DISP=OLD
//SYSIN       DD    *
  REPRO       INDATASET  (VSAM.INPUT)
              OUTDATASET (VSAM.OUTPUT)
```

SPECIFYING A STARTING POINT

In addition to the parameters that identify the input and output data sets, there are several optional parameters that can be included in the REPRO command. Some of these parameters are used to select the records from the input data set that are to be loaded into the new VSAM data set. The FROMKEY (FKEY) parameter can be used to specify the key value of the first record in the input data set to be placed into the output data set. In the following example, including the FROMKEY parameter causes the load process to begin with the input record whose key is 0142.

```
FROMKEY (0142)
```

The value specified in the FROMKEY parameter can be an actual key value or it can be a generic key value. As we mentioned in Chapter 4, a generic key is shorter than an actual key and identifies the beginning characters of a key value. If a generic key is specified, copying begins with the first record whose key matches the characters coded in the FROMKEY parameter. If our keys are 4 bytes in length, the following REPRO command references a generic key:

```
FROMKEY (014)
```

Suppose the input data set contains records whose key values are as follows:

```
0042
0122
0141
0147
0207
```

In this case, AMS begins the loading process with the record for 0141, since it is the first record in the input data set whose key value begins with the generic key characters 014. VSAM handles generic keys by padding the generic key value to the right with the appropriate number of bytes of binary zeros before performing the key value comparison.

The FROMADDRESS (FADDR) parameter can be used to identify the relative byte address of the record with which to begin loading. This parameter is only used when the input data set is a VSAM KSDS or ESDS. By including the following parameter, loading begins with the input record whose RBA is 512.

```
FADDR (512)
```

The FROMNUMBER (FNUM) parameter can be used to specify the relative record number of the first record to be loaded. This parameter applies only to an input data set organized as a VSAM RRDS. With the following FNUM parameter, the first record to be loaded is the record whose relative record number is 100.

```
FNUM (100)
```

The SKIP parameter can be used to specify the number of input records to be skipped before loading. The following SKIP parameter causes 500 records of the input data set to be skipped, and loading begins with the 501st input record.

```
SKIP (500)
```

SPECIFYING AN ENDING POINT

As we have discussed, the FROMKEY, FROMADDRESS, FROMNUMBER, and SKIP parameters can all be used to specify where in the input data set to begin loading. Similar parameters are available for indicating where in the input data set the load should end. The TOKEY parameter can be used to give the key value (actual key or generic key) of the last record to be loaded. With the following parameters, all records from the input data set are loaded between and including those whose key values are or begin with 0288 and 0477:

```
FROMKEY (0288)
TOKEY   (0477)
```

The TOADDRESS (TADDR) parameter can be used to specify the RBA of the last record to be loaded (KSDS or ESDS); or the TONUMBER (TNUM) parameter can be used to specify the last record's relative record number (RRDS). COUNT can be used to specify the number of records to be processed. With the following parameters, VSAM skips the first 100 records in the input data set and then loads the next 1000 records:

```
SKIP  (100)
COUNT (1000)
```

In specifying both a starting point and an ending point, complementary parameters must be used for each. For example, if the FROMKEY parameter is used to specify where to start loading, then the TOKEY parameter or the COUNT parameter must be used to specify where to stop loading. A combination of the TOADDRESS or TONUMBER parameters in combination with the FROMKEY parameter is not valid. The *Access Method Services Reference* manual for your operating system version and catalog facility can be consulted to determine all valid parameter combinations.

MULTIPLE FUNCTIONS

Combinations of AMS commands can be coded in the same job step to perform multiple AMS functions. The following job step shows a commonly used AMS command combination that creates a new VSAM data set and then immediately loads records into it:

```
//LOAD        EXEC  PGM=IDCAMS
//SYSPRINT    DD    SYSOUT=A
//IN1         DD    DSN=ISAM.INPUT,DISP=OLD,DCB=DSORG=IS
//OUT1        DD    DSN=EMPLOYEE.KSDS,DISP=OLD,
//                  UNIT=3380,VOL=SER=DSK001,AMP='AMORG'
//SYSIN       DD    *
  DEFINE     CLUSTER                                          -
                (NAME        (EMPLOYEE.KSDS)                  -
                 KEYS        (0 4)                            -
                 VOLUMES     (DSK001)                         -
                 CYLINDERS   (10 1)                           -
                 RECORDSIZE  (26 26)                          -
                 FREESPACE   (25 25))

  REPRO      INFILE  (IN1)                                    -
             OUTFILE (OUT1)
```

Notice in the preceding job step that the DD statement for the VSAM data set contains UNIT, VOLUME, and AMP parameters. The AMP='AMORG' parameter identifies the data set as a VSAM data set. The UNIT, VOLUME, and AMP parameters are necessary because the data set is not cataloged when the step begins. The DEFINE command creates a catalog entry for the data set; however, the JCL is processed before the DEFINE command executes, and the job step will fail unless UNIT and VOLUME information are provided. As discussed in Chapter 3, the AMP='AMORG' parameter is necessary only when UNIT and VOLUME information (or DUMMY) is included on the DD statement. This is due to the fact that when UNIT and VOLUME information are explicitly coded, the operating system does not search the catalog to locate the data set and, therefore, has no way of knowing that the file is a VSAM data set.

Notice in the preceding job step that each of the two AMS commands is terminated properly. When combining AMS commands in a single step, avoid inadvertently including a continuation character on a line containing the last parameter of a command.

LOADING IN STAGES

The REPRO command can be used to resume loading a VSAM data set that has already had records placed in it. This is useful in many situations. For example, after the initial records of a data set are loaded, it may be necessary to add new records to it at a later time. If no manipulation of the data is required, there is no need for a special user-written update program. In order to resume the load process, the data set being loaded must not have been defined as a reusable data set. (See Chapter 4.) The following job step can be used to add records to an existing non-reusable KSDS cluster.

```
//LOAD       EXEC  PGM=IDCAMS
//SYSPRINT   DD    SYSOUT=A
//SAMIN      DD    DSN=EMPLOYEE.QSAM,DISP=OLD,
//                 UNIT=3380,VOL=SER=DSK001
//VSAMOUT    DD    DSN=EMPLOYEE.KSDS,DISP=OLD
//SYSIN      DD    *
  REPRO      INFILE  (SAMIN)
             OUTFILE (VSAMOUT)
```

The data set containing records to be added is defined by the SAMIN DD statement; the partially loaded KSDS is defined by the VSAMOUT DD statement. VSAM merges the records by key value and appropriately updates the index. In the preceding job step, any records in the input data set whose key values match records already in the output data set are ignored. If the REPLACE (REPL) parameter is included, as in the following job step, VSAM replaces any records in the output data set with records from the input data set that have matching key values:

```
//LOAD       EXEC   PGM=IDCAMS
//SYSPRINT   DD     SYSOUT=A
//SAMIN      DD     DSN=NEWRECS,DISP=OLD,
//                  UNIT=3380,VOL=SER=DSK001
//VSAMOUT    DD     DSN=EMPLOYEE.KSDS,DISP=OLD
//SYSIN      DD     *
  REPRO      INFILE  (SAMIN)                                 -
             OUTFILE (VSAMOUT)                               -
             REPLACE
```

REUSABLE DATA SETS

If the output cluster was defined as reusable by including the REUSE parameter in the DEFINE command used to create it, the REPRO command can be used to set the high-used RBA to zero and load a new set of records into the data set, whether or not the reusable data set already contains data records. The following example includes the REUSE parameter:

```
REPRO      INFILE  (SAMIN)                                     -
           OUTFILE (VSAMOUT)                                   -
           REUSE
```

With the above REPRO command, the RBA of the output data set is reset to 0 before the load begins, and any existing records are replaced with the new records. The REUSE parameter effectively makes the output cluster appear to be empty. The REUSE parameter is only useful when included in a REPRO statement that identifies a reusable data set. If the REUSE parameter is included for an output data set that was not defined with the REUSE option, the REPRO statement will fail unless the non-reusable data set is empty.

RECOVERY

The REPRO command can be used to resume loading after the failure of a load. As discussed in Chapter 4, the SPEED and RECOVERY options of the DEFINE command determine whether recovery is possible after a load failure. If the RECOVERY parameter was used to invoke preformatting, then recovery from a system failure is possible. On the other hand, if the SPEED parameter was specified in the DEFINE command, it may not be possible to recover from a failure, and the load process may have to start from the beginning.

In using the REPRO command to resume loading, the VERIFY command should be issued before the REPRO command in order to update the cluster's catalog entry. Box 5.2 shows the syntax of the VERIFY command and describes its syntax. Since the catalog will probably be incorrect after a load failure, this step is ordinarily necessary before the load process can be resumed successfully. Either the FILE or DATASET parameter must be included in the VERIFY command. The FILE parameter is used to specify the name of the DD statement that defines the VSAM data set; the DATASET parameter explicitly names the

BOX 5.2 The VERIFY command

```
VERIFY     {FILE(ddname[/password])|
              DATASET(entryname[/password])}
```

FILE The FILE parameter specifies the name, and optional password, of the DD statement that describes the cluster or alternate index to be verified.

DATASET The DATASET (DS) parameter specifies the name, and optional password, of the cluster or alternate index to be verified.

VSAM data set and requires no DD statement. The following job step uses a VERIFY command to update the catalog entry followed by a REPRO command to resume loading:

```
//VERIFY     EXEC   PGM=IDCAMS
//SYSPRINT   DD     SYSOUT=A
//SAMIN      DD     DSN=EMPLOYEE.QSAM,DISP=OLD,
//VSAMOUT    DD     DSN=EMPLOYEE.KSDS,DISP=OLD
//SYSIN      DD     *
  VERIFY     FILE     (VSAMOUT)
  REPRO      INFILE   (SAMIN)                      -
             OUTFILE  (VSAMOUT)                    -
             FROMKEY  ('0465')
```

In the preceding job step, the FROMKEY parameter is used to bypass records that have already been loaded, and loading resumes with the record whose key value begins with the value *JONES*. The FILE parameter is used to identify the VSAM data set in the above VERIFY command; however, alternatively, the DATASET parameter could have been used and the VSAMOUT DD statement omitted.

THE ALTER COMMAND

The ALTER command can be used to change most of the attributes that are specified at the time a VSAM object is defined, and similar options are available on the ALTER command for specifying data set attributes as are available on the DEFINE command. Box 5.3 shows the syntax of the ALTER command and describes those ALTER parameters that are not available on the DEFINE command. An example of one use of the ALTER command is to allocate

BOX 5.3 The ALTER command

```
ALTER     [NEWNAME(newname)]
          [ADDVOLUMES(volser[ volser...])]
          [REMOVEVOLUMES(volser[ volser...])]
          [INHIBIT|UNINHIBIT]
          [NULLIFY(
              [AUTHORIZATION(MODULE|STRING)]
              [CODE]
              [CONTROLPW]
              [EXCEPTIONEXIT]
              [MASTERPW]
              [OWNER]
              [READPW]
              [RETENTION]
              [UPDATEPW]
          [additional DEFINE command parameters]
```

NEWNAME The NEWNAME (NEWNM) parameter is the counterpart of the DEFINE command NAME subparameter and is used to change the name of the object being altered.

ADDVOLUMES The ADDVOLUMES (AVOL) parameter is the counterpart of the DEFINE command VOLUMES subparameter and is used to specify additional volumes that can be used if the object needs additional space.

REMOVEVOLUMES The REMOVEVOLUMES (RVOL) parameter is used to remove a volume from the list of available volumes. If the volume already contains part of the data set, the volume is not removed from the list.

INHIBIT | UNINHIBIT The INHIBIT (INH) and UNINHIBIT (UNINH) parameters specify whether or not a data set is to be accessible by read operations.

NULLIFY The NULLIFY (NULL) parameter is used to remove protection options that are currently in effect for the object. The AUTHORIZATION, CODE, EXCEPTIONEXIT, OWNER, RETENTION, and passwords of a data set can be removed using NULLIFY.

varying amounts of free space in different parts of a data set as it is being loaded. For example, suppose that for a specialized application, we require free space to be allocated in the following way:

- The control intervals at the beginning of the data set that contain the records up to the record whose key value is 2999 initially should contain 33 percent free space.
- The control intervals that contain the records between those with key values 3000 and 5999 initially should contain 40 percent free space.
- The control intervals that contain the records from 6000 to the end of the data set initially should contain 25 percent free space.

The following job step defines a cluster, assigns an explicit name to the data component of the cluster, and loads records up to the record whose key value is JONES. It then alters the free space information in the catalog entry, loads the records between keys JONES and SMITH, alters the free space information again, and then loads the records from SMITH to the end of the data set:

```
//DEFINE     EXEC  PGM=IDCAMS
//SYSPRINT   DD    SYSOUT=A
//ISAMIN     DD    DSN=ISAM.INPUT,DISP=OLD,DCB=DSORG=IS
//VSAMOUT    DD    DSN=EMPLOYEE.KSDS,DISP=OLD,
//           UNIT=3380,VOL=SER=DSK001,AMP='AMORG'
//SYSIN      DD    *
  DEFINE   CLUSTER                                       -
             (NAME        (EMPLOYEE.KSDS.CLUSTER)        -
              KEYS        (0  4)                         -
              VOLUMES     (DSK001)                       -
              CYLINDERS   (10 1)                         -
              RECORDSIZE  (26 26)                        -
           DATA                                          -
             (NAME        (EMPLOYEE.KSDS.DATA)           -
              FREESPACE   (33 33))

  REPRO    INFILE     (ISAMIN)                           -
           OUTFILE    (VSAMOUT)                          -
           TOKEY      (2999)

  ALTER    EMPLOYEE.KSDS.DATA                            -
           FREESPACE (40 40)

  REPRO    INFILE     (ISAMIN)                           -
           OUTFILE    (VSAMOUT)                          -
           FROMKEY    (3000)                             -
           TOKEY      (5999)

  ALTER    EMPLOYEE.KSDS.DATA                            -
           FREESPACE (25 25)

  REPRO    INFILE     (ISAMIN)                           -
           OUTFILE    (VSAMOUT)                          -
           FROMKEY    (6000)
```

Notice in the preceding job step that ALTER commands are used to change the FREESPACE attribute initially set in the DEFINE command. The ALTER command can be used to change any of the data set attributes originally set through the DEFINE command. Some parameters, such as FREESPACE, affect only the data or index components. So when one of these attributes is changed, it must be done for the affected component only. To make this easier, it is good practice to give an explicit name to the component that will be altered, as in the preceding example. If a name is not explicitly given to the component, VSAM creates a unique name for it. That name would have to be determined and then coded in each ALTER command.

In the preceding example, we knew the free space requirements in advance and were able to set them at the time of data set creation and loading. However, in many cases, data set attributes must be changed at a later time. For example, suppose the retention period for a data set is about to be reached and the decision is made to keep the data set for another year. The following ALTER command causes VSAM to change the retention period:

```
ALTER    EMPLOYEE.KSDS
         FOR (365)
```

6 DISPLAYING AND DELETING VSAM DATA

AMS provides comprehensive facilities for displaying the contents of VSAM objects, for listing the contents of catalogs, and for deleting objects that are no longer required. This chapter begins by describing the PRINT command that is used to display the contents of VSAM data sets and other objects. Next, we examine the LISTCAT command that is used to display the information contained in VSAM catalog entries. Finally, we examine the DELETE command and discuss the options that are available for removing entries from the VSAM catalog and for physically deleting their associated objects.

THE PRINT COMMAND

AMS provides a powerful PRINT command that can be used to display the contents of all types of VSAM data sets. The complete syntax of the PRINT command and descriptions of its parameters are shown in Box 6.1. The following job step shows an example of the PRINT command in its simplest form:

```
//PRINT      EXEC  PGM=IDCAMS
//SYSPRINT   DD    SYSOUT=A
//SAMPFILE   DD    DSN=EMPLOYEE.KSDS,DISP=OLD
//SYSIN      DD    *
  PRINT      INFILE (SAMPFILE)
```

As with other AMS job steps, the SYSPRINT DD statement identifies the printed output produced by AMS and the SYSIN DD statement identifies the utility control statements that follow in the input stream. The INFILE parameter is used in the above example to specify the name of the DD statement that identifies the VSAM data set to be printed. As with the REPRO command, the name of the cluster can either be specified directly with the INDATASET (IDS) parameter or indirectly using INFILE and an associated DD statement.

BOX 6.1 The PRINT command

```
PRINT      {INFILE(ddname[/password])|
              INDATASET(entryname[/password])}

           [CHARACTER|DUMP|HEX
           [FROMKEY(key)|FROMADDRESS(address)|
              FROMNUMBER(number)|SKIP(count)]
           [OUTFILE(ddname)]
           [TOKEY(key)|TOADDRESS(address)|
              TONUMBER(number)|COUNT(count)]
```

INFILE	The INFILE (IFILE) parameter specifies the name of the DD statement that describes the input object.
INDATASET	The INDATASET (IDS) parameter specifies the name of the input object.
CHARACTER	The CHARACTER (CHAR) parameter specifies that AMS should display the output in character format.
DUMP	The DUMP parameter (the default) specifies that AMS should display the output in both hexadecimal and character format, as in a virtual storage dump.
HEX	The HEX parameter specifies that AMS should display the output in hexadecimal format.
FROMKEY	The FROMKEY (FKEY) parameter specifies the full or generic key value that defines the starting point of the print operation. (KSDS clusters, alternate indexes, catalogs, and ISAM data sets only.)
FROMADDRESS	The FROMADDRESS (FADDR) parameter specifies the RBA value that defines the starting point of the print operation. (KSDS and ESDS clusters only.)
FROMNUMBER	The FROMNUMBER (FNUM) parameter specifies the relative record number that defines the starting point of the print operation. (RRDS clusters only.)
SKIP	The SKIP parameter specifies the number of records to skip before displaying records.
OUTFILE	The OUTFILE (OFILE) parameter specifies the name of the output DD statement when it is other than SYSPRINT.

BOX 6.1 *(Continued)*

TOKEY	The TOKEY parameter specifies the full or generic key value that defines the ending point of the print operation. (KSDS clusters, alternate indexes, catalogs, and ISAM data sets only.)
TOADDRESS	The TOADDRESS (TADDR) parameter specifies the RBA value that defines the ending point of the print operation. (KSDS and ESDS clusters only.)
TONUMBER	The TONUMBER (TNUM) parameter specifies the relative record number that defines the ending point of the print operation. (RRDS clusters only.)
COUNT	The COUNT parameter specifies the number of records to include in the print operation.

SEPARATING THE LISTING

The listing produced by the PRINT command is placed in the SYSPRINT data set unless otherwise specified. If desired, the OUTFILE parameter can be included to cause the listing to be written in a different data set. The following job step includes a DD statement named PRTFILE that defines the data set into which the listing should be placed.

```
//PRINT      EXEC  PGM=IDCAMS
//SYSPRINT   DD    SYSOUT=A
//PRTFILE    DD    SYSOUT=A
//SAMPFILE   DD    DSN=EMPLOYEE.KSDS,DISP=OLD
//SYSIN      DD    *
  PRINT   INFILE  (SAMPFILE)
          OUTFILE (PRTFILE)
```

Notice that the preceding job step includes two SYSOUT data sets: one for the listing of the EMPLOYEE.KSDS data set and one for other AMS output.

SELECTING SPECIFIC RECORDS

Another option of the PRINT command can be used to select specific records in the data set for printing. The same options for selecting records are available with the PRINT command as are available with the REPRO command. The first record to be printed is identified in a FROMKEY, FROMADDRESS, FROMNUMBER, or SKIP parameter. The last record to be printed is identified in a TOKEY, TOADDRESS, TONUMBER, or COUNT parameter. As with the REPRO command, generic keys can be specified in the FROMKEY and TOKEY parameters. If both a first record and a last record are identified, the two parameters must be of complementary types. The following PRINT command includes both FROMKEY and TOKEY parameters:

```
PRINT      INFILE  (VSAMFILE)                                  -
           FROMKEY (JONES)                                     -
           TOKEY   (SMITH)
```

The following set of PRINT commands shows how the SKIP and COUNT parameters can be combined to print selected records from various parts of the data set:

```
PRINT      INFILE  (VSAMFILE)                                  -
           COUNT   (100)
PRINT      INFILE  (VSAMFILE)                                  -
           SKIP    (1000)                                      -
           COUNT   (100)
PRINT      INFILE  (VSAMFILE)                                  -
           SKIP    (1000)                                      -
           COUNT   (100)
PRINT      INFILE  (VSAMFILE)                                  -
           SKIP    (1000)                                      -
           COUNT   (100)
```

OUTPUT FORMAT

The CHARACTER (CHAR), DUMP, and HEX parameters can be used to specify the format of the output listing. CHARACTER specifies that the records are to be printed in character format. HEX specifies that the records are to be printed in hexadecimal format. DUMP (the default) causes the records to be displayed in both character and hexadecimal format, in a similar manner to a virtual storage dump. The following PRINT command requests the listing to be displayed in character format.

```
PRINT      INFILE  (VSAMFILE)                                  -
           FROMKEY (JONES)                                     -
           COUNT   (1000)                                      -
           CHARACTER
```

THE LISTCAT COMMAND

Another command provided by AMS is the LISTCAT (LISTC) command; its syntax and parameter descriptions are shown in Box 6.2. LISTCAT is used to list the information in a VSAM catalog. All parameters for the LISTCAT command are optional. For example, the following LISTCAT job step causes the entire contents of the catalog to be displayed:

```
//PRINT      EXEC   PGM=IDCAMS
//SYSPRINT   DD     SYSOUT=A
//SYSIN      DD     *
  LISTC
```

BOX 6.2 The LISTCAT command

```
LISTCAT  [ALIAS]
            [ALTERNATEINDEX]
            [CLUSTER]
            [DATA]
            [GENERATIONDATAGROUP]
            [INDEX]
            [NONVSAM]
            [PAGESPACE]
            [PATH]
            [USERCATALOG]
         [CREATION] (days)
         [ENTRIES(entryname[/password]
            [ entryname[/password]...])|
           LEVEL(level)]
         [EXPIRATION(days)]
         [NAME|HISTORY|VOLUME|ALLOCATION|ALL]
         [OUTFILE(ddname)]

         [CATALOG(catname[/password])]
```

Optional parameters for VSAM catalogs only

```
         [SPACE]
         [NOTUSABLE]
```

Optional parameter for ICF catalogs only

```
         [FILE(ddname)]
```

Positional Parameters The LISTCAT command can optionally begin with one or more positional parameters that identify the types of catalog entries that AMS is to display.

CREATION The CREATION (CREAT) parameter specifies a number of days; entries of the specified type are listed only if they were created the specified number of days ago or earlier.

ENTRIES The ENTRIES (ENT) parameter specifies the names of the catalog entries to display.

LEVEL The LEVEL (LVL) parameter specifies the high-level qualifier or qualifiers of the catalog entries to be listed.

EXPIRATION The EXPIRATION (EXPIR) parameter specifies a number of days; entries of the specified type are listed only if they will expire in the specified number of days or earlier.

(Continued)

BOX 6.2 *(Continued)*

<u>NAME</u>	The <u>NAME</u> parameter (the default) specifies that AMS should display only the name and entry type for the selected catalog entries.
HISTORY	The HISTORY (HIST) parameter specifies that AMS should display the name, entry type, ownerid, creation date, and expiration date for the selected catalog entries.
VOLUME	The VOLUME (VOL) parameter specifies that AMS should display HISTORY information plus the volume serial numbers and device type for all selected catalog entries.
ALLOCATION	The ALLOCATION parameter (ALLOC) specifies that AMS should display VOLUME information plus detailed information concerning space allocation for the selected catalog entries.
ALL	The ALL parameter specifies that AMS should display all the information contained in the catalog for the selected catalog entries.
OUTFILE	The OUTFILE (OFILE) parameter specifies the name of the output DD statement when it is other than SYSPRINT.
CATALOG	The CATALOG (CAT) parameter specifies the name and optional password of the catalog that contains the selected entries.
SPACE	The SPACE (SPC) parameter is an additional positional parameter that specifies that AMS is to display catalog entries for VSAM data spaces. (VSAM catalogs only; not valid for ICF catalogs.)
NOTUSABLE	The NOTUSABLE (NUS) parameter specifies that only selected entries that have the "unusable" indicator set should be listed. The unusable indicator is set when a system failure damages the object's catalog entry. (VSAM catalogs only; not valid for ICF catalogs.)
FILE	The FILE parameter specifies the name of the DD statement that describes the devices and volumes that contain information in the VVDS. (ICF catalogs only; not valid for VSAM catalogs.)

In most installations, the above job step would cause a quite lengthy listing to be prepared, so LISTCAT parameters normally are used to limit the display to only those entries of immediate interest. The first group of parameters listed in Box 6.2 causes the listing to be limited to only entries of a specific type. For example, you can request information only about clusters, as in the following LISTCAT command:

```
LISTCAT CLUSTER
```

With the above LISTCAT command, only information about cluster entries in the catalog will be displayed. To request a listing of information about the data and index components associated with all clusters, the following command can be used:

```
LISTCAT CLUSTER DATA INDEX
```

The other parameters shown in Box 6.2 can be used to display information about a variety of VSAM and non-VSAM objects. This chapter discusses catalog information for VSAM clusters; consult the *Access Method Services Reference* manual for your operating system version and catalog facility for further information on displaying catalog information for other types of objects.

DISPLAYING SPECIFIC ENTRIES

The ENTRIES (ENT) parameter can be used to specify a list of names of the objects for which catalog entries are to be displayed. The following job step lists catalog entries for two objects named PAYROLL.MASTER and PAYROLL.CHECKS.

```
//PRINT      EXEC   PGM=IDCAMS
//SYSPRINT   DD     SYSOUT=A
//SYSIN      DD     *
  LISTC    ENT(PAYROLL.MASTER PAYROLL.CHECKS)
```

The ENTRIES parameter can be combined with one or more entry type parameters to further limit the display to only those entries that are of interest.

SEPARATING THE LISTING

When listing catalog entries, the listing normally is written to the data set identified in the SYSPRINT DD statement. As with the PRINT command, the listing alternatively can be sent to a different data set by including the OUTFILE parameter in the PRINT command and coding a corresponding DD statement in the JCL for the job step. In the following job step, the listing is written to the data set defined by a DD statement named CATFILE; all other AMS output is written to the SYSPRINT data set:

```
//PRINT      EXEC  PGM=IDCAMS
//SYSPRINT   DD    SYSOUT=A
//CATFILE    DD    SYSOUT=C
//SYSIN      DD    *
  LISTC   ENT(PAYROLL.MASTER  PAYROLL.CHECKS)          -
          OUTFILE (CATFILE)
```

SPECIFYING THE FIELDS TO BE LISTED

The above form of the LISTCAT command displays a minimum amount of information for the selected catalog entries. Parameters are available to request additional information, as follows:

- The NAME parameter is used to specify the name and the type of each listed entry. NAME is the default, and name and type information is displayed if this parameter is omitted from the LISTC command.
- The HISTORY (HIST) parameter is used to list the NAME information plus the owner name, creation date, and expiration date.
- The VOLUME (VOL) parameter is used to list the HISTORY information plus the volume serial numbers and device type corresponding to each entry.
- The ALLOCATION (ALLOC) parameter is used to list the VOLUME information plus detailed space allocation information.
- The ALL parameter is used to obtain a listing of all fields for each displayed catalog entry.

GENERIC NAMES

The name or names that are coded in the ENTRIES parameters can be full names of VSAM or non-VSAM objects, or they can be generic names. A generic name uses an asterisk (*) instead of a simple name at one or more levels to refer to objects that have *any* simple name at that level. For example, the following job step lists catalog entry for all objects that have two simple names and whose second qualifier is *ARBEN*:

```
//PRINT      EXEC  PGM=IDCAMS
//SYSPRINT   DD    SYSOUT=A
//CATFILE    DD    SYSOUT=C
//SYSIN      DD    *
  LISTC   ENT(*.ARBEN)
```

The LEVEL parameter provides an alternative to the above method for specifying a generic name. When one or more initial qualifiers are specified in a LEVEL parameter, the parameter refers to all objects whose names begin with the specified qualifiers, no matter how long their names are. The following job step lists catalog entries for all the objects whose names begin with the qualifier *MARTIN:*

```
//PRINT      EXEC  PGM=IDCAMS
//SYSPRINT   DD    SYSOUT=A
//CATFILE    DD    SYSOUT=C
//SYSIN      DD    *
  LISTC   LEVEL(MARTIN)
```

THE DELETE COMMAND

The DELETE command is used to remove an entry for a VSAM object from the catalog and optionally to free up the space the data set occupies. Box 6.3 shows the syntax and parameter descriptions for the DELETE command. Notice that a variety of VSAM and non-VSAM objects can be deleted with the DELETE command. As with the LISTCAT command, if no information about an entry type is provided, VSAM deletes all components associated with the specified name. The following job step deletes the cluster, index, and data components of the KSDS cluster named EMPLOYEE.KSDS:

```
//DELETE     EXEC  PGM=IDCAMS
//SYSPRINT   DD    SYSOUT=A
//SYSIN      DD    *
  DELETE     EMPLOYEE.KSDS
```

In the preceding job step, the DELETE command is coded in its simplest form; the only required parameter for DELETE is the positional parameter that names the object to be deleted. The above job step removes the VSAM.MASTER entry from the catalog and frees up the space occupied by the VSAM.MASTER object.

Normally, the DELETE command fails unless the expiration date for the specified object has been reached or exceeded. The PURGE and NOPURGE parameters can be used to specify whether or not the expiration date should be ignored. The NOPURGE keyword (the default) specifies that the data set is to be deleted only if the retention period has been reached or exceeded. PURGE indicates that the expiration date is to be ignored, and the data set is deleted regardless of the expiration date.

The ERASE and NOERASE parameters are used to override the ERASE option that was specified when the object was defined or last altered. The ERASE keyword causes the space occupied by the data set to be overwritten with binary zeros; the NOERASE keyword causes the data set's space to be freed up but not overwritten. The ERASE and NOERASE keywords cause their respective actions to take place whether or not the ERASE option is in effect for the object. The following job step causes the space to be overwritten whether

BOX 6.3 The DELETE command

```
DELETE    (entryname[/password)[ entryname[/password]...])
          [ALIAS]
             [ALTERNATEINDEX]
             [CLUSTER]
             [GENERATIONDATAGROUP]
             [NONVSAM]
             [PAGESPACE]
             [PATH]
             [USERCATALOG]
          [ERASE|NOERASE]
          [FILE(ddname)]
          [FORCE|NOFORCE]
          [PURGE|NOPURGE]
          [SCRATCH|NOSCRATCH]

          [CATALOG(catname[/password])]
```

Optional parameter for VSAM catalogs only

```
             [SPACE]
```

Optional parameters for ICF catalogs only

```
             [TRUENAME]
             [VVR]
             [RECOVERY|NORECOVERY]
```

Positional Parameters — The DELETE command can optionally begin with one or more more positional parameters that identify the types of objects that AMS is to delete.

ERASE | NOERASE — The ERASE (ERAS) and NOERASE (NERAS) parameters specify whether or not AMS should overwrite the object with binary zeros when it is deleted.

FILE — The FILE parameter specifies the name of a DD statement that describes the unit and volume on which the object being deleted resides.

FORCE | NOFORCE — The FORCE (FRC) and NOFORCE (NFRC) parameters specify whether or not the specified object, such as a generation data group or user catalog, should be deleted whether or not it is currently empty.

BOX 6.3 *(Continued)*

PURGE ¦ NOPURGE	The PURGE (PRG) and NOPURGE (NPRG) parameters specify whether or not the specified object should be deleted even if its expiration date has not been reached.
SCRATCH ¦ NOSCRATCH	The SCRATCH (SCR) and NOSCRATCH (NSCR) parameters specify whether or not the associated entry is to be removed from the volume's volume table of contents (VTOC) as well as having its catalog entry removed.
CATALOG	The CATALOG (CAT) parameter specifies the name and optional password of the catalog that contains the catalog entries for the objects being deleted.
SPACE	The SPACE (SPC) parameter is an additional positional parameter that specifies that a VSAM data space is to be deleted. (VSAM catalogs only; not valid for ICF catalogs.)
TRUE-NAME	The TRUENAME (TNAME) parameter is an additional positional parameter that specifies that AMS is to delete a truename entry for an object. (ICF catalogs only; not valid for VSAM catalogs.)
VVR	The VVR parameter is an additional positional parameter that specifies that AMS is to delete a VVR entry from a VVDS. (ICF catalogs only; not valid for VSAM catalogs.)
RECOVERY ¦ NORECOVERY	The RECOVERY (RCVRY) and NORECOVERY (NRCVRY) parameters are used only when replacing ICF catalogs with imported copies. (ICF catalogs only; not valid for VSAM catalogs.)

or not the ERASE parameter was specified in the DEFINE command and regardless of the cluster's expiration date:

```
//DELETE     EXEC  PGM=IDCAMS
//SYSPRINT   DD    SYSOUT=A
//IN1        DD    DSN=VSAM.MASTER,DISP=OLD
//SYSIN      DD    *
  DELETE     (VSAM.MASTER)                              -
             ERASE PURGE                                -
             FILE (IN1)
```

Notice in the preceding job step that a FILE parameter and an associated DD statement for the VSAM data set have been included. A DD statement that identifies the data set should normally be included when the data set is being physically erased. This ensures that the volume containing the data set is properly mounted. If the FILE parameter and its associated DD statement are not coded, AMS attempts to allocate the data set dynamically. Notice also that the disposition in the DD statement for the data set to be deleted is KEEP (the default when DISP=OLD is coded). A disposition of DELETE is not coded in the DD statement because *AMS*, and not job management, is being used to delete the data set. The DELETE command can also refer to a group of objects to be deleted by using generic names as described for the LISTCAT command.

7 MODAL COMMANDS

The commands that we have discussed so far in this book are classified as *functional* commands; each performs a specific task according to the specific parameters that are included with it. AMS also provides another set of commands called *modal* commands. Modal commands are used to control the sequence in which a set of functional commands is executed. We will begin this discussion of modal commands by examining the condition code that each functional command sets after it completes its execution.

CONDITION CODES

As we have seen, an AMS job step can execute any number of functional commands. In some situations, it is not possible to predict in advance which of the functional commands will execute successfully. We can determine, during the execution of an AMS step, whether a functional command has executed properly by using a modal command to test the *condition code* value that is returned by that functional command. AMS sets this value after it completes the processing specified by each functional command. Modal commands can be used to test condition code values at any point in an AMS command sequence. Then, based on the condition code values that are returned, modal commands can be used to change the execution sequence of the functional commands that follow. Most AMS functional commands return one of five condition code values, as described in Box 7.1.

IF-THEN-ELSE COMMAND SEQUENCES

Box 7.2 shows the general syntax of an IF-THEN-ELSE modal command sequence. The IF keyword is used to specify a logical expression that tests the condition code values returned by one or more previously executed AMS functional commands. Notice that following the THEN and optional ELSE keywords can be a single AMS functional command or a set

BOX 7.1 AMS command condition codes

Code	Interpretation
0	**Normal Completion.** The functional command completed its processing successtully.
4	**Minor Error.** Processing is able to continue, but a minor error occurred, causing a warning message to be issued. All of the processing specified on the command may not have been completed. For example, AMS returns a condition code of 4 when it is unable to locate one or more of the catalog entries specified in a LISTCAT command.
8	**Major Error.** Processing is able to continue, but a more severe error occurred, causing major command specifications to be bypassed. For example, AMS returns a condition code of 8 when it is unable to locate a catalog entry specified in a DELETE or ALTER command.
12	**Logical Error.** A logical error generally results when inconsistent parameters are specified in a functional command, causing the entire command to be bypassed. For example, AMS returns a condition code of 12 when required parameters are missing or when invalid parameter values are specified.
16	**Severe Error.** A severe error is one that not only affects the AMS command causing the error condition, but also causes the remainder of the AMS command stream to be flushed. For example, AMS returns a condition code of 16 when it is unable to open one of the data sets required to process a set of AMS commands, such as the SYSPRINT data set.

of functional commands delimited by the DO and END keywords. The THEN clause can also be followed by another IF keyword to create complex IF-THEN-ELSE logic. We will first look at examples of simple IF-THEN-ELSE command sequences that do not use DO groups; we will then see how DO groups can be used to create more complex command sequences. Box 7.3 shows the operators that can be used to construct IF-THEN-ELSE logical expressions.

An IF command must include a THEN clause. The functional command or DO group specified in the THEN clause is executed when the logical expression specified in the previous IF is *true*. An ELSE clause can optionally be included to specify a functional command or DO group to be executed when the logical expression is *false*.

A modal command uses the LASTCC keyword to test the condition code value returned by the most recent functional command, or it uses the MAXCC keyword to test the maximum condition code value that was returned by any of the previous functional commands executed in the job step. The following com-

BOX 7.2 IF-THEN-ELSE command sequence

```
IF    {LASTCC|MAXCC} comparand number
      THEN[ command|
         DO
         command-set
         END]
      [ELSE[ command|
         DO
         command-set
         END]]
```

BOX 7.3 Logical expression operators

Operator	Interpretation
EQ or =	equal
NE or − =	not equal
GT or >	greater than
LT or <	less than
GE or >=	greater than or equal to
LE or <=	less than or equal to

mand sequence shows how an IF-THEN-ELSE command sequence can use both the THEN and ELSE clauses:

```
DEFINE CLUSTER
          (NAME          (VSAM.RELREC.FILE)          -
           VOLUMES       (DSK001)                    -
           CYLINDERS     (10 5)                      -
           RECSZ         (80 80))                    -
           NUMBERED
IF LASTCC = 0                                        -
    THEN                                             -
        REPRO   INFILE   (IN1)                       -
                ODS      (VSAM.RELREC.FILE)
    ELSE                                             -
        LISTC   ENTRIES  (VSAM.RELREC.FILE)          -
                ALL
```

The preceding AMS command sequence begins by issuing a DEFINE command for a new RRDS cluster. The DEFINE command is followed by an IF-THEN-ELSE modal command sequence that tests the condition code returned by the DEFINE command. If the DEFINE command executes successfully, the condition code returned by DEFINE is 0, the REPRO command in the THEN clause is executed, and the new RRDS is loaded. If the DEFINE command does not execute successfully, the condition code returned by DEFINE is greater than 0, the LISTC command in the ELSE clause is executed, and the catalog entry for the new data set is displayed to help to determine what went wrong.

Notice how continuation characters are used in the above example. The final line of each AMS functional command does not include a continuation character; but each line that contains a modal command clause does include a continuation character to indicate that the next line belongs to the same modal command sequence.

DO GROUPS

As mentioned above, a DO group can be used when a sequence of multiple functional commands must be executed in a single THEN or ELSE clause. A DO group begins with the DO keyword and ends with an END keyword. All of the commands within a DO group are treated as a single unit with respect to the IF-THEN-ELSE logic. The following IF statement includes a THEN clause with a DO group:

```
IF LASTCC LT 4                                              -
    THEN                                                    -
        DO                                                  -
            REPRO    INFILE      (IN1)                      -
                     OUTFILE     (OUT1)                     -
                     TOKEY       (0499)

            ALTER    FREESPACE   (25 25)

            REPRO    INFILE      (IN1)                      -
                     OUTFILE     (OUT1)                     -
                     FROMKEY     (0500)
        END
```

In the preceding example, if the highest condition code returned by any previous functional commands is less than 4, the indicated REPRO...ALTER...REPRO command sequence is executed. Although this example does not include an ELSE clause, one could have been included specifying either a single functional command or another complete DO group.

NULL COMMANDS

If a THEN keyword or an ELSE keyword is not immediately followed by a functional command, or does not include a continuation character indicating that a functional command follows on the next line, then a null THEN or ELSE clause is assumed. This allows IF and THEN clauses to be included that specify no action to be performed. For example, the following modal command sequence uses a null THEN clause to produce identical results as the previous modal command sequence:

```
IF LASTCC GE 4                                          -
  THEN                                                  -
  ELSE                                                  -
      DO                                                -
           REPRO    INFILE      (IN1)                   -
                    OUTFILE     (OUT1)                  -
                    TOKEY       (0499)

           ALTER    FREESPACE   (25 25)

           REPRO    INFILE      (IN1)                   -
                    OUTFILE     (OUT1)                  -
                    FROMKEY     (0500)
     END
```

THE SET COMMAND

Box 7.4 shows the syntax of the SET modal command that can be used to set the current or maximum condition value to some specific value. The following SET commands can be used to reset the value of the previous and maximum condition code values to 0:

```
SET LASTCC=0
SET MAXCC=0
```

BOX 7.4 The SET command

```
SET     {MAXCC|LASTCC}=number
```

If a SET LASTCC command sets the value for the last condition code to a value that is greater than the current value of the maximum condition code, the maximum condition code value is also set to the higher value. The following SET command can be used to bypass the execution of all following functional commands:

```
SET LASTCC=16
```

THE PARM COMMAND

Box 7.5 shows the syntax of the PARM command and describes its parameters. The PARM command can be used to set the values of a number of AMS parameters. These parameter values can alternatively be set using the PARM parameter of the EXEC statement that invokes the AMS program. Most of these parameters are used infrequently; however, changing the margins of the input command stream can be useful if some commands in a command stream are not

BOX 7.5 PARM command parameters

```
PARM    [GRAPHICS(CHAIN(chain)|TABLE(mnsame))]
        [MARGINS(left-margin right-margin)]
        [TEST({ [TRACE
                [AREAS(area-id[ area-id ...])
                [FULL ((dump-id[ count1[ count2]])
                     [(dump-id ...) ...])]|
                OFF})]
```

GRAPHICS The GRAPHICS parameter provides information concerning graphics character sets or user-supplied graphics tables that are to be used in special-purpose printing applications.

MARGINS The MARGINS parameter specifies the left and right margins to control which positions of SYSIN input records are to be scanned for AMS commands.

TEST Various keywords can be included following the TEST parameter to control diagnostic aids that are used to help in debugging complex command sequences.

ordinarily executed but are included as comments should they be needed to perform some special processing. The following example illustrates this:

```
Pos
 2
 |
     DEFINE CLUSTER                                                  -
                (NAME       (VSAM.RELREC.FILE)                       -
                 VOLUMES    (DSK001)                                 -
                 CYLINDERS  (10 5)                                   -
                 RECSZ      (80 80))                                 -
                 NUMBERED
 /*  LISTC                                                              */
```

Normally, AMS scans positions 2 through 72 of the command statements in the SYSIN data set. In the above command sequence, when normal margins of 2 and 72 are in effect, the line containing the LISTC command is treated as a comment. If the margins are changed to 4 and 60, as in the following example, only positions 4 through 60 are scanned, the /* and */ characters are not processed by AMS, and the LISTC line is treated as an AMS command and is executed:

```
Pos
 2
 |
    MARGIN (4 50)
    DEFINE CLUSTER                                                  -
            (NAME       (VSAM.RELREC.FILE)                          -
             VOLUMES    (DSK001)                                    -
             CYLINDERS  (10 5)                                      -
             RECSZ      (80 80))                                    -
             NUMBERED
 /*  LISTC                                                                      */
```

8 CATALOGS AND DATA SPACES

The *catalog* is the central repository for all the attribute information that is associated with VSAM objects. This chapter discusses the catalog facilities that VSAM provides, shows how catalogs are searched, and describes the procedures that are used for defining user catalogs. Both VSAM catalogs and ICG catalogs are discussed. The AMS commands that are used to define VSAM catalog data spaces and non-VSAM objects are also examined.

USER CATALOGS

Every computing system that uses VSAM has one catalog, called the *master catalog,* that contains information about system data sets and other VSAM and non-VSAM objects that are required by all users of the computing system. In all but the smallest installations, information about data specific to individual applications is generally not stored in the master catalog. Instead, information about application-specific data generally is distributed among many individual *user catalogs*.

Figure 8.1 shows a master catalog and two user catalogs. When a user catalog is created, an entry for it is stored in the master catalog that contains its name and a pointer to the volume on which it resides. A catalog search ordinarily begins at the level of the master catalog, and VSAM employs the user catalog entry to locate the user catalog in which the required entries are stored. In most cases, the high-level qualifier of the data set names of all entries in the user catalog is the same as the name of the user catalog. For example, in Fig. 8.1, all the entries in the EMPLOYEE user catalog should begin with the qualifier EMPLOYEE, and all the catalog entries in the INVENT user catalog should begin with the qualifier INVENT.

Although it is not *necessary* that all entries in a user catalog begin with a high-level qualifier that is the same as the name of the user catalog, by following this convention catalog searches can be made automatic, and the name of the user catalog need not be explicitly stated in AMS commands. Also, when a

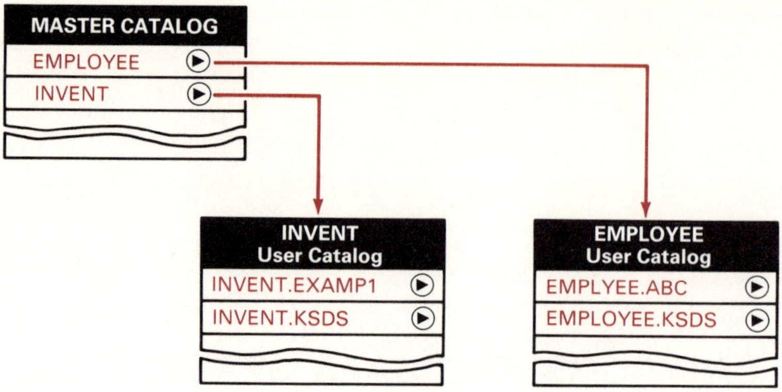

Figure 8.1 Catalog relationships.

DEFINE command is issued for a new object, its entry will be placed into the appropriate user catalog if the highest level qualifier of the object's name matches that of the appropriate user catalog. We will have more to say later in this chapter about how catalog searches work.

Often a different user catalog is used for each major application system. Only the people working directly with an application need be concerned with the catalog entries for that system. When the data associated with an application are not being used, the user catalog can be physically removed from the system, if desired, in order to protect the catalog from inadvertent modification. User catalogs provide many benefits. By spreading entries among several user catalogs, the average size of each catalog can be made small. This generally minimizes the time spent making catalog searches; it also reduces contention by limiting the number of requests that are made to each catalog. A smaller catalog also helps to minimize the effects of system and hardware failures because fewer entries are affected. Using a separate user catalog for each application also simplifies the task of transporting the application to some other computing system.

CATALOG FACILITIES

The way in which the master catalog and user catalogs are structured depends on the types of catalogs that are used by the individual installation. As we introduced in Chapter 1, there are three major types of catalogs that can be used in a computing system that implements VSAM. The following are brief descriptions of the three major catalog facilities.

- **OS CVOLs.** OS CVOLs (short for operating system control volumes) are implemented by standard job management facilities. They keep track of unit and volume information only for non-VSAM data sets. OS CVOLs generally have been replaced by the higher performance VSAM catalog facilities.

- **VSAM Catalogs.** VSAM catalogs can be used to keep track of the attributes and locations of VSAM data sets. They can also be used to maintain unit and volume information for non-VSAM data sets and in place of OS CVOLs for many purposes.
- **ICF Catalogs.** The *Integrated Catalog Facility* (ICF) is a high-performance replacement for the older VSAM catalogs and OS CVOLs. ICF catalogs can be used to maintain information about both VSAM and non-VSAM data sets. All of the functions of OS CVOLs and VSAM catalogs are provided by ICF catalogs.

Most of the material in this book applies equally to VSAM catalogs and to ICF catalogs. However, there are some differences between the two, and this chapter discusses those differences. OS CVOLs are beyond the scope of this course because they are only used to keep track of non-VSAM objects. In reading the following information on the two major types of VSAM catalogs, keep in mind that it is possible for all three types of catalogs to coexist in the same computing system. However, the trend is toward the use of ICF catalogs to handle all catalog functions.

VSAM CATALOGS

A VSAM catalog is implemented in the form of a KSDS. When a given volume contains a VSAM catalog (either the VSAM master catalog or a VSAM user catalog), the catalog must be the first VSAM object stored on that volume. A VSAM catalog *owns* the volume on which it resides. All the VSAM objects that are defined on a volume containing a VSAM catalog must be cataloged there. A catalog can also own other volumes; however, those volumes cannot also contain other VSAM catalogs. When the first VSAM object on a volume that does not contain a VSAM catalog is defined, that volume becomes the property of the catalog that contains its catalog entry. The catalog entries for all future VSAM objects that are defined on that volume must also be stored in the catalog that owns the volume.

VSAM CATALOG DATA SPACES

Before a volume can be used to store VSAM objects, one or more data spaces must be created on it when VSAM catalogs are used. A data space is an area of direct access storage that is under the exclusive control of VSAM. Space for VSAM objects, such as clusters and alternate indexes, is allocated from within data spaces. A data space can be created automatically or data spaces can be created explicitly by using the DEFINE SPACE command. In many cases, all the space on a volume is allocated to a single data space at the time that a VSAM user catalog is created, so that only VSAM objects can be stored on the volume. In other cases, data spaces occupy only some of the space on a volume, which leaves the remaining space available for use by non-VSAM objects.

When VSAM catalogs are used, the VTOC of a direct access storage volume generally contains entries only for non-VSAM data sets and for VSAM data spaces. Information about individual VSAM data sets is not stored in the VTOC; instead, that information is stored in a VSAM catalog. The relationship between a VSAM catalog and the VTOCs of the two volumes it owns is shown in Fig. 8.2. Notice that the two non-VSAM data sets have entries in both the catalog and the VTOC, but that the VSAM data sets have only catalog entries.

ICF CATALOGS

The catalog structure used by ICF is different than the structure used for VSAM catalogs. ICF catalogs do not own the volumes on which they reside, and a volume can have as many ICF catalogs on it as desired. Also, data spaces are not used with ICF catalogs; all the available space on a volume is available for use by both VSAM and non-VSAM objects. As with VSAM catalogs, ICF supports a master catalog and any number of user catalogs. Each ICF catalog consists of the following parts:

- **Basic Catalog Structure.** A *basic catalog structure* (BCS) contains general information about the VSAM and non-VSAM objects defined in a particular ICF catalog. A BCS is implemented in the form of a KSDS.
- **VSAM Volume Data Sets.** A *VSAM volume data set* (VVDS) contains information about the VSAM data sets stored on a particular volume. Each volume that contains one or more VSAM objects contains one VVDS. If a VVDS does not exist on a volume when a VSAM object is defined there, VSAM automatically creates a VVDS. A VVDS is implemented in the form of an ESDS.

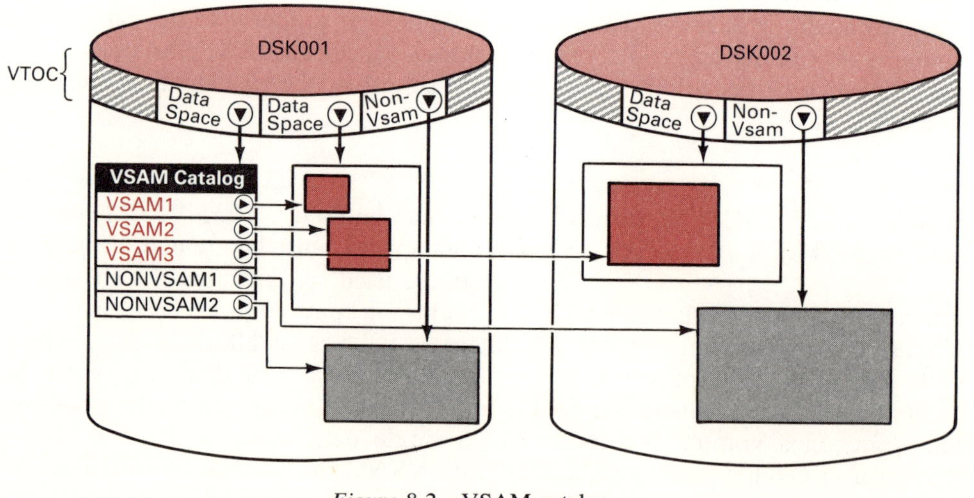

Figure 8.2 VSAM catalog.

Figure 8.3 shows a volume that contains an ICF catalog and an additional volume that contains data sets whose entries are stored in the catalog on the first volume. The BCS keeps track of all non-VSAM objects, whether they are on the same volume as the BCS or on different volumes. The BCS also keeps track of some of the information about the VSAM objects that it describes; however, the VVDS on each of the volumes that store VSAM data sets contains additional information about the VSAM data sets on that volume. To simplify the diagram, we have not shown the VTOC entries that are also stored on each volume. With ICF catalogs, all VSAM and non-VSAM objects have VTOC entries as well as ICF catalog entries.

Since the concept of volume ownership does not apply with ICF catalogs, it is possible for multiple ICF catalogs to refer to VSAM and non-VSAM objects that reside on a given volume. When this is the case, each volume still has a single VVDS, and its entries are shared by the various basic catalog structures that own VSAM objects on that volume. Up to 36 ICF catalogs can own VSAM objects on a given volume. Figure 8.4 illustrates the situation when multiple ICF catalogs refer to VSAM objects on a given volume.

CATALOG SEARCHING

There are a number of ways that VSAM determines which catalog to use when a catalog search is required. These same methods are used for both VSAM catalogs and ICF catalogs. An AMS command can explicitly specify the

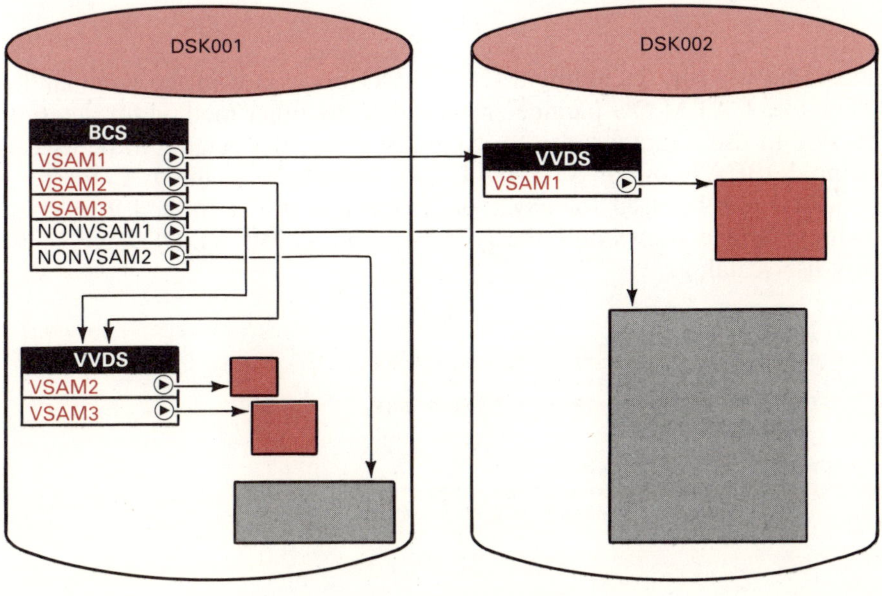

Figure 8.3 ICF catalog.

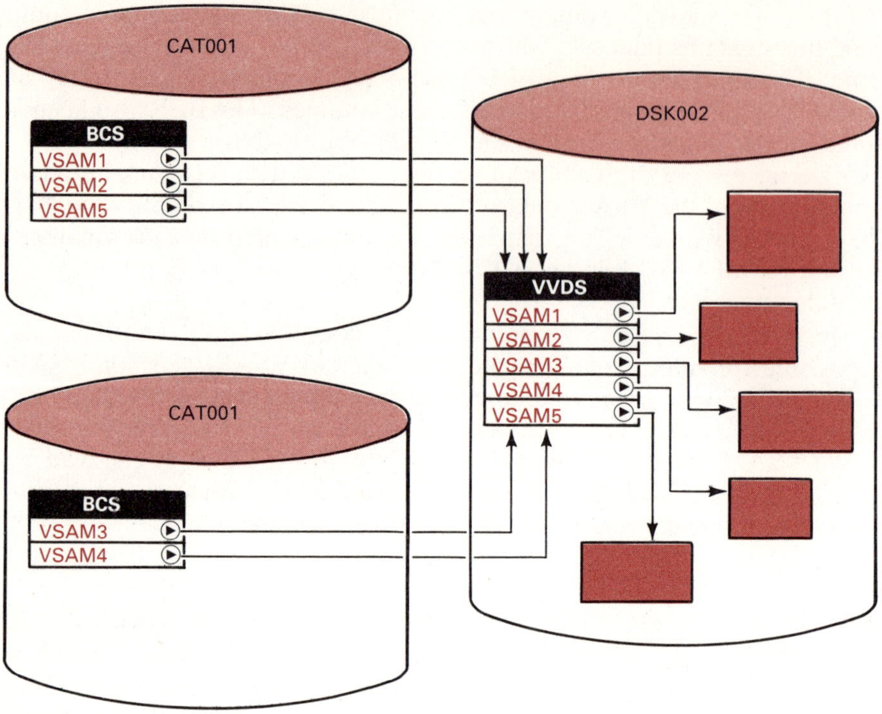

Figure 8.4 Multiple catalogs referring to one volume.

catalog to be used by including a CATALOG parameter in the command. The inclusion of a CATALOG parameter overrides any other method for determining the catalog to use. Another way to explicitly define the catalog to be used is by including JOBCAT and/or STEPCAT DD statements in the JCL for the job. This method can be used for any type of job and is not limited to AMS. The following example shows how the JOBCAT and STEPCAT DD statements can identify user catalogs:

```
//EXAMPLE  JOB   ...
//JOBCAT   DD    DSN=MARTCTLG,DISP=SHR
//STEP1    EXEC  PGM=PROG1
//STEPCAT  DD    DSN=EMPLOYEE,DISP=SHR
            :
//STEP2    EXEC  PGM=PROG1
//STEPCAT  DD    DSN=EMPLOYEE,DISP=SHR
//         DD    DSN=MARTCTLG,DISP=SHR
            :
//STEP3    EXEC  PGM=PROG1
            :
```

In the above example, the JOBCAT DD statement identifies the user catalog named MARTCTLG, and STEPCAT DD statements identify EMPLOYEE and MARTCTLG. The catalog specified in the JOBCAT DD statement defines the catalog that will be searched if no catalog is specified for a step either through an AMS CATALOG parameter or through a STEPCAT DD statement. In the above example, the EMPLOYEE user catalog will be searched for STEP1, both the EMPLOYEE and MARTCTLG user catalogs will be searched for STEP2 (the EMPLOYEE user catalog will be searched first), and the MARTCTLG user catalog will be searched for STEP3.

If no JOBCAT or STEPCAT DD statements are included, and no CATALOG parameters are specified in AMS commands, job management or AMS attempts to interpret the initial qualifier of the data set name as the name of a user catalog. If the initial qualifier matches the name of a user catalog, that user catalog is searched. If the initial qualifier of the data set name does not match that of a user catalog, the master catalog is searched.

THE DEFINE UCAT/MCAT COMMANDS

Master catalogs and user catalogs are defined by issuing the DEFINE MASTERCATALOG (MCAT) or the DEFINE USERCATALOG (UCAT) command. These two commands have the same set of parameters and subparameters. A master catalog must be defined during system generation, and only a single master catalog can exist in the system. If the DEFINE MASTERCATALOG command is issued in a system for which the master catalog already exists, AMS creates a user catalog instead. It is possible, during system initialization, to designate any user catalog as the master catalog for the system; however, the choice of a master catalog is not under the control of individual computing system users.

Box 8.1 shows the syntax of the DEFINE UCAT and DEFINE MCAT commands. Most of the subparameters are the same as those for a DEFINE CLUSTER command for a KSDS. This is because VSAM catalogs and the BCS components of ICF catalogs are implemented in the form of KSDS clusters. Those parameters that are different from DEFINE CLUSTER parameters are described in Box 8.2. Notice that a few parameters apply only to ICF catalogs, and one parameter applies only to VSAM catalogs. More parameters are provided for ICF catalogs because many catalog attributes that have standard values in VSAM catalogs can be explicitly defined for ICF catalogs.

Both VSAM catalogs and ICF catalogs can be defined having different attributes for their index and data components, so the INDEX and DATA parameters can be coded just as they are in defining a KSDS. Box 8.3 shows the syntax of the DATA and INDEX subparameter strings that can be coded in DEFINE MCAT and DEFINE UCAT commands. Again, ICF catalogs offer more flexibility. The following DEFINE USERCATALOG command creates a user catalog named MARTCTLG on volume 407263.

```
DEFINE  UCAT    (NAME       (MARTCTLG)                    -
                    VOLUME     (DSK001)                   -
                    TRACKS     (15 3)                     -
                    FOR        (9999))
```

RECOVERABLE VSAM CATALOGS

When defining a VSAM catalog, the RECOVERABLE subparameter can be included to indicate that a recoverable catalog is desired. This parameter is not valid when defining an ICF catalog. When the RECOVERABLE option is chosen for a VSAM catalog, AMS creates a catalog recovery area (CRA) on *each volume* owned by the catalog. The CRA is created automatically when the first VSAM object is created on a volume. Each time a new VSAM object is defined in a recoverable VSAM catalog, duplicate catalog information is placed in the CRA on the volume containing the new object. The duplicate entries in all of the volumes owned by a user catalog can be used to re-create the user catalog in case a hardware or software failure causes the user catalog itself to be damaged.

BOX 8.1 The DEFINE UCAT/MCAT commands

```
DEFINE   USERCATALOG | MASTERCATALOG
           (subparameter  [subparameter] ... [subparameter])

         [DATA    (subparameter  [subparameter] ... [subparameter])]
         [INDEX   (subparameter  [subparameter] ... [subparameter])]
         [CATALOG (catname[/password])]
```

USERCATALOG | MASTERCATALOG The subparameters included in the required USERCATALOG (UCAT) or MASTERCATALOG (MCAT) subparameter list assign attributes to the catalog as a whole.

DATA The subparameters included in the optional DATA subparameter list assign attributes to the data component of the catalog.

INDEX The subparameters included in the optional INDEX subparameter list assign attributes to the index component of the catalog.

CATALOG The optional CATALOG (CAT) parameter specifies the name and optional password of the master catalog.

BOX 8.2 DEFINE UCAT/MCAT subparameters

```
DEFINE   USERCATALOG|MASTERCATALOG
         (NAME(entryname)
         {CYLINDERS(primary[ secondary])|
           RECORDS(primary[ secondary])|
           TRACKS(primary[ secondary])}
         VOLUME(volser)

         [ATTEMPTS(number|2)]
         [AUTHORIZATION(entrypoint[ string])]
         [BUFFERSPACE(size)|3072]
         [CODE(code)]
         [CONTROLPW(password)]
         [DESTAGEWAIT|NODESTAGEWAIT]
         [FILE(ddname)]
         [MASTERPW(password)]
         [MODEL(entryname[/password][ catname[/password]])]
         [OWNER(ownerid)]
         [READPW(password)]
         [RECORDSIZE(average maximum)]
         [TO(date)|FOR(days)]
         [UPDATEPW|password)]
         [WRITECHECK|NOWRITECHECK])
```

Optional parameter for VSAM catalogs only

```
         [RECOVERABLE|NOTRECOVERABLE])
```

Optional parameters for ICF catalogs only

```
         [BUFND(number)]
         [BUFNI(number)]
         [CONTROLINTERVALSIZE(size)]
         [FREESPACE(CI-percent[ CA-percent]|0 0)]
         [IMBED|NOIMBED]
         [REPLICATE|NOREPLICATE]
         [SHAREOPTIONS(crossregion[ crosssystem]|3 4)]
         [STRNO(number|2)]
         [VSAMCATALOG|ICFCATALOG]
```

Parameter for VSAM Catalogs Only

RECOVERABLE | NOTRECOVERABLE

The RECOVERABLE (RVBL) and NOTRECOVERABLE (NRVBL) parameters specify whether or not a catalog recovery area is to be created on each volume owned by the catalog.

(Continued)

BOX 8.2 *(Continued)*

Parameters for ICF Catalogs Only

BUFND — The BUFND (BFND) parameter specifies the number of buffers to be used in transferring records between the data component of the catalog and virtual storage.

BUFNI — The BUFNI (BFNI) parameter specifies the number of buffers to be used in transferring records between the data component of the catalog and virtual storage.

STRNO — The STRNO parameter specifies the number of concurrent requests for positioning that can be made.

VSAMCATALOG | ICFCATALOG — The VSAMCATALOG (VSAMCAT) and ICFCATALOG (ICFCAT) parameters specify which type of catalog is to be defined by this command.

BOX 8.3 DEFINE catalog DATA and INDEX subparameters

```
DEFINE DATA
         ([BUFFERSPACE(size)|3072]
         [CYLINDERS(primary[ secondary])|
           RECORDS(primary[ secondary])|
           TRACKS(primary[ secondary])]

         [DESTAGEWAIT|NODESTAGEWAIT]
         [RECORDSIZE(average maximum)]
         [WRITECHECK|NOWRITECHECK]
```

Optional parameters for ICF catalogs only

```
         [BUFND(number)]
         [CONTROLINTERVALSIZE(size)]
         [FREESPACE(CI-percent[ CA-percent]|0 0)])
```

BOX 8.3 *(Continued)*

```
DEFINE INDEX
        ([CYLINDERS(primary)|
          RECORDS(primary)|
          TRACKS(primary)]
        [DESTAGEWAIT|NODESTAGEWAIT]
        [WRITECHECK|NOWRITECHECK]
```

Optional parameters for ICF catalogs only

```
        [BUFNI(number)]
        [CONTROLINTERVALSIZE(size)]
        [IMBED|NOIMBED]
        [REPLICATE|NOREPLICATE])
```

ICF CATALOG SPACE ALLOCATION

Space is allocated to an ICF catalog in a similar manner as it is allocated to a KSDS. Space can be allocated in terms of cylinders, tracks, or records, and separate space subparameters can be specified for the index and data components of the catalog if desired. The space requested for an ICF user catalog is assigned to the BCS component. Space is reserved automatically for the VVDS on each volume when the first VSAM object is defined on that volume.

VSAM CATALOG SPACE ALLOCATION

Since a VSAM catalog owns the volume on which it resides, the VSAM catalog must be the first VSAM object stored on a volume. When a VSAM catalog is defined, AMS automatically defines a data space on that volume and then allocates space for the VSAM catalog from within that data space. Space for a VSAM catalog can be allocated in terms of cylinders, tracks, or records, and separate space allocation subparameters can be specified for the index and data components if desired. If space is allocated only to the catalog as a whole, and separate SPACE subparameters are not specified for the index and data components, the entire data space is assigned to the catalog. If separate index and data component space allocation subparameters are coded, the SPACE parameter for the catalog as a whole defines the size of the data space that is created, and the SPACE subparameters that are specified for the data and index components determine the portion of the data space that is assigned to the catalog. The remainder of the data space becomes available for other VSAM objects.

ESTIMATING CATALOG SPACE REQUIREMENTS

The amount of space to assign to either an ICF catalog or a VSAM catalog depends on the type and number of VSAM and non-VSAM catalog entries that will be stored in the catalog. In many cases, a cylinder of space will provide more than enough room. If detailed information is desired about precisely estimating the space requirements for catalogs, the *Catalog User's Guide* reference manual for your operating system version and catalog facility should be consulted.

ALTERING AND DELETING CATALOGS

As with other VSAM objects, the ALTER parameter can be used to change a user catalog's attributes after it has been defined. The example below defines a new expiration date and nullifies the CODE parameter for the catalog named EMPLOYEE.

```
ALTER    EMPLOYEE                                              -
           TO       (81001)                                    -
           NULLIFY (CODE)
```

In order to delete a user catalog, all of its catalog entries should first be deleted. AMS will reject a DELETE command for a catalog that is not empty unless the FORCE parameter is included. The following command deletes the user catalog named EMPLOYEE, no matter what the current expiration date for the catalog is:

```
DELETE EMPLOYEE                                                -
         USERCATALOG                                           -
         PURGE
```

When deleting a user catalog, including the FORCE parameter causes AMS to delete the user catalog and the catalog entries for all the objects cataloged in it. However, the contents of the objects are not erased.

THE DEFINE SPACE COMMAND

As mentioned earlier, data spaces are used only in conjunction with VSAM catalogs; ICF catalogs do not use data spaces. A data space can be defined implicitly for a new VSAM object by coding the UNIQUE parameter in the DEFINE command for the object. This causes a new data space, of the requested size, to be defined for the sole use of that object. An empty data space can also be defined explicitly through the use of the DEFINE SPACE command. The empty data space then becomes available for storing VSAM objects that are defined using the default option of <u>SUBALLOCATION.</u> Box 8.4 shows the

BOX 8.4 The DEFINE SPACE command

```
DEFINE   SPACE
         ({CANDIDATE|
         {CYLINDERS(primary[ secondary])|
           RECORDS(primary[ secondary])|
             RECORDSIZE(average maximum)|
           TRACKS(primary[ secondary])}
         VOLUMES(volser[ volser...])
         [FILE(ddname)])

   [CATALOG(catname[/password])]
```

CANDIDATE	The CANDIDATE (CAN) parameter specifies that the volumes listed in the command are to be reserved for future use by the catalog in effect for this DEFINE SPACE command.
CYLINDERS ¦ RECORDS ¦ TRACKS	The CYLINDERS (CYL), RECORDS (REC), and TRACKS (TRK) parameters are used to allocate direct access space to the data space.
RECORDSIZE	The RECORDSIZE (RECSZ) parameter is used when requesting space in terms of records to define the average and maximum record length to be used in allocating space.
VOLUMES	The VOLUMES (VOL) parameter specifies the volume serial numbers of the volumes to reserve or the volumes on which the data space is to be allocated.
FILE	The FILE parameter specifies the name of the DD statement that provides UNIT and VOLUME information for the data space.
CATALOG	The CATALOG (CAT) specifies the name of the user catalog to which ownership of the volume or volumes is to be assigned.

syntax of the DEFINE SPACE parameter and describes its parameters. The following is an example of a DEFINE SPACE command:

```
DEFINE SPACE                                           -
       (VOLUMES    (DSK001)                            -
        CYLINDERS (100 20))                            -
    CATALOG        (EMPLOYEE)
```

The CANDIDATE parameter of the DEFINE SPACE command can be used to reserve a volume for future use by a particular VSAM catalog. The CANDIDATE option prevents some other user from creating a user catalog on that volume, but does not allocate any of the volume's available space. DEFINE commands can be issued later to allocate space on the volume. The following DEFINE command assigns the ownership of volume DSK003 to the EMPLOYEE user catalog:

```
DEFINE SPACE                                        -
         (VOLUMES  (DSK003)                         -
          CANDIDATE)                                -
       CATALOG     (EMPLOYEE)
```

The DELETE command can be used to remove a data space. Any VSAM objects residing on it should be deleted before the data space itself is deleted. The following command deletes all *empty* data spaces on volume DSK002. Data spaces that are not empty are not deleted.

```
DELETE SPACE   (DSK002)                             -
       CATALOG (EMPLOYEE)
```

The FORCE parameter can be included in a DELETE SPACE command to delete all data spaces on a volume regardless of their contents. As a result, ownership of the volume is automatically released. FORCE is often used to recover space owned by a catalog that was damaged by a system or hardware failure. The FORCE parameter should be used with caution because the catalog entries associated with the deleted objects are not deleted automatically. The use of the FORCE parameter in deleting a data space may result in catalog entries that refer to objects that no longer exist.

THE DEFINE NONVSAM COMMAND

Both ICF catalogs and VSAM catalogs can be used to store entries for non-VSAM objects as well as for VSAM objects. A catalog entry for a non-VSAM data set does not contain a detailed description of the data set. Only the data set name, its volume number, device type, and information such as the data set's creation and expiration dates are included. Information about the data set's attributes, such as record length and block size, is stored in the data set's label. Catalog entries for non-VSAM data sets ordinarily are created using the DISP=CATLG parameter in the DD statement; however, the AMS DEFINE NONVSAM command can also be used to create catalog entries for non-VSAM data sets. Box 8.5 shows the syntax of the DEFINE NONVSAM command and describes its parameters. Catalog entries for non-VSAM data sets can be deleted by issuing a DELETE command that names the entry being deleted.

BOX 8.5 The DEFINE NONVSAM command

```
DEFINE    NONVSAM
            (NAME(entryname)
            DEVICETYPES(devtype[ devtype...])
            VOLUMES(volser[ volser...])

            [FILESEQUENCENUMBERS(number[ number...])
            [OWNER(ownerid)])
            [TO(date)|FOR(days)])

        [CATALOG(catname[/password])]
```

NAME	The NAME parameter specifies the name of the non-VSAM data set being defined.
DEVICETYPES	The DEVICETYPES (DEVT) parameter specifies the device types on which the non-VSAM data set resides.
VOLUMES	The VOLUMES (VOL) parameter specifies the volume serial numbers of the volumes on which the non-VSAM data set resides.
FILESEQUENCENUMBERS	The FILESEQUENCENUMBERS (FSEQN) parameter specifies the file sequence numbers of the non-VSAM data set.
OWNER	The OWNER parameter specifies the owner identifier of the non-VSAM data set.
TO ¦ FOR	The TO and FOR parameters specify the expiration date to be assigned to the non-VSAM data set.
CATALOG	The CATALOG (CAT) parameter specifies the name of the catalog into which the new catalog entry is to be placed.

9 ALTERNATE INDEXES

In this chapter, we discuss the alternate index facilities provided by VSAM. An alternate index is similar to the prime index of a KSDS, but indexes a cluster based on the values of some field other than the prime key. An alternate index can provide an additional way of sequencing the data in a KSDS and can also be used to index an ESDS. This chapter shows how to define an alternate index, how to load it with data using the information contained in the cluster it indexes, and how to define a path that associates an alternate index with its base cluster.

ALTERNATE KEYS

As we have seen, records can be retrieved from a KSDS based on the value of the primary key field that was chosen for the cluster when it was defined. However, an application may also need to retrieve records based on the values contained in other fields. For example, suppose an application retrieves records from a KSDS named EMPLOYEE.KSDS that have the format shown in Fig. 9.1. The primary key for the record is Emp-Number, so the program normally performs direct KSDS retrievals by supplying an Emp-Number value in each direct retrieval request. Suppose the application needs access to records based on Emp-Name values as well. One way that this can be done is by searching the KSDS sequentially until the record with the desired Emp-Name value is located. For a large file, the processing time this would require might be prohibitive. Another solution might be to create a separate file that has the Emp-Name field as the primary key and the corresponding Emp-Number value stored in another field in the record. This file might be used to find the Emp-Number value, which can then be used to perform a direct retrieval in the original employee file. Using a second file creates new problems because both files must be kept in synchronization as employee records are added, deleted, and updated.

VSAM provides a feature that allows records to be retrieved directly from

EMPLOYEE

Emp-Number	Emp-Name	Emp-Region	Emp-Dept
0 3	4 23	24	25 26

Figure 9.1 Employee record format.

a KSDS based on fields other than the field designated as the primary key. The key field chosen when the KSDS is defined is called the *primary key*. Additional fields that can be used to gain direct access to records are called *alternate keys*. Any field in a record can be defined as an alternate key, as long as the field is fixed in size and begins in the same position in each record in the file. Records are maintained in logical sequence based on primary key values via the KSDS index; this index is called the *prime index*. Records can also be maintained in logical sequence based on values of alternate keys via additional indexes called *alternate indexes*. Alternate indexes are created with the DEFINE command in the same way that a KSDS cluster is defined. Later in this chapter, we will examine examples of DEFINE commands for alternate indexes.

THE BASE CLUSTER

Before continuing our discussion of alternate indexes, we will briefly review the structure of a VSAM KSDS that uses only a prime index. Figure 9.2 repeats the employee record layout and shows a typical record that might be stored in the EMPLOYEE.KSDS cluster. The original KSDS cluster, consisting of an index and a data component, is called the *base cluster*. The base cluster that contains our employee records is keyed on the Emp-Number field. In order to retrieve the employee record for *Hall,* Hall's employee number, *0512,* must be known.

Figure 9.3 shows the structure of the index and data components of the base cluster. For clarity, only the key value and part of the Employee-Name field is shown for each record. In order to locate record 0512, VSAM searches

EMPLOYEE

Emp-Number	Emp-Name	Emp-Region	Emp-Dept
0 3	4 23	24	25 26

0512	HALL	1	23

Figure 9.2 Employee record occurrence.

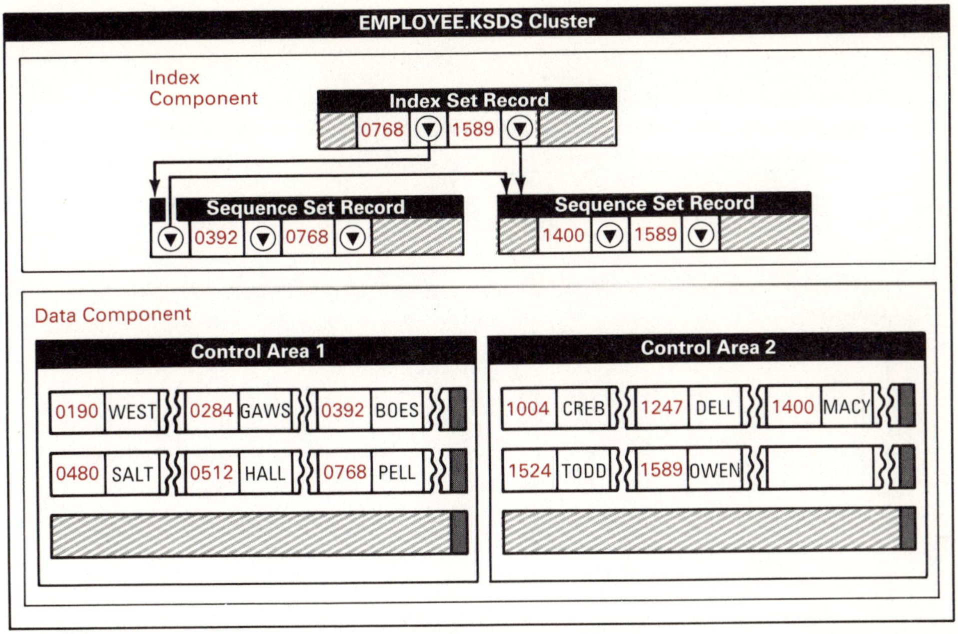

Figure 9.3 EMPLOYEE.KSDS cluster.

the index set for a key value that is greater than or equal to *0512*. In this case, the desired index entry contains the employee number *0768*. This index set entry points to a sequence set record which is then searched in a similar manner. Since there is only one sequence set record per control area, the sequence set entry narrows the search to a particular control interval. VSAM then reads this control interval into virtual storage in order to locate the desired employee record.

INDEXING A KSDS

If our application requires that we be able to perform similar index searches based on the Emp-Name field as well as on the Emp-Number field, we must construct an alternate index based on Emp-Name values. Figure 9.4 shows an alternate index named EMPLOYEE.NAMEIX that does this. The alternate index is implemented in the form of a separate KSDS cluster that itself consists of an index component and a data component. The index component of the alternate index has a structure that is similar to the index component of the base cluster. Just as with the base cluster, the index component of the alternate index is searched to locate a data record in the data component of the alternate index. The data component of the alternate index, however, does not contain complete employee records as does

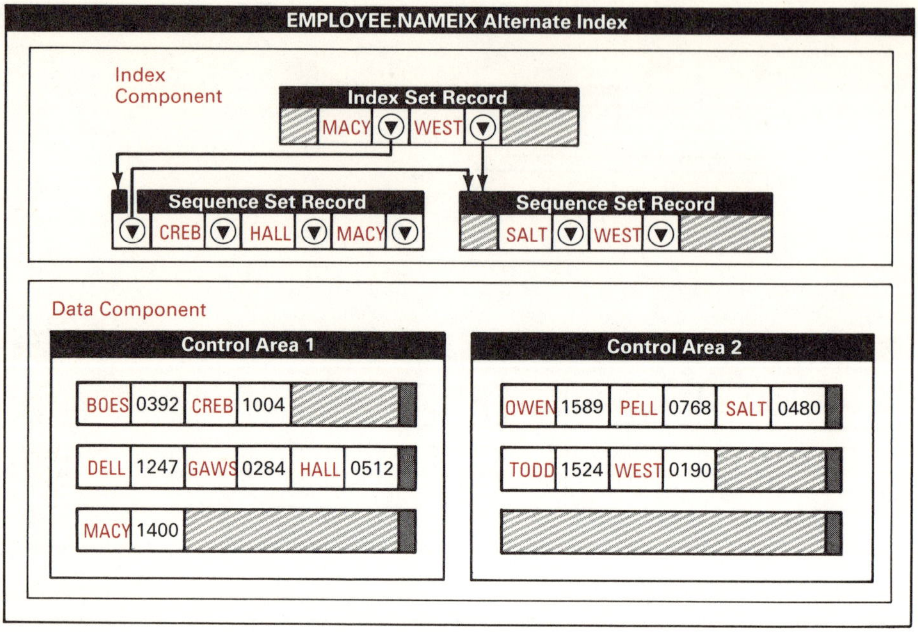

Figure 9.4 EMPLOYEE.NAMEIX alternate index.

the base cluster. Instead, each record in the data component of the alternate index contains an alternate key value and a pointer to the corresponding record in the base cluster.

When an alternate index is used to index a KSDS base cluster, as in our employee example, each pointer record in the alternate index data component contains the primary key value of the corresponding record in the KSDS base cluster. In order to retrieve a record from a KSDS base cluster using the alternate index, the application program issues a retrieval request that passes to VSAM an alternate key value. VSAM then proceeds as follows:

- VSAM searches the index component of the alternate index to locate the appropriate control interval in the *alternate index* data component.
- VSAM reads in the control interval from the alternate index data component and locates the record that corresponds to the supplied alternate key value. This record contains the primary key value of the desired base cluster record.
- The primary key value obtained from the alternate index is used to search the prime index to locate the control interval in the *base* cluster that contains the desired employee record.
- The control interval is read from the base cluster and the desired record is extracted from it and passed to the application program.

The above processing steps show that when an alternate index is used to retrieve a record from a KSDS cluster, VSAM performs two separate index searches to locate the desired record. The first index search uses the alternate index to determine the primary key value of the desired record. The second index search uses the prime index to locate the desired data record in the base cluster.

INDEXING AN ESDS

The base cluster that is indexed by an alternate index does not have to be a KSDS; ESDS clusters can also be referenced by alternate indexes. RRDS clusters cannot be indexed by alternate indexes, nor can reusable data sets of any type be indexed. The structure of an alternate index that indexes an ESDS is similar to that of an alternate index that indexes a KSDS. Figure 9.5 shows what the EMPLOYEE.NAMEIX alternate index would look like if the base Employee cluster were implemented as an ESDS instead of a KSDS. One major difference is that an ESDS base cluster has no prime index component. Therefore, each data record in the alternate index data component contains an alternate key value and a direct relative byte address (RBA) pointer into the data component of the ESDS.

To retrieve a record from an ESDS base cluster using an alternate key

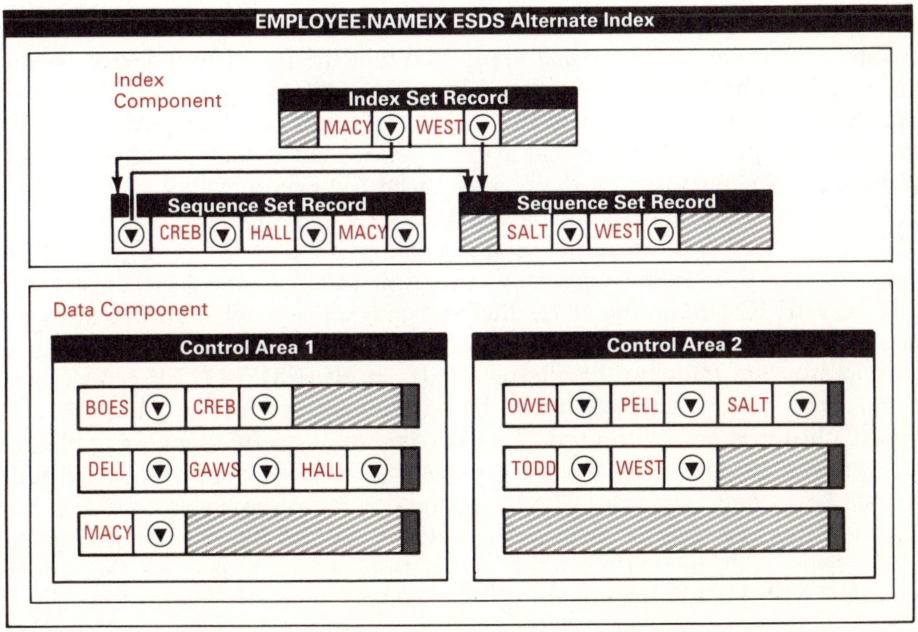

Figure 9.5 EMPLOYEE.NAMEIX ESDS alternate index.

value, the application program again issues a retrieval request that identifies the alternate key and supplies an alternate key value. VSAM then proceeds as follows:

- VSAM searches the index component of the alternate index to locate the appropriate control interval in the alternate index data component.
- VSAM reads in the control interval and locates the particular record in the data component that corresponds to the supplied alternate key value. This record contains a direct RBA pointer to the desired record in the data component of the ESDS base cluster.
- The control interval that contains the desired record is read from the data component of the ESDS, and the desired record is extracted from it based on the RBA value obtained from the alternate index.

The above processing steps show that when an alternate index is used to index an ESDS cluster, only one index search is required to locate a record in the ESDS. The alternate index points directly into the records in the data component of the ESDS.

PATHS

The combination of an alternate index and the base cluster that it indexes is called a *path*. A path has a separate set of attributes, such as password and retention period, that are defined separately from the attributes that apply to either the alternate index or the base cluster alone. The DEFINE command is used to create a path in the same way that a KSDS is defined. Later in this chapter we will see examples of DEFINE commands for paths. Before a path can be defined, its associated alternate index and base cluster must first be defined using DEFINE commands.

The relationships between the EMPLOYEE.KSDS base cluster, the EMPLOYEE.NAMEIX alternate index, and a path named EMPLOYEE.NAME are shown in Fig. 9.6. If an application program refers to the base cluster itself (EMPLOYEE.KSDS) in the JCL, alternate indexes are not used to satisfy processing requests; the base cluster is referenced directly. Similarly, when an application program refers to the alternate index itself (EMPLOYEE.NAMEIX) in the JCL, records are retrieved from the data component of the alternate index; the base cluster is not referenced. This is sometimes useful when an application simply needs to determine the prime key that is associated with a particular alternate key value. The most often used application of an alternate index, however, is to access records from a base cluster via an alternate index. To use the alternate index in this way, the application program specifies the name of the *path* (EMPLOYEE.NAME) in the JCL. Then, when the path is opened, the program is given access to the base cluster via the alternate index defined for

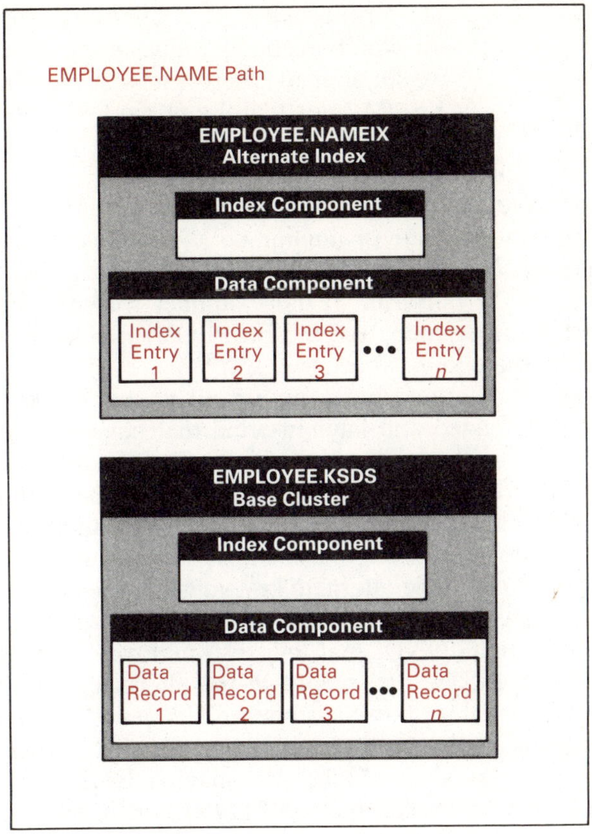

Figure 9.6 Component relationships.

the path. An application program works with a path in the same way that it works with a KSDS cluster. The program supplies an alternate key value in each I/O request, and VSAM searches the alternate index to find the corresponding alternate key/pointer pair. Then VSAM either searches the prime index (for a KSDS) or follows the direct RBA pointer (for an ESDS) to locate the desired record in the base cluster.

Any number of alternate indexes can be defined (using separate DEFINE commands) that apply to the same base cluster; each must be given its own unique path name and set of attributes. Also, multiple paths can be defined that apply to the same alternate index/base cluster pair, each of which can have its own unique set of attributes. In this manner, a separate password and other attributes can be assigned to each potential user of an alternate index/base cluster pair.

NONUNIQUE ALTERNATE KEY VALUES

The prime index of a KSDS must define a key field for which each key value in the data set is unique. If we attempt to insert a new record into a KSDS, and VSAM finds that the prime key value of the new record matches the key value of a record already in the data set, the insert operation fails. When defining an alternate index, it is often desirable to choose alternate keys that do not have unique values. VSAM allows an alternate index to be defined as having either unique or nonunique key values. If we define an alternate index as having *unique* key values, VSAM does not allow duplicate alternate key values. For the purposes of our example, we will assume that no two employees have the same name, and the EMPLOYEE.NAMEIX alternate index contains unique alternate key values.

If we define the alternate index as having *nonunique* key values, VSAM allows records to be loaded and later inserted that have the same alternate key value. There is onc rccord in the data component of the alternate index for each unique alternate key value, but each one may contain multiple pointers to associated records in the base cluster that have the same alternate key value. The nonunique key feature allows a program to retrieve multiple records from the base cluster that have the same alternate key value. For example, there are many records in the employee data set for each region. If we set up an alternate index named EMPLOYEE.REGIONIX that indexes employee records based on Emp-Region values, there will be one record in the alternate index data component for each Emp-Region value; but each one will contain multiple pointers to all the employee records in the base cluster that have that particular Emp-Region value (see Fig. 9.7). By opening the path named EMPLOYEE.REGION for sequential access, consisting of the EMPLOYEE.REGIONIX alternate index and the EMPLOYEE.KSDS base cluster, we can sequentially retrieve all the employee records for a particular region.

UPGRADE SET

When updates are applied to a base cluster, it is possible that the alternate indexes associated with the base cluster will also need to be updated. VSAM can be directed to perform all required alternate index updates automatically by specifying the UPGRADE option when the alternate index is defined. All alternate indexes associated with a base cluster that were defined specifying the UPGRADE option are known as that base cluster's *upgrade set*. When a base cluster is opened for output, VSAM also opens all alternate indexes in the base cluster's upgrade set. When the base cluster is updated, corresponding updates are applied as required to all alternate indexes in the upgrade set. It is the responsibility of the application program to ensure that required updates are applied to those alternate indexes that are not members of the base cluster's upgrade set.

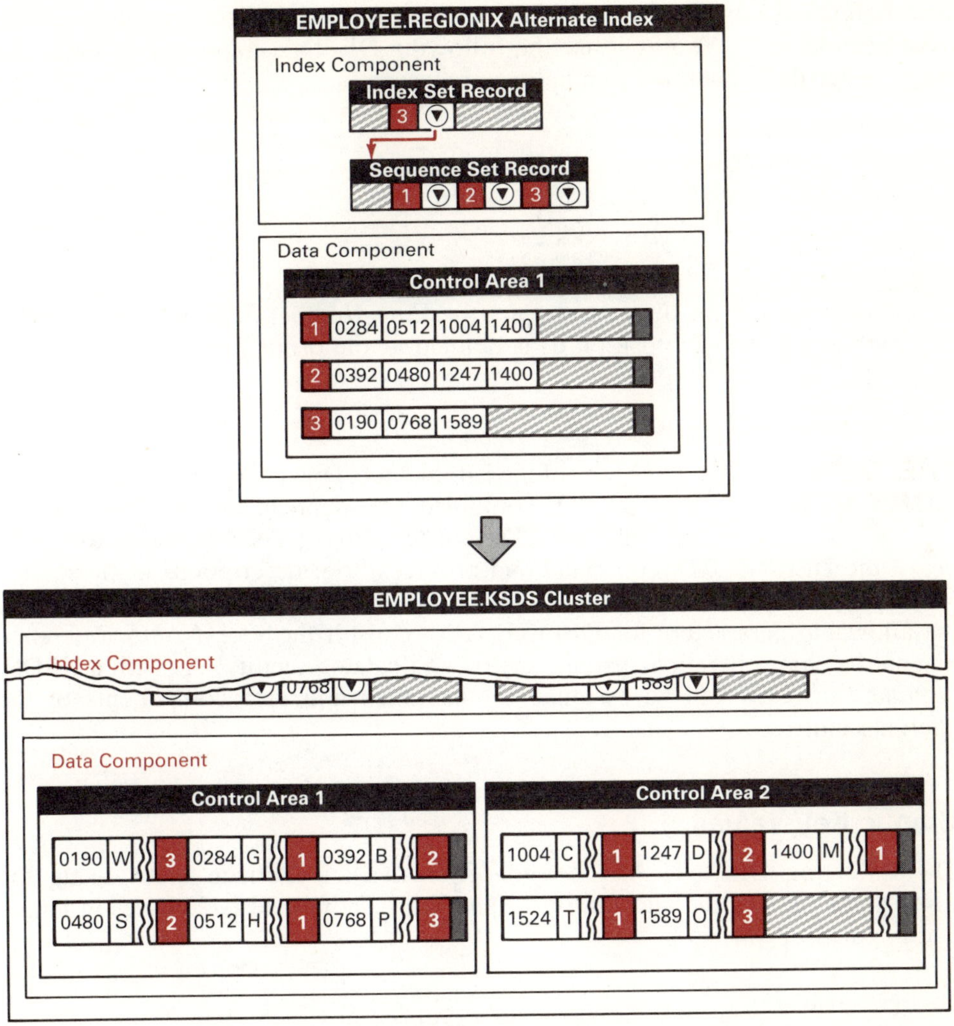

Figure 9.7 EMPLOYEE.REGIONIX alternate index.

DEFINING ALTERNATE INDEXES

As stated earlier, an alternate index is defined in a similar manner as a KSDS cluster. The DEFINE ALTERNATEINDEX (DEFINE AIX) command is used to create a catalog entry for the alternate index, to allocate direct access space for it, and to associate the alternate index with a base cluster. The BLDINDEX command is then issued to load the appropriate values into the new alternate index. Before issuing the DEFINE command for an alternate index, the associated base cluster must already have been defined.

And before issuing the BLDINDEX command, the base cluster must already have been loaded. We might use the following DEFINE command to define the base cluster that contains our employee records:

```
DEFINE CLUSTER                                              -
          (NAME           (EMPLOYEE.KSDS)                   -
           KEYS           (4 0)                             -
           VOLUMES        (DSK001)                          -
           CYLINDERS      (5 1)                             -
           RECORDSIZE     (26 26)                           -
           FREESPACE      (25 33))
```

Notice that in the above example, the Emp-Number field, which is 4 bytes in length and begins in position 0, is defined as the prime key.

THE DEFINE AIX COMMAND

Many of the parameters of the DEFINE ALTERNATE-INDEX command are identical to those used to define a KSDS cluster. Box 9.1 shows the partial syntax of the DEFINE AIX command and provides brief descriptions of those DEFINE parameters that are unique to alternate indexes. For a complete list of all the allowable parameters for DEFINE AIX, consult the *VSAM AMS Reference* manual for your operation system version and catalog facility. As with a KSDS, separate attributes can be assigned to the index and data components of the alternate index.

Unique Key Values

The following DEFINE AIX command creates an alternate index using the Emp-Name field as the alternate key. The Emp-Name field is 20 bytes in length and begins in position 4.

```
DEFINE AIX                                                  -
          (NAME           (EMPLOYEE.NAMEIX)                 -
           RELATE         (EMPLOYEE.KSDS)                   -
           KEYS           (20 4)                            -
           VOLUMES        (DSK001)                          -
           CYLINDERS      (3 1)                             -
           RECORDSIZE     (29 29)                           -
           FREESPACE      (25 25))                          -
           UNIQUEKEY                                        -
           UPGRADE
```

The DEFINE command names the alternate index EMPLOYEE.NAMEIX, and the RELATE (REL) parameter associates this alternate index with the EMPLOYEE.KSDS base cluster. This example assumes that no two employees have the same name, so UNIQUEKEY is included.

The RECORDSIZE parameter is coded just as on the DEFINE CLUSTER command; however, it refers to the record in the data component of the alternate index, not to the record in the base cluster. For an alternate index with unique alternate key values, each alternate index record is made up of the following:

- 5 bytes of control information
- An alternate key value
- A pointer into the base cluster

If the base cluster is a KSDS, each pointer consists of a primary key value. Thus, the length of an EMPLOYEE.NAMEIX alternate index data record is 29 bytes, determined as follows:

- 5 bytes of control information
- 20 bytes for an Emp-Name alternate key value
- 4 bytes for an Emp-Number primary key value

Nonunique Key Values

When defining an alternate index that uses nonunique alternate key values, variable-length records are used in the data component of the alternate index to allow for alternate key values that have multiple pointers to records in the base cluster. Using our employee record example, suppose we assume that the number of employees in each region will range from a minimum of 20 to a maximum of 50. The Emp-Region field is 1 byte in length, and each alternate index data record must allow room for 20 to 50 pointers, each containing a primary key value. The minimum length of an EMPLOYEE.REGIONIX alternate index data record is 86 bytes, determined in the following manner:

- 5 bytes of control information
- 1 byte for an alternate key value
- 80 bytes for 20 Emp-Number prime key values

The maximum length of an EMPLOYEE.NAMEIX alternate index data record is 206 bytes, determined as follows:

- 5 bytes of control information
- 1 byte for an Emp-Region alternate key value
- 200 bytes for 50 Emp-Number prime key values

BOX 9.1 The DEFINE ALTERNATEINDEX command

```
DEFINE   ALTERNATEINDEX
            (NAME(entryname)
             RELATE(entryname[/password])
             {CYLINDERS(primary[ secondary])|
               RECORDS(primary[ secondary])|
               TRACKS(primary[ secondary])}
             [UNIQUEKEY|NONUNIQUEKEY]
             [UPGRADE|NOUPGRADE]
             [optional DEFINE CLUSTER subparameters]

          [DATA
             [UNIQUEKEY|NONUNIQUEKEY]
             [optional DEFINE DATA subparameters]

          [INDEX
             [optional DEFINE INDEX subparameters]

          [CATALOG(catname[/password])]
```

NAME The NAME parameter is used to give a name to the alternate index being defined.

RELATE The RELATE (REL) parameter is required and names the base cluster corresponding to the alternate index. Although an alternate index can be created for any existing key-sequenced or entry-sequenced cluster, one cannot be defined for a relative record cluster, a reusable VSAM data set, a catalog, or another alternate index.

CYLINDERS
RECORDS
TRACKS The CYLINDERS (CYL), RECORDS (REC), and TRACKS (TRK) parameter are used to allocate space to the alternate index in the same manner as space is allocated to a KSDS cluster.

UNIQUEKEY The UNIQUEKEY (UNQK) parameter tells VSAM that there is only one base record corresponding to each alternate key in the alternate index.

NONUNIQUEKEY The NONUNIQUEKEY (NUNQK) parameter is included if each alternate key value can be included in multiple records in the base cluster.

BOX 9.1 *(Continued)*

UPGRADE	The UPGRADE (UPG) parameter makes the alternate index part of the base cluster's upgrade set. The alternate index will then automatically be kept current whether the base cluster is updated by itself or as part of a path.
NOUPGRADE	The NOUPGRADE (NUPG) parameter prevents an automatic upgrade and should be used with caution. In certain applications, it is more efficient for the user to maintain the alternate index. But in most cases, it is better to let VSAM do an automatic index upgrade.
Additional Subparameters	Most of the optional subparameters that can be coded following the CLUSTER, DATA, and INDEX parameters when defining a KSDS cluster can also be coded following the AIX, DATA, and INDEX parameters when defining an alternate index.

The following DEFINE command might be used to define the EMPLOYEE.REGIONIX alternate index, assuming that the average record length of an alternate index data record is 150 bytes:

```
DEFINE AIX                                                    -
       (NAME          (EMPLOYEE.REGIONIX)                     -
        RELATE        (EMPLOYEE.KSDS)                         -
        VOLUMES       (DSK001)                                -
        CYLINDERS     (2 1)                                   -
        FREESPACE     (30 20)                                 -
        KEYS          (1 24)                                  -
        RECORDSIZE    (150 206))                              -
        NONUNIQUEKEY
```

The KEYS parameter tells VSAM that the Emp-Region field is one character long, beginning in position 24. Since neither UPGRADE nor NOUPGRADE is specified, the default value, UPGRADE, is assumed, and the alternate index is included in the upgrade set of the EMPLOYEE.KSDS base cluster.

ESDS Indexes

When choosing a data component record size for an alternate index that indexes an ESDS, 4 bytes are required for each RBA pointer. So the alternate index data record length for an alternate index with unique keys that indexes an ESDS is determined as follows:

- 5 bytes of control information
- Room for one alternate key value
- 4 bytes for an RBA pointer

If an index that references an ESDS has nonunique keys, the minimum and maximum lengths of an alternate index data record are determined as follows:

- 5 bytes of control information
- Room for one alternate key value
- Minimum and maximum number of 4-byte RBA pointers

THE BLDINDEX COMMAND

The DEFINE command for an alternate index creates a catalog entry that describes the alternate index and points to its related base cluster. After the alternate index catalog entry has been defined, the BLDINDEX command is issued to load the alternate index. Box 9.2 shows the syntax of the BLDINDEX (BIX) command and briefly describes each of its parameters. The processing performed by AMS in response to BLDINDEX consists of the following three steps:

1. AMS reads the base cluster sequentially and constructs alternate key/pointer pairs from each data record in the base cluster. As discussed earlier, if the base cluster is a KSDS, each pointer consists of a prime key value; if the base cluster is an ESDS, each pointer consists of an RBA pointer.
2. AMS sorts the alternate key/pointer pairs into ascending alternate key sequence. For a large base cluster, the sort may have to be carried out using work files that must be referenced in the JCL.
3. AMS uses the sorted alternate key/pointer pairs to load records into the data component of the alternate index. Control information is added to each alternate key/pointer pair that tells VSAM the length of the alternate key, describes whether the pointers are prime keys or RBA's, indicates whether the keys are unique or nonunique, and gives the length of each prime key pointer.

Internal Sorting

Depending on the size of the alternate index being built, AMS must use either an internal sort or an external sort. An internal sort is one that can take place

BOX 9.2 The BLDINDEX command

```
BLDINDEX {INFILE(ddname[/password])|
            INDATASET(entryname[/password])}
          {OUTFILE(ddame[/password]
             [ ddname[/password]...])|
            OUTDATASET(entryname[/password
               [ entryname[/password]...])}
          [EXTERNALSORT|INTERNALSORT]
          [WORKFILES(ddname ddname)]
          [CATALOG(catname[/password])]
```

INFILE The INFILE (IFILE) parameter identifies a DD statement that describes the base cluster or a path that points to the base cluster.

INDATASET The INDATASET (IDS) parameter names the base cluster or a path that points to the base cluster.

OUTFILE The OUTFILE (OFILE) parameter identifies a DD statement that describes the alternate index being loaded. Multiple alternate indexes can be built using the same base cluster by including a DD statement for each one.

OUTDATASET The OUTDATASET (ODS) parameter names the alternate index being loaded. Multiple alternate indexes can be built by listing all of them in this parameter.

EXTERNAL-SORT The EXTERNALSORT (ESORT) parameter specifies that two work data sets should be created for the purpose of performing an external sort of alternate key/pointer pairs.

INTERNALSORT The INTERNALSORT (ISORT) parameter (the default) specifies that an internal sort of alternate key/pointer pairs should be performed if possible.

WORKFILES The WORKFILES (WFILE) parameter specifies the names of two DD statements that define work data sets to be used if an external sort is required. This parameter is required only if an external sort is necessary and if the names of the DD statements that define the work data sets are other than IDCUT1 and IDCUT2.

CATALOG The CATALOG (CAT) parameter specifies the name of the user catalog into which the catalog entries for the two sort work data sets are to be placed.

directly in virtual storage. The following job step shows an example of an AMS step that loads the EMPLOYEE.NAMEIX alternate index using an internal sort:

```
//STEP1        EXEC     PGM=IDCAMS
//SYSPRINT     DD       SYSOUT=A
//BASEIN       DD       DSN=EMPLOYEE.KSDS,DISP=OLD
//AIXOUT       DD       DSN=EMPLOYEE.NAMEIX,DISP=OLD
//SYSIN        DD       *
  BLDINDEX     INFILE  (BASEIN)                              -
               OUTFILE (AIXOUT)
```

The only two parameters included in the above BLDINDEX command are parameters that name the DD statements in the job step that describe the base cluster (BASEIN) and the alternate index itself (AIXOUT). The above step assumes that the EMPLOYEE base cluster has already been defined and loaded and that the EMPLOYEE.NAMEIX alternate index has already been defined. Since no information was provided concerning the type of sort that should be performed, the default option of INTERNALSORT is assumed and AMS attempts to perform the sort in the available virtual storage.

Since the base cluster and the alternate index have already been defined before the BLDINDEX step is run, the IDS and ODS parameters can be used instead of INFILE and OUTFILE. The following example uses the IDS and ODS parameters to identify the base cluster and the alternate index:

```
//STEP1        EXEC     PGM=IDCAMS
//SYSPRINT     DD       SYSOUT=A
//SYSIN        DD       *
  BLDINDEX     IDS (EMPLOYEE.KSDS)                           -
               ODS (EMPLOYEE.NAMEIX)
```

External Sorting

For very large base clusters, there may not be enough virtual storage available to handle an internal sort of the alternate key/pointer pairs. In order to prevent the BLDINDEX step from failing due to insufficient virtual storage space, we can provide sort work data sets for AMS to use if they become necessary. If they are provided, and we request an internal sort, AMS will invoke an external sort using the supplied work data set information if not enough virtual storage is available to handle an internal sort. The job step shown below illustrates the use of sort work data sets.

```
//STEP1        EXEC     PGM=IDCAMS
//SYSPRINT     DD       SYSOUT=A
//BASECL       DD       DSN=EMPLOYEE.KSDS,DISP=OLD
//ALTIND       DD       DSN=EMPLOYEE.REGIONIX,DISP=OLD
//WORK1        DD       VOL=SER=DSK001,UNIT=3380,
//             DISP=OLD,AMP='AMORG'
//WORK2        DD       VOL=SER=DSK002,UNIT=3380,
//             DISP=OLD,AMP='AMORG'
//SYSIN        DD
  BLDINDEX     INFILE  (BASECL)                              -
               OUTFILE (ALTIND)                              -
               WFILE   (WORK1 WORK2)
```

Since no ESORT parameter is included in the above BLDINDEX command, AMS attempt an internal sort. If not enough virtual storage is available, AMS then uses two sort work data sets to perform an external sort. The two sort work DD statements must specify a volume that has available space for two ESDS clusters. AMS automatically defines and opens these data sets; they do not have to be defined in advance.

If the two sort work data sets are defined using DD statements named IDCUT1 and IDCUT2, the WFILE parameter can be omitted; AMS automatically will look for DD statements having these names if an external sort is required. The following job step shows an example of this:

```
//STEP1       EXEC    PGM=IDCAMS
//SYSPRINT    DD      SYSOUT=A
//BASECL      DD      DSN=EMPLOYEE.KSDS,DISP=OLD
//ALTIND      DD      DSN=EMPLOYEE.REGIONIX,DISP=OLD
//IDCUT1      DD      VOL=SER=DSK001,UNIT=3380,
//            DISP=OLD,AMP='AMORG'
//IDCUT2      DD      VOL=SER=DSK002,UNIT=3380,
//            DISP=OLD,AMP='AMORG'
//SYSIN       DD
  BLDINDEX    INFILE  (BASECL)                                -
              OUTFILE (ALTIND)                                -
```

THE DEFINE PATH COMMAND

As we have already discussed, an alternate index by itself is of limited use. To access the data records in the base cluster via the alternate index, the alternate index must be connected to its associated base cluster by defining a path. Box 9.3 shows the syntax of the DEFINE PATH command and briefly describes each of its parameters. The example below defines the EMPLOYEE.NAME path.

```
DEFINE PATH                                                   -
         (NAME       (EMPLOYEE.NAME)                          -
          PATHENTRY (EMPLOYEE.NAMEIX))
```

The above path definition gives a name to the path and specifies the name of the alternate index it references. The base cluster is not specified because the alternate index definition specifies the name of the base cluster.

The DEFINE PATH command supports many of the same parameters as the DEFINE CLUSTER and DEFINE AIX commands. A path can be given its own set of attributes, such as passwords, expiration date, retention period, and owner name. If desired, any of these attributes can be different from those defined for the underlying alternate index and base cluster. This allows a user to specify a path name and its password without having to know the password that protects either the underlying alternate index or the base cluster.

In the example, the <u>UPDATE</u> or NOUPDATE option was omitted, so the default value of <u>UPDATE</u> takes effect. The UPDATE option specifies that the

BOX 9.3 The DEFINE PATH command

```
DEFINE   PATH
           (NAME(entryname)
            PATHENTRY(entryname[/password])
            [ATTEMPTS(number|2)]
            [AUTHORIZATION(entrypoint[ string])]
            [CODE(code)]
            [CONTROLPW(password)]
            [MASTERPW(password)]
            [MODEL(entryname[/password][ catname[/password]])]
            [OWNER(ownerid)]
            [READPW(password)]
            [TO(date)|FOR(days)]
            [UPDATEPW|password)]
            [CATALOG(catname[/password])]
```

Optional parameter for VSAM recoverable catalogs only

```
            [FILE(ddname)]
```

Optional parameter for ICF catalogs only

```
            [RECATALOG|NORECATALOG]
```

NAME	The NAME parameter specifies the name of the path being defined.
PATHENTRY	The PATHENTRY (PENT) parameter specifies the name of the alternate index when the path consists of an alternate index and a base cluster. This parameter specifies the name of the base cluster when the path defines an alias for a base cluster.
ATTEMPTS	The ATTEMPT (ATT) parameter specifies the maximum number of times the operator can enter a password.
AUTHORIZATION	The AUTHORIZATION (AUTH) parameter specifies information about a security verification routine to be used in conjunction with this path.
CODE	The CODE parameter specifies a code name to be used in password prompting messages for the path.
CONTROLPW	The CONTROLPW (CTLPW) parameter assigns a control password to the path.

BOX 9.3 *(Continued)*

MASTERPW	The MASTERPW (MRPW) parameter assigns a master password to the path.
MODEL	The MODEL parameter specifies the name of an existing path entry to be used as a model in defining this path.
OWNER	The OWNER parameter identifies the owner of the path.
READPW	The READPW (RDPW) parameter assigns a read password to the path.
TO ¦ FOR	The TO and FOR parameters are used to assign an expiration date to the path.
UPDATEPW	The UPDATEPW (UPDPW) parameter assigns an update password to the path.
CATALOG	The CATALOG (CAT) parameter identifies the user catalog into which the catalog entry for the path is to be placed.
FILE	The FILE parameter specifies the name of a DD statement in the JCL that identifies unit and volume information for the recovery volume associated with the alternate index or path identified in the PATHENTRY parameter. (Used with VSAM recoverable catalogs only.)
RECATALOG **NORECATALOG**	The RECATALOG (RCTLG) and NORECATALOG (NRCTLG) parameters specify whether or not an entry for the path already exists in the VVDS on the primary volume. (Used with ICF catalogs only.)

base cluster's upgrade set should be opened when this path is opened. Note that this does not guarantee that the alternate index defined by the path is part of the base cluster's upgrade set. The alternate index specified by the path will be automatically updated only if the UPGRADE option was specified (explicitly or by default) when the alternate index itself was defined. If NOUPDATE is specified for a path, the base cluster's upgrade set is not opened when the path is opened. This, in effect, overrides the UPGRADE parameters that were coded for all the alternate indexes in the base cluster's upgrade set.

ALIAS NAMES

The DEFINE PATH command has a number of other uses in addition to associating an alternate index and a base cluster. It can also refer to the base cluster alone, or some other VSAM object, to define an *alias,* or alternate name, for the object. (AMS provides a DEFINE ALIAS command, but it is used only to give an alternate name to a non-VSAM data set or to a user catalog.) The NAME parameter is used to define the alias name, and the PATHENTRY (PENT) parameter is used to refer to the existing name of the cluster. A new set of attributes can then be assigned to the alias name. For example, an alias name could be used to assign an alternate set of protection attributes to a cluster. The DEFINE PATH command can also refer to an already existing path. For example, an alias name could be defined with the NOUPDATE option to allow special-purpose applications to update the base cluster without affecting the alternate indexes in the upgrade set.

The example below defines a password-protected alias, named MARTIN.SECRET.FILE, for the EMPLOYEE.KSDS base cluster:

```
DEF PATH                                              -
       (NAME       (MARTIN.SECRET.FILE)               -
        PATHENTRY (EMPLOYEE.KSDS)                     -
        MASTERPW   (MARTMAST)                         -
        READDPW    (MARTREAD))
```

DELETING PATHS

Many of the utility functions that we have already described for VSAM clusters can also be applied to a path. For example, the following AMS commands can be used to delete the EMPLOYEE.NAME path:

```
DELETE EMPLOYEE.NAME                                  -
       PURGE                                          -
       PATH
```

Deleting the path has no effect on the catalog entries for the related alternate index and base cluster. The PATH keyword tells AMS what type of catalog entry is being deleted. If AMS discovers that the EMPLOYEE.NAME catalog entry is not a path, the DELETE command fails. If the PATH keyword is omitted, AMS deletes any object that has the specified name.

DELETING ALTERNATE INDEXES

As mentioned above, deleting a path does not cause its associated VSAM objects to be deleted. However, deleting an alternate index *does* cause all of its associated paths to be automatically deleted. This is because a path that associates a base cluster with an alternate index has no meaning if the alternate index no longer exists. The following DELETE command deletes the EMPLOYEE.NAMEIX alternate index and any paths that are associated with it:

```
DELETE EMPLOYEE.NAMEIX                                    -
       AIX                                                -
       PURGE                                              -
       ERASE                                              -
       FILE (AIXDD)
```

When a base cluster is deleted, all paths and alternate indexes associated with the base cluster are deleted automatically. VSAM does this because neither paths nor alternate indexes have any meaning if the base cluster no longer exists.

PRINTING A CLUSTER VIA A PATH

The PRINT command can be used to print the contents of a cluster, a path, or an alternate index. The following job step prints the contents of the EMPLOYEE.KSDS cluster via the path named EMPLOYEE.NAME:

```
//STEP5      EXEC   PGM=IDCAMS
//SYSPRINT   DD     SYSOUT=A
//MYINPUT    DD     DSN=EMPLOYEE.NAME,DISP=SHR
//SYSIN      DD     *
  PRINT      INFILE (MYINPUT)                             -
             CHARACTER
```

In the above example, EMPLOYEE.NAME is the name of a path that associates the EMPLOYEE.NAMEIX alternate index with the base cluster EMPLOYEE.KSDS. When a path name is specified in a PRINT command, the base cluster data records are printed in order by alternate key values. The above job step prints employee records in employee name order. If the specified data set is an alternate index, the alternate index data records are listed in alternate key sequence.

The parameters that limit printing to certain records can also be used when printing via a path. For example, the following command lists only the employee records for the employees in region D.

```
PRINT      IDS     (EMPLOYEE.REGION)                      -
           FROMKEY (D) -
           TOKEY   (D)
```

DEFINING AND LOADING IN ONE STEP

In most of the previous examples, a separate step was used for each AMS command. However, a single job step can be coded that defines a cluster, loads it, defines and builds an alternate index, and defines a path. It is important, however, to code the various AMS commands in the proper sequence. The following summarizes the sequence in which the steps must be performed:

- A cluster must be defined before an alternate index can be defined for it.
- An alternate index must be defined and its associated base cluster must be loaded before the alternate index can be loaded.
- Both the alternate index and base cluster components must be defined before an associated path can be defined.

10 PASSWORD PROTECTION

VSAM provides security facilities that allow passwords to be associated with VSAM objects to protect them from unauthorized access or modification. This chapter describes the four levels of passwords that can be associated with a VSAM object, explains how password values are provided to VSAM, and shows how to invoke the password protection facilities for VSAM objects. The various AMS parameters that control password processing are also described.

All types of VSAM objects can have passwords associated with them. An object's passwords are recorded in the object's catalog entry; therefore, any one who has unlimited access to a catalog can also learn the passwords for all the objects listed in that catalog. For this reason, the master catalog and user catalogs can themselves have passwords associated with them. Non-VSAM objects, such as non-VSAM data sets and generation data groups, cannot have VSAM passwords associated with them; however, standard operating system password protection facilities can be used to protect non-VSAM objects.

SUPPLYING THE PASSWORD

The correct password can be supplied in a variety of ways during processing. For example, the required password can be supplied by the application program, either by compiling the password directly into the program code (not recommended) or by supplying it at the time the data set is opened. If the job that runs the program is a batch job, and the program does not supply the password, the system operator is prompted for the password when the data set is opened. If the program is invoked from a terminal, for example, via TSO or SPF, the terminal user is prompted for the password.

PASSWORD LEVELS

There are four separate passwords that can be associated with a VSAM object; each of these is specified via one of the password subparameters of the DEFINE command. The syntax for those DEFINE parameters associated with password protection is given in Box 10.1. Each of the four passwords allows the user to issue a different subset of I/O requests against various parts of a VSAM object. Box 10.1 describes the level of access that each password permits. Notice that the subparameters are listed in order, with the first subparameter listed providing the most restrictive level of access. Supplying the password for a higher level of access also permits all levels of access provided by lower level passwords.

BOX 10.1 Levels of password protection

```
DEFINE    CLUSTER

          [READPW(password)]
          [UPDATEPW|password)]
          [CONTROLPW(password)]
          [MASTERPW(password)]
```

READPW The READPW subparameter specifies the password that a user must supply if the object will be read only. For example, a user who provides the read password for a data set can read records from the data set but cannot change, insert, or delete records.

UPDATEPW The UPDATEPW subparameter specifies the password that a user must supply if the user needs to update the object. A user who provides a data set's update password can retrieve, update, insert, and delete records.

CONTROLPW The CONTROLPW subparameter specifies the password that a user must supply if the user needs to have access to the object at the control interval level. At this level, the user can access the control information stored in the object's control intervals as well as the data stored in them.

MASTERPW The MASTERPW subparameter specifies the password that a user must supply in order to have full access to all components of the object, including control information, data, index, and password information in the object's catalog entry. The master password must be supplied if the object is password protected and the user wishes to issue an ALTER or DELETE command for the object.

SPECIFYING PASSWORD PROTECTION

As mentioned above, passwords are assigned to an object when the object is defined. Passwords can be changed for an object at any time by issuing an ALTER command for the object. Each password associated with a VSAM object is a 1-to-8 character simple name. Special characters, such as punctuation marks, can be included in a password if the entire password is enclosed between two single quotation marks. If a quotation mark is to be used as part of the password, each single quotation mark must be coded as two quotation marks. For example, a read password of AA'BBB is defined as follows:

```
READPW='AA''BBB'
```

A password can be specified in hexadecimal form by first coding an X and then enclosing the hexadecimal value in single quotes. The following example defines the password ABCDEFGH:

```
MASTERPW=X'C1C2C3C4C5C6C7C8'
```

The passwords assigned to an object limit access to the data stored in the object and also to the information in the object's catalog entries. By supplying an object's read, update, or control password in a LISTCAT command, all the catalog fields can be printed for the data set except those containing the passwords themselves. Only the master password gives access to the password fields in the object's catalog entry. As shown in Box 10.1, only the master password allows an object's catalog entry to be altered or deleted.

USER SECURITY VERIFICATION ROUTINE

Another level of security can be provided by including the AUTHORIZATION subparameter when defining a VSAM object. This parameter names a *user security verification* exit routine. VSAM passes control to this installation- or user-supplied routine after verifying that a correct read, update, or control password has been specified. This routine might ask for additional information from the system operator or terminal user, or it might simply record information about this particular access to the object. The routine decides whether or not to permit access and passes an appropriate return code to VSAM. The user security verification routine is not executed if the user supplies the master password instead of the read, update, or control password. The following AUTHORIZATION parameter specifies a user security verification routine.

```
AUTH (CLEAR ENTRYCODE275)
```

CLEAR is the name of the security verification routine. VSAM passes the character string ENTRYCODE275 to the routine at the same time it passes control to it. Information on coding a user security verification exit routine is presented in Chapter 24.

PASSWORD PROMPTING

As mentioned earlier, if an appropriate password is not supplied by the application program at the time the object is opened, the system operator or terminal user is prompted for a password. Ordinarily, the name of the object being opened is included in the prompt. In some cases, it is not desirable, for security purposes, to allow the system operator or terminal user to know the actual name of the object being opened. In such cases, the CODE parameter can be included when the object is defined to define a 1- to 8-character code name to be supplied in place of the object's name when password prompting is required. For example, if the following subparameter is included in the DEFINE command for an object, the code name SECRET1 is displayed instead of the object's name in a password prompt:

```
CODE=SECRET1
```

When issuing password prompts, VSAM ordinarily gives the system operator or terminal user two tries to supply a correct password before causing the OPEN attempt to fail. If a particular password contains an unusual character combination, it might be desirable to allow more than two tries. The number of allowable attempts can be defined by including the ATTEMPTS subparameter in the DEFINE command, as in the following example:

```
ATT (4)
```

The above parameter gives the operator four attempts to supply a correct password. If the correct password is not supplied after four tries, the OPEN operation fails.

LEVELS OF PROTECTION

Although passwords can be supplied to control all four levels of access to a VSAM object, all four passwords need not be specified when an object is defined. For example, if only update, control, and master passwords are specified for an object, users can gain read access to the object without supplying a password. A password is required only if a user needs to update the object or perform some other function protected by one of the higher level passwords. And by specifying only a master password, users can have unlimited access to the records and control intervals of an object, but the object can be protected from unauthorized deletion or unauthorized alteration of its catalog entry.

If a password is defined at any level, VSAM uses that as the password for any higher level passwords that are not specified. For example, if only a control password is specified, that value is also used as the master password. For example, the following DEFINE command assigns CPW as the control password; CPW is also assigned by default as the master password:

```
DEFINE CLUSTER                                          -
         (NAME        (EMPLOYEE.KSDS)                   -
          READPW      (RPW)                             -
          UPDATEPW    (UPW)                             -
          CONTROLPW   (CPW))
```

If only a read password is specified, that value is assigned by default as the password for update, control interval, and full access as well. The following DEFINE command assigns RPW as the read password, the update password, the control password, and the master password:

```
DEFINE CLUSTER                                          -
         (NAME        (EMPLOYEE.KSDS)                   -
          READPW      (RPW))
```

ACCESSING PASSWORD-PROTECTED OBJECTS

As mentioned earlier, passwords can be supplied by the application program, or they can be entered by the system operator or terminal user. When including a password in an AMS command, the password can be specified following the name of the data set, for example, in an IDS or ODS parameter, or following the name of the DD statement in an INFILE or OUTFILE parameter. The name and the password are separated with a slash. In the example below, MYSECRET is a password for the data set described by the DD statement VSAMIN.

```
INFILE (VSAMIN/MYSECRET)
```

The ALTER command can be used to change a password once it has been defined. The current master password must be supplied in the ALTER command for any ALTER operation that changes a password-protected object. For example, the following ALTER command changes the master password of the EMPLOYEE.KSDS cluster from EMPPW27 to EMP28PW. It also changes the update password to EMPUPDR and nullifies the read password so that no password will be needed for read access. The control password, if one was previously defined, remains unchanged.

```
ALTER  EMPLOYEE.KSDS/EMPPW27                              -
          MRPW     (EMP28PW)                              -
          UPDPW    (EMPUPDR)                              -
          NULLIFY (RDPW) . . .
```

PROTECTING DATA AND INDEX COMPONENTS

Since each of the catalog entries associated with a VSAM object can have its own attributes associated with it, separate passwords can be specified for the cluster, data, and index components of a KSDS. Separate AUTHORIZATION and ATTEMPTS parameters can be included for each component as well. Passwords can be assigned to individual components by including the appropriate password subparameter in the DATA and/or INDEX subparameter string. The following example shows how separate read passwords can be assigned to the cluster, data, and index components of a cluster.

```
DEFINE CLUSTER                                            -
          (NAME (EMPLOYEE.KSDS.CLUSTER)                   -
           RDPW (CLREAD)                                  -
            :
         INDEX                                            -
          (NAME (EMPLOYEE.KSDS.IXPART)                    -
           RDPW (IXREAD)
         DATA                                             -
          (NAME (EMPLOYEE.KSDS.DATAPART)                  -
           RDPW (DATAREAD)
```

Passwords can also be assigned to the data and index components of a KSDS cluster without protecting the cluster as a whole. This protects the individual components of a cluster from unauthorized access, but leaves the cluster as a whole open for unrestricted access. The data and index component names rarely will be used for normal access, so there is not often a need for four separate passwords for each component; in many cases only a read password is specified. One useful combination is to define all four levels of protection at the cluster level and then to define the cluster's master password as the read password for the data and index components.

Ordinarily, if passwords are specified for the cluster as a whole, and different passwords are not specified for the data or index components, the same set of passwords is assigned to each component of the cluster as well as to the cluster as a whole. However, a protection problem can exist when passwords are defined for the cluster and are defined as null at some levels for either the data or index components. An enterprising programmer could then access the data and index components separately without having to supply a password.

A null password might be inadvertently assigned to a component by defining a high-level password for the component and not defining lower level passwords. For example, look at the following DEFINE command example:

```
DEFINE   CLUSTER                                          -
           (NAME        (EMPLOYEE.KSDS.CLUSTER)           -
            READPW      (CL-RPW)                          -
            UPDATEPW    (CL-UPW)                          -
            CONTROLPW   (CL-CPW)                          -
            MASTERPW    (CL-MPW)                          -
              :
         DATA                                             -
           (NAME        (EMPLOYEE.KSDS.DATA)              -
            MASTERPW    (DATA-MPW)
```

In the above example, notice that all four password levels are defined for the cluster. Since no passwords are defined for the index component, these same four passwords protect the index component of the cluster; it cannot be opened individually without supplying the appropriate password. However, notice that a separate master password is supplied for the data component. Since the master password, and no lower level passwords, are specified for the data component, the read, update, and control passwords for the data component are set to null. This means that read, update, or control interval access can be gained to the data component of this cluster without supplying a password, even though the cluster itself and the index are protected by passwords. A combination of parameters that avoids this problem is as follows:

```
DEFINE   CLUSTER                                          -
           (NAME        (EMPLOYEE.KSDS.CLUSTER)           -
            READPW      (CL-RPW)                          -
            UPDATEPW    (CL-UPW)                          -
            CONTROLPW   (CL-CPW)                          -
            MASTERPW    (CL-MPW)                          -
              :

         DATA                                             -
           (NAME        (EMPLOYEE.KSDS.DATAPART)          -
            READPW      (DATA-MPW)
```

With the above parameters, the password DATA-MPW is assigned as the read, update, control, and master password for the data component; it must be supplied in order for a program to access the data component in any way.

CATALOG PASSWORD PROTECTION

Passwords can be assigned to the master catalog and to user catalogs to restrict access to the catalog entries contained in them. The same four levels of password protection can be assigned to a catalog as are assigned to any other VSAM object. The passwords that are associated with a VSAM catalog work in conjunction with the passwords that protect the individual objects whose entries are stored in that catalog.

To list the contents of catalog entries that are not password protected, no password need be supplied, even though the catalog itself might have a read password associated with it. However, to list the contents of the catalog entry for a password-protected VSAM object, the read (or higher) password for the entry itself or the read (or higher) password for the catalog that contains the entry must be specified in the LISTCAT statement.

For example, suppose the catalog entry for a cluster named EMPLOYEE.KSDS is stored in a user catalog named EMPLOYEE. The read password of the EMPLOYEE.KSDS cluster is EMP01, and the read password of the EMPLOYEE catalog is MARTINXX. Either of the following LISTCAT statements could be used to obtain a listing of the contents of the EMPLOYEE catalog entry:

```
LISTCAT ENTRIES (EMPLOYEE.KSDS/EMP01)
        CATALOG (EMPLOYEE)

LISTCAT ENTRIES (EMPLOYEE.KSDS)
        CATALOG (EMPLOYEE/MARTINXX)
```

In each of the above LISTCAT statements, the CATALOG parameter is used to supply the name of the user catalog that contains the catalog entry for EMPLOYEE.KSDS. In the first statement, the ENTRIES parameter supplies the read password of the EMPLOYEE.KSDS cluster; in the second statement, the CATALOG statement supplies the read password for the EMPLOYEE user catalog. Either password allows access to the catalog entry for the EMPLOYEE.KSDS cluster.

The read password is all that is required to list most information contained in a catalog entry. However, if information is desired about the password entries for an object, the master password must be specified. Either the master password for the object itself or the master password for the catalog can be supplied to list information about the passwords for an object.

To modify the catalog entry of a password-protected object, the master password of either the entry itself or the master password of the catalog can be supplied in the ALTER or DELETE command. To create a new catalog entry in a password-protected catalog, the update (or higher) password for the catalog must be supplied. A catalog's control password must be known to gain access to its control intervals. The catalog's master password must be supplied to delete the catalog itself.

AMS PASSWORD REQUIREMENTS

It is sometimes easy to determine the combination of passwords that is required to perform a given AMS function; in other cases, this is not so straightforward. For example, to print an object or copy it, the object's read password is all that is required. And to DEFINE a new object, the update password of the catalog itself must be supplied. However, as shown above, altering or deleting an entry requires the master password for either the object or the catalog. Other relationships are even more complex, such as when constructing an alternate index for a password-protected base cluster. The *Access Method Services Reference* manual for your operating system version and catalog facility should be consulted to determine the specific password requirements for complex AMS functions. Note, however, that any operation can be specified for an object if that object's master password is supplied.

11 BACKUP AND RESTORE OPERATIONS

As every data processing practitioner knows, the ability to back up and later restore the contents of data files is a key data processing requirement. Data sets can be damaged by system failures, hardware failures, or even power failures. The need for backups is particularly acute with VSAM data sets because the data are often updated in place rather than writing out a new copy each time updates are made. This chapter shows how the REPRO command can be used to make backup copies of data sets and how to restore their contents if they become damaged. The EXPORT and IMPORT commands are also examined; they provide an alternative method to REPRO for backing up and restoring VSAM objects. We conclude this chapter by showing how to make backup copies of VSAM and ICF catalogs.

THE REPRO COMMAND

We have already seen in Chapter 5 how to use the REPRO command to load a VSAM data set from a sequential input source. REPRO can also be used to copy the contents of a VSAM data set into another VSAM data set or into a sequential data set, thus creating a backup copy. The data set can later be restored, if desired, in the same manner as it was initially loaded. Box 11.1 repeats the partial syntax for the REPRO command (again omitting the encryption parameters). REPRO parameters are described in Box 5.1.

In many situations, REPRO is the preferred command to use for creating backup copies. The REPRO command can be used to make backup copies of clusters, alternate indexes, sequential data sets, indexed-sequential data sets, and catalogs. It can produce either a sequential data set or a VSAM cluster as output. The backed-up copy that REPRO creates can be read by conventional application programs. For example, if REPRO is used to read a KSDS cluster as input and to produce an identical KSDS cluster as output, the backup is

BOX 11.1 The REPRO command

```
REPRO {INFILE(ddname[/password][ ENVIRONMENT(DUMMY)])|
         INDATASET(entryname[/password][ ENVIRONMENT(DUMMY)])}
      {OUTFILE(ddname[/password])|
         OUTDATASET(entryname[/password])}

      [FROMKEY(key)|FROMADDRESS(address)|
         FROMNUMBER(number)|SKIP(count)]
      [REPLACE|NOREPLACE]
      [REUSE|NOREUSE]
      [TOKEY(key)|TOADDRESS(address)|
      TONUMBER(number)|COUNT(count)]
```

Optional parameters for ICF catalogs only

```
      [ENTRIES(entryname[/password]
        [entryname[/password]...])|
        LEVEL(level)]
      [FILE(ddname)]
      [MERGECAT|NOMERGECAT]
```

identical to the original data set and can be processed, if desired, using the same application programs that process the original cluster. Similarly, if the REPRO command is used to produce a sequential data set backup of a VSAM cluster, the resulting sequential data set can be processed by an application program that can accept a conventional sequential data set as input. As we will see later, when EXPORT is used to create a backup copy of a VSAM object, only the IMPORT command can be used to read that backup copy. Also, the REPRO command allows the user to select certain parts of a data set to copy or restore, and a backup copy produced by REPRO can be merged with other data sets if necessary.

SEQUENTIAL BACKUP

The following AMS job step shows an example of a REPRO command that creates a backup copy of the EMPLOYEE.KSDS cluster, placing the copy in a sequential tape data set:

```
//BACKUP      EXEC  PGM=IDCAMS
//SYSPRINT    DD    SYSOUT=A
//VSAMDD      DD    DSN=EMPLOYEE.KSDS,DISP=OLD
//TAPEDD      DD    DSN=EMPLOYEE.TAPE.BACKUP,
//                  DISP=(NEW,KEEP),
//                  VOL=SER=TP0042,UNIT=3400-3
//SYSIN       DD    *
  REPRO    INFILE  (VSAMDD)
           OUTFILE (TAPEDD)
```

Should it later become necessary to restore the EMPLOYEE.KSDS cluster after a failure, AMS can be used to delete the cluster and then redefine it. The new data set is then reloaded using another REPRO command. The following job step can be used to accomplish this:

```
//BACKUP      EXEC   PGM=IDCAMS
//SYSPRINT    DD     SYSOUT=A
//TAPEDD      DD     DSN=EMPLOYEE.TAPE.BACKUP,
//            DISP=(OLD),
//            VOL=SER=TP0042,UNIT=3400-3
//VSAMDD      DD     UNIT=3380,VOL=SER=DSK001,DISP=OLD
//SYSIN       DD     *
DELETE   EMPLOYEE.KSDS
DEFINE   CLUSTER
           (NAME         (EMPLOYEE.KSDS)                    -
            VOLUMES      (DSK001)                           -
            CYLINDERS    (42)                               -
            RECORDSIZE   (26 26)                            -
            KEYS         (4  0)                             -
            FREESPACE    (25 30))                           -
            IMBED
REPRO    INFILE          (TAPEDD)                           -
         ODS             (EMPLOYEE.KSDS)
```

VSAM CLUSTER BACKUP

The REPRO command can also be used to copy a VSAM cluster into another VSAM cluster instead of into a sequential data set. This is shown in the following example:

```
//COPY        EXEC    PGM=IDCAMS
//SYSPRINT    DD      SYSOUT=A
//VSAM        DD      UNIT=3380,VOL=SER=DSK001,DISP=OLD
//SYSIN       DD      *
    DEFINE    CLUSTER
                (NAME          (EMPLOYEE.BACKUP)            -
                 VOLUMES       (DSK001)                     -
                 CYLINDERS     (42)                         -
                 RECORDSIZE    (26 26)                      -
                 KEYS          (4 0)                        -
                 FREESPACE     (25 30))                     -
                 IMBED
    REPRO     IDS              (EMPLOYEE.KSDS)              -
              ODS              (EMPLOYEE.BACKUP)
```

Notice that in the above job step, a DEFINE command is used to create a new VSAM data set to contain the backup copy. Normally, a VSAM cluster is copied into another cluster that has the same format as the original cluster. For example, a KSDS is normally copied into another KSDS and not into an ESDS. However, AMS allows a VSAM cluster to be copied into one having a different format if desired.

MERGING DATA

As discussed above, the normal REPRO restore procedure involves deleting the original cluster, redefining it, and then reloading it. This is the only way that REPRO can be used to completely replace a damaged cluster with its backup copy. Copying a backup copy into a cluster that is not empty normally has undesirable results that are not useful when implementing backup and restore procedures. For example, if the output data set is a nonempty ESDS, the records in the backup copy are added to the end of the ESDS. If the target data set is a nonempty KSDS, records from the backup copy are merged into the output cluster according to key values. Records in the input data set that match records already in the output cluster are ordinarily dropped; however, records in the output cluster can be replaced with records from the input data set by including the REPLACE parameter in the REPRO command. This is illustrated in the following example:

```
REPRO  IDS (EMPLOYEE.INPUT)                                -
       ODS (EMPLOYEE.KSDS)                                 -
       REPLACE
```

If the REPLACE is included, when VSAM finds a record in the input data set that has the same key value as a record in the output cluster, it replaces the record in the output cluster with the matching record from the input data set. Input records without a matching record in the output cluster are inserted in their proper places.

OTHER REPRO PARAMETERS

A restore operation that uses REPRO has the same options as a REPRO load operation. As discussed in Chapter 5, the SKIP, FROMKEY, FROMADDRESS, or FROMNUMBER parameters can be used to begin reloading from a specified point, and the COUNT, TOKEY, TOADDRESS, or TONUMBER can be used to specify a stopping point. These parameters can be used in conjunction with the REPLACE parameter to replace the records in selected portions of a data set.

EXPORTING AND IMPORTING DATA

As can be seen from the previous examples, the REPRO command copies only the data records from an input data set; the input data set's catalog information is not copied along with the data. In order to restore the data set using REPRO, the information that was used originally to define the backed-up data set must be supplied in a new DEFINE command before the data set can be restored. The EXPORT command, on the other hand, creates a *portable copy* of a VSAM object that also contains information about the catalog entries associated with the object. An exported portable copy is always contained in a non-VSAM sequential data set, which must be processed using the IMPORT command in order to create a new copy of the original exported object.

THE EXPORT COMMAND

The EXPORT command can be used to create a portable copy of a VSAM cluster, an alternate index, or an ICF catalog. Box 11.2 shows the syntax of the EXPORT command and describes its parameters. When EXPORT is issued with the PERMANENT option (the default), AMS creates a portable copy of the source VSAM object and then attempts to delete the original object after the backup operation has been completed successfully. If the TEMPORARY option is specified, AMS does not delete the original object, but instead makes a notation in the object's catalog entry indicating that an exported copy of the data set now exists.

The delete attributes currently in effect for the data set control EXPORT delete processing when the PERMANENT option is used. For example, if the ERASE option is in effect for the cluster, the cluster is overwritten with binary zeros whenever it is deleted, and the deletion does not take place if the retention period has not expired. EXPORT command parameters can be used to override the delete options in effect for the cluster. The ERASE or NOERASE options can be included in the EXPORT command to override the ERASE option in effect for the cluster. Also, the PURGE parameter can be included to direct VSAM to delete the original data set whether or not its retention period has expired.

The job step shown below creates a backup copy of the EMPLOYEE.KSDS cluster. In this example, the EXPORT command causes AMS to copy the data set and its catalog information to a 3400-3 tape data set.

```
//BKUP        EXEC  PGM=IDCAMS
//SYSPRINT    DD    SYSOUT=A
//TAPEOUT     DD    DSN=EMPLOYEE.TAPE.BACKUP,
//            UNIT=3400-3,DISP=(NEW,CATLG)
//SYSIN       DD    *
  EXPORT   EMPLOYEE.KSDS                                -
           OUTFILE (TAPEOUT)                            -
           TEMPORARY
```

The name of the VSAM data set to be exported is the first positional parameter following the EXPORT keyword. If the data set being exported is password protected, its master password must be provided.

THE IMPORT COMMAND

The IMPORT command is used to reload a VSAM object from a portable copy created with EXPORT. Box 11.3 shows the syntax of the IMPORT command and describes its parameters. AMS begins processing an IMPORT request by searching the target catalog to see if an entry exists with the same name as

BOX 11.2 The EXPORT command

```
EXPORT   entryname[/password]
         {OUTFILE(ddname)|OUTDATASET(entryname)}

         [ERASE|NOERASE]
         [INFILE(ddname)]
         [INHIBITSOURCE|NOINHIBITSOURCE]
         [INHIBITTARGET|NOINHIBITTARGET]
         [PURGE|NOPURGE]
         [TEMPORARY|PERMANENT]
```

Entryname — The required positional parameter gives the name and optional password of the object being exported. EXPORT can be used to create a copy of a cluster, an alternate index, or an ICF catalog.

OUTFILE — The OUTFILE (OFILE) parameter specifies the name of the DD statement that describes the data set that will contain the portable copy.

OUTDATASET — The OUTDATASET (ODS) parameter specifies the name of the data set that will contain the portable copy. (Either OUTFILE or OUTDATASET must be specified for EXPORT.)

ERASE | NOERASE — The ERASE (ERAS) and NOERASE (NERAS) parameters specify whether or not AMS should overwrite the exported object with binary zeros when it is deleted. (Valid only for clusters and alternate indexes.)

INFILE — The INFILE (IFILE) parameter specifies the name of the DD statement that describes the object being exported.

INHIBITSOURCE | NOINHIBITSOURCE — The INHIBITSOURCE (INHS) and NOINHIBITSOURCE (NINHS) parameters specify whether or not AMS should mark the object being exported as being accessible only for retrieval after the export operation.

INHIBITTARGET | NOINHIBITTARGET — The INHIBITTARGET (INHT) and NOINHIBITTARGET (NINHT) parameters specify whether or not AMS should mark the portable copy of the object being exported

BOX 11.2 *(Continued)*

	as being accessible only for retrieval after the export operation.
PURGE | <u>**NOPURGE**</u>	The PURGE (PRG) and <u>NOPURGE</u> (<u>NPRG</u>) parameters specify whether or not the object being exported should be deleted, even if its expiration date has not been exceeded. (Applies only when the PERMANENT option is in effect.)
TEMPORARY | <u>**PERMANENT**</u>	The TEMPORARY (TEMP) and <u>PERMANENT</u> (<u>PERM</u>) parameters specify whether or not the object being exported should be deleted after the EXPORT operation has been completed successfully. (Valid for clusters and alternate indexes only. ICF catalogs must be exported as TEMPORARY, which is the default value for this parameter when an ICF catalog is exported.)

the object being imported. If a catalog entry does not already exist, AMS uses the catalog information included in the portable copy to define a new catalog entry. It then reloads the object. If a catalog entry does exist, IMPORT checks the catalog entry to see if it has been marked as exported by a previous EXPORT operation that included the TEMPORARY option. If this is the case, IMPORT assumes the data set is being restored from the appropriate exported copy. IMPORT then deletes the old object, defines a new catalog entry for it using the catalog information in the exported copy, and then reloads the object. If a catalog entry exists, but it is not marked as having been previously exported, the IMPORT operation fails. The delete processing performed by the IMPORT command is handled in a similar manner as for the EXPORT command, and is controlled by the delete options in effect for the VSAM object. These options can be overridden by including the appropriate parameters in the IMPORT command.

The following job step uses the IMPORT command to cause AMS to reload the data set that was exported in the previous example.

```
//RESTORE     EXEC   PGM=IDCAMS
//SYSPRINT     DD    SYSOUT=A
//TAPEIN       DD    DSN=EMPLOYEE.TAPE.BACKUP,DISP=OLD
//SYSIN        DD    *
  IMPORT   INFILE (TAPEIN)
           ODS    (EMPLOYEE.KSDS)
```

BOX 11.3 The IMPORT command

```
IMPORT   {INFILE(ddname)|INDATASET(entryname)}
         {OUTFILE(ddname[/password])|
            OUTDATASET(entryname[/password])}

         [ERASE|NOERASE]
         [INTOEMPTY]
         [OBJECTS
            ((entryname
               [FILE(ddname)]
               [(KEYRANGES((lowkey highkey)[lowkey highkey)...]))]
               [NEWNAME(newname)]
               [ORDERED|UNORDERED]
               [VOLUME(volser[ volser...])])
            [entryname...)...])]
         [PURGE|NOPURGE]
         [SAVRAC|NOSAVRAC]

         [CATALOG(catname[/password])]
```

INFILE The INFILE (IFILE) parameter specifies the name of the DD statement that describes the portable copy of the object being imported.

INDATASET The INDATASET (IDS) parameter specifies the name of the data set that contains the portable copy of the object being imported.

OUTFILE The OUTFILE (OFILE) parameter specifies the name of the DD statement that describes the object being imported.

OUTDATASET The OUTDATASET (ODS) parameter specifies the name of the object being imported.

ERASE | NOERASE The ERASE (ERAS) and NOERASE (NERAS) parameters specify whether or not AMS should overwrite the original copy of the object being imported with binary zeros. (Valid only when importing an object that was exported previously using the TEMPORARY option.)

INTOEMPTY The INTOEMPTY (IEMPTY) parameter specifies that the object is being imported into an already existing empty data set.

BOX 11.3 *(Continued)*

OBJECTS	The OBJECTS (OBJ) parameter specifies the original name of the object being imported and assigns a new name and/or selected attributes to the object being imported.
PURGE ¦ <u>NOPURGE</u>	The PURGE (PRG) and <u>NOPURGE</u> (<u>NPRG</u>) parameters specify whether or not the original copy of the object being imported should be deleted, even if its expiration date has not been exceeded. (Valid only when importing an object that was previously exported using the TEMPORARY option.)
SAVRAC ¦ <u>NOSAVRAC</u>	The SAVRAC and <u>NOSAVRAC</u> parameters specify whether or not the RACF profile that already exists for the object being imported is to be used.
CATALOG	The CATALOG (CAT) parameter specifies the name of the catalog into which the catalog entry for the object being imported is to be placed.

INDATASET can be used instead of INFILE, since EMPLOYEE.TAPE.BACKUP is cataloged and is available for dynamic allocation. When IMPORT discovers that the data set already exists in the target system, it checks to see if EXPORT marked the data set as having been exported. Since this is the case, the old copy of the data set is deleted and is then redefined using the catalog information included in the portable copy. The data set is then reloaded.

EXPORTING TO OTHER SYSTEMS

In addition to being used for making backup copies, the EXPORT and IMPORT commands can also be used to move VSAM data from one computing system to another. A number of EXPORT and IMPORT parameters are used specifically for this purpose. The INHIBITSOURCE (INHS) can be included in the EXPORT command to cause AMS to mark the original object for read-only access. This prevents any program from making changes to the data set after the EXPORT operation has been performed. The INHIBITTARGET (INHT) can also be included to similarly mark the portable copy of the data set as read only. This read-only restriction can later be removed from either the original VSAM object or the backup copy by using the ALTER command.

IMPORTING FROM OTHER SYSTEMS

If a data set is being imported into a system for the first time or if a cluster is being reloaded that previously was permanently exported, IMPORT automatically defines a catalog entry in the target system using the information contained in the exported copy. This information includes the INHIBIT attribute if INHIBITTARGET (INHT) was coded in the EXPORT command when the exported copy was created. The CATALOG parameter can be included in the IMPORT command to tell AMS the name of the catalog to be used in constructing the new catalog entry for the imported data set.

CHANGING CLUSTER ATTRIBUTES

The OBJECTS parameter can be used to change the name and selected attributes of the VSAM object being imported. The command shown below uses the OBJECTS parameter to define a new name for the object and specifies the serial number of the volume onto which the imported copy should be placed. We are including a DD statement for the new volume to ensure that it is mounted when the IMPORT command is executed. The new name is used in the OUTDATASET parameter and not the original name of the exported cluster. The OBJECTS subparameter list is enclosed in a double set of parentheses in order to allow multiple objects to be specified.

```
//RESTORE     EXEC   PGM=IDCAMS
//SYSPRINT    DD     SYSOUT=A
//TAPEIN      DD     DSN=EMPLOYEE.TAPE.BACKUP,DISP=OLD
//NEWVOL      DD     UNIT=3380,VOL=SER=DSK001,DISP=OLD
//SYSIN       DD     *
  IMPORT  INFILE      (TAPEIN)                           -
          ODS         (EMPLOYEE.NEWNAME)                 -
          OBJECTS     ((EMPLOYEE.KSDS                    -
                        NEWNAME   (EMPLOYEE.NEW.KSDS)    -
                        VOLUMES   (DSK001)))
```

Only selected attributes can be changed with the OBJECTS parameter. Other attributes can be changed by issuing an ALTER command after the object has been reloaded. In order to change a few attributes, including space allocation and some performance options, such as IMBED or REPLICATE, it is necessary to define a new catalog entry for the object before reloading it with IMPORT. The following example shows how EXPORT and IMPORT can be used to reorganize the EMPLOYEE.KSDS cluster and assign new space allocation and performance attributes to it in the process:

```
//REORG      EXEC    PGM=IDCAMS
//SYSPRINT   DD      SYSOUT=A
//TEMP       DD      UNIT=SYSDA,SPACE=(CYL,20),
//           DSN=&&TEMP
//SYSIN      DD      *
  EXPORT   EMPLOYEE.KSDS                                    -
           OUTFILE  (TEMP)                                  -
           PERMANENT
           PURGE
  DEFINE   CLUSTER
             (NAME          (EMPLOYEE.KSDS)                 -
              VOLUMES       (DSK001)                        -
              CYLINDERS     (25   5)                        -
              RECORDSIZE    (26   26)                       -
              FREESPACE     (20   25)                       -
              KEYS          (0    4)                        -
              IMBED                                         -
              REPLICATE
  IMPORT   INFILE           (TEMP)                          -
           ODS              (EMPLOYEE.KSDS)                 -
           TOEMPTY
```

The EXPORT command copies the EMPLOYEE.KSDS cluster to a temporary sequential data set defined by the TEMP DD statement. Since PERMANENT is specified, AMS deletes the cluster after completing the EXPORT operation. The DEFINE command then creates a new catalog entry for the EMPLOYEE.KSDS cluster. The IMPORT command, which includes the TOEMPTY parameter, then causes the original cluster's data to be loaded into the new cluster that we just defined. When the TOEMPTY parameter is included in the IMPORT command, AMS does not delete the catalog entry when it finds one with the same name as the object being imported. Instead, it verifies that the cluster is indeed empty and then loads the data from the portable copy into that cluster.

The above method should sometimes be used instead of the OBJECTS parameter, even when changing attributes that can be changed in the OBJECTS parameter. For example, the OBJECTS parameter should not ordinarily be used to change the device type because the space allocation is not automatically adjusted. For example, four cylinders on a 3350 device do not represent the same amount of direct access space as four cylinders on a 3380. When changing from one device type to another, a new catalog entry should be defined for the data set before importing it, in order to assign the proper amount of direct access to the imported data set.

EXPORTING ALTERNATE INDEXES

The EXPORT and IMPORT commands can be used to back up and restore alternate indexes as well as clusters. When the PERMANENT option is used to export an alternate index, all paths associated with the alternate index are deleted; and when a cluster that has paths and alternate indexes associated with it is exported using the PERMANENT option, all alternate index and path entries are automatically deleted. This means that alternate indexes associated with a base cluster should be exported before the base cluster itself is exported. And when these objects are then imported, the base cluster should be imported first, followed by all of its alternate indexes. Backing up and restoring in this sequence ensures that all catalog entries for the cluster, its alternate indexes, and its paths are backed up and restored properly.

IMPORT/EXPORT VS. REPRO

The use of the EXPORT and IMPORT commands for backup and restore operations has many advantages over the use of REPRO. As we have seen, using EXPORT and IMPORT avoids the necessity of issuing DELETE and DEFINE commands before a restore operation, although a new catalog entry can be defined for an object if desired. Also, data set attributes are written automatically to the backup copy so that when the object is restored its catalog entry is reconstructed automatically. Because the catalog information is recorded with the backup copy, the data set can be restored properly, even if the original data set's catalog entry becomes damaged. A final advantage to using EXPORT for backups is that it can be used to back up alternate indexes and catalogs as well as clusters.

An advantage that REPRO has over EXPORT/IMPORT is that the copy created by EXPORT cannot be read by application programs; it can ordinarily be processed only by IMPORT. REPRO can create either a sequential copy or a VSAM copy of a VSAM cluster, so a REPRO copy can be used as direct input to a program that can access the data. REPRO can also be used to merge data from a backup copy. And REPRO parameters, such as FROMKEY and TOKEY, can be used to replace or copy only certain parts of a data set; EXPORT and IMPORT operate only on the entire object.

COPYING CATALOGS

Both VSAM and ICF catalogs can be copied using the REPRO command. ICF catalogs can also be exported and imported using the EXPORT and IMPORT commands. Just as with VSAM data sets, copying a catalog with the REPRO command requires that both the input and the output catalogs be defined before the REPRO command is executed. The output catalog must also be empty before issuing the REPRO. When either the REPRO or EXPORT command is executed for an ICF catalog, a copy of the catalog is made and the catalog remains connected to the master catalog and available for use. When IMPORT is executed to load a new user catalog, a new copy of the user catalog is created in the destination system, but the user catalog is not connected automatically to the master catalog in the destination system. In order to connect and disconnect user catalog entries properly, the EXPORT DISCONNECT and IMPORT DISCONNECT commands can be used. The syntax of the EXPORT DISCONNECT and IMPORT CONNECT commands is shown in Box 11.4.

The following job step shows how an ICF user catalog can be exported to a sequential data set and its user catalog entry removed from the master catalog. After executing the following command sequence, the catalog entries in the EMPLOYEE user catalog are no longer available via implicit catalog searches. The user catalog can then be deleted from the source system if desired.

```
//EXPORT     EXEC    PGM=IDCAMS
//SYSPRINT   DD      SYSOUT=A
//TAPEOUT    DD      UNIT=3400-2,DISP=(,KEEP),
//           VOL=SER=TP0001,DSN=BACKUP
//SYSIN      DD      *
    EXPORT EMPLOYEE                                         -
           OUTFILE   (TAPEOUT)
    EXPORT EMPLOYEE                                         -
           DISCONNECT
```

BOX 11.4 The EXPORT DISCONNECT and IMPORT CONNECT commands

```
EXPORT   usercatname[/password]
         DISCONNECT

IMPORT   CONNECT
         OBJECTS ((usercatname
            DEVICETYPE(devtype)
            VOLUMES(volser)))

         [CATALOG(catname[/password])]
```

Usercatname The required position parameter specifies the name of the user catalog to be disconnected.

DISCONNECT The DISCONNECT (DCON) parameter causes the specified user catalog entry to be removed from the master catalog.

CONNECT The CONNECT (CON) parameter causes the specified user catalog entry to be placed into the master catalog.

(Continued)

BOX 11.4 *(Continued)*

OBJECTS	The OBJECTS (OBJ) parameter specifies the name, device type, and volume serial number of the user catalog.
CATALOG	The CATALOG (CAT) parameter specifies the name and optional password of the catalog into which the user catalog entry is to be placed. (Used to specify a catalog other than the master catalog or to specify the password for a password-protected master catalog.)

The following job step shows how the EMPLOYEE user catalog can be imported into a new system and a user catalog entry built for it in the destination system. This example assumes that the EMPLOYEE user catalog does not yet exist in the system into which it is being imported:

```
//IMPORT     EXEC     PGM=IDCAMS
//SYSPRINT   DD       SYSOUT=A
//TAPEIN     DD       UNIT=3400-2,DISP=OLD,
//           VOL=SER=TP0001,DSN=BACKUP
//NEWVOL     DD       UNIT=3380,VOL=SER=DSK001,DISP=OLD
//SYSIN      DD       *
    IMPORT OUTDATASET (EMPLOYEE)                                  -
           INFILE     (TAPEIN)                                    -
           OBJECTS    ((EMPLOYEE)                                 -
                       VOLUMES    (DSK001))
    IMPORT CONNECT                                                -
           OBJECTS    (EMPLOYEE)                                  -
           DEVICETYPE (3380)                                      -
           VOLUMES    (DSK001)
```

Notice in the above examples that the EXPORT DISCONNECT and IMPORT CONNECT commands do not cause any user catalog data to be exported or imported. These commands concern only the user catalog entry that is stored in the master catalog. The actual exporting and importing of user catalog data are handled by conventional REPRO, EXPORT, and IMPORT commands as separate steps.

ADDITIONAL CATALOG COMMANDS

Box 11.5 lists some additional AMS commands that can be issued when performing backup and restore operations on VSAM and ICF catalogs. Since these commands normally are issued only by system programmers in conjunction with recovering from system failures, they are beyond the scope of this book. Consult the *AMS Reference* and *Catalog User's Guide* manuals for your operating system version and catalog facility for more information on these commands.

BOX 11.5 Additional catalog commands

Commands used with VSAM Catalogs

CNVTCAT	The CNVTCAT (CNVTCT) command can be used to convert an OS CVOL into a VSAM catalog.
EXPOR-TRA	The EXPORTRA (XPRA) command can be used to create a portable copy of a VSAM recoverable catalog using the catalog recovery areas on the volumes owned by the catalog.
IMPOR-TRA	The IMPORTRA (MPRA) command can be used to recover the contents of a VSAM recoverable catalog using the portable copy created by EXPORTRA.
LISTCRA	The LISTCRA (LISTR) command can be used to list the contents of a catalog recovery area.
RESETCAT	The RESETCAT (RCAT) command can be used to synchronize the contents of a VSAM recoverable catalog with the individual catalog recovery areas that are stored on the volumes owned by the catalog.

Commands used with ICF Catalogs

CNVTCAT	The CNVTCAT (CNVTCT) command can be used to convert an OS CVOL or a VSAM catalog into an ICF catalog.
DIAGNOSE	The DIAGNOSE (DIAG) command can be used to scan either the BCS or VVDS components of an ICF catalog to detect errors in the catalog structure.

PART III COBOL PROGRAMMING

12 COBOL ESDS PROCESSING

When processing VSAM data sets, clauses in various COBOL statements must be coded to specify which type of VSAM cluster is to be processed and what type of access to the data is desired. This chapter discusses those COBOL programming options that are unique to programs that process ESDS clusters. Sequential ESDS load, retrieval, and update programs are discussed. The following two chapters discuss KSDS and RRDS clusters.

ESDS SELECT STATEMENT

Box 12.1 shows the format of the SELECT statement for an ESDS cluster. The following SELECT statement is typical of one used in a program that sequentially loads an ESDS:

```
SELECT ESDS-FILE
    ASSIGN TO AS-ESDSDD
    ORGANIZATION IS SEQUENTIAL
    ACCESS IS SEQUENTIAL
    FILE STATUS IS STATUS-KEY.
```

As with SELECT statements for non-VSAM data sets, the *file-name* parameter names an FD statement in the FILE SECTION. For an ESDS, the ddname parameter in the ASSIGN TO clause must be preceded by the characters "AS-". As with other COBOL ASSIGN TO clauses, the ddname parameter names the DD statement in the JCL that describes the ESDS. (The class and device fields that are part of the formal SELECT statement syntax for the ASSIGN TO clause are not shown, since in the IBM environment these serve only as documentation and generally are not included.) The ORGANIZATION IS SEQUENTIAL clause identifies the data set as an ESDS, and the ACCESS IS SEQUENTIAL clause indicates that the program will process the records sequentially. Both the ORGANIZATION and ACCESS clauses are optional when

BOX 12.1 SELECT statement syntax for ESDS

```
FILE-CONTROL.
    SELECT OPTIONAL file-name
    ASSIGN TO AS-ddname-1 [AS-ddname-2 ...]

    [RESERVE integer {AREA|AREAS}]
    [ORGANIZATION IS SEQUENTIAL]
    [ACCESS MODE IS SEQUENTIAL]
    [PASSWORD IS data-name-1]
    [FILE STATUS IS data-name-2].
```

processing an ESDS because if either or both of these clauses are omitted, SEQUENTIAL is assumed. The PASSWORD clause allows the VSAM password protection option to be used. This clause specifies the name of a data item, generally defined in the WORKING STORAGE section of the DATA DIVISION, that is used to contain a password. If the PASSWORD clause is included, the data item it identifies must be defined using the following PICTURE clause:

```
PICTURE X(8)
```

Two of the four types of passwords are most useful with COBOL programs: the *read* password and the *update* password. For a sequential load program, the update password must be used so that records can be written into the data set.

The final clause in the SELECT statement is the FILE STATUS clause. This clause defines a data item into which VSAM places a 2-byte numeric code after each I/O function is performed. The program can examine this code to determine the results of each I/O operation. The data item referenced in the FILE STATUS clause should be defined using either of the following sets of PICTURE and VALUE clauses:

```
PICTURE XX VALUE 0.
PICTURE 99 VALUE 0.
```

VSAM FD ENTRY

The FD entry for a VSAM data set contains fewer pieces of information than is typical in an FD for a non-VSAM data set. The same FD format is used for ESDS, KSDS, and RRDS clusters. The only required clause is LABEL RECORDS; the RECORDING MODE and REPORT clauses *must not* be specified. The following FD is typical of a VSAM FD entry:

```
FD  ESDS-FILE
        LABEL RECORDS ARE STANDARD
        DATA RECORD IS ESDS-RECORD
01  ESDS-RECORD    PIC X(100).
```

The LABEL RECORDS clause is required and can specify either STANDARD or OMITTED; however, in the IBM implementations of COBOL, this clause serves only as documentation. STANDARD is normally specified, since label records are never omitted for VSAM data sets. A RECORD CONTAINS clause can be included, if desired, to explicitly define the record length. The BLOCK CONTAINS, DATA RECORDS, and VALUE OF clauses serve only as documentation and are ignored if coded. The program does not have to specify information about the physical characteristics of a VSAM data set, since this information is obtained from the catalog entry when the data set is opened.

SEQUENTIAL ESDS LOAD

The PROCEDURE DIVISION statements used to read and write ESDS records are identical to those used to process conventional sequential data sets. A program to load an ESDS sequentially begins by issuing an OPEN statement to open the data set. Box 12.2 shows the syntax of the OPEN statement for processing VSAM data sets. The following OPEN statement opens an ESDS described by an FD named ESDS-FILE:

```
OPEN OUTPUT ESDS-FILE.
```

BOX 12.2 The OPEN statement

```
OPEN {INPUT    file-name-1 [file-name-2] ...
      OUTPUT   file-name-1 [file-name-2] ...
      I-O      file-name-1 [file-name-2] ...
      EXTEND   file-name-1 [file-name-2] ...} ...
```

Following are descriptions of the four available options that can be specified in a VSAM OPEN statement. These options apply for KSDS and RRDS clusters as well as for ESDS clusters.

- **INPUT.** When opened for INPUT, records can be retrieved from the data set.
- **OUTPUT.** When opened for OUTPUT, records can be written into the data set.
- **I-O.** When opened for I-O, records can be both read and written.

- **EXTEND.** When opened for EXTEND, ACCESS MODE IS SEQUENTIAL must be either specified or implied, and records that are written into the data set are written after any existing records.

For a sequential load operation, the data set normally is opened for OUTPUT, and records are written into the data set using WRITE statements. Box 12.3 shows the syntax of the WRITE statement used for writing new records into an ESDS. As shown in the following example, the only required parameter is the file name defined in the FD for the data set; the FROM clause is optional.

```
WRITE ESDS-FILE.
```

BOX 12.3 WRITE statement syntax for ESDS

```
WRITE record-name
   [FROM identifier].
```

After all the records have been loaded, the program issues a CLOSE statement. As shown in Box 12.4 and in the following example, the CLOSE statement for a VSAM data set has the same format as for any other data set.

```
CLOSE ESDS-FILE.
```

BOX 12.4 The CLOSE statement

```
CLOSE file-name-1 [WITH LOCK]
      [file-name-2 [WITH LOCK]] ...
```

Figure 12.1 shows the skeleton coding that could be used to build a program to sequentially load an ESDS. These statements will load records into the data set in the physical sequence in which they are presented to the load program. Notice that the password protection feature is used in this program. When the OPEN statement is executed, the password value contained in the UPDATE-PASSWORD data item is compared against the update password, and all higher level passwords, currently in effect for the data set. If the supplied value matches an appropriate password, open processing completes normally. If the value does not match, an I/O error occurs and the data set is not opened.

```
IDENTIFICATION DIVISION.
            :
ENVIRONMENT DIVISION.
            :
INPUT-OUTPUT SECTION.
FILE-CONTROL.
    SELECT ESDS-FILE
        ASSIGN TO AS-ESDSDD
        PASSWORD IS UPDATE-PASSWORD
        FILE STATUS IS STATUS-KEY.
            :
DATA DIVISION.
FILE SECTION.
FD  ESDS-FILE
    LABEL RECORDS ARE STANDARD.
01  ESDS-RECORD         PIC X(100).
            :
WORKING-STORAGE SECTION.

01  UPDATE-PASSWORD     PIC X(8)    VALUE ...
01  STATUS-KEY          PIC XX      VALUE ZERO.
01  ERROR-RECORD.
    03 ERROR-MESSAGE    PIC X(37).
    03 ERROR-STATUS     PIC XX.

PROCEDURE DIVISION.

DECLARATIVES.

FILE-ERROR SECTION.
    USE AFTER STANDARD ERROR PROCEDURE ON ESDS-FILE.
    MOVE 'I/O ERROR ON ESDSDD--STATUS KEY IS '
        TO ERROR-MESSAGE.
    MOVE STATUS-KEY TO ERROR-STATUS.
    WRITE ERROR-RECORD.
    STOP RUN.
    END DECLARATIVES.

LOAD-DATA-SET.
            :
    OPEN OUTPUT ESDS-FILE.
            :
    WRITE ESDS-RECORD.
            :
    CLOSE ESDS-FILE.
            :
```

Figure 12.1 Sequential ESDS load.

I/O ERROR HANDLING

When an error occurs in processing an I/O function (such as OPEN, CLOSE, READ, or WRITE), the I/O operation fails and control is returned to the program. If no provision for error handling has been provided in the program, return is passed to the statement following the one that caused the error. It is then the responsibility of the program to determine whether or not the I/O operation completed normally. A better way to handle I/O errors is to include in the DECLARATIVES section a routine to be executed whenever an I/O error occurs.

Errors that occur during data set processing usually are caused during testing by something that the programmer has neglected to do. So it is usually sufficient to issue a descriptive message and then simply terminate the program when an I/O error occurs. The problem can then be corrected and the program rerun. To help in identifying the cause of the error, it is useful to include the FILE STATUS clause in the SELECT statement, as in the SELECT statement example shown earlier. The contents of the FILE STATUS data item can then be included in the descriptive message to help in diagnosing the cause of the I/O error.

The USE statement immediately after the section header in the DECLARATIVES section indicates when the routine is to be invoked. The USE AFTER STANDARD ERROR PROCEDURE ON ESDS-FILE statement indicates that the routine is to be executed whenever an I/O error occurs in processing the ESDS-FILE data set. Multiple routines can be specified if the program processes more than one VSAM data set. Each one is then coded as a separate section in DECLARATIVES, and each one identifies its associated data set in the USE statement.

SEQUENTIAL ESDS RETRIEVAL

After an ESDS has been loaded, records can be retrieved from it using READ statements. The syntax of the READ statement used for retrieving records sequentially from an ESDS is shown in Box 12.5. The following example shows that a READ statement for an ESDS is identical in format to a READ statement used to retrieve records sequentially from a non-VSAM sequential data set.

```
READ ESDS-FILE
     AT END MOVE HIGH-VALUES TO EOF-SWITCH.
```

BOX 12.5 READ statement syntax for sequential ESDS retrieval

```
READ file-name RECORD

    [INTO identifier]
    [AT END imperative-statement].
```

```
                    :
INPUT-OUTPUT SECTION.
FILE-CONTROL.
    SELECT ESDS-FILE
        ASSIGN TO AS-ESDSDD
        PASSWORD IS READ-PASSWORD
        FILE STATUS IS STATUS-KEY.
                    :
DATA DIVISION.
FILE SECTION.
FD  ESDS-FILE
    LABEL RECORDS ARE STANDARD.
01  ESDS-RECORD          PIC X(100).
                    :
WORKING-STORAGE SECTION.
01  READ-PASSWORD        PIC X(8)    VALUE ...
01  STATUS-KEY           PIC XX      VALUE ZERO.
                    :
PROCEDURE DIVISION.
                    :
RETRIEVE-RECORDS.
    OPEN INPUT ESDS-FILE.
                    :
    READ ESDS-FILE
        AT END MOVE HIGH-VALUES TO EOF-SWITCH.
                    :
    CLOSE ESDS-FILE.
                    :
```

Figure 12.2 Sequential ESDS retrieval.

The READ statement identifies the name of the FD that describes the data set being read and specifies a statement to be executed when the end of the file is reached.

Figure 12.2 shows the skeleton coding around which an ESDS retrieval program could be created. The same SELECT statement and FD are used as those in the ESDS load program. The read password can be specified this time instead of the update password, since records are only being retrieved and not updated. The I/O error routine in the DECLARATIVES section is not shown; the one from the load program can be used here as well. Notice that as with the load program, the same PROCEDURE DIVISION statements are used to retrieve records sequentially from an ESDS as are used to read a non-VSAM data set.

SEQUENTIAL ESDS UPDATE

New records cannot be added to an existing ESDS by inserting a new record between two existing records; however, existing records in an ESDS can be updated in place. The REWRITE statement is used for this purpose. Box 12.6 shows the syntax of the REWRITE statement used to update ESDS records. The following example shows that REWRITE is similar in format to WRITE and specifies the name of the record defined in the FD:

```
REWRITE ESDS-RECORD.
```

BOX 12.6 REWRITE statement syntax for ESDS

```
REWRITE record-name

    [FROM identifier]
```

Figure 12.3 shows the skeleton coding that could be used to build a program that sequentially updates ESDS records. The SELECT, FD, and DECLARATIVES are again unchanged from the previous two programs. Because records will be written into the data set, the update password is required for password-protected data sets.

In the PROCEDURE DIVISION, the data set is opened as I-O because records in the ESDS are both read and written. To update a record, the program begins by retrieving records using conventional READ statements. When the desired record has been read, the changes are first applied to the record in the work area. The program then writes the new version of the record back into the data set by issuing a REWRITE statement. Like the WRITE statement, REWRITE can include a FROM clause if the updated record resides in some place other than in the record work area identified in the FD. The REWRITE statement can also be used to logically (but not physically) delete a record from the data set. To do this, the program moves HIGH-VALUES to the first byte of the record in the work area and then issues a REWRITE for the record. HIGH-VALUES in the first byte of a record flags the record as deleted. Most programs that process VSAM data sets bypass ESDS records that have been flagged in this manner.

When sequentially updating in place, keep these points in mind. A record must first be read into the work area using a READ statement before a REWRITE statement can be issued for it; the REWRITE statement always applies to the record read most recently. However, the REWRITE statement need not be issued for each record that is read; only the records that are changed need to be rewritten. One last restriction for an ESDS that contains variable-length records—the record length of a record cannot be changed when updating an ESDS.

In some cases, it is desirable to update an ESDS by reading the old version

```
            :
FILE-CONTROL.
    SELECT ESDS-FILE
        ASSIGN TO AS-ESDSDD
        PASSWORD IS UPDATE-PASSWORD
        FILE STATUS IS STATUS-KEY.
            :
DATA DIVISION.
FILE SECTION.
FD  ESDS-FILE
    LABEL RECORDS ARE STANDARD.
01  ESDS-RECORD.
    05  VSAM-FLAG           PIC X.
            :
WORKING-STORAGE SECTION.
01  UPDATE-PASSWORD         PIC X(8)    VALUE ...
01  STATUS-KEY              PIC XX      VALUE ZERO.
            :
PROCEDURE DIVISION.
            :
    OPEN I-O ESDS-FILE.
            :
    READ ESDS-FILE
        AT END MOVE HIGH-VALUES TO EOF-SWITCH.
            :
    CLOSE ESDS-FILE.
            :
CHANGE-ROUTINE.
            :
        Code to update record in ESDS_RECORD work area.
            :
    REWRITE ESDS-RECORD.
            :
DELETE-ROUTINE.
    MOVE HIGH-VALUES TO VSAM-FLAG.
    REWRITE ESDS-RECORD.
            :
```

Figure 12.3 Sequential ESDS update.

of the data set and writing a new version into a separate new data set. Such a program operates in an identical manner to an update program for a non-VSAM sequential data set. The program opens the input data set for INPUT and the output data set for OUTPUT. It then issues READS for the input records and WRITES for the output records. The program terminates by issuing a CLOSE for both data sets. When updating in this fashion, records are physically deleted simply by not writing them into the output data set. Records in the input data set that have already been flagged as deleted can be dropped by the program. No restrictions apply to changing the sizes of variable-length records if an ESDS is updated in this manner.

EXTENDING AN ESDS

Although new records cannot be inserted between existing records in an ESDS, new records can be added to the end of the data set. An operation of this type is sometimes called *extending* the data set. Figure 12.4 shows the skeleton coding that could be used to construct a program for extending an ESDS. The program is almost identical to the program used to load the data set initially; the only difference is the addition of the EXTEND keyword to the OPEN statement. EXTEND indicates that the data set is to be opened in such a way as to cause new records to be written after any existing records in the data set.

```
              :
FILE-CONTROL.
    SELECT ESDS-FILE
        ASSIGN TO AS-ESDSDD
        PASSWORD IS UPDATE-PASSWORD
        FILE STATUS IS STATUS-KEY.
              :
DATA DIVISION.
FILE SECTION.
FD  ESDS-FILE
    LABEL RECORDS ARE STANDARD.
01  ESDS-RECORD          PIC X(100).
              :
WORKING-STORAGE SECTION.
01  UPDATE-PASSWORD      PIC X(8)    VALUE ...
01  STATUS-KEY           PIC XX      VALUE ZERO.
              :
PROCEDURE DIVISION.
              :
    OPEN EXTEND ESDS-FILE.
              :
    WRITE ESDS-RECORD.
              :
    CLOSE ESDS-FILE.
              :
```

Figure 12.4 Extending an ESDS.

13 COBOL KSDS PROCESSING

This chapter discusses techniques that can be used in COBOL programs to process VSAM data sets that are organized as KSDS clusters. With a KSDS, records are handled based on the values of their symbolic keys, and records can be accessed either sequentially, in symbolic key order, or directly, by specifying the symbolic key value of the desired record. This chapter begins by looking at the skeleton coding for a program that sequentially loads a KSDS. We then continue by seeing how KSDS records can be retrieved in both primary key and alternate key sequence. Next, we look at examples of KSDS update programs that update records sequentially and directly. Finally, we look at a load program that directly loads a new KSDS according to key field values.

KSDS SELECT STATEMENT

The format of the SELECT statement used to define a VSAM KSDS is shown in Box 13.1. Notice that its format is somewhat different from that of the SELECT statement used with an ESDS. The first difference is not evident in the formal syntax description. In the ASSIGN clause for a KSDS, the *ddname* parameter must not be preceded by the ''AS-'' characters as in the ASSIGN clause for an ESDS. An example of a KSDS SELECT statement is shown below:

```
SELECT KSDS-FILE
    ASSIGN TO KSDSDD
    ORGANIZATION IS INDEXED
    RECORD KEY IS EMP-NUMBER
    ACCESS MODE IS SEQUENTIAL
    FILE STATUS IS STATUS-KEY.
```

The ORGANIZATION clause must specify INDEXED when processing a VSAM KSDS, and the ACCESS clause indicates how the program will access the records. The above SELECT clause is for a sequential load program, so the keyword SEQUENTIAL is included. The RECORD KEY clause tells which

BOX 13.1 SELECT statement syntax for KSDS

```
FILE-CONTROL.
   SELECT file-name
   ASSIGN TO ddname-1 [ddname-2 ...]
   ORGANIZATION IS INDEXED
   RECORD KEY IS data-name-3
      [PASSWORD IS data-name-1]

   [RESERVE integer {AREA|AREAS}
   [ACCESS MODE IS {SEQUENTIAL|RANDOM|DYNAMIC}]
   [ALTERNATE RECORD KEY IS data-name-4
      [PASSWORD IS data-name-5]
      [WITH DUPLICATES]]
   [FILE STATUS IS data-name-2].
```

data item in the record description for the data set is the key field. Most of the SELECT statement clauses can be coded in any order; however, for a KSDS, the PASSWORD used to gain access to records in primary key sequence must follow the RECORD KEY clause. This is to distinguish the password from a separate password that might be used to gain access to records in alternate key sequence. Alternate key KSDS retrieval is discussed later in this chapter.

SEQUENTIAL KSDS LOAD

Records are written into a KSDS using WRITE statements. As shown in Box 13.2, the WRITE statement for a KSDS can include an optional INVALID KEY clause. The following WRITE statement uses the INVALID key clause to specify a statement to be executed when VSAM detects an invalid key error:

```
WRITE KSDS-RECORD
      INVALID KEY PERFORM KEY-ERROR-ROUTINE.
```

If the INVALID KEY clause is omitted, an I/O error occurs when a problem with a key value is detected, and the routine specified in the DECLARATIVES section is executed. If no INVALID KEY statement or DECLARA-

BOX 13.2 WRITE statement syntax for KSDS

```
WRITE record-name

   [FROM identifier]
   [INVALID KEY imperative-statement].
```

TIVES routine is specified, the WRITE statement fails, and processing resumes with the next sequential statement.

Figure 13.1 shows the skeleton coding that can be used to construct a program to sequentially load a KSDS. I/O errors can occur when processing KSDS clusters, so an error processing routine is often included in the DECLARATIVES section. The error routine shown in Fig. 13.1 is identical to the one

```
                 :
INPUT-OUTPUT SECTION.
FILE-CONTROL.
    SELECT KSDS-FILE
        ASSIGN TO KSDSDD
        ORGANIZATION IS INDEXED
        ACCESS IS SEQUENTIAL
        RECORD KEY IS EMP-NUMBER
            PASSWORD IS UPDATE-PASSWORD
        FILE STATUS IS STATUS-KEY.
                 :
DATA DIVISION.
FILE SECTION.
FD  KSDS-FILE
    LABEL RECORDS ARE STANDARD.
01  KSDS-RECORD.
    05  EMP-NUMBER       PIC 9999.
                 :
WORKING-STORAGE SECTION.

01  UPDATE-PASSWORD     PIC X(8)    VALUE ...
01  STATUS-KEY          PIC XX      VALUE ZERO.
01  ERROR-RECORD.
    03 ERROR-MESSAGE    PIC X(37).
    03 ERROR-STATUS     PIC XX.

PROCEDURE DIVISION.

DECLARATIVES.

FILE-ERROR SECTION.
    USE AFTER STANDARD ERROR PROCEDURE ON KSDS-FILE.
    MOVE 'I/O ERROR ON KSDSDD--STATUS KEY IS '
        TO ERROR-MESSAGE.
    MOVE STATUS-KEY TO ERROR-STATUS.
    WRITE ERROR-RECORD.
    STOP RUN.
    END DECLARATIVES.

BEGIN-PROCESSING.
    OPEN OUTPUT KSDS-FILE.
                 :
    WRITE KSDS-RECORD
        INVALID-KEY ...
                 :
    CLOSE KSDS-FILE.
                 :
```

Figure 13.1 Sequential KSDS load.

used in the ESDS load program in Chapter 12; it simply displays a descriptive message and terminates the program when an I/O error occurs. More comprehensive error detection and recovery routines can be coded if desired.

The I/O statements used to sequentially load a KSDS are similar to those used to load an ESDS. The data set is opened as OUTPUT, and the records are written with WRITE statements. After all the records have been loaded, the data set is closed. In a sequential load program, records must be presented to the load program in ascending sequence by primary key value. VSAM checks each key value as it is loaded; if VSAM detects an out-of-sequence condition, the WRITE operation fails. If the INVALID KEY option is included in the WRITE statement, as shown in Fig. 13.1, the statement in the INVALID KEY clause is executed when an out-of-sequence condition occurs. If the INVALID KEY clause is not included in the WRITE statement, an out-of-sequence condition causes control to be passed to the I/O error routine specified in the DECLARATIVES.

SEQUENTIAL KSDS RETRIEVAL

After a KSDS has been loaded, programs can retrieve records from it. When records are sequentially retrieved from a KSDS using READ statements, VSAM passes records to the program in ascending sequence according to their key values. The syntax of the READ statement for a KSDS is shown in Box 13.3. As shown in the following example, the NEXT keyword is optional for a sequential KSDS retrieval:

```
READ KSDS-FILE
     AT END MOVE HIGH-VALUES TO EOF-SWITCH.
```

Figure 13.2 shows the skeleton coding that could be used to build a program that retrieves records sequentially from a KSDS. In this example, we are assuming that the key field for the KSDS is the EMP-NUMBER field. The SELECT statement and FD entry are similar to those used in the sequential KSDS load program in Fig. 13.1. Since the data set is only being read by this program, the PASSWORD parameter could reference the read password instead

BOX 13.3 READ statement syntax for sequential KSDS retrieval

```
READ file-name [NEXT] RECORD

   [INTO identifier]
   [AT END imperative-statement].
```

```
                :
INPUT-OUTPUT SECTION.
FILE-CONTROL.
    SELECT KSDS-FILE
        ASSIGN TO KSDSDD
        ORGANIZATION IS INDEXED
        ACCESS IS SEQUENTIAL
        RECORD KEY IS EMP-NUMBER
            PASSWORD IS READ-PASSWORD
        FILE STATUS IS STATUS-KEY.
                :
DATA DIVISION.
FILE SECTION.
FD  KSDS-FILE
    LABEL RECORDS ARE STANDARD.
01  KSDS-RECORD.
    05  EMP-NUMBER      PIC 9999.
                :
WORKING-STORAGE SECTION.
01  READ-PASSWORD       PIC X(8)   VALUE ...
01  STATUS-KEY          PIC XX     VALUE ZERO.
                :
PROCEDURE DIVISION.
                :
    OPEN INPUT KSDS-FILE.
                :
    READ KSDS-FILE
        AT END MOVE HIGH-VALUES TO EOF-SWITCH.
                :
    CLOSE KSDS-FILE.
                :
```

Figure 13.2 Sequential KSDS retrieval.

of the update password. For simplicity, we have omitted the error processing routine, but the same one that is used in the load program could be used for KSDS retrieval.

The PROCEDURE DIVISION statements used to sequentially retrieve records from a KSDS are the same as those used for sequential ESDS retrieval. The data set is opened as INPUT, and the records are accessed sequentially by issuing READ statements until the end of the data set is reached. Finally, the data set is closed. VSAM retrieves records beginning with the record whose EMP NUMBER value is lowest and continues retrieving records in ascending sequence according to their EMP-NUMBER values.

SKIP-SEQUENTIAL KSDS RETRIEVAL

When processing a KSDS, it is not necessary to start at the beginning of the data set and sequentially read all the records. Instead, only selected records from the data set can be read and records in other parts of the data set can be skipped. To do this, the program issues a START statement that provides the key value of the record at which sequential processing is to begin. The syntax of the START statement is shown in Box 13.4. When no KEY clause is included in the START statement, as in the following example, VSAM performs an *equal* comparison and locates the record in the data set whose key value is equal to the value in the RECORD KEY data item:

```
START KSDS-FILE
      INVALID KEY KEY-ERROR-ROUTINE.
```

Alternatively, the START statement can include a KEY clause to explicitly define the test to be performed. When using the KEY option, any of the tests shown in Box 13.4 can be specified. After executing the following statements, VSAM will be positioned on the first record in the data set whose key value is greater than or equal to 0050:

```
MOVE "0050" TO EMP-NUMBER.
START KSDS-FILE
      KEY IS NOT < EMP-NUMBER.
```

After a START statement is executed, the next READ statement begins sequentially retrieving records starting from the point specified in the START statement. At any time, the program can issue another START statement to begin subsequent sequential retrievals from a new starting point. The START statement can be used any number of times during the execution of a program and can cause VSAM to move forward or backward in the data set to locate each required sequential retrieval point.

Figure 13.3 shows the skeleton coding that can be used to build a program that uses the START statement to perform skip-sequential retrieval. The coding shows the retrieval of records beginning with the one whose EMP-NUMBER

BOX 13.4 The START statement

```
START file-name

   [KEY IS {EQUAL TO |
            = |
            GREATER THAN |
            > |
            NOT LESS THAN |
            NOT <            } data-name]

   [INVALID KEY imperative-statement].
```

```
          :
INPUT-OUTPUT SECTION.
FILE-CONTROL.
    SELECT KSDS-FILE
        ASSIGN TO KSDSDD
        ORGANIZATION IS INDEXED
        ACCESS IS SEQUENTIAL
        RECORD KEY IS EMP-NUMBER
            PASSWORD IS READ-PASSWORD
        FILE STATUS IS STATUS-KEY.
          :
DATA DIVISION.
FILE SECTION.
FD  KSDS-FILE
    LABEL RECORDS ARE STANDARD.
01  KSDS-RECORD.
    05  EMP-NUMBER       PIC 9999.
          :
PROCEDURE DIVISION.
          :
    OPEN INPUT KSDS-FILE.
    MOVE '1057' TO EMP-NUMBER.
    START KSDS-FILE
        INVALID KEY
            PERFORM NOT-FOUND-ROUTINE.
    READ KSDS-FILE
        AT END MOVE HIGH-VALUES TO EOF-SWITCH.
    PERFORM PROCESS-RECORDS
        UNTIL EMP-NUMBER IS GREATER THAN '3644'
        OR END-OF-FILE.
          :
    CLOSE KSDS-FILE.
          :
PROCESS-RECORDS.
          :
    READ KSDS-FILE
        AT END MOVE HIGH-VALUES TO EOF-SWITCH.
          :
```

Figure 13.3 Skip-sequential KSDS retrieval.

value is 1057 and ending with record 3644. Processing begins by moving the key field value of the first record to be sequentially retrieved to the RECORD KEY data item. The START statement is then issued, which causes VSAM to locate that record in the data set. The first READ statement then causes record 1057 to be retrieved. Note that the START statement does not retrieve a record; it simply causes VSAM to establish position on the specified record. The next READ statement causes that record to be read into the work area. If no record corresponding to the specified test in the START statement is found, the statement in the INVALID KEY clause is executed. If no INVALID KEY clause is included, an I/O error occurs.

GENERIC KEY RETRIEVAL

The KEY clause of the START statement must refer either to the RECORD KEY data item defined for the data set or to a data item that is subordinate to the RECORD KEY data item and aligned on the left with it. For example, the coding in Fig. 13.4 retrieves only records for employees whose key values begin with the digits 80. The START statement specifies a generic key that identifies the first record in the data set whose EMP-NUMBER value begins with the digits 80. The first READ statement then retrieves that record. Subsequent reads retrieve the records that follow.

```
 .
 .
DATA DIVISION.
FILE SECTION.
FD  KSDS-FILE
    LABEL RECORDS ARE STANDARD.
01  KSDS-RECORD.
    05  EMP-NUMBER.
        10  EMP-GROUP          PIC 99.
        10  EMP-NO             PIC 99.
            :
PROCEDURE DIVISION.
            :
    OPEN INPUT KSDS-FILE.
    MOVE '80' TO EMP-GROUP.
    MOVE '00' TO EMP-NO.
    START KSDS-FILE
        KEY IS EQUAL EMP-GROUP
        INVALID KEY
            MOVE 'NO' TO FOUND-SW.
    IF RECORD-FOUND
        PERFORM READ-KSDS-RECORD
        PERFORM PROCESS-RECORDS
           UNTIL EMP-GROUP IS GREATER THAN '80'
           OR END-OF-FILE-REACHED.
            :
    CLOSE KSDS-FILE.
            :
PROCESS-RECORDS.
            :
    PERFORM READ-KSDS-RECORD.
            :
READ-KSDS-RECORD.
    READ KSDS-FILE
        AT END MOVE HIGH-VALUES TO EOF-SWITCH.
            :
```

Figure 13.4 Generic key retrieval.

ALTERNATE KEY SEQUENTIAL KSDS RETRIEVAL

Records in a KSDS can be processed sequentially using either the *primary key,* as in the preceding examples, or using an *alternate key*. Suppose that our KSDS is indexed by an alternate index that uses EMP-NAME as an alternate key. Figure 13.5 shows the skeleton coding that could be used to build a program to sequentially retrieve records from this KSDS in EMP-NAME sequence. Notice the SELECT statement has an ALTER-

```
                  :
INPUT-OUTPUT SECTION.
FILE-CONTROL.
    SELECT KSDS-FILE
        ASSIGN TO KSDSDD
        ORGANIZATION IS INDEXED
        ACCESS IS SEQUENTIAL
        RECORD KEY IS EMP-NUMBER
            PASSWORD IS READ-PASSWORD
        ALTERNATE RECORD KEY IS EMP-NAME
            PASSWORD IS ALT-READ-PASSWORD
            WITH DUPLICATES
        FILE STATUS IS STATUS-KEY.
                  :
DATA DIVISION.
FILE SECTION.
FD  KSDS-FILE
    LABEL RECORDS ARE STANDARD.
01  KSDS-RECORD.
    05  EMP-NUMBER        PIC 9999.
    05  EMP-NAME          PIC X(25).
                  :
WORKING-STORAGE SECTION.
01  READ-PASSWORD         PIC X(8)   VALUE ...
01  ALT-READ-PASSWORD     PIC X(8)   VALUE ...
01  STATUS-KEY            PIC XX     VALUE ZERO.
                  :
PROCEDURE DIVISION.
                  :
    OPEN INPUT KSDS-FILE.
                  :
MOVE . . . TO EMP-NAME.
START KSDS-FILE KEY=EMP-NAME
    INVALID KEY ...
IF RECORD-FOUND
    READ KSDS-FILE
        AT END MOVE HIGH-VALUES TO EOF-SWITCH.
                  :
   CLOSE KSDS-FILE.
                  :
```

Figure 13.5 Sequential KSDS retrieval via alternate key.

NATE RECORD KEY clause as well as a RECORD KEY clause. The ALTERNATE RECORD KEY clause identifies the alternate key field.

If the data set is password protected, PASSWORD clauses must be coded following both the RECORD KEY and the ALTERNATE RECORD KEY clauses. To establish the alternate key as the key to be used in performing sequential retrieval, the program issues a START statement that uses the RECORD KEY clause to identify EMP-NAME instead of EMP-NUMBER. Subsequent READ statements then cause records to be retrieved in sequence according to the values contained in the EMP-NAME fields. When the WITH DUPLICATES clause is coded in the ALTERNATE RECORD KEY clause in the SELECT statement, all records having each alternate key value are retrieved. If the WITH DUPLICATES clause is omitted, only the first record having a given alternate key field value is read.

Records can be sequentially retrieved via the prime key and via an alternate key in the same run of a program. Multiple alternate keys can also be referenced in the same program. A new START statement, specifying a new primary or alternate key name, begins a new sequence of sequential retrievals using the specified key field.

Keep in mind that retrieval efficiency is generally lower when retrieving records in alternate key sequence rather than in primary key sequence. VSAM maintains the records in each control interval in primary key sequence, so retrieving records in alternate key sequence may cause VSAM to move from control interval to control interval in satisfying each alternate key sequential retrieval request.

SEQUENTIAL KSDS UPDATE

A KSDS can be sequentially updated in a similar manner to updating an ESDS in place. When performing a sequential KSDS update, the original data set serves as both input and output. Records can be retrieved, changed, and then rewritten to the data set if desired. With a KSDS, VSAM allows all types of updating to be performed. For example, the size of a variable-length KSDS record can be changed, records can be physically deleted from the data set, and new records can be inserted between existing records.

Figure 13.6 shows the skeleton coding that could be used to create a sequential KSDS update program. The SELECT statement and FD entries are similar to those in the previous KSDS examples. As with a sequential retrieval program, the ACCESS IS SEQUENTIAL clause is optional, since SEQUENTIAL is the default value. The OPEN statement this time specifies I-O, indicating that the data set will be used for both input and output.

As with the sequential retrieval programs we have already seen, READ statements in the update program cause VSAM to retrieve records from the data set in ascending sequence according to key values. To update a record that has been retrieved, the program makes any required changes to the record in the

```
                :
INPUT-OUTPUT SECTION.
FILE-CONTROL.
    SELECT KSDS-FILE
        ASSIGN TO KSDSDD
        ORGANIZATION IS INDEXED
        ACCESS IS SEQUENTIAL
        RECORD KEY IS EMP-NUMBER
        FILE STATUS IS STATUS-KEY.
                :
DATA DIVISION.
FILE SECTION.
FD  KSDS-FILE
    LABEL RECORDS ARE STANDARD.
01  KSDS-RECORD.
    05  EMP-NUMBER ...
                :
PROCEDURE DIVISION.
                :
    OPEN I-O KSDS-FILE.
                :
    READ KSDS-FILE
        AT END MOVE HIGH-VALUES TO EOF-SWITCH.
                :
    CLOSE KSDS-FILE.
                :
CHANGE-ROUTINE.
                :
    REWRITE KSDS-RECORD
        INVALID KEY ...
                :
DELETE-ROUTINE.
    DELETE KSDS-FILE RECORD.
                :
ADD-ROUTINE.
                :
    WRITE KSDS-RECORD
        INVALID KEY ...
                :
```

Figure 13.6 Sequential KSDS update.

work area and then issues a REWRITE statement. The syntax of the REWRITE statement used for a KSDS is shown in Box 13.5. As in the following example, the REWRITE statement for a KSDS can include an optional INVALID KEY clause to specify a statement to be executed when a problem is detected with a key value:

```
REWRITE KSDS-RECORD
        INVALID KEY PERFORM KEY-ERROR-ROUTINE.
```

BOX 13.5 REWRITE statement syntax for KSDS

```
REWRITE record-name

   [FROM identifier]
   [INVALID KEY imperative-statement].
```

When a REWRITE statement is executed, the record in the data set is replaced with the new version in the work area. The length of a variable-length KSDS record can be changed, if desired, before executing the REWRITE statement. The only restriction to updating a KSDS record is that its key value must not be modified. If the program inadvertently changes the key field value, the REWRITE statement fails and the INVALID KEY clause, if specified, is executed.

COBOL provides a DELETE statement that can be used to delete records from a KSDS. Its syntax is shown in Box 13.6. As with the READ statement, the DELETE statement specifies the file name defined in the FD. The following DELETE statement physically removes the most recently read record from its control interval:

```
DELETE KSDS-FILE RECORD
       INVALID KEY PERFORM KEY-ERROR-ROUTINE.
```

After a DELETE statement is issued, the space formerly occupied by the deleted record is freed up, the records in the control interval are rearranged, and the free space pool is updated. Thus, the space in the control interval previously occupied by a deleted record becomes immediately available for use by other records.

The WRITE statement is used to add a new record to a KSDS. The same WRITE statement syntax is used as for a sequential KSDS load (see Box 13.2). Before executing the WRITE statement, the program ordinarily builds the new record in the work area, thus placing the key value of the new record into the RECORD KEY data item. Alternatively, the record can be built in an area of working storage and can be moved to the work area by including the FROM

BOX 13.6 The DELETE statement

```
DELETE file-name RECORD

   [INVALID KEY imperative-statement].
```

clause in the WRITE statement. If a record with the specified key value already exists in the data set, the statement in the INVALID KEY clause is executed.

When adding records to a KSDS that is defined with ACCESS IS SEQUENTIAL, the records must be added in ascending sequence according to key values. As with the READ statement, however, a new sequence of sequential record additions can be begun at any time by issuing a START statement that defines a new starting point.

EXTENDING A KSDS

A KSDS can be extended by adding new records to the end of the data in the same manner as for an ESDS. The coding for extending a KSDS is similar to the coding used to load a new KSDS, as shown in Fig. 13.7. The SELECT statement and FD entries are the same as for the KSDS load program; the OPEN statement specifies EXTEND instead of OUTPUT. Conventional WRITE statements are used to add records to the end of the data set. As with a KSDS load, the records must be presented to the program in ascending sequence according to key value, and all key values must be greater than the key values of any

```
          :
INPUT-OUTPUT SECTION.
FILE-CONTROL.
    SELECT KSDS-FILE
        ASSIGN TO KSDSDD
        ORGANIZATION IS INDEXED
        ACCESS IS SEQUENTIAL
        RECORD KEY IS EMP-NUMBER
        FILE STATUS IS STATUS-KEY.
          :
DATA DIVISION.
FILE SECTION.
FD  KSDS-FILE
    LABEL RECORDS ARE STANDARD.
01  KSDS-RECORD.
    05  EMP-NUMBER        PIC 9999.
          :
PROCEDURE DIVISION.
          :
    OPEN EXTEND KSDS-FILE.
          :
    WRITE KSDS-RECORD
        INVALID KEY ...
          :
    CLOSE KSDS-FILE.
          :
```

Figure 13.7 Extending a KSDS.

records currently stored in the data set. If the key value of a new record fails to meet either condition, the statement specified in the INVALID KEY clause is executed.

DIRECT KSDS RETRIEVAL

All the examples shown thus far in this chapter have processed KSDS clusters using the ACCESS IS SEQUENTIAL clause in the SELECT statement. Alternatively, a KSDS can be processed directly by changing that clause to ACCESS IS RANDOM. By using ACCESS IS RANDOM, a program can retrieve, update, delete, or add a specific record by moving a key value to the RECORD KEY data item before issuing the I/O request.

When directly retrieving a record from a KSDS, the program moves the key value of the desired record to the RECORD KEY data item before issuing the READ. VSAM then locates the requested record in the data set and places it in the work area. The format of the READ statement used for a direct KSDS retrieval is shown in Box 13.7. Notice that in the following READ statement example, no AT END clause is used. However, the optional INVALID KEY clause is specified, which causes the KEY-ERROR-ROUTINE procedure to be executed if the requested record cannot be found:

```
READ KSDS-FILE
     INVALID KEY PERFORM KEY-ERROR-ROUTINE.
```

The skeleton coding that could be used to build a direct KSDS retrieval program is shown in Fig. 13.8. The data set is opened as INPUT since records will be retrieved. A transaction file is read that specifies the key values of the records that are to be retrieved. A field in each transaction record called TRANS-KEY contains a key value. Before each READ statement is executed, the key value in TRANS-KEY is moved to the RECORD KEY area—in this case EMP-NUMBER. VSAM then uses the key value in EMP-NUMBER to locate each record.

BOX 13.7 READ statement syntax for direct KSDS retrieval

```
READ file-name RECORD

   [INTO identifier]
   [INVALID KEY imperative-statement].
```

```
                    :
INPUT-OUTPUT SECTION.
FILE-CONTROL.
    SELECT KSDS-FILE
        ASSIGN TO KSDSDD
        ORGANIZATION IS INDEXED
        ACCESS IS RANDOM
        RECORD KEY IS EMP-NUMBER
            PASSWORD IS READ-PASSWORD
        FILE STATUS IS STATUS-KEY.
                    :
DATA DIVISION.
FILE SECTION.
FD  KSDS-FILE
    LABEL RECORDS ARE STANDARD.
01  KSDS-RECORD.
    05  EMP-NUMBER      PIC 9999.
                    :
WORKING-STORAGE SECTION.
01  NOT-FOUND-SWITCH   PIC XXX VALUE 'NO'.
    88 NOT-FOUND               VALUE 'YES'.
                    :
PROCEDURE DIVISION.
                    :
    OPEN INPUT KSDS-FILE.
                    :
    MOVE TRANS-KEY TO EMP-NUMBER.
    READ KSDS-FILE
        INVALID KEY
            MOVE 'YES' TO NOT-FOUND-SWITCH.
    IF NOT-FOUND
        PERFORM NOT-FOUND-ROUTINE
    ELSE
        PERFORM PROCESS-RECORD.
                    :
    CLOSE KSDS-FILE.
                    :
```

Figure 13.8 Direct KSDS retrieval.

DIRECT KSDS UPDATE

A KSDS can also be directly updated. When ACCESS IS RANDOM is specified and the data set is opened for I-O, all types of update operations can be performed. Figure 13.9 shows the skeleton coding that could be used to create a direct KSDS update program. Notice that the program contains separate subroutines for adding, changing, and deleting records.

Records are added to a KSDS by issuing WRITE statements. The key value contained in the RECORD KEY data item dictates where the new record will be placed in the data set. The KSDS index is searched to locate the appropriate control interval for each new record, and the records already in the control interval are rearranged to make room for it. Control interval and control area

```
                :
INPUT-OUTPUT SECTION.
FILE-CONTROL.
    SELECT KSDS-FILE
        ASSIGN TO KSDSDD
        ORGANIZATION IS INDEXED
        ACCESS IS RANDOM
        RECORD KEY IS EMP-NUMBER
            PASSWORD IS UPDATE-PASSWORD
        FILE STATUS IS STATUS-KEY.
                :
DATA DIVISION.
FILE SECTION.
FD  KSDS-FILE
    LABEL RECORDS ARE STANDARD.
01  KSDS-RECORD.
    05  EMP-NUMBER        PIC 9999.
                :
PROCEDURE DIVISION.
                :
    OPEN I-O KSDS-FILE.
                :
ADD-ROUTINE.
    MOVE TRANS-ADD-RECORD TO KSDS-RECORD.
    WRITE KSDS-RECORD
        INVALID KEY
            MOVE 'YES' TO DUPLICATES-SW.
                :
CHANGE-ROUTINE.
    MOVE TRANS-CHANGE-RECORD TO KSDS-RECORD.
    REWRITE KSDS-RECORD
        INVALID KEY
            MOVE 'YES' TO NOT-FOUND-SW.
                :
DELETE-ROUTINE.
    MOVE TRANS-KEY TO EMP-NUMBER.
    DELETE KSDS-FILE RECORD
        INVALID KEY
            MOVE 'YES' TO NOT-FOUND-SW.
                :
    CLOSE KSDS-FILE.
                :
```

Figure 13.9 Direct KSDS update.

splits are performed when necessary. If a record with the same key value as the new record already exists in the data set, the WRITE operation fails and the statement in the INVALID KEY clause is executed.

A REWRITE statement is issued to update a specified record. When ACCESS IS RANDOM is in effect, the REWRITE statement does not refer to the previous record read, as with sequential updating. Instead, the program normally builds the updated version of the record in the work area, thus moving the key value of the record to be updated into the RECORD KEY data item. The REWRITE statement is then executed and the record in the work area replaces the corresponding record in the data set. The program can, of course, issue a READ statement for the record prior to issuing the REWRITE, but this is not a requirement. If no record is found that has the specified key value, the statement specified in the INVALID KEY clause is executed.

Records are removed from the data set by issuing DELETE statements. The value in the RECORD KEY data item is used to locate the record to be deleted, and the record is physically deleted from its control interval. If no record having the specified key value is found, the statement specified in the INVALID KEY clause is executed. As with REWRITE, it is not necessary to read a record before deleting it. If the record is not read first, the key value of the record to be deleted must be moved into the RECORD KEY data item before issuing the DELETE statement.

ALTERNATE KEY DIRECT KSDS RETRIEVAL

Records can be retrieved via alternate key values when ACCESS IS RANDOM is in effect. For example, Fig. 13.10 shows the skeleton coding that could be used to create a program that retrieves records using the EMP-NAME alternate key. Here the SELECT statement contains an ALTERNATE RECORD KEY clause naming EMP-NAME as the alternate key. To directly retrieve a record based on an EMP-NAME value, the program moves the desired EMP-NAME value to the ALTERNATE RECORD KEY data item and then issues a READ statement that specifies the EMP-NAME key field.

In order to directly update a record based on an alternate key value, the record must first be retrieved using the alternate key value. The prime key value must then be extracted from the record and moved to the data item referenced by the RECORD KEY clause before the REWRITE statement can be issued. However, if the RECORD KEY data item is in the record work area, the RECORD KEY data item is loaded automatically with the appropriate PRIME KEY value when the record is retrieved, and the REWRITE statement can be issued at any time after the READ. The following three restrictions exist for updating records via alternate key values:

- A PUT operation that replaces an existing record must not change the value of the prime key.
- A PUT operation that replaces an existing record must not change the value of the alternate key that was used to retrieve the record.
- A PUT operation that inserts a new record using an alternate key defined with the UNIQUEKEY attribute must not insert a record that has an alternate key value equal to that of an existing record.

```
                    :
INPUT-OUTPUT SECTION.
FILE-CONTROL.
    SELECT KSDS-FILE
        ASSIGN TO KSDSDD
        ORGANIZATION IS INDEXED
        ACCESS IS RANDOM
        RECORD KEY IS EMP-NUMBER
            PASSWORD IS READ-PASSWORD
        ALTERNATE RECORD KEY IS EMP-NAME
            PASSWORD IS NAME-READ-PASSWORD
        FILE STATUS IS STATUS-KEY.
                    :
DATA DIVISION.
FILE SECTION.
FD  KSDS-FILE
    LABEL RECORDS ARE STANDARD.
01  KSDS-RECORD.
    05  EMP-NUMBER          PIC 9999.
    05  EMP-NAME            PIC X(25).
                    :
PROCEDURE DIVISION.
                    :
    OPEN INPUT KSDS-FILE.
                    :
    MOVE TRANS-NAME TO EMP-NAME
    READ KSDS-FILE
        KEY IS EMP-NAME
        INVALID KEY
            MOVE 'YES' TO NOT-FOUND-SWITCH.
        IF NOT-FOUND
            PERFORM NOT-FOUND-ROUTINE
        ELSE
            PERFORM PROCESS-RECORD.
                    :
        CLOSE KSDS-FILE.
                    :
```

Figure 13.10 Direct KSDS retrieval via alternate key.

DIRECT KSDS LOAD

The load programs we have looked at thus far have all required that the records be presented to the load program in ascending key sequence. When ACCESS IS RANDOM is specified, records can be loaded into a KSDS in any sequence. A direct KSDS load program functions in the same manner as an update program that adds records to an existing KSDS. In fact, the previous direct KSDS update program could be used to load a KSDS simply by using a transaction file that contains all add transactions. For a direct KSDS load, the KSDS is opened either as OUTPUT or I-O, and conventional WRITE statements are used to write new records into the data set. VSAM uses the key value contained in the RECORD KEY data item in determining where in the data set to write each new record.

In actual practice, direct KSDS load programs are seldom used. More processing time is required than for an equivalent sequential load, since the index must be searched and updated each time a record is written. Also, after a sequential KSDS load, control intervals contain records that are in physical sequence from one control interval to the next. With a direct KSDS load, all the initial records are written into the first control interval until it is filled. Then a control interval split occurs, and all subsequent records are written into the first two control intervals until a third is required, at which point another control interval split occurs, and so on. Thus, by the time the direct load is finished, control intervals tend to be scattered throughout KSDS in no particular order. This causes later sequential retrieval efficiency to be lower than if a sequential load had been used.

DYNAMIC KSDS PROCESSING

The same program can combine sequential processing and direct processing by specifying ACCESS MODE IS DYNAMIC in the SELECT statement. When this option is chosen, the program can issue both sequential and direct I/O statements as required. For example, to directly retrieve a specific record from the data set, the following READ statement might be issued:

```
READ KSDS-FILE
     INVALID KEY PERFORM ERROR-ROUTINE.
```

If the program determines that records should now be retrieved sequentially from that point, it could issue a sequence of sequential READ statements, such as the following:

```
READ KSDS-FILE NEXT
     AT END MOVE HIGH-VALUES TO EOF-SWITCH.
```

In the above examples, the first direct READ statement has a similar effect as a START statement for sequential retrieval. It directly retrieves a record and positions VSAM on the next record should subsequent sequential retrievals be required. When ACCESS MODE IS DYNAMIC is in effect, sequential READ statements must specify the NEXT keyword to distinguish them from other direct READ statements.

14 COBOL RRDS PROCESSING

The final type of VSAM data set is the relative record data set. Records in an RRDS are stored in fixed-length slots, and COBOL programs work with RRDS records based on their relative record numbers, or slot numbers. In this final chapter on COBOL programming, we discuss the COBOL techniques that are used in working with RRDS clusters. Much of the coding that we will show for working with an RRDS is similar to the coding used with ESDS and KSDS clusters. We will begin, as we did in the previous two chapters, by discussing the sequential load process.

RRDS SELECT STATEMENT

Box 14.1 shows that the SELECT statement syntax for an RRDS is similar to that for a KSDS. The ORGANIZATION clause must specify ORGANIZATION IS RELATIVE, and the optional RELATIVE KEY clause can be coded in place of the RECORD KEY clause used with a KSDS. As shown in the following example, the SEQUENTIAL keyword must be specified in the ACCESS IS clause for a sequential RRDS load.

```
SELECT RRDS-FILE
   ASSIGN TO KSDSDD
   ORGANIZATION IS RELATIVE
   RELATIVE KEY IS RR-NUMBER
        ACCESS IS SEQUENTIAL
   FILE STATUS IS STATUS-KEY.
```

For sequential access, the RELATIVE KEY clause is not required. If it is coded, VSAM places the relative record number of each record that is processed into the specified data item. A data field referenced by the RELATIVE KEY clause must be an unsigned numeric data item; its size is determined by how

BOX 14.1 SELECT statement syntax for RRDS

```
FILE-CONTROL.
    SELECT file-name
    ASSIGN TO ddname-1 [ddname-2 ...]
    ORGANIZATION IS RELATIVE

    [RESERVE integer {AREA|AREAS}]
    [ACCESS MODE IS {SEQUENTIAL|RANDOM|DYNAMIC}]
    [RELATIVE KEY IS dataname-1]}
    [PASSWORD IS data-name-2]
    [FILE STATUS IS data-name-3].
```

many slots are contained in the RRDS. The RELATIVE KEY data item cannot be a data item that is contained in the record work area.

SEQUENTIAL RRDS LOAD

In performing a sequential RRDS load, it is important to realize that records are not loaded into the RRDS in sequence according to their key values. The logical sequence according to the values of any symbolic keys that might be contained in the records bears no relationship to physical sequence according to relative record numbers. This is because a hashing or randomizing algorithm is generally used, tending to scatter the records of an RRDS more or less randomly through the data set.

One technique for loading an RRDS sequentially is to write a program that reads the records to be loaded and writes out a new file of records that has the relative record number of each record attached to it. The program must use the same randomizing algorithm that will be used by programs that access the RRDS. The records are then sorted into relative record number sequence. Either before or after the sort, synonyms must be handled by determining alternate relative record numbers for sets of records that randomize to the same relative record number. The final sorted data set then contains a record for each slot in the RRDS that will contain an active record and can be read by the sequential RRDS load program. The load program must write dummy records into those slots that will not initially contain an active record. The sequential load program we will look at in this chapter assumes that the input data set read by the load program already has the records sorted into relative record number sequence and that there is a record in the input data set for each slot in the RRDS.

Figure 14.1 shows the skeleton coding that could be used to construct a sequential RRDS load program. The FD entry is coded in the same manner as the FD for an ESDS or KSDS. As with ESDS and KSDS clusters, a routine can

```
                :
 INPUT-OUTPUT SECTION.
 FILE-CONTROL.
     SELECT RRDS-FILE
         ASSIGN TO RRDSDD
         ORGANIZATION IS RELATIVE
         ACCESS IS SEQUENTIAL
         PASSWORD IS UPDATE-PASSWORD
         FILE STATUS IS STATUS-KEY.
                :
 DATA DIVISION.
 FILE SECTION.
 FD  RRDS-FILE
     LABEL RECORDS ARE STANDARD.
 01  RRDS-RECORD.
     05  EMP-NUMBER ...
                :
 WORKING-STORAGE SECTION.
 01  UPDATE-PASSWORD     PIC X(8)    VALUE ...
 01  STATUS-KEY          PIC XX      VALUE ZERO.
 01  ERROR-RECORD.
     03 ERROR-MESSAGE    PIC X(37).
     03 ERROR-STATUS     PIC XX.

 PROCEDURE DIVISION.

 DECLARATIVES.

 FILE-ERROR SECTION.
     USE AFTER STANDARD ERROR PROCEDURE ON RRDS-FILE.
     MOVE 'I/O ERROR ON RRDSDD--STATUS KEY IS '
         TO ERROR-MESSAGE.
     MOVE STATUS-KEY TO ERROR-STATUS.
     WRITE ERROR-RECORD.
     STOP RUN.
     END DECLARATIVES.

 BEGIN-PROCESSING.
                :
     OPEN OUTPUT RRDS-FILE.
                :
     WRITE RRDS-RECORD.
                :
     CLOSE RRDS-FILE.
                :
```

Figure 14.1 Sequential RRDS load.

be included in DECLARATIVES to handle I/O errors. The I/O statements are identical to those used in a sequential KSDS load program. The data set is opened as OUTPUT, and each record is loaded in ascending slot number sequence using conventional sequential WRITE statements. After all the records are loaded, the data set is closed.

SEQUENTIAL RRDS RETRIEVAL

During sequential retrieval of RRDS records, the records are passed to the retrieval program in relative record number sequence. A record that sequentially retrieves RRDS records also retrieves dummy records, so the program must contain logic to bypass these empty slots. Figure 14.2 shows the skeleton coding that could be used to build a program to sequentially retrieve records from an RRDS.

The SELECT statement has the same format as the SELECT statement used to load the data set, and the I/O statements are the same as those used to sequentially retrieve records from an ESDS or KSDS. Keep in mind, however, that when sequentially retrieving records from an RRDS, records are retrieved in relative record number sequence; the VSAM software has no knowledge of any symbolic keys that might be contained in the records.

```
                :
INPUT-OUTPUT SECTION.
FILE-CONTROL.
    SELECT RRDS-FILE
        ASSIGN TO RRDSDD
        ORGANIZATION IS RELATIVE
        ACCESS IS SEQUENTIAL
        PASSWORD IS UPDATE-PASSWORD
        FILE STATUS IS STATUS-KEY.
                :
DATA DIVISION.
FILE SECTION.
FD  RRDS-FILE
    LABEL RECORDS ARE STANDARD.
01  RRDS-RECORD.
    05  EMP-NUMBER ...
                :
WORKING-STORAGE SECTION.
01  UPDATE-PASSWORD        PIC X(8)   VALUE ...
01  STATUS-KEY             PIC XX     VALUE ZERO.
                :
PROCEDURE DIVISION.
                :
    OPEN OUTPUT RRDS-FILE.
                :
    READ RRDS-FILE.
        AT END MOVE HIGH-VALUES TO EOF-SWITCH.
                :
    CLOSE RRDS-FILE.
                :
```

Figure 14.2 Sequential RRDS retrieval.

```
                    :
INPUT-OUTPUT SECTION.
FILE-CONTROL.
    SELECT RRDS-FILE
        ASSIGN TO RRDSDD
        ORGANIZATION IS RELATIVE
        ACCESS IS SEQUENTIAL
        RELATIVE KEY IS RR-NUMBER.
                    :
DATA DIVISION.
FILE SECTION.
FD  RRDS-FILE
    LABEL RECORDS ARE STANDARD.
01  RRDS-RECORD.
                    :
WORKING-STORAGE SECTION.
01  RR-NUMBER     PIC 999   VALUE  ZERO.
                    :
PROCEDURE DIVISION.
                    :
    OPEN INPUT RRDS-FILE.
    MOVE 047 TO RR-NUMBER.
    START RRDS-FILE
        INVALID KEY
            MOVE 'YES' TO NOT-FOUND-SW.
                    :
    READ RRDS-FILE
        AT END MOVE HIGH-VALUES TO EOF-SWITCH.
                    :
    CLOSE RRDS-FILE.
```

Figure 14.3 Skip-sequential RRDS retrieval.

SKIP-SEQUENTIAL RRDS RETRIEVAL

As with sequential KSDS retrieval, a START statement can be used to specify a starting point for a series of sequential RRDS retrievals. Figure 14.3 shows the skeleton coding that could be used to create a program to perform skip-sequential RRDS retrieval. A RELATIVE KEY clause must be coded in the SELECT statement if START statements will be issued. The relative record number of the desired starting point is moved into the RELATIVE KEY data item, and the START statement is executed. VSAM then positions itself on the desired slot. The next sequential READ statement that is issued then retrieves that record. Subsequent READ statements retrieve records in slot number sequence from that point. A new START statement can be issued at any time to move forward or backward in the data set to begin a new sequence of sequential retrievals.

SEQUENTIAL RRDS UPDATE

Updating in place can be done with an RRDS in a similar manner as for an ESDS. To update a record, the record is read and is then rewritten back into the same slot; as with an ESDS, and RRDS record's length cannot be changed. New records cannot be inserted between two existing records, but a record can be added to the data set by replacing an existing dummy record with an active record. The DELETE statement can be issued to delete a record; VSAM responds by rewriting the slot with binary zeros, thus converting it into a dummy record.

The skeleton coding that could be used to build a sequential RRDS update program is shown in Fig. 14.4. The SELECT statement and FD entry are the same as for sequential retrieval. The OPEN statement specifies I-O, indicating that the data set can be both read and written. READ statements cause records

```
          :
INPUT-OUTPUT SECTION.
FILE-CONTROL.
    SELECT RRDS-FILE
        ASSIGN TO RRDSDD
        ORGANIZATION IS RELATIVE
        ACCESS IS SEQUENTIAL
        RELATIVE KEY IS RR-NUMBER
        FILE STATUS IS SEQUENTIAL
          :
DATA DIVISION.
FILE SECTION.
FD  RRDS-FILE
    LABEL RECORDS ARE STANDARD.
01  RRDS-RECORD.
          :
PROCEDURE DIVISION.
          :
    OPEN I-O RRDS-FILE.
          :
    READ RRDS-FILE
        AT END MOVE HIGH-VALUES TO EOF-SWITCH.
          :
    CLOSE RRDS-FILE.
          :
CHANGE-ROUTINE.
          :
    REWRITE RRDS-RECORD.
          :
DELETE-ROUTINE.
    DELETE RRDS-FILE RECORD.
          :
```

Figure 14.4 Sequential RRDS update.

to be retrieved in ascending slot number sequence. A record is updated by making changes to the record in the work area and then issuing a REWRITE statement. Records are deleted by issuing DELETE statements. The record rewritten or deleted is always the one most recently read. Since new slots cannot be added to an RRDS, the WRITE statement is not used in a sequential RRDS update program.

DIRECT RRDS RETRIEVAL

The process of retrieving RRDS records directly is similar to the process of directly retrieving KSDS records. The only difference is that the record to be retrieved is identified by its relative record number rather than by a symbolic key value. A direct RRDS retrieval program normally makes use of a hashing or randomizing algorithm to convert a symbolic key value to a relative record number before each direct retrieval.

The skeleton coding that could be used to retrieve records directly from an RRDS is shown in Fig. 14.5. The SELECT statement is similar to the SELECT statement used to sequentially retrieve RRDS records, and the I/O statements are similar to those used in direct KSDS retrieval. The relative record number of the desired record is placed in the RELATIVE KEY data item prior to issuing each READ. If the specified slot is empty, the INVALID KEY statement is executed.

DIRECT RRDS UPDATE

A direct RRDS update program is similar to a direct KSDS update. Records can be added, deleted, and changed. With an RRDS, any field in the existing record can be changed, but the record's length cannot be modified. Figure 14.6 shows the skeleton coding that could be used to create a direct RRDS update program. The SELECT statement and FD entries are the same as those for direct retrieval. The OPEN statement specifies I-O.

A new record can be added to an empty slot by moving the relative record number of the empty slot to the RELATIVE KEY data item and then issuing a WRITE statement. If the specified slot is not empty, the statement specified in the INVALID KEY clause is executed.

The REWRITE statement is used to update existing records. The new version of the record is built in the work area and the relative record number of the record to be changed is moved to the RELATIVE KEY data item. The REWRITE statement is then issued to update the record in the data set. The record can be first read if desired, but this is not a requirement. If the slot referenced by the REWRITE statement is an empty slot, the statement specified in the INVALID KEY clause is executed.

Records are removed from an RRDS by issuing DELETE statements. The program moves the relative record number of the record to be deleted to the

```
                :
INPUT-OUTPUT SECTION.
FILE-CONTROL.
    SELECT RRDS-FILE
        ASSIGN TO RRDSDD
        ORGANIZATION IS RELATIVE
        ACCESS IS RANDOM
        RELATIVE KEY IS RR-NUMBER
        PASSWORD IS READ-PASSWORD
        FILE STATUS IS STATUS-KEY.
                :
DATA DIVISION.
FILE SECTION.
FD  RRDS-FILE
    LABEL RECORDS ARE STANDARD.
01  EMP-RECORD.
    05  EMP-NUMBER ...
                :
WORKING-STORAGE SECTION.
01  RR-NUMBER    PIC 999 ...
                :
PROCEDURE DIVISION.
                :
    OPEN INPUT RRDS-FILE.
                :
    PERFORM OBTAIN-RR-NUMBER
    MOVE OBTAINED-RR-NUMBER TO RR-NUMBER.
    READ RRDS-FILE
        INVALID KEY
            MOVE 'YES' TO NOT-FOUND-SWITCH.
    IF NOT-FOUND
        PERFORM NOT-FOUND-ROUTINE
    ELSE
        PERFORM PROCESS-RECORD.
                :
    CLOSE RRDS-FILE.
                :
```

Figure 14.5 Direct RRDS retrieval.

RELATIVE KEY data item and then issues a DELETE statement. VSAM responds by filling the indicated slot with binary zeros, thus converting the record into an empty slot. If the slot is already empty when the DELETE statement is executed, the statement specified in the INVALID KEY clause is executed. As with the REWRITE statement, it is not necessary to read a record before deleting it.

Regardless of whether the program issues a READ, WRITE, REWRITE, or DELETE, the relative record number must be moved to the RELATIVE KEY data item prior to issuing the I/O statement. However, if a REWRITE or DELETE statement is issued for a record that has just been read, the RELATIVE KEY data item already contains the correct relative record number.

```
                 :
INPUT-OUTPUT SECTION.
FILE-CONTROL.
    SELECT RRDS-FILE
        ASSIGN TO RRDSDD
        ORGANIZATION IS RELATIVE
        ACCESS IS RANDOM
        RELATIVE KEY IS RR-NUMBER
        PASSWORD IS UPDATE-PASSWORD
        FILE STATUS IS STATUS-KEY.
                 :
DATA DIVISION.
FILE SECTION.
FD  RRDS-FILE
    LABEL RECORDS ARE STANDARD.
01  RRDS-RECORD
    05  EMP-NUMBER ...
                 :
PROCEDURE DIVISION.
                 :
     OPEN I-O RRDS-FILE.
                 :
ADD-ROUTINE.
    PERFORM OBTAIN-RR-NUMBER.
    MOVE OBTAINED_RR_NUMBER TO RR-NUMBER.
    WRITE RRDS-RECORD
        INVALID KEY
            MOVE 'YES' TO DUPLICATES-SW.
                 :
CHANGE-ROUTINE.

    PERFORM OBTAIN-RR-NUMBER.
    MOVE OBTAINED_RR_NUMBER TO RR-NUMBER.
    REWRITE RRDS-RECORD
        INVALID KEY ...
                 :
DELETE-ROUTINE.

    PERFORM OBTAIN-RR-NUMBER.
    MOVE OBTAINED_RR_NUMBER TO RR-NUMBER.
    DELETE RRDS-FILE RECORD
        INVALID KEY ...
                 :
    CLOSE RRDS-FILE.
                 :
```

Figure 14.6 Direct RRDS update.

DIRECT RRDS LOAD

With a KSDS, the normal practice is to load the data set sequentially; as discussed in Chapter 13, a direct KSDS load is normally inefficient and is to be avoided. However, with an RRDS, random load programs are often used. This is because of the extra processing time involved in sorting the records to be loaded into relative record number sequence and handling synonyms.

Figure 14.7 shows the skeleton coding that could be used to build a direct RRDS load program. ACCESS IS RANDOM is specified in the SELECT statement and the data set is opened as OUTPUT. WRITE statements are used to write records into the data set. The program operates as if the data set consists of all empty slots, even though the data set may or may not be preformatted before the program executes. The INVALID KEY option should be coded to allow the program to handle synonyms.

DYNAMIC RRDS RETRIEVAL

As with a KSDS, sequential and direct retrieval of RRDS records can be combined in the same program. Figure 14.8 shows the skeleton coding for a

```
              :
INPUT-OUTPUT SECTION.
FILE-CONTROL.
    SELECT RRDS-FILE
        ASSIGN TO RRDSDD
        ORGANIZATION IS RELATIVE
        ACCESS IS RANDOM
        RELATIVE KEY IS RR-NUMBER
        FILE STATUS IS STATUS-KEY.
              :
DATA DIVISION.
FILE SECTION.
FD  RRDS-FILE
    LABEL RECORDS ARE STANDARD.
01  RRDS-RECORD.
    05  EMP-NUMBER ...
              :
WORKING-STORAGE SECTION.
01  STATUS-KEY   PIC XX ...
01  RR-NUMBER    PIC 999 ...
              :
PROCEDURE DIVISION.
              :
    OPEN OUTPUT RRDS-FILE.
              :
    PERFORM CALCULATE-RR-NUMBER.
    WRITE RRDS-RECORD
        INVALID KEY
            MOVE 'YES' TO DUPLICATES-SW.
              :
   CLOSE RRDS-FILE.
              :
```

Figure 14.7 Direct RRDS load.

```
                 :
INPUT-OUTPUT SECTION.
FILE-CONTROL.
    SELECT RRDS-FILE
        ASSIGN TO RRDSDD
        ORGANIZATION IS RELATIVE
        ACCESS IS DYNAMIC
        RELATIVE KEY IS RR-NUMBER
        FILE STATUS IS STATUS-KEY.
                 :
DATA DIVISION.
FILE SECTION.
FD  RRDS-FILE
    LABEL RECORDS ARE STANDARD.
01  RRDS-RECORD.
    05  EMP-NUMBER ...
                 :
WORKING-STORAGE SECTION.
01  RR-NUMBER ... .
                 :
PROCEDURE DIVISION.
                 :
    OPEN INPUT RRDS-FILE.
                 :
    MOVE TRANS-RR-NUMBER TO RR-NUMBER.
    READ RRDS-FILE
        INVALID KEY
            MOVE 'YES' TO NOT-FOUND-SWITCH.
                 :
    READ RRDS-FILE NEXT
        AT END MOVE HIGH-VALUES TO EOF-SWITCH.
            MOVE 'YES' TO EOF-SWITCH
                 :
    CLOSE RRDS-FILE.
                 :
```

Figure 14.8 Dynamic RRDS retrieval.

program that performs both sequential and direct retrievals. The ACCESS IS DYNAMIC clause is specified in the SELECT statement, and the data set is opened for INPUT. The statements used to retrieve records directly are the same as those in Fig. 14.5. For a direct retrieval, the relative record number of the desired record is moved to the RELATIVE KEY data item, and a READ statement with an INVALID KEY clause is issued. To begin sequential retrieval from that point, a sequence of READ statements is issued that includes the NEXT keyword and an AT END clause.

DYNAMIC RRDS UPDATE

Records can also be updated when ACCESS IS DYNAMIC is in effect. Records can be added, changed, and deleted directly, as in the direct RRDS update program shown in Fig. 14.6. Records that are being sequentially retrieved can also be updated, as in the sequential update program shown in Fig. 14.4. The SELECT statement and FD entry are the same as they are for dynamic retrieval, and the data set is opened for I-O.

This concludes the three chapters on COBOL programming techniques for working with VSAM data sets. The chapters in Part IV discuss programming techniques for working with VSAM data sets in PL/I programs. Techniques similar to those discussed in Part III are covered.

PART IV PL/I PROGRAMMING

15 PL/I ESDS PROCESSING

PL/I provides similar facilities as COBOL for processing the three types of VSAM data sets. In PL/I, much of the procedural code used to process VSAM data sets is similar to that used for processing non-VSAM data sets. This chapter discusses those PL/I programming techniques that apply to programs that process ESDS clusters. Sequential ESDS load, retrieval, and update programs are discussed. The following two chapters discuss PL/I programming techniques for accessing KSDS and RRDS clusters.

ESDS FILE DECLARATION ATTRIBUTES

The file declaration attributes that are supplied for a file determine the characteristics of that file. As with other types of files, most file description attributes can be specified either in the DECLARE (DCL) statement for the file or in an OPEN statement that refers to that DCL. In the examples in these chapters, we will specify all file description attributes in the DCL. So the OPEN statements that we show are optional and can be omitted if desired. Box 15.1 shows the attributes that are most often coded in DCL statements for ESDS clusters. The following file declaration is typical of one used in a program that sequentially loads an ESDS:

```
DCL ESDS FILE FILE
              RECORD
              SEQUENTIAL
              OUTPUT
              ENV (VSAM);
```

The ENVIRONMENT (ENV) attribute in the DCL defines the file as one that processes a VSAM data set. The type of cluster being processed (ESDS, KSDS, or RRDS) is specified when the file is defined, and the same set of DCL keywords generally can be used to process a VSAM data set of any type. The

BOX 15.1 File declaration syntax for ESDS

```
DCL    file-name FILE RECORD SEQUENTIAL
       ENV(VSAM [PASSWORD (password-specification)])
       {INPUT|OUTPUT|UPDATE};
```

PASSWORD option in the ENV attribute refers to either a character literal or character variable that defines the 8-byte password. A number of additional options are allowed in the ENV attribute; for a complete list, consult the *Programmer's Guide* for your particular PL/I compiler. Two of the four password types are most useful with PL/I programs: the *read* password and the *update* password. For a sequential load program, the update password must be used in order to allow records to be written into the data set.

SEQUENTIAL ESDS LOAD

The procedural code used to read and write ESDS records is similar to the code used to process a conventional sequential data set. A program to sequentially load an ESDS optionally begins by issuing an OPEN statement to open the data set. As with other types of files, if the OPEN statement is omitted, the file is automatically opened when required; however, we feel that it is good programming practice to explicitly open and close all files. Box 15.2 shows the syntax of the OPEN statement for processing VSAM data sets. The following OPEN statement opens an ESDS described by a DCL for a file named ESDS_FILE:

```
OPEN FILE (ESDS_FILE).
```

BOX 15.2 The OPEN statement

```
OPEN FILE(file-reference)
   [,FILE (file-reference)]...;
```

As mentioned earlier, the OPEN statement can also include file description attributes that were not specified in the file declaration. The same attributes need not be specified in both the file declaration and the OPEN statement, and there should be no conflict between the two.

For a sequential load operation, the data set generally is opened with a file description attribute of OUTPUT, and records are written into the data set using WRITE statements. Box 15.3 shows the syntax of the WRITE statement used for writing new records into an ESDS. As shown in the following example, the only required parameter is the file name defined in the FD for the data set:

```
WRITE FILE (ESDS_FILE);
```

BOX 15.3 WRITE statement syntax for ESDS

```
WRITE FILE (file-reference)

   [FROM (reference)]
   [KEYTO (RBA-reference)];
```

The FROM option generally is also included to specify the name of a work area that contains the record being written. If the KEYTO option is included, it should reference a full word variable. VSAM places into the KEYTO variable the RBA of each record that is written. This value can then be used to record the RBAs of records, which can later be used to retrieve the records directly.

After all the records have been loaded, the program optionally issues a CLOSE statement. As shown in Box 15.4 and in the following example, the CLOSE statement for a VSAM data set has the same format as for any other data set.

```
CLOSE FILE (ESDS_FILE);
```

BOX 15.4 The CLOSE statement

```
CLOSE FILE (file-reference)

      [,FILE (file-reference)]...;
```

Figure 15.1 shows the file declaration and procedural code that could be used to build a program to sequentially load an ESDS. These statements will load records into the data set in the physical sequence in which they are presented to the load program. Notice that the password protection feature is used in this program. When the OPEN statement is executed, the password specified

```
                    :
ON KEY (ESDS_FILE) CALL ERROR;
                    :
DCL ESDS_FILE FILE
              RECORD
              SEQUENTIAL
              OUTPUT
              ENV(VSAM PASSWORD('ESDSPSWD'));
DCL 1 ESDS_RECORD        CHAR (100);
                    :
LOAD_DATA_SET:
                    :
    OPEN FILE (ESDS_FILE);
                    :
    WRITE FILE (ESDS_FILE)
          FROM (ESDS_RECORD);
                    :
    CLOSE FILE (ESDS_FILE);
                    :
ERROR:
                    :
    [Code to handle invalid key error.]
                    :
```

Figure 15.1 Sequential ESDS load.

in the PASSWORD option of the ENV attribute is compared against the update, and all higher level passwords, currently in effect for the data set. If the supplied value matches the appropriate password, open processing completes normally. If the value does not match, an I/O error occurs and the data set is not opened.

I/O ERROR HANDLING

When an error occurs in processing a PL/I I/O function, such as READ, or WRITE, the I/O operation fails and control is returned to the program. If no provision for error handling has been provided in the program, control is returned to the statement following the one that caused the error. It is then the responsibility of the program to determine whether or not the I/O operation completed normally. A better way to handle I/O errors is to include an ON KEY statement to specify the code to be executed whenever an I/O error occurs.

Errors that occur during data set processing are often caused during program testing by something that the programmer has neglected to do. So when an I/O error occurs, it is often sufficient to issue a descriptive message and then simply terminate the program. The error can then be corrected and the program rerun. All the program examples in this chapter use this type of error handling.

In other cases, certain types of errors are expected to occur regularly during normal processing. For example, a direct update program should be able to handle record-not-found errors and duplicate-record errors. To handle these, the program can test a return code that VSAM sets after each I/O request. The ONCODE built-in function can be used to test the return code. The use of the ONCODE function is introduced in Chapter 16, where we discuss programs that work with KSDS clusters.

SEQUENTIAL ESDS RETRIEVAL

After an ESDS has been loaded, records can be retrieved from it using READ statements. The most commonly used READ options for retrieving VSAM records are shown in Box 15.5. The following example shows that a READ statement for an ESDS is similar in format to a READ statement used to retrieve records sequentially from a non-VSAM sequential data set.

```
READ FILE (ESDS_FILE)
     INTO (ESDS_RECORD);
```

BOX 15.5 The READ statement

```
READ FILE (file-reference)

   [INTO (reference)]
   [KEY (expression)]
   [KEYTO (reference)];
```

The above READ statement specifies the name of the file declaration used to define the VSAM data set and gives the name of the work area into which VSAM should place the record. The KEY option can be used to pass key values to VSAM that describe the specific record to be read. With an ESDS, the KEY option normally specifies a full word value into which the *program* places the RBA of the record to retrieve. As with the WRITE statement, the KEYTO option of the READ statement is used to specify the name of a full word variable into which *VSAM* places the RBA of each record that is retrieved. The KEYTO option can be used when retrieving records sequentially in order to record the RBAs of the retrieved records.

Figure 15.2 shows the file declaration and procedural code around which a sequential ESDS retrieval program could be created. The only difference between the file declaration in this program and the one for the load program is that the file declaration for the retrieval program specifies INPUT instead of

```
                :
ON KEY (ESDS_FILE) CALL ERROR;
                :
DCL ESDS_FILE FILE
              RECORD
              SEQUENTIAL
              INPUT
              ENV(VSAM PASSWORD('ESDSPSWD'));
DCL 1 ESDS_RECORD        CHAR (100);
                :
READ_DATA_SET:
                :
    OPEN FILE (ESDS_FILE);
                :
    READ FILE (ESDS_FILE)
         INTO (ESDS_RECORD);
                :
    CLOSE FILE (ESDS_FILE);
                :
ERROR:
                :
    [Code to handle invalid key error.]
                :
```

Figure 15.2 Sequential ESDS retrieval.

OUTPUT. If the data set being read is password protected, the *read* password can be specified instead of the *update* password. Notice that, as with the load program, the same type of procedural code is used to sequentially retrieve records from an ESDS as is used to read a non-VSAM data set.

SEQUENTIAL ESDS UPDATE

New records cannot be added to an existing ESDS by inserting new records between existing records; however, existing records in an ESDS can be updated in place. The REWRITE statement is used for this purpose. Box 15.6 shows the most commonly used REWRITE statement options. The following example shows that REWRITE is similar in format to WRITE and specifies the name of the file defined in the file declaration:

```
REWRITE FILE (ESDS_FILE)
        FROM (ESDS_RECORD;
```

BOX 15.6 The REWRITE statement

```
REWRITE FILE (file-reference)

   [FROM (reference)]
   [KEY (RBA-expression)];
```

Figure 15.3 shows the file declaration and procedural code that could be used to build a program that sequentially updates ESDS records. If the data set is password protected, the update password is required because records will be written into the data set. To update a record, the program begins by retrieving records using conventional READ statements. When the desired record has been read, the changes are first applied to the record in the work area. The program then writes the new version of the record back into the data set by issuing a REWRITE statement. Like the WRITE statement, REWRITE can optionally include the FROM option to identify the work area. It can also include the KEY option to give the RBA of a particular record to update.

The REWRITE statement can also be used to logically [but not physically] delete a record from an ESDS. To do this, the program moves hexadecimal ''FF'' to the first byte of the record in the work area and then issues a REWRITE statement for the record. Hexadecimal ''FF'' in the first byte of a record flags it as a deleted record. As shown in Fig. 15.3, this can conveniently be done by using the HIGH built-in function. Most programs that process VSAM data sets bypass ESDS records that have been flagged as deleted.

When writing a sequential update-in-place program, keep the following points in mind. A record must first be read into the work area using a READ statement before a REWRITE statement can issued for it, and the REWRITE statement always applies to the record most recently read. However, the REWRITE statement need not be issued for each record read; only the records that are changed need to be rewritten. One last restriction for an ESDS that contains variable-length records: the record length of an existing ESDS record cannot be changed.

In some cases, it is desirable to update an ESDS by reading the old version of the data set and writing a new version into a separate new data set. Such a program operates in an identical manner to an update program for a non-VSAM sequential data set. The program uses two sequential file declarations: one specifying INPUT for the file being read and one specifying OUTPUT for the file being written. It then issues READS for the input records and WRITES for the output records. When updating a file in this fashion, records are physically de-

```
              :
ON KEY (ESDS_FILE) CALL ERROR;
              :
DCL HIGH BUILTIN;
DCL ESDS_FILE FILE
              RECORD
              SEQUENTIAL
              INPUT
              ENV(VSAM PASSWORD('ESDSPSWD'));
DCL 1 ESDS_RECORD,
      5 VSAM_FLAG      CHAR (1),
              :
READ_DATA_SET:
              :
    OPEN FILE (ESDS_FILE);
              :
    READ FILE (ESDS_FILE)
         INTO (ESDS_RECORD);
              :
    CLOSE FILE (ESDS_FILE);
              :
CHANGE_ROUTINE:
              :
        Code to modify record in ESDS_RECORD work area
              :
    REWRITE FILE (ESDS_FILE)
            FROM (ESDS_RECORD);
              :
DELETE_ROUTINE:
              :
    VSAM_FLAG = HIGH (1);
    REWRITE FILE (ESDS_FILE)
            FROM (ESDS_RECORD);
              :
ERROR:
              :
    [Code to handle invalid key error.]
              :
```

Figure 15.3 Sequential ESDS update.

leted simply by not writing them into the output data set. Records in the input data set that have already been flagged as deleted can also be dropped by the program. No restrictions apply to changing the sizes of variable-length records if an ESDS is updated in this manner.

EXTENDING AN ESDS

Although new records cannot be inserted between existing records in an ESDS, new records can be added to the end of the data set. An operation of this type is sometimes called *extending* the data set. Figure 15.4 shows the file declaration and procedural code that could be used to construct a program for extending an ESDS. Notice that the code is identical to the code used to load the data set initially. When the data set is opened for output, VSAM detects that the data set already contains records and establishes a position following the last record in the data set. WRITE operations then cause new records to be added to the end of the data set.

```
                   :
ON KEY (ESDS_FILE) CALL ERROR;
                   :
DCL ESDS_FILE FILE
              RECORD
              SEQUENTIAL
              OUTPUT
              ENV(VSAM PASSWORD('ESDSPSWD'));
DCL 1 ESDS_RECORD       CHAR (100);
                   :
LOAD_DATA_SET:
                   :
    OPEN FILE (ESDS_FILE);
                   :
    WRITE FILE (ESDS_FILE)
          FROM (ESDS_RECORD);
                   :
    CLOSE FILE (ESDS_FILE);
                   :
ERROR:
                   :
    [Code to handle invalid key error.]
                   :
```

Figure 15.4 Extending an ESDS.

16 PL/I KSDS PROCESSING

This chapter discusses techniques that can be used in PL/I programs to process VSAM data sets that are organized as KSDS clusters. With a KSDS, records are handled based on the values of their symbolic keys, and records can be accessed either sequentially, in symbolic key order, or directly, by specifying the symbolic key value of the desired record. This chapter begins by examining the file declaration and partial procedural code for a program that sequentially loads a KSDS. We then continue by seeing how KSDS records can be retrieved in both primary key and alternate key sequences. Next, we look at examples of KSDS update programs that update records sequentially and directly. Finally we look at a load program that loads a new KSDS directly in random sequence.

SEQUENTIAL KSDS LOAD

The attributes used most often in the file declaration to process a VSAM KSDS are shown in Box 16.1. Records are written into a KSDS using WRITE statements; the WRITE statement syntax is shown in Box 16.2. A WRITE statement used to write records into a KSDS normally includes a KEYFROM option that specifies a variable containing the symbolic key value of the record being writ-

BOX 16.1 File declaration syntax for KSDS

```
DCL file-name FILE RECORD
   ENV(VSAM [PASSWORD (password-specification)])
   [KEYED]{SEQUENTIAL|DIRECT}
   {INPUT|OUTPUT|UPDATE};
```

BOX 16.2 WRITE statement syntax for KSDS

```
WRITE FILE (file-reference)

   [FROM (reference)]
   [KEYFROM (expression)];
```

ten. In this example, we are assuming that the key field for the KSDS is the 4-byte EMP_NUMBER field.

Figure 16.1 shows the file declaration and procedural code that could be used to construct a program to load a KSDS sequentially. The code used to load a KSDS sequentially is similar to that used when loading an ESDS. The data set is opened using the OUTPUT attribute, and the records are sequentially written using WRITE statements. After all the records have been loaded, the

```
            :
ON KEY (KSDS_FILE) CALL ERROR;
            :
DCL KSDS_FILE FILE
              RECORD
              KEYED SEQUENTIAL
              OUTPUT
              ENV(VSAM);
DCL 1  KSDS_RECORD,
       5  EMP_NUMBER     CHAR (4),
            :
ERROR:
            :
     Code for routine to handle key out of sequence error.
            :
LOAD_DATA_SET:
            :
     OPEN FILE (KSDS_FILE);
            :
     WRITE FILE     (KSDS_FILE)
           FROM     (KSDS_RECORD)
           KEYFROM  (EMP_NUMBER);
            :
     CLOSE FILE (KSDS_FILE);
            :
```

Figure 16.1 Sequential KSDS load.

data set is closed. In a sequential load program, records must be presented to the load program in ascending sequence by primary key value. The program includes an ON KEY statement that specifies the processing to perform should VSAM detect a key value that is out of sequence.

SEQUENTIAL KSDS RETRIEVAL

After a KSDS has been loaded, programs can then retrieve records from it. When records are sequentially retrieved from a KSDS using READ statements, VSAM uses the sequence set of the KSDS index to pass records to the program in ascending sequence according to their key values. Figure 16.2 shows the file declaration and procedural code that could be used to build a program that retrieves KSDS records sequentially.

The procedural code used to sequentially retrieve records from a KSDS is the same as that used for sequential ESDS retrieval. The data set is opened with the INPUT attribute, and the records are accessed sequentially by issuing READ statements until the end of the data set is reached. Finally, the data set is closed. VSAM retrieves records beginning with the record whose key value is lowest and continues retrieving records in ascending sequence according to key value.

```
                  :
ON ENDFILE (KSDS_FILE) GOTO END_OF_FILE;
                  :
DCL KSDS_FILE FILE
              RECORD
              KEYED SEQUENTIAL
              INPUT
              ENV(VSAM);
DCL 1  KSDS_RECORD,
       5  EMP_NUMBER     CHAR (4),
                  :
    OPEN FILE (KSDS_FILE);
                  :
READ_DATA_SET:
                  :
    READ  FILE (KSDS_FILE)
          INTO (KSDS_RECORD);
                  :
END_OF_FILE:
    CLOSE FILE (KSDS_FILE);
                  :
```

Figure 16.2 Sequential KSDS retrieval.

SKIP-SEQUENTIAL KSDS RETRIEVAL

When processing a KSDS, it is not necessary to start at the beginning of the data set and sequentially read all the records. Instead, only selected records from the data set can be read and records in other parts of the data set can be skipped. This is done by first issuing a direct READ request that includes the KEY option to specify the key value of a record to be retrieved. The program then continues by issuing sequential READ statements that omit the KEY option. This causes VSAM to retrieve records sequentially starting with the record that follows the one retrieved by the direct retrieval. For example, after executing the following direct READ statement, VSAM will be positioned on the first record in the data set whose key value is greater than 0050:

```
EMP NUMBER = "0050"
READ FILE (KSDS_FILE)
     INTO (KSDS_RECORD)
     KEY  (EMP_NUMBER);
```

After sequentially retrieving any number of records, the program can issue another direct READ request to begin subsequent sequential retrievals from a new starting point. Direct READ statements can be issued any number of times during the execution of a program and can cause VSAM to move forward or backward in the data set to locate the beginning of each new sequential retrieval point.

Figure 16.3 shows the file declaration and procedural code that can be used to build a program to perform skip-sequential retrieval. The coding shown retrieves a group of records beginning with record 1057 and ending with record 3644. Processing begins by moving the key field value of the first record to be sequentially retrieved to the EMP_NUMBER variable. A direct READ is then issued, which causes VSAM to retrieve the record with key value 1057. The first sequential READ statement then causes the record that follows 1057 to be retrieved.

GENERIC KEY RETRIEVAL

The KEY option in a direct READ statement ordinarily refers to a variable that contains a full key value. However, if the ENV attribute in the file declaration contains the GENKEY option, the KEY option alternatively can refer to a generic, or partial, key value. For example, the coding in Fig. 16.4 retrieves only records for employees whose key values begin with the digits 80. The direct READ statement specifies a generic key to retrieve the first record in the data set whose EMP_NUMBER value begins with the digits 80. The first sequential READ statement then retrieves the records that follow that one. Notice that an explicit test must be made to determine when a record is retrieved that has an EMP GROUP value that is greater than 80. VSAM gives no indication of when this occurs.

```
                 :
ON KEY      (KSDS_FILE) CALL ERROR;
ON ENDFILE (KSDS_FILE) GOTO END_OF FILE;
                 :
DCL KSDS_FILE FILE
              RECORD
              KEYED SEQUENTIAL
              INPUT
              ENV(VSAM);
DCL 1  KSDS_RECORD,
       5  EMP_NUMBER      CHAR (4),
                 :
    OPEN FILE (KSDS_FILE);
                 :
READ_FIRST:

    EMP_NUMBER = '1057';
    READ FILE (KSDS_FILE)
         INTO (KSDS_RECORD)
         KEY  (EMP_NUMBER);
    CALL PROCESS_RECORD

READ_NEXT:

    DO UNTIL (EMP_NUMBER > '3644');
        READ  FILE (KSDS_FILE)
              INTO (KSDS_RECORD);
        CALL PROCESS_RECORD;
    END;
                 :
ERROR:
                 :
    Code for routine to handle record not found error.
                 :
END_OF_FILE

    CLOSE FILE (KSDS_FILE);
                 :
```

Figure 16.3 Skip-sequential KSDS retrieval.

ALTERNATE KEY SEQUENTIAL KSDS RETRIEVAL

Records in a KSDS can be processed sequentially using either the *primary key*, as in the preceding examples, or using an *alternate key*. Suppose that our KSDS is indexed by an alternate index that uses EMP NAME as an alternate key. Figure 16.5 shows the file declaration and procedural code that could be used to build a program to sequentially retrieve records from this KSDS in EMP_NAME sequence. The file declaration and READ statements are coded in the same way as for primary key retrieval. In order for the program to retrieve records in alternate key sequence, the DD statement used

```
                :
ON KEY     (KSDS_FILE) CALL ERROR;
ON ENDFILE (KSDS_FILE) GOTO END_OF FILE;
                :
DCL KSDS_FILE FILE
              RECORD
              KEYED SEQUENTIAL
              INPUT
              ENV(VSAM GENKEY);
DCL 1  KSDS_RECORD,
       5  EMP_NUMBER      CHAR (4),
                :
    OPEN FILE (KSDS_FILE);
                :
READ_FIRST:

    EMP_GROUP = '80';
    EMP_NO = '00';
    READ FILE (KSDS_FILE)
         INTO (KSDS_RECORD)
         KEY  (EMP_GROUP);
    CALL PROCESS_RECORD

READ_NEXT:

    DO UNTIL (EMP_GROUP > '80');
        READ  FILE (KSDS_FILE)
              INTO (KSDS_RECORD);
        CALL PROCESS_RECORD;
    END;
                :
ERROR:
                :
    Code for routine to handle record not found error.
                :
END_OF_FILE

    CLOSE FILE (KSDS_FILE);
                :
```

Figure 16.4 Generic key retrieval.

in executing the program must identify the name of a path instead of the KSDS cluster itself. The only difference in the procedural code is that a direct READ statement must specify an alternate key value instead of a primary key value. For example, in Fig. 16.5, the program issues a direct READ statement that identifies the EMP_NAME variable instead of the EMP_NUMBER variable.

Keep in mind that sequential retrieval efficiency is generally lower when retrieving records in alternate key sequence rather than in primary key sequence. VSAM maintains the records in each control interval in primary key sequence,

```
                 :
ON ENDFILE (ALT_PATH_FILE) GOTO END_OF_FILE;
                 :
DCL ALT_PATH_FILE FILE
              RECORD
              KEYED SEQUENTIAL
              INPUT
              ENV(VSAM);
DCL 1  ALT_PATH_RECORD,
       5  EMP_NUMBER      CHAR (4),
       5  EMP_NAME        CHAR (25),
                 :
    OPEN FILE (ALT_PATH_FILE);
                 :
READ_FIRST:

    EMP_NAME = . . . ;
    READ FILE (ALT_PATH_FILE)
         INTO (ALT_PATH_RECORD)
         KEY  (EMP_NAME);
    CALL PROCESS_RECORD

READ_NEXT:
                 :
    READ  FILE (ALT_PATH_FILE)
          INTO (ALT_PATH_RECORD);
    CALL PROCESS_RECORD;
                 :
END_OF_FILE:

    CLOSE FILE (ALT_PATH_FILE);
                 :
```

Figure 16.5 Sequential KSDS retrieval via alternate key.

and retrieving records in alternate key sequence may cause VSAM to move from control interval to control interval in satisfying each alternate key sequential retrieval request.

SEQUENTIAL KSDS UPDATE

A KSDS can be sequentially updated in a similar manner to updating an ESDS in place. When performing a sequential KSDS update, the original data set serves as both input and output, and records can be retrieved, changed, and then rewritten to the data set if desired. Figure 16.6 shows the file declaration and procedural code that could be used to create a sequential KSDS update program. The file declaration attributes are similar to those in the previous KSDS examples; the only difference is that the UPDATE attribute is specified instead of INPUT or OUTPUT. As with the sequential retrieval programs we have already seen, READ statements in the update program cause VSAM to

```
                :
ON ENDFILE (KSDS_FILE) GOTO END_OF_FILE;
                :
DCL KSDS_FILE FILE
              RECORD
              KEYED SEQUENTIAL
              UPDATE
              ENV(VSAM);
DCL 1  KSDS_RECORD,
       5  EMP_NUMBER     CHAR (4),
                :
    OPEN FILE (KSDS_FILE);
                :
READ_DATA_SET:
                :
    READ  FILE (KSDS_FILE)
          INTO (KSDS_RECORD);
                :
END_OF_FILE:
    CLOSE FILE (KSDS_FILE);
                :
CHANGE_ROUTINE:
                :
    REWRITE FILE (KSDS_FILE)
            FROM (KSDS_RECORD);
                :
DELETE_ROUTINE:
    DELETE FILE (KSDS_FILE);
                :
ADD_ROUTINE:
                :
    WRITE FILE    (KSDS_FILE)
          FROM    (KSDS_RECORD)
          KEYFROM (EMP_NUMBER);
```

Figure 16.6 Sequential KSDS update.

retrieve records from the data set in ascending sequence according to key values.

To update a record that has been previously sequentially retrieved, the program makes any required changes to the record in the work area and then issues a REWRITE statement. When a REWRITE statement is executed, the record in the data set is replaced with the new version. If desired, the length of a variable-length KSDS record can be changed before executing the REWRITE statement. The only restriction to updating a KSDS record is that its key value must not be modified. If the program inadvertently changes the key field value, the REWRITE statement will fail and the code specified in the ON KEY statement will be executed.

PL/I provides a DELETE statement that can be used to delete records from a KSDS; its syntax is shown in Box 16.3. The following DELETE statement physically removes the most recently read record from its control interval:

```
DELETE FILE (KSDS_FILE);
```

After a DELETE statement is issued for a record, the space occupied by the record is freed up, the records in the control interval are rearranged, and the free space pool is updated. Thus, the space in the control interval previously occupied by a deleted record becomes immediately available for use by other records.

The WRITE statement is used to add a new record to a KSDS. The same WRITE statement syntax is used as for a sequential KSDS load (see Fig. 16.1). If a record with the specified key value already exists in the data set, the code specified in the ON KEY statement is executed. When adding records to a KSDS that is defined with the SEQUENTIAL file declaration attribute, records are normally added in ascending sequence according to key values. As with the READ statement, however, a new sequence of sequential record additions can be begun at any time by issuing a new direct READ statement that defines a new starting point.

EXTENDING A KSDS

A KSDS can also be extended by adding new records to the end of the data set in the same manner as for an ESDS. The coding for extending a KSDS is similar to the coding used to load a new KSDS, as shown in Fig. 16.7. As with a KSDS load, the records normally are presented to the program in ascending key value sequence. If a key value is out of sequence for a particular WRITE, the code specified in the ON KEY statement is executed.

BOX 16.3 The DELETE statement

```
DELETE FILE (file-reference)

    [KEY (expression)];
```

```
[Exactly the same as initial load.]

          :
ON KEY (KSDS_FILE) CALL ERROR;
          :
DCL KSDS_FILE FILE
              RECORD
              KEYED SEQUENTIAL
              OUTPUT
              ENV(VSAM);
DCL 1  KSDS_RECORD,
       5  EMP_NUMBER      CHAR (4),
          :
ERROR:
          :
    Code for routine to handle key out of sequence error.
          :
LOAD_DATA_SET:
          :
    OPEN FILE (KSDS_FILE);
          :
    WRITE FILE    (KSDS_FILE)
          FROM    (KSDS_RECORD)
          KEYFROM (EMP_NUMBER);
          :
    CLOSE FILE (KSDS_FILE);
          :
```

Figure 16.7 Extending a KSDS.

DIRECT KSDS RETRIEVAL

So far, all the examples in this chapter have processed KSDS clusters using the SEQUENTIAL file declaration attribute. A KSDS can also be processed directly by changing that attribute to DIRECT. By using the DIRECT file declaration attribute, a program can retrieve, update, delete, or add a record by specifying a key value in the I/O request.

Figure 16.8 shows the file declaration and procedural code for a direct KSDS retrieval program. The data set is opened using a file declaration attribute of INPUT, since records will only be retrieved. Before each READ statement is executed, the key value of the record to be retrieved is moved to the EMP_NUMBER field in the record work area. VSAM then uses the key value in EMP_NUMBER to locate each record. Notice that this is the same method that was used earlier to directly read the first record in a series of skip-sequential retrieval requests.

```
                    :
ON KEY (KSDS_FILE) CALL ERROR;
                    :
DCL KSDS_FILE FILE
              RECORD
              KEYED DIRECT
              INPUT
              ENV(VSAM);
DCL 1   KSDS_RECORD,
        5  EMP_NUMBER      CHAR (4),
                    :
    OPEN FILE (KSDS_FILE);
                    :
READ_RECORD_DIRECT:
                    :
    EMP_NUMBER = . . . ;

    READ  FILE (KSDS_FILE)
          INTO (KSDS_RECORD)
          KEY  (EMP_NUMBER);
                    :
ERROR:

    Code to handle record-not-found condition.
                    :
```

Figure 16.8 Direct KSDS retrieval.

DIRECT KSDS UPDATE

A KSDS can also be directly updated. When the DIRECT and UPDATE file declaration attributes are specified, all types of update operations can be issued for the records in the KSDS. Figure 16.9 shows the file declaration and procedural code that could be used to create a direct KSDS update program. Notice that the program contains separate subroutines for adding, changing, and deleting records.

Records are added to the KSDS by issuing WRITE statements. The key value contained in the EMP_NUMBER variable dictates where the new record will be placed in the data set. The KSDS index is searched to locate the appropriate control interval for the new record, and the records already in the control interval are rearranged to make room for the new record. Control interval and control area splits are performed as necessary.

The REWRITE statement is issued to update a specified record. When the DIRECT file declaration attribute is specified, the REWRITE statement does not refer to the previous record read, as with sequential updating. Instead, the program normally builds the updated version of the record in the work area, thus moving the key value of the record to be updated into the appropriate variable. The REWRITE statement then includes a KEY option that specifies the key

```
                :
DCL ONCODE BUILTIN;
ON KEY KSDS_FILE CALL ERROR;
                :
DCL KSDS_FILE FILE
              RECORD
              KEYED DIRECT
              UPDATE
              ENV(VSAM);
DCL 1  KSDS_RECORD,
       5  EMP_NUMBER      CHAR (4),
                :
    OPEN FILE (KSDS_FILE);
                :
ADD_ROUTINE:
                :
    WRITE FILE    (KSDS_FILE)
          FROM    (KSDS_RECORD)
          KEYFROM (EMP_NUMBER);
                :
CHANGE_ROUTINE:
                :
    REWRITE FILE (KSDS_FILE)
            FROM (KSDS_RECORD)
            KEY  (EMP_NUMBER);
                :
DELETE_ROUTINE:

    DELETE FILE (KSDS_FILE)
           KEY  (EMP_NUMBER);
                :
ERROR:
    SELECT (ONCODE);
        WHEN (51)
            DO;
                [Code to handle record not found condition.]
            END;
        WHEN (52)
            DO;
                [Code to handle duplicate record found condition.]
            END;
        OTHERWISE
            DO;
                [Code to handle all other error conditions.]
            END;
END ERROR;
```

Figure 16.9 Direct KSDS update.

value of the record being rewritten. When the REWRITE statement is executed, the record in the work area replaces the corresponding record in the data set. The program can, of course, issue a READ statement for the record prior to issuing the REWRITE, but this is not a requirement.

Records are removed from the data set by issuing DELETE statements that include the KEY option. The value in the EMP_NUMBER variable is used to locate the record to be deleted, and the record is physically deleted from its control interval. As with REWRITE, it is not necessary to read a record before deleting it. If the record is not read first, the key value of the record to be deleted must be moved into the variable specified in the DELETE statement's KEY option before issuing the DELETE.

THE ONCODE BUILT-IN FUNCTION

In previous examples, the code specified in the ON KEY statement was simple because, generally, only a single error condition was of interest. In a direct update program, however, at least two specific error types are of interest: VSAM might not find the specified record after a REWRITE or DELETE statement is executed, and a record having the specified key value might already exist in the data set for a WRITE operation. The ONCODE built-in function can be used to interrogate the *return code* that is set by each I/O operation. This return code can be tested after each I/O statement or, as in Fig. 16.9, it can be tested in the subroutine executed by the CALL in the ON KEY statement. The meanings of the various return code values are listed in the *Programmer's Guide* manual for your particular compiler. The two values of interest in the update program are as follows:

- 51 Record not found after
- 52 Record with specified key value already exists

ALTERNATE KEY DIRECT KSDS ACCESS

Records can also be retrieved and updated via alternate key values when the DIRECT file declaration attribute is specified. For example, Fig. 16.10 shows the file declaration and procedural code that could be used to create a program that retrieves records using the EMP_NAME alternate key. Again, the program must use a DD statement that refers to the alternate key path rather than to the KSDS cluster itself, and the program must specify alternate key values in the KEY option of the READ statement. The following three restrictions exist for updating records via alternate key values:

- A PUT operation that replaces an existing record must not change the value of the prime key.
- A PUT operation that replaces an existing record must not change the value of the alternate key that was used to retrieve the record.
- A PUT operation that inserts a new record using an alternate index defined with the UNIQUEKEY attribute must not insert a record that has an alternate key value equal to that of an existing record.

```
                    :
ON KEY (ALT_PATH_FILE) CALL ERROR;
                    :
DCL ALT_PATH_FILE FILE
                  RECORD
                  KEYED DIRECT
                  INPUT
                  ENV(VSAM);
DCL 1  ALT_PATH_RECORD,
       5  EMP_NUMBER       CHAR (4),
       5  EMP_NAME         CHAR (25),
                    :
    OPEN FILE (ALT_PATH_FILE);
                    :
READ_RECORD_DIRECT:
                    :
    EMP_NAME = . . . ;

    READ  FILE (ALT_PATH_FILE)
          INTO (ALT_PATH_RECORD)
          KEY  (EMP_NAME);
                    :
ERROR:

    Code to handle record-not-found condition.
                    :
```

Figure 16.10 Direct KSDS retrieval via alternate key.

DIRECT KSDS LOAD

All the load programs we have looked at thus far have required that the records be presented to the load program in ascending key sequence. When the DIRECT file declaration attribute is specified, records can be loaded into a KSDS in any desired sequence. A direct KSDS load program functions in the same manner as an update program that adds records to an existing KSDS. In fact, the previous direct KSDS update program could be used to load a KSDS simply by using a transaction file that contains all add transactions. For a direct KSDS load, the KSDS is opened using a file declaration attribute of either OUTPUT or UPDATE, and conventional WRITE statements are used to WRITE new records into the data set. VSAM uses the key value contained in the variable specified by the WRITE statement KEYFROM option to determine where to write each new record in the data set.

In actual practice, direct KSDS load programs are seldom used. More processing time is required than for an equivalent sequential load, since the index must be searched and updated each time a record is written. Also, after a sequential KSDS load, control intervals contain records that are in physical sequence from one control interval to the next. With a direct KSDS load, all the initial records are written into the first control interval until it is full. Then a control interval split occurs, and all subsequent records are written into those two control intervals until a third is required, at which point another control interval split occurs, and so on. Thus, by the time the direct load is finished, control intervals tend to be scattered throughout KSDS in no particular order. This may cause later sequential retrieval efficiency to be lower than if a sequential load had been used.

17 PL/I RRDS PROCESSING

The final type of VSAM data set is the relative record data set. Records in an RRDS are stored in fixed-length slots, and PL/I programs work with RRDS records based on their relative record numbers. In this final chapter on PL/I programming, we discuss the PL/I techniques that are used in working with RRDS clusters. Much of the coding that we will show for working with an RRDS is similar to the coding used with ESDS and KSDS clusters. We will begin, as we did in the previous two chapters, by discussing the sequential RRDS load process.

SEQUENTIAL RRDS LOAD

Box 17.1 shows that the most commonly used file declaration attributes for an RRDS are the same as those for a KSDS. In performing a sequential RRDS load, it is important to realize that records are not loaded into the data set in sequence according to their key values. The logical sequence of any symbolic keys that might be contained in the records bears no relationship to the physical sequence in which records are stored in the data set. This is because a hashing or randomizing algorithm is generally used, tending to scatter the records of an RRDS more or less randomly through the data set.

BOX 17.1 SELECT statement syntax for RRDS

```
DCL file-name FILE RECORD
   ENV(VSAM [PASSWORD (password-specification)])
   [KEYED]{SEQUENTIAL|DIRECT}
   {INPUT|OUTPUT|UPDATE};
```

One technique for loading an RRDS sequentially is to use a program that reads the records to be loaded and writes out a new file of records that has the relative record number of each record attached to it. The program must use the same randomizing algorithm that will be used by programs that will later access the RRDS. The records are then sorted into relative record number sequence. Either before or after the sort, synonyms must be handled by determining alternate relative record numbers for sets of records that randomize to the same relative record number. The final sorted data set then contains a record for each slot in the RRDS that will contain an active record and can be read by the sequential RRDS load program. The load program must write a dummy record into each slot that will not initially contain an active record. The sequential load program we will look at in this chapter assumes that the input data set read by the load program already has the records sorted into relative record number sequence and that there is a record in the input data set for each slot in the RRDS.

Figure 17.1 shows the file declaration and procedural code that could be used to construct a sequential RRDS load program. The WRITE statement is identical to that used in a sequential KSDS load program. The data set is opened using a file declaration attribute of OUTPUT, and each record is loaded in ascending slot number sequence. After all the records are loaded, the data set is closed.

SEQUENTIAL RRDS RETRIEVAL

During sequential retrieval of an RRDS, the records are passed to the retrieval program in relative record number sequence. A record that retrieves RRDS rec-

```
                    :
DCL RRDS_FILE FILE
              RECORD
              SEQUENTIAL
              OUTPUT
              ENV(VSAM);
DCL 1  RRDS_RECORD
       5  EMP_NUMBER     CHAR (4),
                    :
    OPEN FILE (RRDS_FILE);
                    :
LOAD_DATA_SET:
                    :
    WRITE FILE     (RRDS_FILE)
          FROM     (RRDS_RECORD);
                    :
    CLOSE FILE (RRDS_FILE);
                    :
```

Figure 17.1 Sequential RRDS load.

ords sequentially also retrieves dummy records, so the program must contain logic to bypass these empty slots. Figure 17.2 shows the file declaration and procedural code that could be used to build a program to retrieve records sequentially from an RRDS. Keep in mind, however, that when retrieving RRDS records sequentially, records are retrieved in relative record number sequence; VSAM has no knowledge of any symbolic keys that might be contained in the records.

SKIP-SEQUENTIAL RRDS RETRIEVAL

As with sequential KSDS retrieval, a direct READ statement can be used to specify a starting point for a sequence of sequential RRDS retrievals. Figure 17.3 shows the file declaration and procedural code that could be used to create a program to perform skip-sequential RRDS retrieval. The READ statement specifies the name of a variable that contains the relative record number of the desired record. VSAM then retrieves the record that is in the specified slot. The next sequential READ statement then retrieves the record in the next slot. A new direct READ statement can be issued at any time to move forward or backward in the data set to begin a new series of sequential retrievals.

```
                  :
ON ENDFILE (RRDS_FILE) GOTO END_OF_FILE;
                  :
DCL RRDS_FILE FILE
              RECORD
              SEQUENTIAL
              INPUT
              ENV(VSAM);
DCL 1  RRDS_RECORD,
       5  EMP_NUMBER      CHAR (4),
                  :
     OPEN FILE (RRDS_FILE);
                  :
READ_DATA_SET:
                  :
     READ  FILE (RRDS_FILE)
           INTO (RRDS_RECORD);
                  :
END_OF_FILE:

     CLOSE FILE (RRDS_FILE);
                  :
```

Figure 17.2 Sequential RRDS retrieval.

```
                :
ON KEY      (RRDS_FILE) CALL ERROR;
ON ENDFILE (RRDS_FILE) GOTO END_OF FILE;
                :
DCL RRDS_FILE FILE
              RECORD
              KEYED SEQUENTIAL
              INPUT
              ENV(VSAM);
DCL 1  RRDS_RECORD,
       5  EMP_NUMBER      CHAR (4),
                :
DCL 1  RR_NUMBER          CHAR (3);


    OPEN FILE (RRDS_FILE);
                :
READ_FIRST:

    RR_NUMBER = '047';
    READ FILE (RRDS_FILE)
         INTO (RRDS_RECORD)
         KEY  (RR_NUMBER);
    CALL PROCESS_RECORD

READ_REST:
                :
        READ  FILE (RRDS_FILE)
              INTO (RRDS_RECORD);
        CALL PROCESS_RECORD;
    END;
                :
ERROR:
                :
    Code for routine to handle invalid relative record number error.
                :
END_OF_FILE

    CLOSE FILE (RRDS_FILE);
                :
```

Figure 17.3 Skip-sequential RRDS retrieval.

SEQUENTIAL RRDS UPDATE

Updating in place can be done with an RRDS in a similar manner as for an ESDS. To update a record, the record is read and then rewritten back into the same slot; like an ESDS, an RRDS record's length cannot be changed. New records cannot be inserted between two existing records, but a record can be added by replacing an existing dummy record with an active record. The DELETE statement can be issued to delete a record; VSAM responds by rewriting the slot with binary zeros, thus converting it into a dummy record.

The file declaration and procedural code that could be used to build a sequential RRDS update program is shown in Fig. 17.4. The file declaration attributes include DIRECT and UPDATE. READ statements cause records to be retrieved in ascending slot number sequence. A record is updated by making changes to the record in the work area and then issuing a REWRITE statement. Records are deleted by issuing DELETE statements. The record rewritten or deleted is always the one most recently read. Since new slots cannot be added to an RRDS, the WRITE statement is not used in a sequential RRDS update program.

DIRECT RRDS RETRIEVAL

The process of retrieving RRDS records directly is similar to retrieving KSDS records directly. The only difference is that the record to be retrieved is identi-

```
              :
ON ENDFILE (RRDS_FILE) GOTO END_OF_FILE;
              :
DCL RRDS_FILE FILE
              RECORD
              SEQUENTIAL
              UPDATE
              ENV(VSAM);
DCL 1  RRDS_RECORD,
       5  EMP_NUMBER      CHAR (4),
              :
    OPEN FILE (RRDS_FILE);
              :
READ_DATA_SET:
              :
    READ  FILE (RRDS_FILE)
          INTO (RRDS_RECORD);
              :
END_OF_FILE:

    CLOSE FILE (RRDS_FILE);
              :
CHANGE_ROUTINE:
              :
    REWRITE FILE (RRDS_FILE)
            FROM (RRDS_RECORD);
              :
DELETE_ROUTINE:

    DELETE FILE (RRDS_FILE);
              :
```

Figure 17.4 Sequential RRDS update.

fied by *relative record number* rather than by *symbolic key value*. A direct RRDS retrieval program normally makes use of a hashing or randomizing algorithm to convert a symbolic key value to a relative record number before each direct retrieval.

The file declaration and procedural code that could be used to retrieve records directly from an RRDS is shown in Fig. 17.5. The relative record number of the desired record is placed in the variable identified in the READ statement KEY option prior to issuing each READ. If the specified slot is empty, the code specified in the ON KEY statement is executed.

DIRECT RRDS UPDATE

A direct RRDS update program is similar to a direct KSDS update. Records can be added, deleted, and changed. With an RRDS, any field in the existing record can be changed, but the length of a record cannot be modified. Figure 17.6 shows the file declaration and procedural code that could be used to create

```
                  :
ON KEY (RRDS_FILE) CALL ERROR;
                  :
DCL RRDS_FILE FILE
              RECORD
              KEYED DIRECT
              INPUT
              ENV(VSAM);
DCL 1   RRDS_RECORD,
        5  EMP_NUMBER      CHAR (4),
                  :
DCL 1   RR_NUMBER          CHAR (3);
                  :
    OPEN FILE (RRDS_FILE);
                  :
READ_RECORD_DIRECT:
                  :
    CALL OBTAIN_RR_NUMBER;
    RR_NUMBER = OBTAINED_RR_NUMBER;

    READ  FILE (RRDS_FILE)
          INTO (RRDS_RECORD)
          KEY  (RR_NUMBER);
                  :
ERROR:

    Code to handle invalid relative record number condition.
                  :
```

Figure 17.5 Direct RRDS retrieval.

```
              :
DCL 1  RR_NUMBER          CHAR (3);
DCL ONCODE BUILTIN;
ON KEY RRDS_FILE CALL ERROR;
DCL RRDS_FILE FILE
              RECORD
              KEYED DIRECT
              UPDATE
              ENV(VSAM);
DCL 1  RRDS_RECORD,
       5  EMP_NUMBER      CHAR (4),
              :
ADD_ROUTINE:

    CALL OBTAIN_RR_NUMBER;
    RR_NUMBER = OBTAINED_RR_NUMBER;
    WRITE FILE    (RRDS_FILE)
          FROM    (RRDS_RECORD)
          KEYFROM (RR_NUMBER);
              :
CHANGE_ROUTINE:

    CALL OBTAIN_RR_NUMBER;
    RR_NUMBER = OBTAINED_RR_NUMBER;
    REWRITE FILE (RRDS_FILE)
            FROM (RRDS_RECORD)
            KEY  (RR_NUMBER);
              :
DELETE_ROUTINE:

    CALL OBTAIN_RR_NUMBER;
    RR_NUMBER = OBTAINED_RR_NUMBER;
    DELETE FILE (RRDS_FILE)
           KEY  (RR_NUMBER);
              :
ERROR:
    SELECT (ONCODE);
        WHEN (51)
            DO;
                [Code to handle record not found condition.]
            END;
        WHEN (52)
            DO;
                [Code to handle duplicate record found condition.]
            END;
        OTHERWISE
            DO;
                [Code to handle all other error conditions.]
            END;
END ERROR;
```

Figure 17.6 Direct RRDS update.

a direct RRDS update program. The DIRECT and UPDATE file declaration attributes are used.

A new record can be added to an empty slot by moving the relative record number of the empty slot to the variable identified in the WRITE statement KEY option before issuing the WRITE. If the specified slot is not empty, the code specified in the ON KEY statement is executed.

The REWRITE statement is used to update existing records. The new version of the record is built in the work area and the relative record number of the record to be changed is moved to the variable specified in the REWRITE statement KEY option. The REWRITE statement is then issued to update the record in the data set. The record can be first read if desired, but this is not a requirement. If the slot referenced by the REWRITE statement is an empty slot, the code specified in the ON KEY statement is executed.

Records are removed from an RRDS by issuing DELETE statements. The program moves the relative record number of the record to be deleted to the variable specified in the DELETE statement KEY option and then executes the DELETE. VSAM responds by filling the indicated slot with binary zeros, thus converting the record into an empty slot. If the slot is already empty when

```
                :
DCL ONCODE BUILTIN;
ON KEY RRDS_FILE CALL ERROR;
                :
DCL RRDS_FILE FILE
              RECORD
              KEYED DIRECT
              OUTPUT
              ENV(VSAM);
DCL 1   RRDS_RECORD,
        5  EMP_NUMBER       CHAR (4),
                :
DCL 1   RR_NUMBER           CHAR (3);
                :
     OPEN FILE (RRDS_FILE);
                :
     CALL OBTAIN_RR_NUMBER;
     RR_NUMBER = OBTAINED_RR_NUMBER;

     WRITE FILE    (RRDS_FILE)
           FROM    (RRDS_RECORD)
           KEYFROM (RR_NUMBER);
                :
     CLOSE FILE (RRDS_FILE);
                :
ERROR:
                :
     [Code to handle duplicate record condition.]
                :
END ERROR;
```

Figure 17.7 Direct RRDS load.

the DELETE statement is executed, the code specified in the ON KEY statement is executed. As with the REWRITE statement, it is not necessary to read a record before deleting it.

DIRECT RRDS LOAD

With a KSDS, the normal practice is to load the data set sequentially; as discussed in Chapter 16, a direct KSDS load is normally inefficient and to be avoided. However, with an RRDS, direct load programs are often used. This is because of the extra processing time involved in sorting the records to be loaded into relative record number sequence and handling synonyms.

Figure 17.7 shows the file declaration and procedural code that could be used to build a direct RRDS load program. The file declaration attributes include DIRECT and OUTPUT. WRITE statements are used to write records into the data set in any desired sequence. The program operates as if the data set consists of all empty slots, even though the data set may or may not be preformatted before the program executes. An ON KEY statement should be included to allow the program to handle synonyms.

This concludes the three chapters on PL/I programming techniques for working with VSAM data sets. The chapters in Part V discuss programming techniques for working with VSAM data sets in Assembler Language programs. Techniques similar to those discussed in Part III and Part IV are covered, as well as additional advanced techniques.

PART V ASSEMBLER LANGUAGE PROGRAMMING

18 MACROS AND CONTROL BLOCKS

This chapter begins an investigation of Assembler Language programming techniques for processing VSAM data sets. Many of the chapters in this part present programs that perform similar functions as in the chapters in Parts IV and V. In addition, many advanced functions are also discussed that are difficult to implement using high-level languages, such as COBOL and PL/I. Assembler Language programs that access VSAM data sets issue *macros* that reference VSAM *control blocks*. Conventional access methods use a DCB to contain fields of information that are used to control access to the data set during processing. The DCB is replaced in VSAM with three control blocks called the *access method control block* (ACB), the *request parameter list* (RPL), and the *exit list* (EXLST). These control blocks are chained together and are referenced by OPEN and CLOSE macros and by request macros, such as GET and PUT. We will begin by examining the OPEN, CLOSE, and request macros; we will then discuss the macros that are used to generate and work with VSAM control blocks.

OPEN AND CLOSE MACROS

In working with the information in a VSAM data set, the main macros used are the same as those used with other access methods. For example, an OPEN macro must be issued before a VSAM data set can be accessed. Then a CLOSE macro is issued when processing is completed. After issuing the OPEN macro, request macros can be issued to work with the information in the data set.

Box 18.1 shows the syntax of the OPEN and CLOSE macros. Notice that the syntax is similar to that of the OPEN and CLOSE macros used with non-VSAM data sets. The *address* parameter refers to an ACB instead of a DCB. Note that the *options* parameter is not used in working with VSAM objects and must be omitted. However, if more than one data set is opened or closed with

BOX 18.1 The OPEN and CLOSE macros

```
[label]   OPEN    (address,[(options)],...)

[label]   CLOSE   (address,[(options)],...)
                  [,TYPE=T]
```

a single OPEN or CLOSE macro, the extra comma is required to indicate that the options parameter is omitted.

The TYPE=T temporary close option causes VSAM to complete outstanding I/O operations and to update catalog information without completely closing the data set. This allows a program to continue accessing the data set without having to issue a new OPEN macro for it.

REQUEST MACROS

A request macro is one that specifies some I/O operation to be performed. Brief descriptions of the four VSAM request macros that are used most often follow:

- **ERASE.** The ERASE macro is used to delete a record from a VSAM data set.
- **PUT.** The PUT macro is used to store a record into a VSAM data set. It is used for all output operations, including loading a record into a new data set, adding a record to the end of a data set, inserting a record between two existing records, and updating an already existing record.
- **GET.** The GET macro is used to retrieve a record from the data set or to read a record that might later be updated or deleted.
- **POINT.** The POINT macro is used to establish a position within the data set so that retrieval can later begin at that point.

Box 18.2 shows the syntax of the four main request macros. GET, PUT, and POINT are used much in same way as they are used with other access methods. ERASE is used in a similar manner as the other three. There are two additional request macros that are used less often than the above four:

- **ENDREQ.** The ENDREQ macro is used to terminate an I/O request. For example, it might be used to release exclusive control of a VSAM object or to cancel the positioning previously established with a GET or POINT macro.

BOX 18.2 Request macros

```
[label]   GET     RPL=address

[label]   PUT     RPL=address

[label]   POINT   RPL=address

[label]   ERASE   RPL=address
```

- **CHECK.** The CHECK macro can be issued after issuing an asynchronous I/O request to wait for the completion of that request. Asynchronous processing is discussed in Appendix C.

VSAM CONTROL BLOCKS

The OPEN, CLOSE, and request macros each refer to a VSAM control block. The control blocks contain information about the data set itself and about the types of requests that are being made. These control blocks are different from the ones used with conventional data sets. We will examine the purpose of each control block and see how they are chained together to control I/O operations.

The ACB

A major function of the ACB is to provide the name of the DD statement that defines the particular VSAM object being processed. It also identifies the types of access that will be allowed to the VSAM data set, specifies the number and sizes of buffers, indicates the locations of message areas and passwords, and defines the location of the EXLST control block. The ACB is referenced in the OPEN and CLOSE macros and performs functions that are roughly analogous to the DCB used with conventional access methods.

The RPL

Each request macro, such as GET or PUT, can be used to perform a variety of functions. In order to provide complete information about a particular I/O request, each request macro points to an RPL that contains a list of request parameters. One parameter specified in the RPL is the name or address of the data set's ACB. Thus, a GET or PUT request points to an RPL, which in turn points to an ACB. In addition to the ACB address, the RPL contains the following information:

- The type of I/O access being requested.
- The I/O area or buffer address to be used for input or output.
- The location of key values to be used when keyed access is requested.
- Logical record size.

To summarize, the ACB contains general information about the data set itself, and the RPL contains information about one specific I/O request that is being made. The reason that access type is specified in both the ACB and the RPL is that VSAM allows a data set to be accessed in different ways within the same program. For example, a VSAM KSDS might be opened to allow both sequential and direct access. This is accomplished by specifying both sequential and direct access in the ACB. However, one execution of a specific request macro, such as a GET, must specify a single access type: either sequential or direct. Therefore, the RPL is used to indicate which of the two access types specified in the ACB should be used for each particular request. Figure 18.1 shows the relationship between the ACB and an RPL that references it. Notice that bits in the ACB are set to allow both sequential and direct access. Each GET request then references an RPL that indicates the type of access to be used for that request.

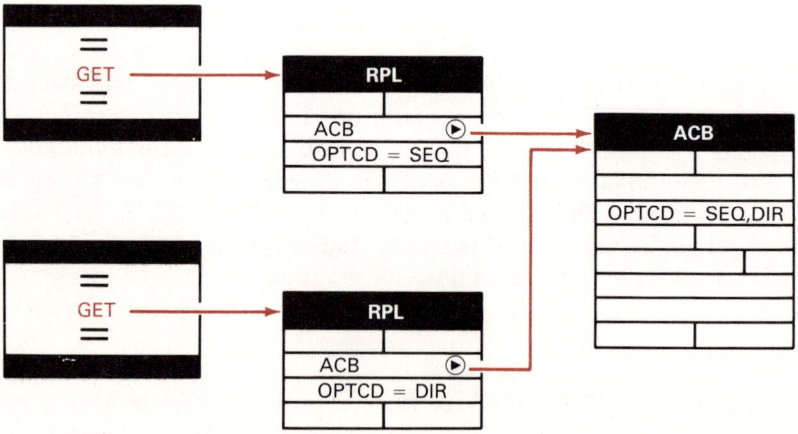

Figure 18.1 ACB and RPL relationships.

The EXLST

The ACB points to an EXLST control block. An EXLST control block contains information about exit routines that are entered automatically when specified events occur during the processing of the data set. For example, an exit routine that is commonly used when reading a data set sequentially is the *end-of-data exit*. Brief descriptions of the five available exits are provided later in this chapter when we discuss the EXLST macro that is used to generate an EXLST control block.

CONTROL BLOCK RELATIONSHIPS

Figure 18.2 shows the relationships between the ACB, RPL, and EXLST control blocks and the macros that reference them. The ACB contains general information about the VSAM object being processed. The RPL contains specific information about a specific access request. The EXLST points to exit routines that are executed when certain events occur. OPEN and CLOSE macros refer

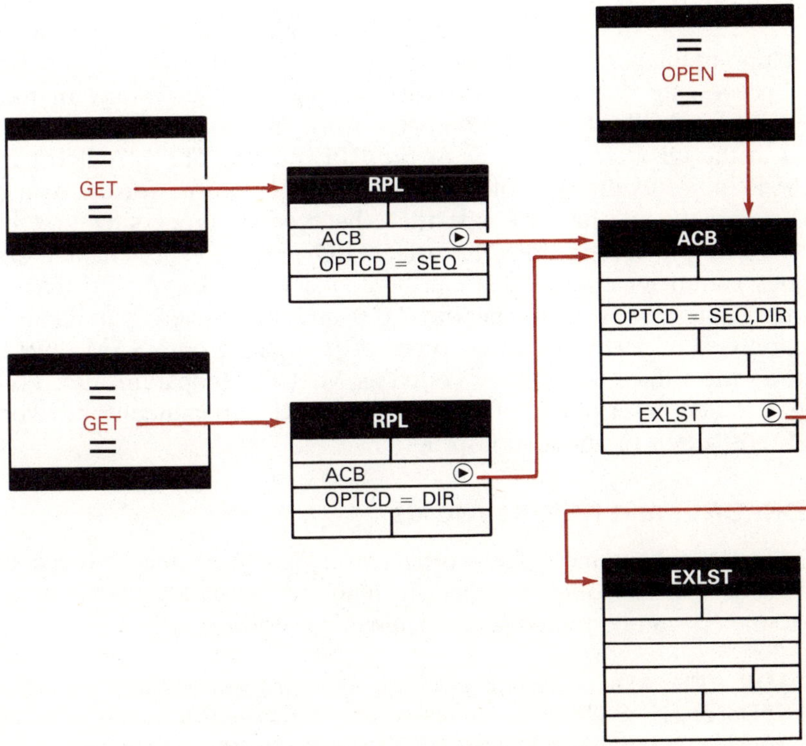

Figure 18.2 Control block relationships.

to the data set's ACB. Request macros, such as GETs and PUTs, refer to a specific RPL. Note that many ACBs can point to the same EXLST and many RPLs can point to the same ACB.

CONTROL BLOCK MACROS

VSAM provides a set of macros that can be used to generate VSAM control blocks in a program. The ACB, RPL, and EXLST macros are used to generate their respective control blocks at assembly time; these macros are included in the program at the point at which the control block is desired and generate lists of addresses and values that the application program and VSAM use for communication. The GENCB macro can be used to generate any VSAM control block at execution time. The technique of generating control blocks at execution time rather than at assembly time is useful in writing reentrant programs, which are discussed in Appendix D.

THE ACB MACRO

Box 18.3 shows the syntax of the ACB macro and provides brief descriptions of ACB macro parameters. An important parameter in the ACB macro is MACRF. It describes the types of processing that can be specified for the data set. Many of the codes specified in the ACB MACRF parameter work in conjunction with the codes specified in the OPTCD parameter of the RPL macro. The MACRF parameter of the ACB indicates the type of processing that is *allowed* for the data set; the OPTCD parameter of the RPL specifies the type of processing that is to be performed in a *particular execution* of an I/O request. This chapter discusses the various parameter options that can be coded in ACB and RPL macros. The following chapters show how specific ACB and RPL macro parameter combinations are used to perform various types of processing on VSAM objects. Box 18.4 shows the values that can be coded as MACRF subparameters. Following are more detailed descriptions of the ACB MACRF subparameter keywords that are used most often in application programs.

The ADR, CNV, and KEY Keywords

These MACRF subparameter keywords specify the way in which records will be addressed in the I/O requests that are made to the data set. One or more of these parameters can be included; their meanings follow:

- **ADR.** The ADR keyword specifies *addressed access*, and applies only to KSDS or ESDS clusters. Addressed access means that access to records will be made by supplying an RBA value as a search argument in each I/O request.
- **CNV.** The CNV keyword specifies *control interval access*, and applies to all types of clusters. Control interval access means that access will be to entire

BOX 18.3 ACB macro parameters

```
[label]    ACB      [AM=VSAM]
                    [,BSTRNO=number]
                    [,BUFND=number]
                    [,BUFNI=number]
                    [,BUFSP=number]
                    [,CATALOG=YES|NO]
                    [,CRA=SCRA|UCRA]
                    [,DDNAME=ddname]
                    [,EXLST=address]
                    [,MACRF=(code)]
                    [,MAREA=address]
                    [,MLEN=number]
                    [,PASSWD=address]
                    [,STRNO=number]
```

AM= VSAM Specifies that the access method in use is VSAM. Since this is the only allowable keyword, and it is the default, this parameter is normally not coded.

BSTRNO Specifies the number of strings allocated for access to the base cluster of a path. Typically, one string is required for each concurrent positioning request that is required. Strings are allocated dynamically as required, but specifying a number that is too low or too high may have an effect on performance and/or virtual storage utilization. See the *VSAM Reference* manual for more specific information.

BUFND Specifies the number of I/O buffers that VSAM is to use for data records.

BUFNI Specifies the number of I/O buffers that VSAM is to use for index records.

BUFSP Specifies the total number of bytes of virtual storage space VSAM is to use for both data and index buffers.

CATA-LOG Specifies whether a catalog is being opened as a catalog or as a conventional VSAM data set.

CRA Specifies that a catalog recovery area is to be created either in system storage or in user storage.

DDNAME Gives the name of the DD statement in the JCL that further defines the VSAM object described by this ACB.

EXLST Specifies the address of the EXLST control block to be chained to this ACB.

(Continued)

BOX 18.3 *(Continued)*

MACRF Specifies one or more codes that indicate the kinds of processing that will be performed using this ACB. Commonly used MACRF codes are described in the chapters that follow. For a complete list, see Box 18.4.

MAREA Specifies the address of a message area to be used during executions of OPEN and CLOSE macros. This message area can be optionally used to contain information about errors that occur during OPEN and CLOSE processing.

MLEN Specifies the length of the message area referenced by the MAREA parameter.

PASSWD Specifies the address of a field that contains a password. The first byte of the field contains the length of the password field. A zero in the length field indicates no password.

STRNO Specifies the number of requests that will require concurrent data set positioning. VSAM automatically increases this value if required, but specifying a number that is either too low or too high may have an effect on performance and/or virtual storage utilization.

BOX 18.4 ACB MACRF subparameter values

```
MACRF   ([ADR][,CNV][,KEY]
          [,CFX|NFX]
          [,DDN|DSN]
          [,DFR|NDF]
          [,DIR][,SEQ][,SKP]
          [,ICI|NCI]
          [,IN|OUT]
          [,NIS|SIS]
          [,NRM|AIX]
          [,NRS|RST]
          [,NSR|LSR|GSR]
          [,NUB|UBF])
```

BOX 18.4 *(Continued)*

ADR ¦ CNV ¦ <u>KEY</u>	These parameters control the way individual records are accessed. ADR indicates addressed access by RBA value, CNV indicates control interval access, and <u>KEY</u> (the default) indicates keyed access by symbolic key or relative record number.
CFX ¦ <u>NFX</u>	CFX specifies that VSAM control blocks and I/O buffers are to be fixed in real storage.
<u>DDN</u> ¦ DSN	DSN specifies that shared control block connection is to be made based on common data set names. With DDN, sharing is based on common ddnames. Chapter 23 discusses sharing of VSAM resources.
DFR ¦ <u>NDF</u>	DFR specifies that the writing of I/O buffers is to be deferred until a WRTBFR request is issued.
DIR ¦ <u>SEQ</u> ¦ SKP	These parameters control the way the data set as a whole is accessed. DIR indicates direct access, <u>SEQ</u> (the default) indicates sequential access, and SKP indicates skip-sequential access.
ICI ¦ <u>NCI</u>	ICI specifies that processing is to be limited to control interval processing for increased performance.
<u>IN</u> ¦ OUT	IN specifies that records will be retrieved from the data set; OUT specifies that records will be written into the data set.
<u>NIS</u> ¦ SIS	SIS specifies that control interval splits are to occur at the insertion point rather than roughly at the midpoint.
<u>NRM</u> ¦ AIX	AIX specifies that the alternate index, rather than the base cluster, is to be processed when the object to which the ACB refers is a path.

(Continued)

BOX 18.4 *(Continued)*

NRS ¦ RST	NRS specifies that the data set is not reusable; RST specifies that the data set is reusable.
NSR ¦ LSR ¦ GSR	These parameters are used to control resource sharing. Shared resources are discussed in Chapter 23.
NUB ¦ UBF	UBF specifies that the user program, rather than VSAM, is to manage the VSAM I/O buffers. When the UBF option is in effect, the work area specified in the RPL refers to an entire I/O buffer rather than to an individual record work area.

control intervals rather than to the individual data records stored in them. Access to entire control intervals is beyond the scope of this book. Consult the material on advanced applications in the *VSAM User's Guide* for additional information on control interval access.

- **KEY.** The KEY keyword, the default, specifies *keyed access*, and applies only to KSDS or RRDS clusters. Keyed access means that access to records will be made by supplying a key value as a search argument in each I/O request. For a KSDS, a key value consists of a prime key or alternate key value; for an RRDS, a key value consists of a relative record number.

For KSDS or RRDS clusters, both the ADR and KEY values can be included if RPLs specifying both addressed and keyed access will be used in the same program.

The DIR, SEQ, AND SKP Keywords

These MACRF subparameter keywords specify the type of access that will be made by I/O requests. One or more of these parameters can be coded. Following are the meanings of each keyword:

- **DIR.** The DIR keyword indicates that RPLs will request direct access to records. Direct access applies to ESDS, KSDS, and RRDS clusters.

- **SEQ.** The SEQ keyword, the default, indicates that RPLs will request sequential access to records. Sequential access applies to ESDS, KSDS, and RRDS clusters.
- **SKP.** The SKP keyword indicates that RPLs will request skip-sequential access to records. Skip-sequential access applies only to KSDS and RRDS clusters.

Both DIR and SEQ can be specified if RPLs will request both direct and sequential access to records in the same program. If keyed access to records is specified, the SKP keyword can be included as well.

The IN and OUT Keywords

These MACRF keywords specify whether request macros will be used to retrieve records from the data set and/or store records into the data set. Both parameters can be coded if records will be both read and written. Following are the meanings of each keyword:

- **IN.** The IN keyword, the default, indicates that request macros are allowed for retrieval of records from a KSDS, ESDS, or RRDS cluster.
- **OUT.** The OUT keyword indicates that request macros are allowed for the following purposes:
  PUT macros can be used to store new records in a KSDS, ESDS, or RRDS cluster. The OUT option is not allowed for addressed access to a KSDS cluster.
  PUT macros can be used to update records in a KSDS, ESDS, or RRDS cluster.
  ERASE macros can be used to delete records from a KSDS or RRDS cluster. ERASE macros are not valid for ESDS clusters.

The NRS and RST Keywords

These keywords specify whether or not the data set is to be marked as reusable when the data set is opened. Either NRS or RST, but not both, can be coded. NRS, the default, causes the data set to be marked as non-reusable; RST causes the high-used RBA in the data set's catalog entry to be reset to 0 when the data set is opened for output. The RST option causes the data set to appear as a new data set when it is opened.

THE RPL MACRO

The RPL macro is used to generate an RPL control block that can be used for one or more I/O requests. Box 18.5 shows the syntax of the RPL macro and describes its parameters. An important parameter of the RPL macro is the OPTCD parameter. It is the counterpart of the MACRF parameter of the ACB macro and describes the processing that is to be performed by a request macro that references the RPL. Box 18.6 shows the subparameters that can be coded in an OPTCD parameter.

BOX 18.5 RPL macro parameters

```
[label]    RPL      [ACB=address]
                    [,AM=VSAM]
                    [,AREA=address]
                    [,AREALEN=number]
                    [,ARG=address]
                    [,ECB=address]
                    [,KEYLEN=number]
                    [,MSGAREA=address]
                    [,MSGLEN=number]
                    [,NXTRPL=address]
                    [,OPTCD=(code)]
                    [,RECLEN=number]
                    [,TRANSID=number]
```

ACB Specifies the address of the ACB that controls access to the data set for which the I/O request applies.

AM=VSAM Specifies that the access method in use is VSAM. Since this is the only allowable keyword, and it is the default, this parameter normally is not coded.

AREA Specifies the address of a work area to be used by this I/O request. Depending on the OPTCD value specified, the work area contains either a data record or the address of the data record in a VSAM buffer.

AREALEN Specifies the length of the work area identified in the AREA parameter.

ARG Specifies the address of a field that contains a search argument.

ECB Specifies the address of an event control block (ECB), generally used only for asynchronous processing requests.

KEYLEN Specifies the length of a generic key supplied in the area defined by the ARG parameter.

MSGAREA Specifies the address of an area that VSAM can use to store an error message after a physical error.

MSGLEN Specifies the length of the area defined in the MSGAREA parameters.

NXTRPL Specifies the address of the next RPL in a chain of RPL control blocks.

BOX 18.5 *(Continued)*

OPTCD	Specifies a code that defines the type of operation requested by the RPL. Commonly used OPTCD codes are described in the chapters that follow. For a complete list, see Box 18.6.
RECLEN	Specifies the length of a record being stored as a result of a PUT request.
TRANSID	Specifies a number that relates to modified buffers in a shared resource application. The use of shared VSAM resources is introduced in Chapter 23.

BOX 18.6 RPL OPTCD parameter values

```
OPTCD  ([ADR|CNV|KEY]
        [,DIR|SEQ|SKP]
        [,ARD|LRD]
        [,FWD|BWD]
        [,ASY|SYN]
        [,NSP|NUP|UPD]
        [,KEQ|KGE]
        [,FKS|GEN]
        [,NWAITX|WAITX]
        [,LOC|MVE])
```

ADR ¦ CNV ¦ <u>KEY</u>	These are the RPL counterparts to the same keywords in the ACB macro and control the way individual records are accessed. If one of these keywords is coded in the RPL, the ACB to which it refers must also have that keyword coded. ADR indicates addressed access by RBA value, CNV indicates control interval access, and <u>KEY</u> (the default) indicates keyed access by symbolic key or relative record number.

(Continued)

BOX 18.6 *(Continued)*

DIR ¦ SEQ ¦ SKP	These are the RPL counterparts to the same keywords in the ACB macro and control the way the data set as a whole is accessed. If one of these keywords is coded in the RPL, the ACB to which it refers must also have that keyword coded. DIR indicates direct access, SEQ (the default) indicates sequential access, and SKP indicates skip-sequential access.
ARD ¦ LRD	ARD specifies that an argument supplied in the request determines the record to be located; LRD causes VSAM to establish position on the last record in the data set. Either ARD or LRD, but not both, can be coded. If LRD is specified, BWD must also be specified.
FWD ¦ BWD	FWD specifies that processing is to proceed in a forward direction; BWD indicates that processing is to proceed in a backward direction.
ASY ¦ SYN	ASY specifies asynchronous processing, in which the program continues executing after an I/O request is initiated. Asynchronous processing is discussed in Appendix C.
NSP ¦ NUP ¦ UPD	NSP is valid only when used in conjunction with the DIR access option and causes VSAM to keep track of current position for subsequent sequential access. NUP specifies that a retrieved record will not be later updated or deleted. UPD indicates that a retrieved record can later be updated or deleted.

BOX 18.6 *(Continued)*

<u>KEQ</u> ¦ KGE	<u>KEQ</u> specifies that key arguments must equal the symbolic key or relative record number in searching for a record; KGE specifies that when key values do not match, the record having the next higher key value will be accessed.
<u>FKS</u> ¦ GEN	<u>FKS</u> indicates that key arguments contain full key value; GEN indicates that a key argument can contain a generic, or partial, key value.
<u>NWAITX</u> ¦ WAITX	WAITX specifies that the UPAD exit routine is to be executed at appropriate times. Exit routines are discussed in Chapter 24.
LOC ¦ <u>MVE</u>	LOC specifies that records are to be processed in the I/O buffer; <u>MVE</u> specifies that VSAM is to move records to and from a user work area for I/O requests.

THE EXLST MACRO

The EXLST macro is used to generate a control block that describes the addresses of exit routines that are to be executed at appropriate times. Box 18.7 shows the syntax of the EXLST macro and describes its parameters. The use of the EXLST macro will be discussed in the remaining chapters in this part.

THE GENCB MACRO

As mentioned earlier, the GENCB macro is used to generate VSAM control blocks at execution time. Instead of generating lists of addresses and values, the GENCB macro generates executable code and a parameter list that causes a specified ACB, RPL, or EXLST to be constructed when the program executes. Box 18.8 shows the syntax of the GENCB macro. The additional parameters that are coded in the GENCB macro are the same as those coded in an ACB, RPL, or EXLST macro.

BOX 18.7 EXLST macro parameters

```
[label]    EXLST    [,AM=VSAM]
                    [,EODAD=address[,A|N][,L])]]
                    [,JRNAD=address[,A|N][,L])]]
                    [,LERAD=address[,A|N][,L])]]
                    [,SYNAD=address[,A|N][,L])]]
                    [,UPAD=address[,A|N][,L])]]
```

AM=VSAM Specifies that the access method in use is VSAM. Since this is the only allowable keyword, and it is the default, this parameter is normally not coded.

EODAD Specifies the address of the routine to be executed when VSAM detects the end of the data set while performing sequential access.

JRNAD Specifies the address of the routine to be executed for journalizing changes that are made to a VSAM data set.

LERAD Specifies the address of the routine to be executed when VSAM detects a logical error in processing an I/O request.

SYNAD Specifies the address of the routine to be executed when VSAM detects a physical error in processing an I/O request.

UPAD Specifies the address of the routine to be executed for user processing during a VSAM request. This routine is given control during the processing of all VSAM executable macros, with the exception of GENCB, MODCB, SHOWCB, and TESTCB.

ACCESSING CONTROL BLOCK FIELDS

In addition to providing macros for generating VSAM control blocks, VSAM also provides a set of macros that can be used to test and manipulate the information stored in them. These are the MODCB, TESTCB, and SHOWCB macros. Each of these macros has parameters that apply to each of the three VSAM control blocks—the ACB, the RPL, and the EXLST. It is possible to extract information from a VSAM control block directly and then to manipulate it in the same manner that is used to manipulate certain fields in a DCB. However, this practice is discouraged by IBM. The use

BOX 18.8 The GENCB macro

```
[label]   GENCB   BLK={ACB|RPL|EXLST}
                  [,controlblockparm],...
```

BOX 18.9 The MODCB, TESTCB, and SHOWCB macros

```
[label]   MODCB  {ACB=address|RPL=address|EXLST=address}
                 [,controlblockparm],...

[label]   TESTCB {ACB=address|RPL=address|EXLST=address}
                 [,controlblockparm],...

[label]   SHOWCB {ACB=address|RPL=address|EXLST=address}
                 ,AREA=address
                 ,LENGTH=number
                 ,FIELDS=(parmkeyword[,...])
```

of the MODCB, TESTCB, and SHOWCB macros avoids the necessity of knowing the specific format of VSAM control blocks and protects the application program from changes that might be made in the future to the formats of those control blocks.

Box 18.9 shows the general syntax of the MODCB, TESTCB, and SHOWCB macros. The additional parameters that are coded in these macros are the same as those coded in an ACB, RPL, or EXLST macro. The MODCB macro is used to modify control block field values, the TESTCB macro is used to test control block fields against specified values, and the SHOWCB macro is used to extract field values from specified control block fields. Figure 18.3 shows examples of MODCB, TESTCB, and SHOWCB. Following are descriptions of the processing performed by each of the macros in Fig. 18.3:

- **CHANGE1 MODCB Macro.** This macro changes the value of the MACRF parameter to IN in an ACB named INFILE.
- **CHANGE2 MODCB Macro.** This macro changes the OPTCD value to KEY in an RPL named EXRPL.

```
CHANGE1  MODCB ACB=INFILE,                                          *
               MACRF=(IN)

CHANGE2  MODCB RPL=EXRPL,                                           *
               OPTCD=(KEY)

CHANGE3  MODCB EXLST=ADDRLIST,                                      *
               EODAD=END1

TESTER   TESTCB RPL=EXRPL,                                          *
               RECLEN=200
         BE    NEXT
          :
*
DISPLAY  SHOWCB RPL=EXRPL,                                          *
               AREA=RECAREA,                                        *
               LENGTH=8,                                            *
               FIELDS=(RECLEN,AREA)
          :
RECAREA  DS    F                            ADDR OF REC LENGTH FIELD
RECADDR  DS    F                            ADDR OF RECORD IN BUFFER
```

Figure 18.3 MODCB, TESTCB, and SHOWCB examples.

- **CHANGE3 MODCB Macro.** This macro stores the end-of-data exit address corresponding to the label END1 into the EXLST named ADDRLIST.
- **TESTER TESTCB Macro.** This macro compares the RECLEN value in an RPL named EXRPL against the RECLEN value of 200 and sets the condition code bits in the same manner as a compare instruction. The BE instruction that follows it tests the condition code bits set by TESTCB.
- **DISPLAY SHOWCB Macro.** This macro extracts the field values for the RECLEN and AREA fields from the RPL named EXRPL and places them into the data area named RECL.

VSAM MACRO PARAMETERS

There are various ways that parameters can be coded in the various VSAM macros. Before we begin further descriptions of how the actual macros are used, we must discuss the general rules that govern the coding of macro parameters. There are basically four types of values that can be specified in VSAM macro parameters. The four parameters of the ACB macro provide a good illustration of each of these parameter types. The following ACB macro includes four parameters, each of which is of a different parameter type:

```
EXACB    ACB  AM=VSAM,                                             *
              DDNAME=EXDD01,                                       *
              BUFNI=200,                                           *
              EXLST=EXIT01
```

VSAM Character String

The AM parameter shows an example of a parameter value that uses a *VSAM character string*. The syntax description of a macro parameter of this type normally lists, in uppercase type, one or more keywords to choose from, each of which has a specific meaning to VSAM. The default keyword value, if there is one, is underlined. In the above example, the only allowable value for the AM= character string is "VSAM". So when the AM parameter is included in an ACB macro, it must be coded as shown. Other macro parameters that use a VSAM character string allow us to make a choice from among a set of allowable character string values. The main characteristic of this type of parameter value specification is that VSAM defines the allowable character string values that can be coded and interprets each character string in a particular way.

Literal Character Strings

DDNAME is an example of parameter that uses a *literal character string*. A macro parameter of this type is described in a syntax diagram by a lowercase, underlined keyword that is other than *address* or *number*. With this type of parameter, we are allowed to specify any desired character string that has some meaning in our program. For example, the character string coded in a DDNAME parameter must match the name of one of the DD statements included in the JCL. The description of the macro parameter in the *VSAM Reference* manual lists any restrictions that apply in the specification of the literal character string. For example, with the DDNAME parameter, the macro parameter description explains that the character string must be a valid 1- to 8-character DD statement name.

Numeric Value

BUFNI is an example of a parameter that uses a *numeric value*. A macro parameter that is of this type is indicated by the word *number* in the syntax description. The *VSAM Reference* manual's description of the parameter describes any restrictions that apply to the specified value. As with any Assembler Language instruction, it is not necessary to code an actual number in a parameter that uses a numeric value; any valid numeric expression can be used. The expression will be translated into an integer value during assembly. For example, the following example produces the same result as our original example:

```
EXACB    ACB  AM=VSAM,                                        *
              DDNAME=EXDD01,                                  *
              BUFNI=BUFFER,                                   *
              EXLST=EXIT01
      :
BUFFER   EQU   200
```

Address Values

The EXLST macro in the above ACB shows an example of a parameter value that consists of a virtual storage *address*. A macro parameter that uses an address is indicated by the word *address* in a syntax diagram. In the example, EXIT01 is the label on a corresponding EXLST macro. There are many types of virtual storage address references; the type of address that can be specified for a macro parameter that uses an address value depends on whether the macro is one that generates a control block, such as the ACB macro above, or one that generates executable code and a parameter list, such as GET, PUT, and GENCB.

ADDRESS TYPES

The only type of address reference that can be used in a control block generating macro, such as an ACB, RPL, or EXLST, is one that references a label in the program. With executable macros such as GET, PUT, and GENCB, a number of other types of addresses can be specified in address-type parameters. In order to see how they work, it is necessary to have an understanding of how addresses are handled within the macro. The following sections discuss the various types of addresses that can be used in executable macros.

A-Type Addresses

VSAM uses parameter lists to pass information between itself and the application program. Suppose we coded the following EXLST parameter in a GENCB macro:

```
INFILE   GENCB EXLST=INEXIT, . . .
```

For the EXLST parameter, the GENCB macro generates an A-type address constant, which, after link editing, will contain the virtual storage address of the location referenced by the label INEXIT. That address constant would then be used by VSAM to locate the exit list. An important restriction with an A-type address constant reference is that the label that is coded cannot be part of a DSECT. If a label in a DSECT must be referenced, the address must be passed in a register, or an S-type address constant reference must be used.

Register Notation

All executable VSAM macros allow address values to be specified using register notation. The following GENCB macro assumes that the address of the appropriate EXLST control block is contained in register 2 before the macro is executed:

```
INFILE   GENCB EXLST=(2), . . .
```

The code generated by the above macro reserves a 4-byte area to hold the exit list ACB address and then stores the contents of register 2 into that 4-byte area. As with any Assembler Language instruction, an actual number does not have to be coded in parentheses. Any expression can be coded as long as the expression produces a numeric register value. The following example produces the same result as the previous one.

```
INFILE   GENCB   EXLST=(REG2), . . .
   :
REG2     EQU     2
```

Direct S-Type Addresses

Executable macros can also generate S-type address constants. An S-type address constant generates a 2-byte base-displacement address. Suppose we coded the following parameter in a GENCB macro:

```
INFILE   GENCB   EXLST=(S,INEXIT), . . .
```

The above EXLST parameter causes the macro to generate, as before, a 4-byte area, which will be used to contain the address of INEXIT. It also generates code that will convert, at execution time, the base-displacement address of INEXIT into an absolute virtual storage address and then store the generated absolute address into the 4-byte area. This method can be used in place of register notation when the referenced label is part of a DSECT.

Indirect Addresses

The example below shows an example of an indirect address reference. The label referenced in the EXLST parameter is not the exit list itself. Instead, the label is that of a 4-byte area that contains the address of the exit list:

```
INFILE   GENCB   EXLST=(*,ADDREXIT), . . .
   :
ADDREXIT DC      A(INEXIT)
   :
INEXIT   EXLST   ---
```

REENTRANT PROGRAMMING

As we will see in later chapters, there are many uses for the various varieties of addresses that can be specified in executable macros. Register notation and the two types of S-type address references are especially useful when writing reentrant programs. Many of the VSAM macros also have both list and execute forms that are useful in constructing reentrant programs. Reentrant programming techniques, and the macro forms that are used with them, are discussed in Appendix D.

MISCELLANEOUS MACROS

There are a number of additional VSAM macros that are not often used in conventional application programs. Brief descriptions of some of these additional macros are provided in Box 18.10.

BOX 18.10 Additional VSAM macros

ACQRANGE	Used for a mass storage system to stage a continuous portion of a data set.
BLDVRP	Used to build a VSAM resource pool.
CNVTAD	Used to return an RBA value based on an argument supplied by the macro.
DLVRP	Used to delete a VSAM resource pool.
MNTACQ	Used with the CNVTAD macro to prestage needed direct access volumes before they are actually used.
MRKBFR	Used to mark a buffer for output and causes the buffer to be written without issuing a PUT request.
SCHBFR	Used to search for buffers that contain adjacent control intervals.
WRTBFR	Used to write out the contents of buffers whose writing has been deferred.

19 ASSEMBLER ESDS PROCESSING

This chapter and the three that follow present examples of partial programs that use the macros discussed in Chapter 18. This chapter shows the VSAM control block and request macros used to process ESDS clusters, Chapters 20 and 21 shows programs that access KSDS clusters, and Chapter 22 discusses RRDS programming techniques. We begin this chapter by examining the ACB, OPEN, and CLOSE macros that are used with VSAM data sets. We then examine the code for sequentially loading an ESDS, for retrieving records from it, and for updating it in various ways. Techniques for working with reusable data sets are also introduced.

In processing an ESDS in an Assembler Language program, records are read from the data set by issuing GET request macros, and records are written into the data set by issuing PUT macros. There are two basic PUT operation types. The first type is used to *load* records into a new data set or to *add a record to the end* of an already loaded data set; the second type is used to *update* an already existing record. Before an ESDS record can be updated, it must first be retrieved by a GET request indicating that the record may later be updated. The DELETE macro is not valid for an ESDS. In order to delete an ESDS record, it can be flagged as a deleted record by first changing the first byte of the record to a hexadecimal "FF" and using a PUT request to update the record. Most software recognizes such a record as a deleted record; these records are normally dropped during maintenance operations. To illustrate some of the types of processing that can be performed on an ESDS, we will work with an ESDS named VSAM.ESDS that contains 200-byte, fixed-length records. We will begin by looking at the OPEN and CLOSE macros used with VSAM data sets. We will then examine the RPL and request macros that are used to initially load an ESDS.

ACB, OPEN, AND CLOSE

Figure 19.1 shows the OPEN and CLOSE macros that are used in a program to load an ESDS initially. These are coded in a similar manner for all types of VSAM data sets. Notice that both the OPEN and CLOSE macros reference an ACB. The DDNAME parameter in the ACB names the DD statement in the JCL that describes the data set being loaded. Notice that the ACB MACRF coding indicates *addressed* access to the data set. This is the only option that is valid when working with individual data records in an ESDS. *Sequential* access to records is also specified. Direct access to records, based on RBA values, can also be specified for an ESDS, but this option cannot be specified in an RPL that is used to initially load the data set.

Since no exit routines are being used by this program, no EXLST macro is required. The ACB for a load program can specify additional options in the MACRF parameter if the data set will later be read or updated after the initial load phase, but the MACRF options shown in Fig. 19.1 are the only required ones for a sequential ESDS load. Also, some of the parameters shown are default values and can be omitted if desired. In the examples in these chapters, we will sometimes include all applicable parameters, including defaults, when this helps to add clarity to the examples.

In the example in Fig. 19.1, the ACB includes a PASSWD parameter. This is only required if the data set being accessed is password protected. Notice that the PASSWD parameter refers to an area that contains a 1-byte password length field followed by the password value itself. When the OPEN macro is executed, the password value will be compared against the appropriate password value currently in effect for the data set. If the values match, the data set is opened successfully. If the passwords do not match, the OPEN process fails and the OPEN macro sets a nonzero return code. If no password value is specified

```
         :
         OPEN  (LOADACB)                   OPEN ESDS
         LTR   15,15
         BNZ   ERROR
         :
         CLOSE (LOADACB)                   CLOSE ESDS
         LTR   15,15
         BNZ   ERROR
         :
LOADACB  ACB   DDNAME=ESDS,                                     *
               MACRF=(ADR,SEQ,OUT),                             *
               PASSWD=PASS
         :
PASS     DC    X'07'                       PASSWORD LENGTH
         DC    C'READPSS'                  PASSWORD VALUE
         :
```

Figure 19.1 VSAM OPEN and CLOSE macros.

in the ACB for a password-protected data set, the system operator or terminal user is prompted for the password in the usual manner.

ESDS SEQUENTIAL LOAD

Figure 19.2 shows the control block and request macro coding for an ESDS load program. To simplify things, we are assuming that the data set is not password protected. Notice that both the ACB MACRF parameter and the RPL OPTCD parameter include the ADR and SEQ options. The RPL OPTCD parameter includes the MVE option as well, which indicates that move mode requests will be issued. Move mode PUT requests cause each PUT macro to move a record from the specified work area to the appropriate VSAM I/O buffer for later writing into the data set. MVE must be specified when PUTs will be issued. The AREA and AREALEN parameters specify the address and length of the work area that will be used by the program. The program builds in this work area each new record that will be written into the data set. A PUT macro then moves the record from this work area to the VSAM I/O buffer. Finally, the RECLEN parameter is also required when PUT operations are issued. As we will see, the RECLEN parameter is not needed for GET requests; VSAM moves the length of each retrieved record into the RECLEN field in the RPL.

The ESDS is opened and closed using conventional OPEN and CLOSE macros. The only request macro used in loading an ESDS is PUT. Notice that both the OPEN and CLOSE macros refer to the ACB, but that the PUT macros

```
//LOADSTEP EXEC PGM=LOADPROG
//ESDS      DD    DSN=VSAM.ESDS,DISP=OLD
             :
          OPEN   (LOADACB)                  OPEN ESDS
             :
          PUT    RPL=LOADRPL                LOAD RECORD INTO DATA SET
          LTR    15,15
          BNZ    ERROR
             :
          CLOSE  (LOADACB)                  CLOSE ESDS
             :
LOADRPL   RPL    ACB=LOADACB,                                          *
                 AREA=RECWORK                                          *
                 AREALEN=200,                                          *
                 RECLEN=200,                                           *
                 OPTCD=(ADR,SEQ,NUP,MVE)
*
RECWORK   DS     CL200                      RECORD WORK AREA
*
LOADACB   ACB    DDNAME=ESDS,                                          *
                 MACRF=(ADR,SEQ,OUT)
             :
```

Figure 19.2 ESDS sequential load.

refer to the RPL. After VSAM executes each OPEN, CLOSE, or request macro, it places a return code value in register 15 to indicate the result of the operation. A zero value indicates successful completion; any other value indicates that an error has occurred. Since a nonzero value often indicates a parameter conflict, many programs, especially during testing, simply ABEND if a nonzero return code is detected. The resulting dump can then be analyzed to determine the cause of the problem.

ESDS SEQUENTIAL RETRIEVAL

After the VSAM.ESDS data set is successfully loaded, we can then execute programs that retrieve records from it. Figure 19.3 shows the control block and request macros that are used to retrieve records from an ESDS. Following are descriptions of the differences between this program and the previous load program:

- The ACB MACRF parameter specifies an option of IN instead of OUT. Since IN is the default for the IN ¦ OUT keyword pair, this keyword could have been omitted from the MACRF keyword subparameter list.
- The ACB refers to an EXLST macro that specifies the address of an EODAD exit routine to handle end-of-data processing.

```
          :
         OPEN   READACB                   OPEN ESDS
          :
         GET    RPL=READRPL               RETRIEVE RECORD
         LTR    15,15
         BNZ    ERROR
          :
EODRTN   CLOSE  (READACB)                 CLOSE ESDS
          :
READRPL  RPL    ACB=READACB,                                   *
                AREA=RECWORK,                                  *
                AREALEN=200,                                   *
                OPTCD=(ADR,SEQ,NUP,MVE)
*
RECWORK  DS     CL200.
*
READACB  ACB    DDNAME=ESDS,                                   *
                MACRF=(ADR,SEQ,IN),                            *
                EXLST=READLIST
*
READLIST EXLST  EODATA=EODRTN
          :
```

Figure 19.3 ESDS sequential retrieval.

- The RECLEN parameter is omitted from the RPL macro because VSAM stores the length of the record into the RPL KEYLEN field when each record is retrieved.
- GET request macros are issued instead of PUT macros to sequentially retrieve records from the data set.

END-OF-DATA PROCESSING

When records are sequentially retrieved, provision must be made in the program for handling the end-of-file condition. The code in Fig. 19.3 uses an EODAD exit routine to detect and handle end-of-data processing. The EODAD exit routine, the address of which is specified in the EXLST macro, gains control when VSAM detects an end-of-data condition. Notice that the EXLST parameter has been specified in the ACB. This parameter references the EXLST macro named READLIST, which in turn specifies the address of the routine that will gain control when end-of-data occurs.

The conventions that must be followed in saving and restoring registers in exit routines can sometimes be quite involved, but if the exit routine simply closes all files and terminates the program, these conventions can be ignored. Chapter 24 discusses exit routines in detail. If no EODAD exit routine is specified in an EXLST macro, VSAM stores a nonzero return code into register 15 when it detects end-of-data during GET processing. The program could then explicitly test for the specific error condition that indicates end-of-data as an alternative to providing an EODAD exit routine.

To test for specific error conditions, the program must examine both the return code value passed in register 15 and the values placed in the *feedback field* in the RPL. The feedback field is 3 bytes in length and is stored in the three low-order bytes of a full word, as shown in Fig. 19.4. The Return Code byte repeats the contents of register 15; the Function Code and FDBK Code bytes provide additional information about the error. The *VSAM Reference* manual contains descriptions of all possible error conditions. Specifically, end-of-data is indicated by a register-15 return code value of 8 and an RPL FDBK Code value of 4.

To examine the feedback field, the program can issue the SHOWCB macro to place the contents of the feedback field into any desired storage area. A listing of the data areas contained in an RPL can be obtained by assembling an

0	1	2	3
not used	Register 15 Return Code	Function Code	FDBK Code

Figure 19.4 RPL feedback field contents.

RPL and requesting that statements generated by the assembler be displayed. This can be done by omitting the PRINT NOGEN option that is often included at the beginning of the program. The SHOWCB macro, illustrated in Fig. 19.5, can be used to extract the feedback field from the RPL, placing it into a 4-byte area that can be examined by the program. Note that even though the feedback field is 3 bytes in length, SHOWCB returns a fullword value with the three feedback bytes stored in the low-order portion of the fullword.

The RPL parameter of the SHOWCB macro specifies the type of control block from which information is being extracted and the address of that control block. The FIELDS parameter specifies the field or fields that should be extracted from the control block, in this case the FDBK field. The AREA and AREALEN parameters specify the address and length of the storage area into which the extracted field is to be placed. The *VSAM Reference* manual describes the length of each control block field.

ESDS SEQUENTIAL UPDATE

As mentioned previously, there are two types of PUT requests. The one that we have already seen ordinarily is used to load records into a new data set. A load-type PUT request can also be used to store new records into an ESDS that

```
         :
         GET   RPL=READRPL                 RETRIEVE RECORD
         LTR   15,15
         BE    NOERROR
*
         SHOWCB RPL=READRPL,               GET FEEDBACK FIELD FROM RPL     *
               AREA=FEEDBACK,                                              *
               AREALEN=4                                                   *
               FIELDS=FDBK
         :
         Code to test FDBK field for specific errors
         :
READRPL  RPL   ACB=READACB,                                                *
               AREA=RECWORK,                                               *
               AREALEN=200,                                                *
               OPTCD=(ADR,SEQ,NUP,MVE)
*
READACB  ACB   DDNAME=ESDS,                                                *
               MACRF=(ADR,SEQ,IN)
*
RECWORK  DS    CL200                       RECORD WORK AREA
*
FEEDBACK DS    0F                          RPL FEEDBACK FIELD WORK AREA
         DS    C
RTRNCODE DS    C
FUNCCODE DS    C
FDBKCODE DS    C
         :
```

Figure 19.5 Examining the RPL feedback field.

already contains records. When this is done, the new records are added to the end of the data set. A second type of PUT request can be used to update existing ESDS records. Each update-type PUT request must be preceded by a GET request referencing an RPL that indicates the retrieved record is eligible for updating. When an ESDS record is updated, any information in the record can be changed; however, the record's length cannot be modified. Remember that records cannot be physically deleted from an ESDS.

The RPL and request macros in Fig. 19.6 show the sequence of operations that are necessary for sequentially updating ESDS records. Notice that the program uses the same RPL for both the GET and PUT request macros, and that the RPL specifies UPD in the OPTCD parameter. Notice also that the ACB specifies both IN and OUT in the MACRF subparameter list. The RPL does not include a RECLEN parameter, even though RECLEN normally is required when PUT requests are issued. RECLEN could be included, but it is not necessary

```
         :
         OPEN   UPDACB                          OPEN ESDS
         :
READRTN  DS     0H
         :
         GET    RPL=UPDRPL                      RETRIEVE RECORD
         LTR    15,15
         BNZ    ERROR
         :
UPDRTN   DS     0H
         :
         PUT    RPL=UPDRPL                      WRITE RECORD BACK TO DATA SET
         LTR    15,15
         BNZ    ERROR
         :
EODRTN   CLOSE  (UPDACB)                        CLOSE ESDS
         :
UPDRPL   RPL    ACB=UPDACB,                                            *
                AREA=RECWORK,                                          *
                AREALEN=200,                                           *
                RECLEN=200,                                            *
                OPTCD=(ADR,SEQ,UPD,MVE)
*
RECWORK  DS     CL200                           RECORD WORK AREA
*
UPDACB   ACB    DDNAME=ESDS,                                           *
                MACRF=(ADR,SEQ,IN,OUT),                                *
                EXLST=UPDLIST
*
UPDLIST  EXLST  EODATA=EODRTN
         :
```

Figure 19.6 ESDS sequential update.

because each PUT is preceded by a GET, which causes the appropriate record length value to be stored into the RECLEN field of the RPL.

When a record is retrieved sequentially using the UPD option, a subsequent PUT macro causes that same record to be written back into the data set. Changes can be made to any of the record's fields in the work area before issuing the PUT request. Note that each record that is retrieved for updating does not have to be updated. If the program determines that the record does not require updating, the program can bypass the PUT and continue by issuing the next GET request to retrieve the next record in sequence.

```
              :
SEQREAD   DS      0H
              :
          GET     RPL=SEQRPL              RETRIEVE RECORD SEQUENTIALLY
          LTR     15,15
          BNZ     ERROR
*
          SHOWCB RPL=SEQRPL,              GET RBA OF RETRIEVED RECORD      *
                  AREA=SAVERBA                                             *
                  FIELDS=RBA,                                              *
                  LENGTH=4
              :
DIRREAD   DS      0H
*
          MODCB  RPL=DIRRPL               STORE RBA IN DIRECT RPL          *
                  ARG=SAVERBA
*
          GET     RPL=DIRQRPL             RETRIEVE RECORD DIRECTLY
          LTR     15,15
          BNZ     ERROR
              :
SEQRPL    RPL     ACB=READACB,                                             *
                  AREA=RECWORK,                                            *
                  AREALEN=200,                                             *
                  OPTCD=(ADR,SEQ,MVE)
*
DIRRPL    RPL     ACB=READACB,                                             *
                  AREA=RECWORK,                                            *
                  AREALEN=200,                                             *
                  OPTCD=(ADR,DIR,NUP,MVE)
*
RECWORK   DS      CL200                   RECORD WORK AREA
SAVERBA   DS      F                       RECORD RBA SAVE AREA
*
READACB   ACB     DDNAME=ESDS,                                             *
                  MACRF=(ADR,SEQ,DIR,IN),                                  *
                  EXLST=UPDLIST
*
UPDLIST   EXLST EODATA=EODRTN
              :
```

Figure 19.7 ESDS direct RBA retrieval.

ESDS DIRECT RBA RETRIEVAL

ESDS records are most often processed sequentially. However, direct processing of ESDS records is also allowed. To retrieve an ESDS record directly, the relative byte address (RBA) value of the desired record must be known. The program must store the RBA value of the desired record into the appropriate RPL field before issuing each direct GET request. The MODCB macro can be used for this purpose. As an example, Fig. 19.7 shows the control block and request macros that could be used in a program that combines sequential and direct retrieval. A series of sequential GET requests is used to read the data set sequentially. The SHOWCB macro is used to store the RBA value for a selected record into an area named SAVERBA.

Then after the file has been sequentially processed, a direct GET request can be issued to directly retrieve the record for which the RBA value was stored. This is done by issuing a MODCB macro to store the RBA value of the desired record into the ARG field in the RPL. This time we are using two RPLs, one specifying *sequential* access and the other *direct* access. The same RPL can be used if desired by using the MODCB macro to modify the OPTCD parameter from SEQ to DIR before issuing a direct retrieval request.

Although the simple code in Fig. 19.7 saves the RBA value of only one record, similar techniques could be used to store many RBA values in a table or file. Direct access could then be gained to any of the records for which RBA values are available. For an ESDS that contains fixed-length records, the RBA value for any desired record can also be calculated. For example, the RBA value of the first record in our data set of 200-byte records is 0, the RBA value of the second record is 200, the RBA for the third record 300, and so on. A direct update program could also be constructed using RBA techniques. To directly update a record whose RBA is known, simply issue a GET request specifying the RBA value of the desired record and follow it with a PUT request referencing the same RPL. The UPD option must be specified in the RPL if directly retrieved records will be updated.

ESDS SKIP-SEQUENTIAL RBA RETRIEVAL

In addition to issuing GET and PUT requests in processing an ESDS, POINT request macros can also be used. A POINT macro causes VSAM to establish position on a specified record without causing that record to be retrieved. When used with an ESDS, the RBA value of the desired record must be stored in the RPL before issuing the POINT request. A common use of POINT in ESDS processing is to establish position on a particular record in order to begin sequential retrieval from that point. Another POINT macro can be issued at any time to select a new starting point. Figure 19.8 shows the control block and request macro coding that might be used to implement an ESDS skip-sequential RBA retrieval program. Each new series of sequential retrievals is preceded by the execution of a POINT macro that establishes a new

```
         :
         OPEN   READACB                      OPEN ESDS
         :
POSITION DS     0H
         :
         MODCB  RPL=SEQRPL,                  STORE RBA IN RPL
                ARG=SAVERBA
*
         POINT  RPL=SEQRPL                   ESTABLISH POSITION ON RECORD
         :
RETRIEVE DS     0H
         :
         GET    RPL=SEQRPL                   RETRIEVE RECORD SEQUENTIALLY
         LTR    15,15
         BNZ    ERROR
         :
EODRTN   CLOSE  (SEQACB)                     CLOSE ESDS
         :
SEQRPL   RPL    ACB=READACB,                                            *
                AREA=RECWORK,                                           *
                AREALEN=200,                                            *
                OPTCD=(ADR,SEQ,NUP,MVE)
*
RECWORK  DS     CL200                        RECORD SAVE AREA
SAVERBA  DS     F                            RECORD RBA SAVE AREA
*
READACB  ACB    DDNAME=ESDS,                                            *
                MACRF=(ADR,SEQ,IN),                                     *
                EXLST=UPDLIST
*
UPDLIST  EXLST  EODATA=EODRTN
         :
```

Figure 19.8 ESDS skip-sequential RBA retrieval.

starting point. Keep in mind that a new RBA value that matches the RBA value of a record in the data set must be provided in the RPL before each execution of the POINT macro.

REUSABLE DATA SETS

When a VSAM data set that already contains records is opened, those records normally are made available to the program. Existing records can be read from the data set and new records added to it. As discussed in Chapter 4, a data set can be defined as reusable by including the REUSE parameter in the DEFINE command. A reusable data set is one whose high-used RBA pointer can be reset to 0 when the data set is opened, thus making it appear empty to an application program. Reusable data sets are often used as work data sets that will simply be loaded and then immediately read in the same program or job. Any type of

```
//LOADSTEP EXEC PGM=LOADPROG
//ESDS      DD    DSN=VSAM.REUSE,DISP=OLD
           :
           OPEN   (LOADACB)                  OPEN AND RESET HIGH-USED RBA
           :
           PUT    RPL=LOADRPL                LOAD RECORD INTO DATA SET
           LTR    15,15
           BNZ    ERROR
           :
           CLOSE  (LOADACB)                  CLOSE DATA SET
           :
LOADRPL    RPL    ACB=LOADACB,                                          *
                  AREA=RECWORK                                          *
                  AREALEN=200,                                          *
                  RECLEN=200,                                           *
                  OPTCD=(ADR,SEQ,NUP,MVE)
*
RECWORK    DS     CL200                      RECORD WORK AREA
*
LOADACB    ACB    DDNAME=ESDS,                                          *
                  MACRF=(ADR,SEQ,OUT,RST)
           :
```

Figure 19.9 Opening a reusable data set.

VSAM data set, ESDS, KSDS, or RRDS, can be defined as a reusable data set.

In order to reset a reusable data set's high-used RBA to zero, an application program issues an OPEN macro that references an ACB specifying MACRF=RST. An example of this is shown in Fig. 19.9. Notice that the control block and request macros are similar to those used for a load program. The RST keyword in the ACB MACRF subparameter list causes the high-used RBA pointer of the reusable data set to be reset to zero. After the data set is reset, it can be treated in exactly the same way as a data set that has just been created. This means that the usual load mode restrictions are in force after execution of the OPEN. A reusable data set does not necessarily have to be reset. If the RST keyword is omitted from the ACB MACRF parameter, the data set is not reset and the records that are presently stored in it can be accessed by the program. Also note that the RST parameter in the ACB has no effect on a data set that was not defined as a reusable data set; a data set's high-used RBA pointer is reset to zero only if the data set was defined as reusable *and* the RST option is included in the ACB.

20 ASSEMBLER KSDS PROCESSING

This chapter discusses the control block and request macro coding for Assembler Language programs that access KSDS clusters. In this chapter we examine Assembler Language code for loading a KSDS, for retrieving records from it, and for updating a KSDS in various ways. Techniques are discussed for using full and generic keys, processing records in the VSAM buffer, and accessing records in descending sequence.

Figure 20.1 shows the format of the records in a VSAM KSDS that we will access in the program examples in this chapter and in Chapter 21. The KSDS stores records that keep track of inventory on a line of novelty items. The KSDS stores variable-length records that can contain from 1 to 42 part numbers, thus the record size ranges from a minimum of 32 bytes to a maximum of 200 bytes. Notice that the records conform to the KSDS restriction that requires the key field of the record to reside in the fixed portion of the record. We will begin this chapter by examining the control block and request block macros that would be required to load the inventory data set. We will then examine the various options that are available for retrieving records from it. We conclude this chapter by looking at KSDS update functions.

KSDS SEQUENTIAL LOAD

Two restrictions apply for a program that initially loads a KSDS: sequential access must be used and no I/O requests other than PUTs can be issued. These two restrictions are reflected in the MACRF subparameters of the ACB and the OPTCD subparameters of the RPL that the PUT references, as shown in Fig. 20.2. The KEY subparameter of both the ACB and the RPL indicates that we are using keyed access. For a KSDS, this means that records will be processed based on their symbolic key values. The SEQ subparameter of the ACB and RPL indicates that we are processing records sequentially; the OUT subparam-

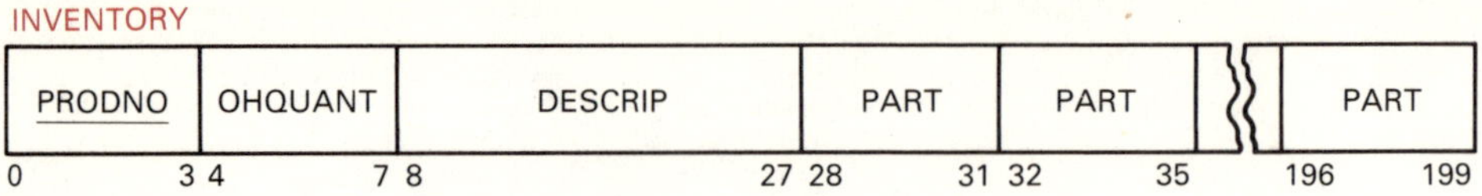

Figure 20.1 Inventory record format.

eter of the ACB MACRF parameter indicates that we will issue PUTs to write records into the data set. The absence of UPD in the RPL OPTCD parameter implies the default of NUP, which indicates no updating is allowed. The MVE keyword (the default) indicates that *move mode* requests will be used to move each record from a work area to the I/O buffer.

During the loading of a KSDS, VSAM automatically builds the index, taking key values directly from each record that is presented to the load program. With our sample inventory data set, the DEFINE command specified that the key is stored in the first four positions of the record, which corresponds to the Product Number field. The records being loaded must be presented to the load program in ascending sequence by key value.

Notice that the work area defined for the records being loaded is large enough to contain the maximum length record that will be loaded (200 bytes). Although we have included an AREALEN parameter in the RPL for documentation purposes, this is not necessary, since we will have to store a record length

```
         :
*
         PUT   RPL=LOADRPL                LOAD RECORD INTO KSDS
         LTR   15,15
         BNZ   ERROR
         :
LOADRPL  RPL   ACB=KSDSACB,                                            *
               AREA=RECORD,                                            *
               AREALEN=200,                                            *
               OPTCD=(KEY,SEQ,NUP,MVE)
*
RECORD   DS    0CL200                     RECORD WORK AREA
*
PRODNO   DS    CL4                        PRODUCT NUMBER (RECORD KEY)
OHQUANT  DS    CL4                        ON HAND QUANTITY
DESCRIP  DS    CL20                       PRODUCT DESCRIPTION
PART     DS    0CL4                       PART NUMBER
*
         DS    42CL4                      ROOM FOR 42 PARTS


LENSAVE  DS    F                          RECORD LENGTH AREA
*
KSDSACB  ACB   DDNAME=KSDS,                                            *
               MACRF=(KEY,SEQ,OUT)
         :
```

Figure 20.2 KSDS sequential load.

value into the RPL before issuing each PUT request to indicate the specific size of each variable-length record. Notice that this is done with the MODCB macro. In this program, we begin by storing the length of each new record into register 5. The MODCB macro references the KSDSRPL RPL and uses the RECLEN parameter to indicate that the record length value is stored in register 5. Code generated by the MODCB macro causes the contents of register 5 to be stored into the appropriate field of the RPL control block.

Following the MODCB macro, we test the contents of register 15 for a nonzero return code. If the MODCB macro executes successfully, KSDSRPL now contains the value from register 5 in its record length field. The PUT macro that references this RPL will then cause a record of the specified length, which is contained in the RECORD work area, to be loaded into the data set.

KSDS SEQUENTIAL RETRIEVAL

There are three methods of access that can be used to retrieve records from a KSDS: sequential, direct, and skip-sequential. Before a direct or skip-sequential retrieval request is issued, an argument must be passed to VSAM, specifying the key value of the desired record. Later examples in this chapter will show how this is done. When sequential retrieval requests are issued, no specific key argument is required. Each new retrieval request causes VSAM to use the KSDS index to retrieve the next record in key value sequence. An example of the control block and request macro coding for a program that retrieves our variable-length inventory records is shown in Fig. 20.3.

The ACB MACRF parameter and the RPL OPTCD parameter are similar to those used in the load program. The only difference is that the ACB MACRF parameter specifies IN for GET macros instead of OUT for PUT macros. Both the ACB and the RPL specify KEY and SEQ for keyed, sequential access to records.

Since we are retrieving variable-length records, the program must be able to determine the length of each record before processing the Part-Number fields. The SHOWCB macro is used for this purpose. In the example shown in Fig. 20.3, the fullword area named LENSAVE is used to contain the length of the record most recently retrieved. The SHOWCB macro uses the AREA and LENGTH parameters to define the LENSAVE fullword; the FIELDS parameter then specifies which RPL field (RECLEN) to place into this area. After executing the SHOWCB macro, the program loads the record length into register 9, which can then be used in any desired manner.

LOCATE MODE GET REQUESTS

In all the program examples we have looked at so far, we have specified an RPL OPTCD subparameter of MVE to indicate *move mode* request macros. As mentioned earlier, MVE must be specified, or implied, when PUT macros will

```
         :
         GET    RPL=SEQRPL                RETRIEVE RECORD SEQUENTIALLY
         LTR    15,15
         BNZ    ERROR
*
         SHOWCB RPL=SEQRPL,               MOVE REC LNGTH TO LENSAVE FIELD *
                AREA=LENSAVE,                                             *
                LENGTH=4,                                                 *
                FIELDS=(RECLEN)
         LTR    15,15
         BNZ    ERROR
*
         L      9,LENSAVE                 LOAD RECORD LENGTH INTO REG 9
         :
*
SEQRPL   RPL    ACB=KSDSACB,                                              *
                AREA=RECORD,                                              *
                AREALEN=200,                                              *
                OPTCD=(KEY,SEQ,NUP,MVE)
*
RECORD   DS     0CL200                    RECORD WORK AREA
*
PRODNO   DS     CL4                       PRODUCT NUMBER (RECORD KEY)
OHQUANT  DS     CL4                       ON HAND QUANTITY
DESCRIP  DS     CL20                      PRODUCT DESCRIPTION
PART     DS     0CL4                      PART NUMBER
*
         DS     42CL4                     ROOM FOR 42 PARTS
*
LENSAVE  DS     F                         RECORD LENGTH SAVE AREA
*
KSDSACB  ACB    DDNAME=KSDS,                                              *
                MACRF=(KEY,SEQ,IN),
         :
```

Figure 20.3 KSDS sequential retrieval.

be issued. However, when GET macros are used, we have the option of processing input records directly in the VSAM I/O buffer rather than requiring VSAM to move each retrieved record to a user work area. This mode of operation is referred to as *locate mode*. Locate mode I/O requests are specified by coding LOC in the OPTCD parameter of the RPL. When locate mode is specified, the areas referred to by the AREA and AREALEN parameters of the RPL do not refer to a record work area. Instead, they refer to a fullword area that is used to contain the address of the retrieved record.

Figure 20.4 shows an example of the control block and request macros used to perform locate mode retrieval requests. In executing each GET request macro, VSAM stores the address of the retrieved record into the fullword RECADDR field defined by the RPL AREA and AREALEN fields. The AREA and AREALEN field must refer to a 4-byte area when LOC is specified in the OPTCD parameter. Notice that in our example, we are using a DSECT to describe the record, and we load register 5 with the address of the record in the buffer to establish addressability on it.

```
         :
         USING RECORD,5                    ESTABLISH ADDRESSABILITY
         :
         GET   RPL=LOCRPL                  RETRIEVE RECORD
         LTR   15,15
         BNZ   ERROR
*
         L     5,RECADDR                   LOAD RECORD ADDRESS INTO REG 5
         :
         (Code to manipulate fields in retrieved record)
         :
LOCRPL   RPL   ACB=KSDSACB,                                           *
               AREA=RECADDR,                                          *
               AREALEN=4,                                             *
               OPTCD=(KEY,SEQ,NUP,LOC)
*
RECADDR  DS    F                           ADDRESS OF RECORD IN I/O BUFFER
RECORD   DSECT
*
PRODNO   DS    CL4                         PRODUCT NUMBER (RECORD KEY)
OHQUANT  DS    CL4                         ON HAND QUANTITY
DESCRIP  DS    CL20                        PRODUCT DESCRIPTION
PART     DS    0CL4                        PART NUMBER
*
         DS    42CL4                       ROOM FOR 42 PARTS
*
KSDSACB  ACB   DDNAME=KSDS,                                           *
               MACRF=(KEY,SEQ,IN)
         :
```

Figure 20.4 Locate mode retrieval.

KSDS DIRECT RETRIEVAL

When processing records sequentially, as in the sequential load and retrieval examples we have examined so far, it is not necessary to explicitly pass a key argument to VSAM before issuing each I/O request. However, in order to retrieve records directly based on a specific symbolic key value, the program must use the RPL ARG parameter to identify the key value of the desired record.

Figure 20.5 shows the control block and request macros that can be used to retrieve records directly from a KSDS. Notice that the only new control block parameter is the ARG parameter in the RPL. The ARG parameter refers to an area in the program that will contain a symbolic key value before each GET request is executed. VSAM uses the key value that it finds in the ARG data area to locate each requested record using the KSDS index. Notice that the ARG parameter in the example in Fig. 20.5 points to the PRODNO field in the record work area. This was done for convenience. The ARG parameter does not have to point to an area in the record work area; a separate work area for the key argument can be used if desired.

The KEQ and KGE subparameters of the RPL OPTCD parameter specify the type of comparison that is to be made in performing the index search. The

```
          :
          MVC    PRODNO,GETKEY             MOVE KEY VALUE TO RECORD AREA
*
          GET    RPL=DIRRPL                RETRIEVE RECORD DIRECTLY
          LTR    15,15
          BNZ    ERROR
          :
DIRRPL    RPL    ACB=KSDSACB,                                            *
                 AREA=RECORD,                                            *
                 AREALEN=200,                                            *
                 ARG=PRODNO,                                             *
                 OPTCD=(KEY,DIR,NUP,MVE)
*
RECORD    DS     0CL200                    RECORD WORK AREA
*
PRODNO    DS     CL4                       PRODUCT NUMBER (RECORD KEY)
OHQUANT   DS     CL4                       ON HAND QUANTITY
DESCRIP   DS     CL20                      PRODUCT DESCRIPTION
PART      DS     0CL4                      PART NUMBER
*
          DS     42CL4                     ROOM FOR 42 PARTS
*
KSDSACB   ACB    DDNAME=KSDS,                                            *
                 MACRF=(KEY,DIR,IN)
          :
```

Figure 20.5 KSDS direct retrieval.

KEQ subparameter (the default) specifies that VSAM should perform an *equal* key value comparison in searching for the requested record. Only a record that has a key value that exactly matches the supplied key value argument satisfies the search. If a record with the desired key value does not exist in the data set, the GET request fails and sets a nonzero return code value. The same method described in Chapter 19 can be used to examine the feedback field of the RPL and test for the record-not-found condition. The KGE subparameter alternatively can be included in the RPL OPTCD parameter to specify a *greater-than-or-equal* key value comparison. When KGE is specified, and VSAM is unable to locate a record that has a key value that is equal to the key value argument, VSAM retrieves the record that has the next higher key value.

GENERIC KEY KSDS RETRIEVAL

We can also use the FKS and GEN subparameter pair to specify whether a full key search or a generic key search is to be performed. FKS (the default) specifies a full key search. When a full key search is specified, each key value argument must be the same size as the actual key field that is defined for the data set. When a generic key search is specified, key arguments can be smaller than the actual key. When a generic key search is requested, the RPL must include a KEYLEN value that defines the length of the argument for each I/O request.

The example in Fig. 20.6 shows a simple example of a generic key search

```
         :
         MVC   PRODNO(2),=C'12'              1ST 2 BYTES OF KEY TO PRODNO
*
         GET   RPL=GENRPL                    RETRIEVE VIA GENERIC KEY VALUE
         LTR   15,15
         BNZ   ERROR
         :
GENRPL   RPL   ACB=KSDSACB,                                            *
               AREA=RECORD,                                            *
               AREALEN=200,                                            *
               ARG=PRODNO,                                             *
               KEYLEN=2,                                               *
               OPTCD=(KEY,DIR,NUP,MVE,GEN)
*
RECORD   DS    0CL200                        RECORD WORK AREA
*
PRODNO   DS    CL4                           PRODUCT NUMBER (RECORD KEY)
OHQUANT  DS    CL4                           ON HAND QUANTITY
DESCRIP  DS    CL20                          PRODUCT DESCRIPTION
PART     DS    0CL4                          PART NUMBER
*
         DS    42CL4                         ROOM FOR 42 PARTS
*
KSDSACB  ACB   DDNAME=KSDS,                                            *
               MACRF=(KEY,DIR,IN)
         :
```

Figure 20.6 KSDS generic key retrieval.

that causes VSAM to locate the first record in the data set whose key value begins with the characters "12". The GET request that performs this generic key retrieval might then be followed by code that sequentially retrieves all of the records whose key values begin with those characters. The code in Fig. 20.6 uses the KEYLEN parameter to specify a key-argument length of 2 bytes. The program could also use the MODCB macro to store a different KEYLEN value into the RPL for each generic key retrieval request if key arguments of varying lengths will be used.

SKIP-SEQUENTIAL KSDS RETRIEVAL

In many applications, sets of records in varying places in the data set must be processed sequentially. A program can be written to perform sequential retrieval of sets of records by using a direct GET request to retrieve the first record of each sequential set and then using a series of sequential GET requests to retrieve the remaining records in each set. The program might use two RPLs, one specifying OPTCD=DIR for the direct GET requests and one specifying OPTCD=SEQ for the sequential GET requests. Alternatively, the program might use the MODCB macro to store the appropriate OPTCD value into the RPL when switching between the direct and sequential GET requests. An advantage to using a direct GET request to establish each new position in the data set is that there is no restriction on which record can be retrieved by each new direct GET request. The GET request can move either forward or backward in the data set relative to the previous direct GET request.

A program that performs true skip-sequential processing specifies OPTCD = SKP in the RPL and always moves forward in the data set. An example is shown in Fig. 20.7. In order to perform skip-sequential processing, the program issues a POINT macro to establish each new position in the data set and then issues a sequence of sequential GET requests to retrieve records beginning with the record located by the POINT. The POINT macro generally refers to the same sequential RPL as is used by the sequential GET requests.

There is an efficiency difference between using a direct GET request to establish each new position in the data set and using true skip-sequential processing. With skip-sequential access, VSAM uses only the sequence set of the

```
         MVC   PRODNO(2),=C'12'          1ST 2 BYTES OF KEY TO PRODNO
*
         POINT RPL=SKIPRPL               POSITION FOR SEQUENTIAL ACCESS
         LTR   15,15
         BNZ   ERROR
*
REPEAT   GET   RPL=SKIPRPL               RETRIEVE ONE RECORD
         LTR   15,15
         BNZ   ERROR
*
         CLC   PRODNO(2),=C'12'          TEST FOR END OF RECORD SET
         BNE   ENDSEQ
          :
        (Code to process record.)
          :
         B     REPEAT
*
ENDSEQ   DS    0H                        END OF RECORD SET
          :
SKIPRPL  RPL   ACB=KSDSACB,                                          *
               AREA=RECORD,                                          *
               AREALEN=200,                                          *
               ARG=PRODNO,                                           *
               KEYLEN=2,                                             *
               OPTCD=(KEY,SEQ,NUP,MVE,KEQ,FKS)
*
*              KEQ AND FKS OPTIONS USED BY POINT ONLY
*
*
RECORD   DS    0CL200                    RECORD WORK AREA
*
PRODNO   DS    CL4                       PRODUCT NUMBER (RECORD KEY)
OHQUANT  DS    CL4                       ON HAND QUANTITY
DESCRIP  DS    CL20                      PRODUCT DESCRIPTION
PART     DS    0CL4                      PART NUMBER
*
         DS    42CL4                     ROOM FOR 42 PARTS
*
KSDSACB  ACB   DDNAME=KSDS,                                          *
               MACRF=(KEY,SEQ,IN)
```

Figure 20.7 KSDS skip-sequential retrieval.

index in searching for each new record. When a direct retrieval is specified, VSAM searches the entire index in satisfying each direct GET request. If the program issues a lot of direct GET requests, and processing always moves forward in the data set, this additional searching is not needed and a program that performs true skip-sequential processing will be more efficient.

BACKWARD ACCESS

In all our sequential retrieval examples so far we have been retrieving records in ascending key value sequence. Ascending sequence is specified by the FWD subparameter of the RPL OPTCD parameter, which is the default. To process records in descending key value sequence, we must include OPTCD=BWD in the RPL. When the BWD option is specified, skip-sequential processing is not allowed.

When backward processing is used, it is often useful to begin a sequential retrieval program by establishing a position on the last record in the data set. OPTCD=LRD can be used for this purpose. A direct GET request that refers to an RPL that specifies LRD will cause the last record to be retrieved, and a POINT request using that RPL will cause position to be established on the last record.

The RPL in Fig. 20.8 includes both the LRD and the BWD options. The LRD keyword causes the POINT macro to establish position on the last record in the data set. The BWD keyword causes each GET request to retrieve the next record in descending key value sequence. The LRD keyword has no effect on sequential GET requests, so the same RPL can be used by both the POINT request and the GET requests.

KSDS UPDATING

The full complement of maintenance functions is allowed when a KSDS is being processed, including adds, changes, and deletes. An *add* operation causes a new record to be inserted in logical key value sequence into a previously loaded data set. A *change* or *update* operation causes an already existing record to be replaced. For a KSDS that contains variable-length records, records can be made either shorter or longer, as desired. A *delete* operation causes an existing record to be physically removed from the data set. The space previously occupied by records that are shortened or deleted from a KSDS is immediately returned to the free space pool for use when records are lengthened or inserted.

KSDS DIRECT RECORD INSERTION

New records can be inserted into a KSDS while processing the data set using either sequential, direct, or skip-sequential processing. While using sequential or skip-sequential processing, the key value of a new

```
         :
         POINT RPL=BACKRPL                     ESTABLISH POSITION ON LAST REC
         LTR   15,15
         BNZ   ERROR
*
REPEAT   GET   RPL=BACKRPL                     RETRIEVE SEQUENTIAL BACKWARDS
         LTR   15,15
         BNZ   ERROR
         :
         (Code to process record.)
         :
         B     REPEAT
         :
BACKRPL  RPL   ACB=KSDSACB,                                                  *
               AREA=RECORD,                                                  *
               AREALEN=200,                                                  *
               OPTCD=(KEY,SEQ,NUP,MVE,LRD,BWD)
*
*                        LRD OPTION USED BY POINT ONLY
*
RECORD   DS    0CL200                          RECORD WORK AREA
*
PRODNO   DS    CL4                             PRODUCT NUMBER (RECORD KEY)
OHQUANT  DS    CL4                             ON HAND QUANTITY
DESCRIP  DS    CL20                            PRODUCT DESCRIPTION
PART     DS    0CL4                            PART NUMBER
*
         DS    42CL4                           ROOM FOR 42 PARTS
*
KSDSACB  ACB   DDNAME=KSDS,                                                  *
               MACRF=(KEY,SEQ,IN)
         :
```

Figure 20.8 KSDS backward sequential retrieval.

record being inserted must be in sequence with respect to the preceding record and the following record in the transaction file. Records can be added while processing the data set in either ascending or descending sequence. While processing a KSDS directly, a new record of any desired key value can be inserted into the data set. VSAM uses the KSDS index to determine where in the data set the new record belongs.

Fig. 20.9 shows the control block and request macros that might be used to directly add a new record to an existing data set. Since the data set contains variable-length records, we are using a MODCB macro to insert the proper record length value into the RPL before issuing the PUT request. Notice that no argument is supplied via the RPL ARG parameter. None is necessary because VSAM takes the key value directly from the record in the work area. The PUT will cause VSAM to place the record in the data set in its proper location according to its key value. The NUP option must be in effect in order to indicate that the PUT request is inserting a new record rather than replacing the record

```
         :
         MVC    RECORD,NEWREC                NEW RECORD TO RECORD AREA
*
         MODCB  RPL=ADDRPL,                  STORE RECORD LENGTH IN RPL       *
                RECLEN=LENSAVE
         LTR    15,15
         BNZ    ERROR
*
         PUT    RPL=ADDRPL                   INSERT NEW RECORD IN DATA SET
         LTR    15,15
         BNZ    ERROR
         :
ADDRPL   RPL    ACB=KSDSACB,                                                  *
                AREA=RECORD,                                                  *
                AREALEN=200,                                                  *
                OPTCD=(KEY,DIR,NUP,MVE)
*
LENSAVE  DS     F
*
RECORD   DS     0CL200                       RECORD WORK AREA
*
PRODNO   DS     CL4                          PRODUCT NUMBER (RECORD KEY)
OHQUANT  DS     CL4                          ON HAND QUANTITY
DESCRIP  DS     CL20                         PRODUCT DESCRIPTION
PART     DS     0CL4                         PART NUMBER
*
         DS     42CL4                        ROOM FOR 42 PARTS
*
KSDSACB  ACB    DDNAME=KSDS,                                                  *
                MACRF=(KEY,DIR,OUT)
         :
```

Figure 20.9 KSDS direct record insertion.

that was most recently retrieved. Since NUP is the default value, this keyword need not be included in the RPL OPTCD parameter.

KSDS DIRECT RECORD UPDATING

Before an existing record can be changed or deleted, it must first be retrieved with a GET request that indicates an intention to update the record. As with record addition, records can be changed while processing a record using any type of access, including sequential, skip-sequential, or direct. Everything we have discussed thus far regarding retrievals also applies to a retrieval that precedes a change or delete. To indicate that a retrieved record is eligible for updating, we must specify the UPD OPTCD keyword in the RPL used for retrieval (see Fig. 20.10). Any required changes are then made to the record in the work area. Finally, a PUT request is issued referring to the same RPL. A PUT request that updates an existing record always uses an RPL that specifies UPD; a PUT request that inserts a new record into a data set always refers to an RPL that specifies (or implies) the NUP option.

```
         MVC   PRODNO,UPDKEY              MOVE KEY VALUE TO KEY ARGUMENT
*
         GET   RPL=UPDRPL                 RETRIEVE RECORD FOR UPDATING
         LTR   15,15
         BNZ   ERROR
          :
         (Code to update record in work area.)
          :
         PUT   RPL=UPDRPL                 WRITE RECORD BACK TO DATA SET
         LTR   15,15
         BNZ   ERROR
          :
UPDRPL   RPL   ACB=KSDSACB,                                            *
               AREA=RECORD,                                            *
               AREALEN=200,                                            *
               ARG=PRODNO,                                             *
               OPTCD=(KEY,DIR,UPD,MVE)
*
RECORD   DS    0CL200                     RECORD WORK AREA
*
PRODNO   DS    CL4                        PRODUCT NUMBER (RECORD KEY)
OHQUANT  DS    CL4                        ON HAND QUANTITY
DESCRIP  DS    CL20                       PRODUCT DESCRIPTION
PART     DS    0CL4                       PART NUMBER
*
         DS    42CL4                      ROOM FOR 42 PARTS
*
KSDSACB  ACB   DDNAME=KSDS,                                            *
               MACRF=(KEY,DIR,IN,OUT)
          :
```

Figure 20.10 KSDS direct record updating.

When modifying the record in the work area, any desired changes can be made to the record with the exception of modifying the key field value. If the key field is changed, the PUT request will fail, causing VSAM to set a nonzero return code value. In order to change a record's key field value, the original record must be deleted from the data set and reinserted using the new key field value. The example in Fig. 20.10 assumes that the record's length does not change. If the record's length will be changed, the PUT request must be preceded by a MODCB macro that stores the new record length value into the RPL.

KSDS DIRECT RECORD DELETION

As with update operations, a delete request must be preceded by a GET request that specifies that an update on that record is allowed. An ERASE macro is then issued, which causes VSAM to remove the record from the data set. An example is shown in Fig. 20.11. The control block and request macros are similar to those in the previous update example.

```
         MVC   PRODNO,RECKEY             MOVE KEY VALUE TO KEY ARGUMENT
*
         GET   RPL=DELRPL                RETRIEVE RECORD FOR DELETION
         LTR   15,15
         BNZ   ERROR
          :
         ERASE RPL=DELRPL                ERASE RECORD
         LTR   15,15
         BNZ   ERROR
          :
DELRPL   RPL   ACB=KSDSACB,                                           *
               AREA=RECORD,                                           *
               AREALEN=200,                                           *
               ARG=PRODNO,                                            *
               OPTCD=(KEY,DIR,UPD,MVE)
          :
*
RECORD   DS    0CL200                    RECORD WORK AREA
*
PRODNO   DS    CL4                       PRODUCT NUMBER (RECORD KEY)
OHQUANT  DS    CL4                       ON HAND QUANTITY
DESCRIP  DS    CL20                      PRODUCT DESCRIPTION
PART     DS    0CL4                      PART NUMBER
*
         DS    42CL4                     ROOM FOR 42 PARTS
*
KSDSACB  ACB   DDNAME=KSDS,                                           *
               MACRF=(KEY,DIR,IN,OUT)
          :
```

Figure 20.11 KSDS direct record deletion.

21 ALTERNATE INDEXES

In this chapter, we will examine the Assembler Language coding necessary to work with VSAM clusters that have alternate indexes associated with them. As an example, we will use an alternate index named INVENT.ALTINDEX that indexes the inventory data set (INVENT.KSDS) that we examined in Chapter 20. The field used to index the base cluster is the 20-character description field from the inventory file. A path named INVENT.DESCRIP associates the secondary index with the base cluster. These alternate index relationships are shown in Fig. 21.1. For the purposes of this example, we will assume that each product has a unique description, and that the INVENT.ALTINDEX alternate index contains unique key values.

Figure 21.2 summarizes all the various VSAM objects that are involved when a single alternate index is associated with our inventory KSDS. As shown, the structure consists of seven objects. The KSDS base cluster is one object, which in turn has an index component and a data component. The alternate index cluster also consists of an index and a data component and is similar in structure to a KSDS. The alternate index normally is used by accessing the path that associates an alternate index with its base cluster. The AMS commands in Fig. 21.3 might be used to define and build our INVENT.ALTINDEX alternate index and to define the INVENT.DESCRIP path that associates INVENT.ALTINDEX with INVENT.KSDS.

ACCESSING RECORDS VIA AN ALTERNATE INDEX

When opening a data set that is indexed by an alternate index, the name of the object specified in the JCL determines whether or not the alternate index is used for access. For example, Fig. 21.4 shows the DD statement and the control block and request macros used to access records sequentially from the INVENT.KSDS data set. Since the DSNAME parameter

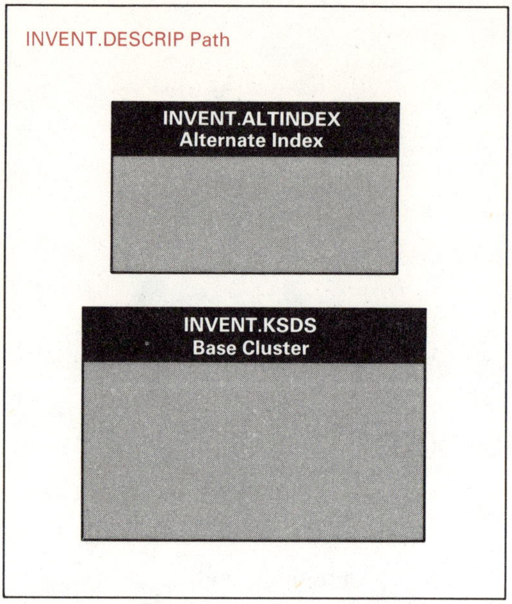

Figure 21.1 Inventory alternate index and path.

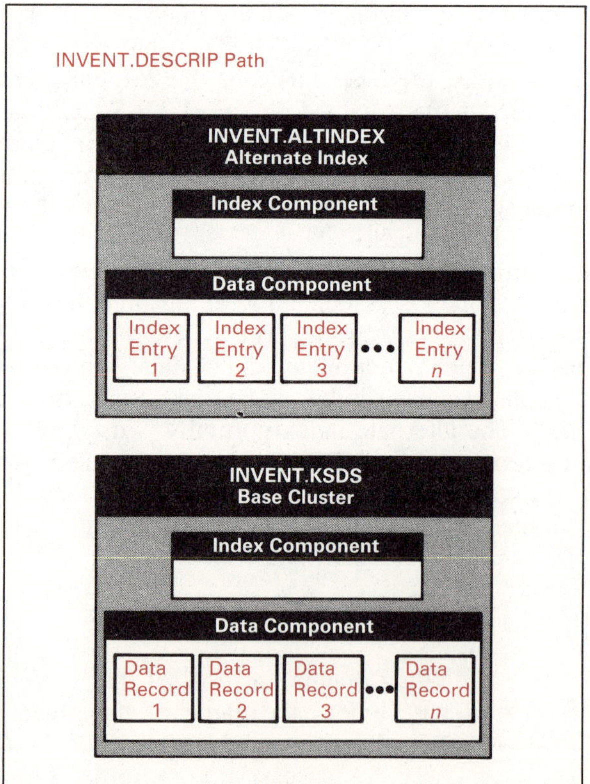

Figure 21.2 Alternate index components.

```
DEFINE    ALTERNATEINDEX                                    -
          (NAME         (INVENT.ALTINDEX)                   -
           RELATE       (INVENT.KSDS)                       -
           KEYS         (7 20)                              -
           TRACKS       (1 1)                               -
           VOLUMES      (DSK001)                            -
           RECORDSIZE   (100 100)                           -
           FILE         (INDEXDD)

BLDINDEX  INDATASET     (INVENT.KSDS)                       -
          OUTDATASET    (INVENT.ALTINDEX)

DEFINE    PATH                                              -
          (NAME         (INVENT.DESCRIP)                    -
           PATHENTRY    (INVENT.ALTINDEX)
```

Figure 21.3 Alternate index and path definition.

```
//KSDS  DD  DSN=INVENT.KSDS,DISP=SHR

          :
         OPEN   (KSDSACB)                 OPEN INPUT
         LTR    15,15
         BNZ    ERROR
          :
         GET    RPL=SEQRPL                RETRIEVE RECORD SEQUENTIALLY
         LTR    15,15
         BNZ    ERROR
          :
         CLOSE  (KSDSACB)                 CLOSE INPUT
         LTR    15,15
         BNZ    ERROR
          :
*
SEQRPL   RPL    ACB=KSDSACB,                                          *
                AREA=RECORD,                                          *
                AREALEN=200,                                          *
                OPTCD=(KEY,SEQ,NUP,MVE)
*
RECORD   DS     0CL200                    RECORD WORK AREA
*
PRODNO   DS     CL4                       PRODUCT NUMBER (RECORD KEY)
OHQUANT  DS     CL4                       ON HAND QUANTITY
DESCRIP  DS     CL20                      PRODUCT DESCRIPTION
PART     DS     0CL4                      PART NUMBER
*
         DS     42CL4                     ROOM FOR 42 PARTS
*
KSDSACB  ACB    DDNAME=KSDS,                                          *
                MACRF=(KEY,SEQ,IN),
          :
```

Figure 21.4 Prime key retrieval.

in the DD statement identifies the base cluster, records will be accessed via the prime key, and records will be retrieved in PRODNO sequence.

Figure 21.5 shows how records can be accessed from the inventory file in alternate key sequence. The only difference between the example in Fig. 21.4 and the example in Fig. 21.5 is the name of the VSAM object coded in the DD statement; the control block and request macros are identical. Since the DD statement in Fig. 21.5 names the path rather than the base cluster, the alternate index will be used to provide access to the base cluster, and inventory records will be sequentially retrieved in DESCRIP sequence rather than PRODNO sequence.

Sequential updates are also made in an identical manner when an alternate key is used for access to the data set. Records to be updated or deleted are first retrieved using an RPL and ACB that access the data set via the alternate key, and PUT and ERASE requests are issued as necessary to update the data set.

```
//KSDS   DD   DSN=INVENT.DESCRIP,DISP=SHR


           :
         OPEN   (KSDSACB)                     OPEN INPUT
         LTR    15,15
         BNZ    ERROR
           :
         GET    RPL=SEQRPL                    RETRIEVE RECORD SEQUENTIALLY
         LTR    15,15
         BNZ    ERROR
           :
         CLOSE  (KSDSACB)                     CLOSE INPUT
         LTR    15,15
         BNZ    ERROR
           :
*
SEQRPL   RPL    ACB=KSDSACB,                                                 *
                AREA=RECORD,                                                 *
                AREALEN=200,                                                 *
                OPTCD=(KEY,SEQ,NUP,MVE)
*
RECORD   DS     0CL200                        RECORD WORK AREA
*
PRODNO   DS     CL4                           PRODUCT NUMBER (RECORD KEY)
OHQUANT  DS     CL4                           ON HAND QUANTITY
DESCRIP  DS     CL20                          PRODUCT DESCRIPTION
PART     DS     0CL4                          PART NUMBER
*
         DS     42CL4                         ROOM FOR 42 PARTS
*
KSDSACB  ACB    DDNAME=KSDS,                                                 *
                MACRF=(KEY,SEQ,IN),
           :
```

Figure 21.5 Alternate key retrieval.

Records are inserted sequentially in a similar manner by issuing PUT requests that refer to an RPL that specifies OPTCD=NUP.

USING MULTIPLE ACBS

In some applications it is useful to concurrently access records via both the prime key and an alternate key. This type of application requires two DD statements, each referenced by a separate ACB in the program. Figure 21.6 shows an example of this. Each of the two GET requests refers to its own RPL, which refers to its own ACB. The two ACBs are opened at the same time, giving the program access to the records in the inventory file either via PRODNO or via DESCRIP.

DIRECT ALTERNATE INDEX ACCESS

When accessing records directly, the ARG parameter of the RPL must reference an area that contains a key value to be used in searching for the desired record. For this reason, the control block and request macro coding for a retrieval program that accesses records via an alternate index is somewhat different from a program that accesses records via the prime key. Specifically, the ARG parameter in the RPL must point to an area that contains an alternate key value rather than a prime key value. The example in Fig. 21.7 shows the control block and request macro coding for a direct retrieval program that allows direct access to inventory records either via the prime key (PRODNO) or the alternate key (DESCRIP). The ARG parameter for the RPL that allows prime key access describes a 4-byte area that contains a PRODNO field value. The ARG parameter for the RPL that allows alternate key access points to a 20-byte area that contains a DESCRIP field value.

Direct updates can also be made using alternate key argument values. Records to be updated or deleted are first retrieved by supplying an alternate key value and an appropriate RPL and ACB. PUT or ERASE requests could then be issued as required to update the data set. Records are inserted directly by supplying the alternate key value of a new record and issuing a PUT request that refers to an RPL that specifies OPTCD=NUP. The following three restrictions exist for updating records via alternate key values:

- A PUT operation that replaces an existing record must not change the value of the prime key.
- A PUT operation that replaces an existing record must not change the value of the alternate key that was used to retrieve the record.
- A PUT operation that inserts a new record using an alternate key defined with the UNIQUEKEY attribute must not insert a record that has an alternate key value equal to that of an existing record.

```
//PRIME      DD  DSN=INVENT.KSDS,DISP=SHR
//ALTINDEX   DD  DSN=INVENT.DESCRIP,DISP=SHR

             :
            OPEN  (PRMACB,,ALTACB)          OPEN BOTH ACBS
            LTR   15,15
            BNZ   ERROR
             :
            GET   RPL=PRMRPL                RETRIEVE VIA PRIME KEY
            LTR   15,15
            BNZ   ERROR
             :
            GET   RPL=ALTRPL                RETRIEVE VIA ALTERNATE KEY
            LTR   15,15
            BNZ   ERROR
             :
            CLOSE (PRMACB,,ALTACB)          CLOSE BOTH ACBS
            LTR   15,15
            BNZ   ERROR
             :
*
SEQRPL      RPL   ACB=PRMACB,                                        *
                  AREA=RECORD,                                       *
                  AREALEN=200,                                       *
                  OPTCD=(KEY,SEQ,NUP,MVE)
*
SEQRPL      RPL   ACB=ALTACB,                                        *
                  AREA=RECORD,                                       *
                  AREALEN=200,                                       *
                  OPTCD=(KEY,SEQ,NUP,MVE)
*
RECORD      DS    0CL200                    RECORD WORK AREA
*
PRODNO      DS    CL4                       PRODUCT NUMBER (RECORD KEY)
OHQUANT     DS    CL4                       ON HAND QUANTITY
DESCRIP     DS    CL20                      PRODUCT DESCRIPTION
PART        DS    0CL4                      PART NUMBER
*
            DS    42CL4                     ROOM FOR 42 PARTS
*
PRMACB      ACB   DDNAME=PRIME,                                      *
                  MACRF=(KEY,SEQ,IN),
*
ALTACB      ACB   DDNAME=ALTINDEX,                                   *
                  MACRF=(KEY,SEQ,IN),
             :
```

Figure 21.6 Using two ACBs.

ERROR CHECKING

As with other types of access, when a logical or physical error occurs, VSAM provides information about the cause of the error by storing information in the 3-byte feedback area in the RPL. Figure 21.8 repeats the format of the RPL feedback area. The Function Code byte of the feedback area is of particular interest to I/O requests

```
//KSDS   DD   DSN=INVENT.DESCRIP,DISP=SHR


              :
         OPEN   (KSDSACB)                   OPEN INPUT
         LTR    15,15
         BNZ    ERROR
              :
         MVC    DESCRIP,INNAME              DESCRIPTION TO ALT KEY ARGUMENT
*
         GET    RPL=DIRRPL                  RETRIEVE VIA ALTERNATE KEY
         LTR    15,15
         BNZ    ERROR
              :
         CLOSE  (KSDSACB)                   CLOSE INPUT
         LTR    15,15
         BNZ    ERROR
              :
*
DIRRPL   RPL    ACB=KSDSACB,                                          *
                AREA=RECORD,                                          *
                AREALEN=200,                                          *
                ARG=DESCRIP,                                          *
                OPTCD=(KEY,DIR,NUP,MVE)
*
RECORD   DS     0CL200                      RECORD WORK AREA
*
PRODNO   DS     CL4                         PRODUCT NUMBER (RECORD KEY)
OHQUANT  DS     CL4                         ON HAND QUANTITY
DESCRIP  DS     CL20                        PRODUCT DESCRIPTION
PART     DS     0CL4                        PART NUMBER
*
         DS     42CL4                       ROOM FOR 42 PARTS
*
KSDSACB  ACB    DDNAME=KSDS,                                          *
                MACRF=(KEY,SEQ,IN),
              :
```

Figure 21.7 Direct alternate key retrieval.

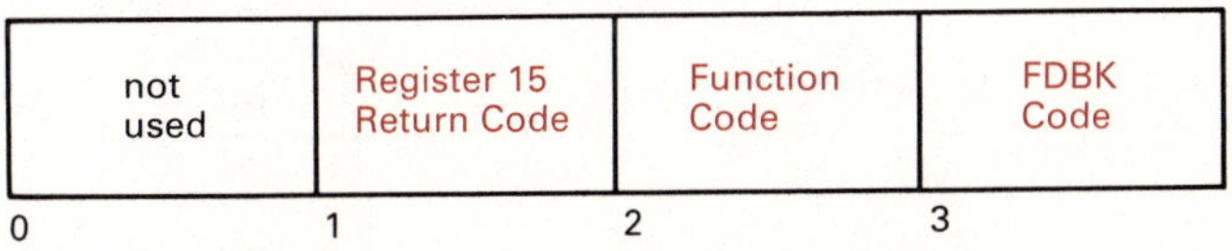

Figure 21.8 RPL feedback field contents.

that use secondary indexes. Box 21.1 shows the meanings of the codes that VSAM stores in the Function Code byte.

RETRIEVING RECORDS WITH NONUNIQUE KEYS

When a program accesses a data set via an alternate index that uses nonunique key values, the processing sometimes becomes more involved than in the previous examples. For example, suppose we have a path named INVENT.OHQUANT that uses an alternate index that indexes the inventory data set based on On-Hand-Quantity values. This allows a program to retrieve inventory records in ascending sequence according to the number of parts of each type that are in stock. The record for the part that has the fewest in stock will be retrieved first, and so on. This is an example of an alternate index that does not have unique key values. For example, it is quite possible that several inventory records might show an OHQUANT value of 10. In this case, each pointer record in the alternate index may point to several records in the inventory data set. A direct or skip-sequential GET request that supplies a given OHQUANT value retrieves the first inventory record in the data set that has that OHQUANT value.

The control block and request macros in Fig. 21.9 show how a program might retrieve all the records in the inventory data set having OHQUANT values that range from 10 to 100. The program uses an RPL that specifies skip-sequential retrieval. It begins by storing the value 10 in the OHQUANT key argument field and then issuing a POINT request. The key argument value and the KGE keyword in the RPL causes VSAM to establish a position on the first record in the data set that has an OHQUANT value that is greater than or equal to 10. The program then proceeds to retrieve records sequentially from that point until the value of the OHQUANT field in the retrieved record is greater than 100.

A program can determine whether or not there are multiple records in the base cluster that have the same key value by examining a code in the feedback

BOX 21.1 FTNCD field values

Code	Function Attempted	Status of Upgrade Set
0	Base Cluster Access	Correct
1	Base Cluster Access	May be Incorrect
2	Alternate-Index Access	Correct
3	Alternate-Index Access	May be Incorrect
4	Upgrade Processing	Correct
5	Upgrade Processing	May be Incorrect

```
//KSDS   DD   DSN=INVENT.OHQUANT,DISP=SHR



          :
         MVC     OHQUANT,=C'0010'

         POINT RPL=SEQRPL                     LOCATE FIRST RECORD
         LTR     15,15
         BNZ     ERROR
*
AGAIN    DS      OH
*
         GET     RPL=SEQRPL                   RETRIEVE RECORD SEQUENTIALLY
         LTR     15,15
         BNZ     ERROR
*
         CLC     OHQUANT,=C'0100'
         BH      DONE
          :
         (Code to process record)
          :
         B       AGAIN
          :

*
SEQRPL   RPL     ACB=KSDSACB,                                            *
                 AREA=RECORD,                                            *
                 AREALEN=200,                                            *
                 ARG=OHQUANT,                                            *
                 OPTCD=(KEY,SKP,NUP,MVE)
*
RECORD   DS      OCL200                       RECORD WORK AREA
*
PRODNO   DS      CL4                          PRODUCT NUMBER (RECORD KEY)
OHQUANT  DS      CL4                          ON HAND QUANTITY
DESCRIP  DS      CL20                         PRODUCT DESCRIPTION
PART     DS      OCL4                         PART NUMBER
*
         DS      42CL4                        ROOM FOR 42 PARTS
*
KSDSACB  ACB     DDNAME=KSDS,                                            *
                 MACRF=(KEY,SKP,IN),
          :
```

Figure 21.9 Nonunique alternate key retrieval.

field. This condition is indicated when the return code set by the GET request is zero, indicating normal completion, and the FDBK Code byte in the feedback area also contains the value 8.

ALTERNATE KEY POINTER COUNTS

When working with a data set that has multiple alternate indexes, it may be possible to use multiple search strategies to retrieve a given record. For ex-

PURCHASE ORDER

PONUMB	PRODNUMB	VENDNUMB	QUANTITY	UNPRICE
0–3	4–7	8–11	12–15	16–23

Figure 21.10 Purchase order record format.

ample, suppose we are working with a file containing purchase order records in which the prime key is a purchase order number. The format of this purchase order record is shown in Fig. 21.10. Notice that each record contains a vendor number field and a part number field, each of which is an alternate key. Note that the alternate indexes using these alternate keys each contain nonunique alternate key values; there may be many records having a particular product number and also many records having a particular vendor number.

```
          :
         MVC   PRODNUMB,INPROD           MOVE ALT KEY VALUE TO ARG
*
         GET   RPL=SEQRPL                LOCATE FIRST RECORD
         LTR   15,15
         BNZ   ERROR
*
         SHOWCB RPL=SEQRPL,              GET COUNT                     *
               AREA=RECCOUNT,                                          *
               LENGTH=4,                                               *
               FIELDS=(AIXPC)
         LTR   15,15
         BNZ   ERROR
*
          :
         (Code to examine record count in RECCOUNT field)
          :
*
SEQRPL   RPL   ACB=KSDSACB,                                            *
               AREA=RECORD,                                            *
               AREALEN=24,                                             *
               ARG=PRODNUMB,                                           *
               OPTCD=(KEY,SEQ,NUP,MVE)
*
RECORD   DS    0CL24                     RECORD WORK AREA
*
PONUMB   DS    CL4                       P. O. NUMBER   (PRIME KEY)
PRODNUMB DS    CL4                       PRODUCT NUMBER (ALT KEY)
VENDNUMB DS    CL4                       VENDOR NUMBER  (ALT KEY)
QUANTITY DS    CL4                       QUANTITY
UNPRICE  DS    CL8                       UNIT PRICE
*
RECCOUNT DS    F                         RECORD COUNT WORK AREA
*
KSDSACB  ACB   DDNAME=KSDS,                                            *
               MACRF=(KEY,SEQ,IN),
          :
```

Figure 21.11 Accessing the record count field.

Suppose we had to satisfy a request for a list of all purchase order records that reference both product number 1143 and vendor number 8888. There are two alternative methods for providing this information. The first alternative is to use the product number alternate index to sequentially retrieve all records with product number 1143, extracting only those records that also have a vendor number of 8888. The other alternative is to use the vendor number alternate index to sequentially retrieve all records with a vendor number of 8888, extracting only those records that also have a product number of 1143.

In a relatively small data set, it may make no practical difference which strategy is used. But in a very large data set, there may be many more records with vendor number 8888 than there are records with product number 1143. It may then be more efficient to sequentially access the records via the product number alternate index rather than the vendor number index. VSAM provides the information needed to choose between the two alternative search strategies. The control block and request macro coding in Fig. 21.11 shows how a program can determine the shortest search path. After a GET request for the first record having a given alternate key value, the AIXPC field in the RPL contains a count of the number of records in the base cluster that have the specified alternate key value. An initial GET request could be issued via each of the alternate indexes to determine a record count for each index. The AIXPC RPL field values can then be compared to determine which search strategy to use for a particular retrieval sequence.

22 ASSEMBLER RRDS PROCESSING

The final type of VSAM data set is the relative record data set. This chapter discusses the VSAM control block and request macro coding used in programs that process RRDS clusters. Both sequential and direct RRDS processing are discussed. An RRDS cluster always stores fixed-length records, each of which is assigned a sequential number called its *relative record number* (sometimes known as its *slot number*). Records are retrieved from an RRDS based on their relative record numbers. In many applications, the relative record number of the desired record may not be known, so a computation is often used to transform a symbolic key value into a relative record number. This process is explored in Appendix B. After an RRDS is loaded initially, some of the data set's slots may not be occupied by active records. Slots that do not contain active records contain dummy records; a slot that contains a dummy record is indicated by a record that contains hexadecimal value "FF" in its first byte.

RELATIVE RECORD I/O OPERATIONS

Only keyed access can be used to process the records in an RRDS; keyed access for an RRDS means access by relative record number, and not by symbolic key value. Any symbolic keys that are involved in processing an RRDS are handled by the application, and VSAM is not aware of them. Records can be retrieved from an RRDS either sequentially—in relative record number sequence—or directly—by supplying the relative record number of the desired record. A new record can be added to an RRDS only by specifying the relative record number of an existing dummy record; VSAM then replaces the dummy record with the new active record. Existing records can be updated in the normal manner, but their lengths cannot be changed. An existing record can be deleted by issuing an ERASE request; VSAM deletes the record by converting it to a dummy record and does not remove it physically from the data set.

RRDS LOADING

As we have seen in Chapters 19 and 20, ESDS and KSDS clusters are initially loaded sequentially using PUT requests that refer to an RPL specifying OPTCD=SEQ. RRDS clusters can be loaded either sequentially or directly using OPTCD=SEQ or OPTCD=DIR, but direct RRDS load programs are more commonly used than sequential loads. An RRDS may or may not be formatted physically with dummy records when it is defined, depending on whether the SPEED or RECOVERY parameter was specified. However, an RRDS load program always operates as if a formatted slot, containing a dummy record, already exists in the data set. So an RRDS load program can always issue direct PUT requests that specify the relative record number of the slot into which each new record is to be placed, just as if the data set is preformatted with dummy records.

An RRDS sequential load program uses the same control block and request macros that are used to sequentially load an ESDS. In performing a sequential RRDS load, it is important to realize that records are not loaded into the RRDS in sequence according to their key values. The logical sequence according to the values of any symbolic keys that might be contained in the records bears no relationship to physical sequence according to relative record numbers. This is because a hashing or randomizing algorithm generally is used, tending to scatter the records of an RRDS more or less randomly through the data set.

One technique for loading an RRDS sequentially is to use a program that reads the records to be loaded and writes out a new file of records that has the relative record number of each record attached to it. The program must use the same randomizing algorithm that will be used by programs that will later access the RRDS. The records are then sorted into relative record number sequence. Either before or after the sort, synonyms must be handled by determining alternate relative record numbers for sets of records that randomize to the same relative record number. The final sorted data set then contains a record for each slot in the RRDS that will initially contain an active record and can be read by the sequential RRDS load program. The load program must explicitly write a dummy record into each slot that will not initially contain an active record.

RRDS DIRECT LOAD

Since it is more common for an RRDS load program to load records directly, the first coding example we will look at in this chapter is for a direct load. The VSAM control block and request block coding shown in Fig. 22.1 can be used to create a direct load program that loads 100-byte records into an RRDS. Notice that the ARG parameter specifies a fullword work area that must contain the relative record number of the record being loaded. For an RRDS, VSAM assumes that a 4-byte argument will be used, so a KEYLEN parameter is not required. For an RRDS direct load program, OPTCD=NUP must be specified or implied.

Before issuing each PUT request, the program invokes a randomizing rou-

```
         :
         OPEN  (RRDSACB)                    OPEN RRDS
         LTR   15,15
         BNZ   ERROR
         :
         MVC   RECORD,INREC                 MOVE RECORD TO WORK AREA
*
         LA    1,RECKEY                     GET SYMBOLIC KEY
         BAL   14,HASH                      BRANCH TO RANDOMIZING ROUTINE
         ST    0,SLOT                       STORE SLOT NUMBER
*
         PUT   RPL=LOADRPL                  LOAD RECORD INTO DATA SET
         LTR   15,15
         BNZ   ERROR
         :
         CLOSE (RRDSACB)                    CLOSE RRDS
         LTR   15,15
         BNZ   ERROR
         :
LOADRPL  RPL   ACB=RRDSACB,                                            *
               AREA=RECORD,                                            *
               AREALEN=100,                                            *
               RECLEN=100,                                             *
               ARG=SLOT,                                               *
               OPTCD=(KEY,DIR,MVE,NUP)
*
         DS    0F
RECORD   DS    0CL100                       RECORD WORK AREA
RECKEY   DS    CL5                          SYMBOLIC KEY
         DC    CL96
*
SLOT     DS    F                            RELATIVE RECORD NUMBER
*
RRDSACB  ACB   DDNAME=RRDS,                                            *
               MACRF=(KEY,DIR,OUT)
```

Figure 22.1 RRDS direct load.

tine that transforms the symbolic key value contained in the record into the relative record number of the slot into which it belongs. The name of the randomizing routine in the example is HASH. Before invoking HASH, the program stores the address of the symbolic key value into register 1; HASH returns in register 0 the relative record number of the appropriate slot. (These conventions are not used by all randomizing routines; they simply provide an example of linkage conventions that might be used.)

For simplicity, the code in Fig. 22.1 does not show any provision for handling synonyms. In actual practice, synonyms will normally occur and must be handled by the load program. To handle synonyms, the program might test the feedback fields when a PUT request fails. A synonym occurs when the load program attempts to store a new record into a slot that already contains an active record. A simple technique for handling synonyms is to write the record into the next available slot and to store the address of that slot in a chain field provided for this purpose in the record that occupies the original slot. Notice in

Fig. 22.1 that the last four bytes of each record are reserved for use as a synonym pointer.

In order to handle synonyms in the above manner, the load program must be able to update the chain field by modifying an existing record. However, the OPTCD=UPD option is required in order to replace an existing record, and the OPTCD=NUP option is required to insert a new record into an empty slot. Since these two OPTCD values are mutually exclusive, the program might use two RPLs—one with OPTCD=NUP for loading records into empty slots and another with OPTCD=UPD for updating chain fields. Alternatively, the MODCB macro could be used to set the appropriate OPTCD value before each PUT operation.

RRDS SEQUENTIAL RETRIEVAL

Figure 22.2 shows the control block and request macros that could be used to sequentially retrieve our 100-byte RRDS records. Notice that the RPL parameters are similar to those used in performing KSDS sequential retrieval. One important difference is that the RPL for RRDS sequential retrieval must include an ARG parameter that specifies a fullword area; VSAM places the relative record number of each retrieved record into this area.

```
         :
         OPEN  (RRDSACB)                    OPEN RRDS
         LTR   15,15
         BNZ   ERROR
         :
         GET   RPL=SEQRPL                   RETRIEVE SEQUENTIALLY
         LTR   15,15
         BNZ   ERROR
         :
         CLOSE (RRDSACB)                    CLOSE RRDS
         LTR   15,15
         BNZ   ERROR
         :
SEQRPL   RPL   ACB=RRDSACB,                                            *
               AREA=RECORD,                                            *
               AREALEN=100,                                            *
               RECLEN=100,                                             *
               ARG=SLOT,                                               *
               OPTCD=(KEY,SEQ,NUP,MVE)
*
RECORD   DS    0CL100                       RECORD WORK AREA
RECKEY   DS    CL5                          SYMBOLIC KEY
         DC    CL95
*
RRDSACB  ACB   DDNAME=RRDS,                                            *
               MACRF=(KEY,SEQ,IN)
```

Figure 22.2 RRDS sequential retrieval.

During sequential RRDS retrieval, records are read only from slots that contain active records; VSAM automatically bypasses dummy records.

RRDS DIRECT RETRIEVAL

Figure 22.3 shows the control block and request macro coding for a program that performs RRDS direct retrieval. The only difference in the control block macro parameters from the previous example is that the ACB MACRF parameter and the RPL OPTCD parameter specify DIR instead of SEQ. The randomizing routine is then used to convert a symbolic key value into a relative record number. The relative record number is stored in the area specified in the RPL ARG parameter before each GET is issued. This program shows how synonyms can be handled using the simple chaining technique described for the RRDS direct load example above.

```
         :
         LA    1,INKEY                       GET SYMBOLIC KEY
         BAL   14,HASH                       BRANCH TO RANDOMIZING ROUTINE
         ST    0,SLOT                        STORE SLOT NUMBER
*
REPEAT   GET   RPL=RRPL                      RETRIEVE RECORD DIRECTLY
         LTR   15,15
         BNZ   ERROR
*
         CLC   RECKEY,INKEY                  CHECK FOR SYNONYM
         BE    FOUND
*
         MVC   SLOT,SYNPTR                   MOVE SYNONYM PTR TO SLOT NO.
         B     REPEAT                        RETRIEVE NEXT RECORD IN CHAIN
*
FOUND    DS    0H
         :
         (Code to process record.)
         :
RRPL     RPL   ACB=RRDSACB,                                                *
               AREA=RECORD,                                                *
               AREALEN=100,                                                *
               RECLEN=100,                                                 *
               ARG=SLOT,                                                   *
               OPTCD=(KEY,DIR,NUP,MVE)
*
         DS    0F
RECORD   DS    0CL100                        RECORD WORK AREA
RECKEY   DS    CL5                           SYMBOLIC KEY
         DC    CL91
SYNPTR   DS    F                             POINTER TO NEXT REC IN CHAIN
*
SLOT     DS    F                             RELATIVE RECORD NUMBER
INKEY    DS    CL5                           SYMBOLIC KEY OF DESIRED RECORD
*
RRDSACB  ACB   DDNAME=RRDS,                                                *
               MACRF=(KEY,DIR,IN)
```

Figure 22.3 RRDS direct retrieval.

After each direct retrieval, the program compares the symbolic key value in the record to the symbolic key value originally passed to the randomizing routine. If these key values are equal, the desired record has been retrieved. If these key values are not equal, a synonym situation probably exists. The program then uses the chain field in the retrieved record to retrieve the next record in the synonym chain.

The error-checking code would examine both the return code set by the GET and the contents of the third byte of the RPL feedback field (the FDBK Code byte) to determine the specific error that occurred. Procedures for exam-

```
         :
         LA    1,INKEY                    GET SYMBOLIC KEY
         BAL   14,HASH                    BRANCH TO RANDOMIZING ROUTINE
         ST    0,SLOT                     STORE SLOT NUMBER
*
REPEAT   GET   RPL=RRPL                   RETRIEVE RECORD DIRECTLY
         LTR   15,15
         BNZ   ERROR
*
         CLC   RECKEY,INKEY               CHECK FOR SYNONYM
         BE    FOUND
*
         MVC   SLOT,SYNPTR                MOVE SYNONYM PTR TO SLOT NO.
         B     REPEAT                     RETRIEVE NEXT RECORD IN CHAIN
*
FOUND    DS    0H
         :
         (Code to update record.)
         :
         PUT   RPL=URPL                   WRITE RECORD BACK TO DATA SET
         LTR   15,15
         BNZ   ERROR
         :
URPL     RPL   ACB=RRDSACB,                                            *
               AREA=RECORD,                                            *
               AREALEN=100,                                            *
               RECLEN=100,                                             *
               ARG=SLOT,                                               *
               OPTCD=(KEY,DIR,UPD,MVE)
*
         DS    0F
RECORD   DS    0CL100                     RECORD WORK AREA
RECKEY   DS    CL5                        SYMBOLIC KEY
         DC    CL91
SYNPTR   DS    F                          POINTER TO NEXT REC IN CHAIN
*
SLOT     DS    F                          RELATIVE RECORD NUMBER
INKEY    DS    CL5                        SYMBOLIC KEY OF DESIRED RECORD
*
RRDSACB  ACB   DDNAME=RRDS,                                            *
               MACRF=(KEY,DIR,IN,OUT)
         :
```

Figure 22.4 RRDS direct update.

ining the RPL feedback area were discussed in Chapter 19. Two specific error conditions are particularly useful in implementing synonym handling.

When the return code is equal to 8 and the RPL FDBK code is equal to hexadecimal 16, a record-not-found condition has occurred. For an RRDS, this indicates that the requested slot contains a dummy record. When the return code is equal to 8 and the RPL FDBK code is equal to hexadecimal CO, VSAM has detected an invalid relative record number. This indicates that the specified slot number was outside the range of relative record numbers defined for the data set.

```
         :
         LA    1,INKEY                       GET SYMBOLIC KEY
         BAL   14,HASH                       BRANCH TO RANDOMIZING ROUTINE
         ST    0,SLOT                        STORE SLOT NUMBER
*
REPEAT   GET   RPL=RRPL                      RETRIEVE RECORD DIRECTLY
         LTR   15,15
         BNZ   ERROR
*
         CLC   RECKEY,INKEY                  CHECK FOR SYNONYM
         BE    FOUND
*
         MVC   SLOT,SYNPTR                   MOVE SYNONYM PTR TO SLOT NO.
         B     REPEAT                        RETRIEVE NEXT RECORD IN CHAIN
*
FOUND    DS    0H
         :
         (Code to update record.)
         :
         PUT   RPL=URPL                      WRITE RECORD BACK TO DATA SET
         LTR   15,15
         BNZ   ERROR
         :
URPL     RPL   ACB=RRDSACB,                                                *
               AREA=RECORD,                                                *
               AREALEN=100,                                                *
               RECLEN=100,                                                 *
               ARG=SLOT,                                                   *
               OPTCD=(KEY,DIR,UPD,MVE)
*
         DS    0F
RECORD   DS    0CL100                        RECORD WORK AREA
RECKEY   DS    CL5                           SYMBOLIC KEY
         DC    CL91
SYNPTR   DS    F                             POINTER TO NEXT REC IN CHAIN
*
SLOT     DS    F                             RELATIVE RECORD NUMBER
INKEY    DS    CL5                           SYMBOLIC KEY OF DESIRED RECORD
*
RRDSACB  ACB   DDNAME=RRDS,                                                *
               MACRF=(KEY,DIR,IN,OUT)
```

Figure 22.5 RRDS direct deletion.

RRDS UPDATE AND DELETE OPERATIONS

As with other types of VSAM data sets, RRDS records can be updated either sequentially or directly. In order to update or delete an RRDS record, it must first be retrieved using an RPL that specifies OPTCD=UPD. A PUT request using that same RPL causes the record to be written back into the data set; and an ERASE request using that RPL causes the record to be deleted. As mentioned earlier, VSAM deletes an RRDS record by converting it into a dummy record. Figures 22.4 and 22.5 show the control block and request macro coding to handle RRDS direct update and delete operations. Sequential updates and deletes are handled in a similar manner, but are not often used with RRDS clusters.

RRDS record insertions are handled in a different manner from KSDS record insertions. Figure 22.6 shows the control block and request macro coding to handle an RRDS direct record insertion operation. A PUT request that inserts a new record into an empty slot need not be preceded by a GET request, and the RPL must specify NUP instead of UPD. Notice that the insertion program operates in an identical manner to an RRDS direct load program and stores in the RPL key argument area the relative record number of the slot into which the new record is to be inserted. If the specified slot contains a dummy record, VSAM replaces the dummy record with the record being inserted. If the specified slot already contains an active record, the PUT request fails.

```
         :
         MVC   RECORD,NEWREC                 MOVE NEW RECORD TO WORK AREA
*
         LA    1,RECKEY                      GET SYMBOLIC KEY
         BAL   14,HASH                       BRANCH TO RANDOMIZING ROUTINE
         ST    0,SLOT                        STORE SLOT NUMBER
*
REPEAT   PUT   RPL=RRPL                      INSERT RECORD DIRECTLY
         LTR   15,15
         BNZ   ERROR
*
         :
URPL     RPL   ACB=RRDSACB,                                              *
               AREA=RECORD,                                              *
               AREALEN=100,                                              *
               RECLEN=100,                                               *
               ARG=SLOT,                                                 *
               OPTCD=(KEY,DIR,NUP,MVE)
*
         DS    0F
RECORD   DS    0CL100                        RECORD WORK AREA
RECKEY   DS    CL5                           SYMBOLIC KEY
         DC    CL91
SYNPTR   DS    F                             POINTER TO NEXT REC IN CHAIN
*
SLOT     DS    F                             RELATIVE RECORD NUMBER
*
RRDSACB  ACB   DDNAME=RRDS,                                              *
               MACRF=(KEY,DIR,OUT)
```

Figure 22.6 RRDS direct insertion.

23 DATA SET SHARING

In many applications, especially with online systems that support many terminals, it is necessary for multiple concurrently executing tasks to have access to the same VSAM data sets. VSAM implements comprehensive facilities for handling data set sharing. These supplement the locking mechanisms that are implemented by the operating system itself. In many applications, both VSAM facilities and operating system facilities must be used to control data integrity. Before we examine these facilities, we will first illustrate how a lack of proper updating controls can result in a loss of either read or write integrity of the data contained in a data set.

READ INTEGRITY

Figure 23.1 shows two programs, executing concurrently in different address spaces, each of which has access to the same VSAM data set. Each program uses its own set of I/O buffers. At point 2, Program A retrieves a record from the data set, and at point 3, Program B retrieves the same record. At point 4, Program A updates the On-Hand-Quantity field in the record and writes the new version of the record back into the data set. Notice at this point that the copy of the record in Program A's buffer and the copy of the record in the data set match, but that the copy of the record in Program B's buffer is now incorrect. This is an example of a loss of *read* integrity. However, the information in the record itself is accurate, so *write* integrity has been maintained.

WRITE INTEGRITY

Figure 23.2 shows how write integrity can be lost when two concurrently executing programs are both allowed to update the On-Hand-Quantity field. We begin with the same sequence as above. Program A retrieves a record, and Program B retrieves that

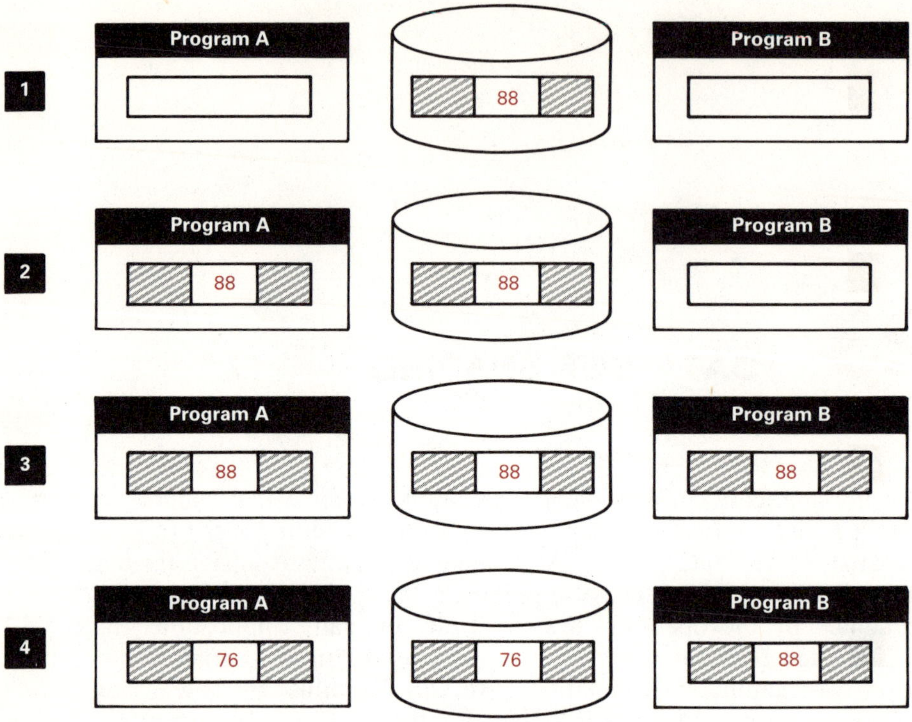

Figure 23.1 Loss of read integrity.

same record. At point 3, Program A updates the On-Hand-Quantity field by deducting 10 from it and writing a new version of the record into the file. At point 4, Program B updates the same record by deducting 5 from the same field and then writes the record back into the data set. Notice that Program B has updated the record based on the old value of the On-Hand-Quantity field. Program B is not aware of the update that has already been made, and when the record is written back into the file, the update that was made by Program A is lost. This makes the value of the On-Hand-Quantity field now stored in the data set incorrect. The value of the On-Hand-Quantity field should contain 63 to reflect the values that both Program A and Program B deducted from it.

VSAM DATA SET SHARING

There are three types of data set sharing that VSAM allows. The first form of sharing is called *subtask sharing*. In this type of sharing, two or more tasks within the same partition or address space access the same VSAM data set. When this level of sharing is used, and one task attempts to update a record in a given control interval, that task is given ownership of the buffer until the

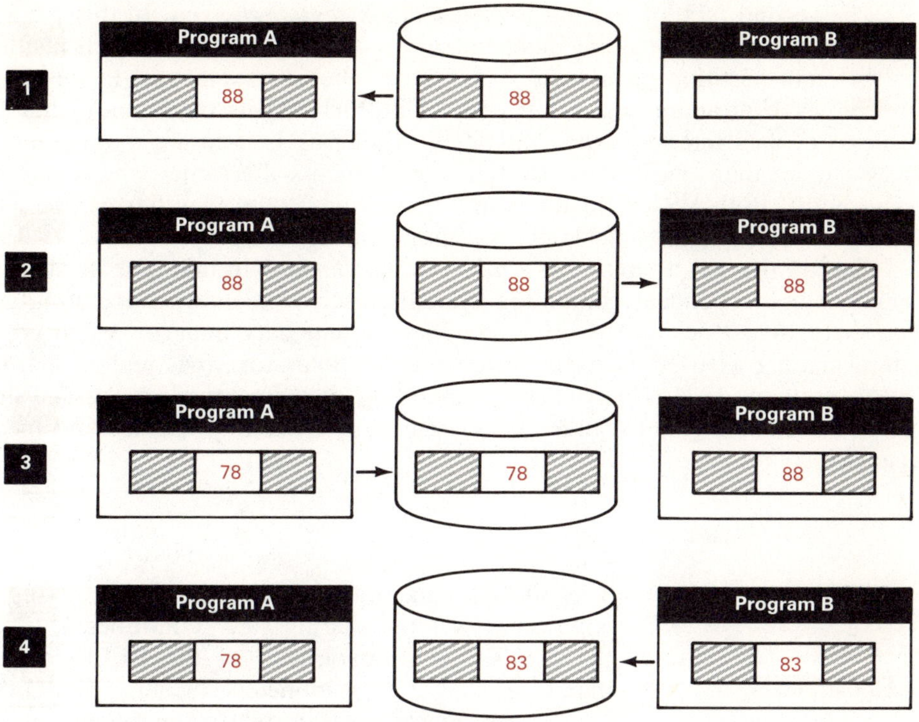

Figure 23.2 Loss of write integrity.

contents of the buffer are written back to the direct access device. During this time no other task is given update access to any of the records in that control interval. VSAM thus guarantees that write integrity is maintained. If read integrity must also be maintained, this must be handled by the application program itself. However, maintaining read integrity is easy to accomplish, since all sharing is handled within the same application program. In order to cause VSAM to properly maintain write integrity for subtask sharing, it is important to ensure that all I/O requests reference the same control block structure. This can be done in any of three ways:

- Common ACB. All I/O requests share the same control block structure if the RPLs they use all refer to the same ACB.
- Common DD Statement Names. I/O requests share the same control block structure if they all refer to ACBs that include the MACRF=DDN option (the default) and all reference the same DD statement.
- Common Data Set Names. I/O requests share the same control block structure if they all refer to ACBs that include the MACRF=DSN option and all reference DD statements that describe the same data set.

The second type of sharing is called *cross-region sharing*. In this form of data set sharing, two or more independent application programs, each residing in a different partition or address space, share the same data set. In this environment, each program has its own set of buffers and its own control blocks. Problems of data integrity when this level of sharing is used are more complex because more than one program might try to access the same control interval concurrently. Both VSAM facilities and operating system facilities can be used to maintain data integrity when cross-region sharing is used.

The third type of sharing is *cross-system sharing*. In this type of sharing, a number of independent computing systems, each with its own operating system, share the same VSAM data set. Maintaining data integrity when cross-system sharing is used is even more complex than for cross-region sharing. VSAM provides less assistance in maintaining data integrity for cross-system sharing, and the user must make heavy use of operating system locking mechanisms.

THE SHAREOPTIONS DEFINE PARAMETER

The VSAM data integrity facilities for cross-region and cross-system sharing are controlled by the SHAREOPTIONS parameter of the DEFINE command. The two subparameters of the SHAREOPTIONS parameter were introduced in Chapter 4 and are summarized in Box 23.1. As we discussed in Chapter 4, the first subparameter of SHAREOPTIONS controls the degree of sharing that is allowed across partitions or address spaces. The second controls the degree of sharing allowed across independent computing systems. Four values are valid for the crossregion subparameter; two values are allowed for the crosssystem subparameter.

In discussing the various SHAREOPTIONS subparameter values, we must differentiate between two categories of users, which we will call *read users* and *write users*. VSAM considers an application program that has opened the data set for input to be a read user; a read user can issue only GET requests. A program that has opened the data set for output is considered to be a write user; a write user can retrieve, update, add, and delete records.

Share Option 1

When share option 1 has been specified for a data set, any number of read users can access that data set. But if a write user gains access to the data set first, no other read or write users can access the data set at the same time. If an application program attempts to open a data set that is already allocated to a write user, the OPEN request fails and VSAM places a nonzero return code in register 15. The OPEN also fails for a write user if one or more read users are already

BOX 23.1 The SHAREOPTIONS subparameter of DEFINE

```
[SHAREOPTIONS(crossregion[ crosssystem]|1 3)]
```

- Share Option 1. Any number of users can share the data set if all users are only reading the data set; only one user at a time can access the data set for updating.
- Share Option 2. Any number of users can share the data set for reading, and at the same time a single user can also access the data set for updating.
- Share Option 3. Any number of users can share the data set for reading and also for updating. Share option 3 is used normally when the applications that access the data set have their own controls for maintaining data integrity; VSAM makes no attempt to ensure data integrity when this share option is specified.
- Share Option 4. Any number of users can share the data set for reading and for updating, and VSAM provides some assistance to applications in maintaining data integrity. With this share option, applications must use the ENQ and DEQ functions to control data integrity. Share option 4 is not valid for ESDS clusters.

accessing the data set when the write user issues the OPEN request. This level of sharing is the most restrictive but guarantees that all users will have access to up-to-date data.

Share Option 2

Share option 2 is less restrictive than share option 1. When share option 2 has been specified in the DEFINE command for a data set, only *one* write user at a time is allowed to open that data set. However, any number of read users can also open the data set while the write user is accessing it. With this option, VSAM ensures write integrity, but does not ensure read integrity. This means that a read user might retrieve a record just before a write user updates it. As soon as the write user stores the updated record back into the data set, the copy of the record in the read user's buffer is out of date, and that user will not be aware of it. Despite the possible loss of read integrity, this level of sharing is appropriate for some applications. For example, it may not be necessary that all users have access to data that is 100 percent up-to-date. And in some cases, the read users may not be using data fields that the write user is updating. If data will be updated and it is required that all users have access to up-to-date data, then share option 1 should be used instead of share option 2.

Share Option 3

With share option 3, all categories of users can share the data concurrently. VSAM does not provide any facilities for controlling data integrity. Because everyone has access to the same data without restriction, all the application programs that access the data set must work together and use operating system facilities, such as the ENQ and DEQ macros, to control data integrity. If appropriate controls are not implemented when this share option is used, both *read* and *write* integrity can be lost.

Share Option 4

Share option 4 is similar to share option 3. With share option 4, all users can share the data concurrently, and operating system facilities must be used by the programs to ensure data integrity. However, VSAM does provide some assistance in maintaining data integrity by refreshing the VSAM I/O buffers as required after each I/O request. After each PUT request, the affected buffers are written back to the data set. And after each GET request, the required control interval is read back into the buffer, even if a copy is already available. This ensures that the data in the buffers and the data in the data set are always in synchronization.

OPERATING SYSTEM LOCKING MECHANISMS

VSAM data integrity facilities can be used in maintaining data integrity for share options 1 and 2, but operating system locking mechanisms must be used to maintain data integrity when share option 3 or 4 is used. When operating system facilities are used to control data integrity, a record, or collection of records, is associated with a named *resource*. A lock is then placed on a record's associated resource before issuing a retrieval request for the record. Thus, a lock can be used to prevent two programs from accessing the same record at the same time.

Two types of locks can be used: *conditional* locks and *unconditional* locks. If a program requests an unconditional lock on a resource that is already locked, the program waits until the lock is removed. If a program requests a conditional lock, the program is immediately given control, but is informed if the requested resource is already locked with a return code.

When programs request locks on more than one resource at a time, it is possible to cause a situation called a *deadlock* or *deadly embrace*. A deadlock occurs when two programs request locks on resources that the other program has already locked. Since neither program can proceed until the other releases its lock, both programs wait indefinitely. The operating system generally recovers from a deadlock by abnormally terminating one of the two programs after a wait time limit has been exceeded. Deadlocks can always be avoided if all applications lock only one record at a time.

THE ENQ AND DEQ MACROS

Locks on resources are requested with the ENQ and DEQ macros. When we use the ENQ and DEQ macros to set and release locks we must name a resource that will be controlled by the lock. The ENQ macro is used to set a lock by enqueueing on a resource; the DEQ macro is used to release a lock. The ENQ and DEQ macros refer to arbitrary resources, the names of which users must agree upon. For example, if two or more users will be sharing a resource, such as a VSAM data set, those users must agree upon and use the same name in referring to a resource that controls access to the data set. The choice of a resource name is arbitrary, and need not have any relationship to the name of the data set itself. The only requirement is that all users sharing a given resource use the *same* name in referring to it.

A resource name consists of a 1- to 8-character *queue name* optionally followed by a 1- to 255-character *resource name*. If the second part is used, it is connected to the first part with a period. For example, SHARE.DATA is a valid resource name. If you are not familiar with the use of the ENQ and DEQ macros, descriptions of their parameters can be found in the manual *Supervisor Services and Macro Instructions* for your operating system version.

ENQUEUEING ON A RESOURCE

Before a VSAM entity that is being shared by others is accessed, the program must issue an ENQ macro that specifies the name of the resource that controls access to the VSAM entity. For example, suppose a number of programs will share a VSAM data set named KSDS.INVENTORY. All users may agree that access to the KSDS.INVENTORY data set will be controlled by a resource named VSAM.KSDS.INVENTORY. In this example, the queue name is VSAM and the resource name is the same as the data set name. To use a lock to control access to the KSDS.INVENTORY data set, each user might agree to issue an ENQ macro before issuing an OPEN request for the data set and to issue a DEQ request after the data set is closed. This would ensure that the data set could be opened by only one user at a time, thus ensuring both read and write integrity. Alternatively, the users might agree to issue an ENQ macro only before opening the data set for updating. This would ensure that only one user at a time would be allowed to update the data set, thus guaranteeing write integrity but not necessarily read integrity.

Notice that the use of locks on resources is dependent on cooperation among all the sharing users. If share option 3 or 4 is in effect and a program chooses to open the KSDS.INVENTORY data set for update without first issuing an ENQ macro on the appropriate resource, the data set will be opened successfully and updates will be allowed, thus potentially causing loss of write integrity.

ASSIGNING RESOURCE NAMES

In the previous example, we associated a resource name with an entire VSAM data set. This means that each time an ENQ macro was issued for the VSAM.KSDS.INVENTORY resource, all other programs will wait when attempting to issue an ENQ macro for that same resource. Such restrictive use of a locked resource might not be appropriate, especially in an online environment, in which a program might lock a resource for a long period of time.

Since resources are totally arbitrary and can be used to control access to anything, it is not necessary to assign a resource to an entire VSAM data set. For example, at the other extreme, we might associate a separate resource with each individual record in a VSAM data set. The resource name might be made up of any desired queue name, followed by a resource name that includes the key value of a specific record. The users could then cooperate by allowing any user to open the data set, but to issue an ENQ macro before retrieving an individual record from the data set. In this way a user is given exclusive control over a single record. No other user is allowed to access that same record until the first user issues a DEQ macro for the record's associated resource. Any user can, however, retrieve and update other records in the data set as required.

This approach is not without its problems, however. By assigning a different resource name to each record, it is possible for users to concurrently update records that happen to reside in the same control interval. When this happens, it is possible for one program to write the contents of the buffer back into the data set, thus nullifying the results of some other user's update. One solution to this problem is to compromise by using the KEYRANGES subparameter of the DEFINE command to define multiple key ranges for the data set, each of which can be associated with a separate resource. When multiple key ranges are specified, the records that belong to one key range will not be stored in the same control interval with the records that belong to some other key range.

ENQ/DEQ EXAMPLE

Figure 23.3 shows examples of the ENQ and DEQ macros used to enqueue on resources that have names made up of the queue name VSAM followed by a name of the form KSDS.INVENT*n*, where *n* is replaced by one of the digits from 0 through 9. We will assume that the data set associated with these resources has been divided into ten key ranges based on the first digit of the key.

After the ENQ is issued, the program tests register 15; a zero in register 15 indicates successful execution. Since no RET parameter is coded in the ENQ macro, RET=NONE is assumed making this an unconditional enqueue request.

```
         MVC    PRODNO,UPDKEY               MOVE KEY VALUE TO KEY ARGUMENT
         MVC    GENKEY,BYTE1                MOVE 1ST BYTE OF KEY TO ENQ PARM
*
         ENQ    (QUEUE,RESOURCE,E,13,SYSTEM)
         LTR    15,15
         BNZ    ERR1
*
         GET    RPL=UPDRPL                  RETRIEVE RECORD FOR UPDATING
         LTR    15,15
         BNZ    ERROR
          :
         (Code to update record in work area.)
          :
         PUT    RPL=UPDRPL                  WRITE RECORD BACK TO DATA SET
         LTR    15,15
         BNZ    ERROR
*
         DEQ    (QUEUE,RESOURCE,13,SYSTEM)
         LTR    15,15
         BNZ    ERR1
          :
UPDRPL   RPL    ACB=KSDSACB,                                           *
                AREA=RECORD,                                           *
                AREALEN=200,                                           *
                ARG=PRODNO,                                            *
                OPTCD=(KEY,DIR,UPD,MVE)
*
RECORD   DS     0CL200                      RECORD WORK AREA
*
PRODNO   DS     0CL4                        PRODUCT NUMBER (RECORD KEY)
BYTE1    DS     C                           FIRST BYTE OF PRODNO
         DS     CL3
OHQUANT  DS     CL4                         ON HAND QUANTITY
DESCRIP  DS     CL20                        PRODUCT DESCRIPTION
PART     DS     0CL4                        PART NUMBER
*
         DS     42CL4                       ROOM FOR 42 PARTS
*
QUEUE    DS     CL8'VSAM    '
RESOURCE DS     CL12'INVENT.KSDS'
GENKEY   DS     C                           FIRST BYTE OF PRODNO

*
KSDSACB  ACB    DDNAME=KSDS,                                           *
                MACRF=(KEY,DIR,IN,OUT)
          :
```

Figure 23.3 ENQ/DEQ example.

BOX 23.2 The ENDREQ macro

```
[label] ENDREQ RPL=address
```

Any nonzero condition code indicates an error condition. If the specified resource is already in use, this program will wait until the program currently using the resource issues a DEQ macro. After the update is complete, the DEQ macro releases the resource.

THE ENDREQ MACRO

When an application program issues a PUT request, either to update an existing record or to add a new record to the data set, the VSAM I/O buffers are updated accordingly. However, the changes may not always be written into the data set at the time the PUT request is issued. VSAM sometimes holds many records in its I/O buffers and defers the writing of those buffers in order to minimize the number of physical I/O operations that it makes. In some cases, however, especially when a VSAM data set is shared between multiple concurrent tasks, it is desirable to explicitly direct VSAM to write out the contents of the I/O buffers. The ENDREQ macro can be used for this purpose. The syntax of the ENDREQ macro is shown in Box 23.2; it simply refers to an RPL. When the ENDREQ macro is issued, VSAM releases exclusive control over any control intervals that it has locked, releases positioning that it may have established in the data set, and writes out the contents of the I/O buffers. Figure 23.4 shows an example of a program that issues the ENDREQ macro to write out the contents of the buffer after a group of sequential updates.

```
         :
REPEAT   DS     0H
         :
         GET    RPL=SRPL
         LTR    15,15
         BNZ    ERROR
*
         CLC    GENK1,GENK2
         BNE    FORCE
         :
         Code to update record
         :
         B      REPEAT

FORCE    ENDREQ RPL=SRPL
         LTR    15,15
         BNZ    ERROR
         :
SRPL     RPL    ACB=KSDSACB,                                          *
                AREA=RECORDS,                                         *
                AREALEN=300,                                          *
                OPTCD=(KEY,SEQ,MVE,UPD,GEN)
         :
```

Figure 23.4 The ENDREQ macro.

24 EXIT ROUTINES

As VSAM processes a data set, a number of exceptional conditions can occur that require special handling if program processing is to continue. In addition, it may be necessary to perform special processing in conjunction with certain types of I/O requests. As introduced in Chapter 18, exit routines can be used to handle these exception conditions and to perform any special processing that is required.

Box 24.1 repeats the syntax of the EXLST macro that can be used to specify the addresses of five exit routines to be executed. The A or N in each EXLST exit routine parameter indicates whether or not a specific exit routine is active (A) or not active (N). When a routine is not active, VSAM does not take the exit when the condition occurs. The N effectively neutralizes the exit. This specification can be useful while a program is being tested. Once the main program testing has been completed, the N can be changed to A so that the exit routine can be tested. It is also possible to change the N to A, or vice versa, at execution time using the MODCB macro. An L indicates that the routine exists in a partitioned data set and that it will be loaded by VSAM when it is needed. If the L is not coded, VSAM assumes that the exit routine is found in the program's load module. In addition to the five exits that can be specified in the

BOX 24.1 The EXLST macro

```
[label] EXLST  [,AM=VSAM]
               [,EODAD=address[,A|N][,L])]]
               [,JRNAD=address[,A|N][,L])]]
               [,LERAD=address[,A|N][,L])]]
               [,SYNAD=address[,A|N][,L])]]
               [,UPAD=address[,A|N][,L])]]
```

EXLST macro, two additional exits, an *exception exit* routine and a *user security verification* exit routine, can be specified in the DEFINE command for a cluster.

An exit routine can either be included, in source form, in the program that invokes it, it can exist as a separate object module and can be link-edited with the program that invokes it, or it can exist in load module form and can be loaded automatically when needed. Figure 24.1 shows the main program coding necessary to use a precoded exit routine that exists in load module form. When the L specification is used in an EXLST exit routine parameter, the EXLST macro does not define the address of the exit routine. Instead, it defines the 1- to 8-character entry point name of the exit routine. In this example, whenever the JRNAD exit is taken, VSAM fetches the load module whose entry point name is JROUT, loads it into memory (if it is not already loaded), and passes control to it.

Instead of using exits, a program can include logic to test for exceptional conditions or to perform any desired processing in conjunction with each I/O request. To test for exceptional conditions after each I/O request is issued, the program can test the value of the return code stored in register 15 and the values stored in the feedback field in the RPL.

THE LERAD EXIT

The LERAD exit is used to handle logical errors that occur during the processing of an I/O request. Logical errors generally indicate that the program requested some action that VSAM found impossible to complete. For example, a logical error occurs if a program issues a direct request for a particular record and VSAM is unable to locate the record. When a logical error occurs, VSAM passes control to the LERAD exit if one is specified in an EXLST macro referenced by the ACB. If no LERAD exit is available, VSAM passes control to the instruction following the macro that caused the logical error. VSAM indicates a logical error by storing the value 8 in register 15. It then places a specific code in the FDBK Code byte of the RPL feedback area to indicate the type of logical error that has occurred. Record-not-found is indicated by a return code value of 8 and a FDBK Code value of hexadecimal 16. A great many different types of logical errors are

```
                :
*
ACB1     ACB    DDNAME=KSDS,                                          *
                EXLST=LIST,                                           *
                MACRF=(KEY,SEQ,OUT)
*
LIST     EXLST  JRNAD=(JNAME,A,L)
JNAME    DC     CL8'JROUT'
                :
```

Figure 24.1 Using a predefined JRNAD exit routine.

possible; some common ones are listed in Box 24.2. The specific values associated with all possible logical errors are documented in the *VSAM Reference* manual for your operating system version.

THE EODAD EXIT

End-of-data normally occurs as a result of issuing a group of sequential GET requests. When a program issues a GET request, and VSAM detects end-of-file, VSAM passes control to the EODAD exit if one is specified in an EXLST macro referenced by the ACB. If no EODAD exit is specified, VSAM considers the end-of-data condition to be a form of logical error and passes control to the LERAD exit. If no EODAD or LERAD exit is available, VSAM passes control to the instruction following the GET request, stores the value 8 in register 15, and places the value 4 into the FDBK Code byte of the RPL feedback field.

THE SYNAD EXIT

A physical error normally occurs as a result of a hardware malfunction and ordinarily is not caused by a programming error. When a physical error occurs, VSAM passes control to the SYNAD exit if one is specified in an EXLST macro referenced by the ACB. If no SYNAD exit is available, VSAM passes control to the instruction following the macro that was executing when the physical error occurred. VSAM indicates a physical error by storing the value hexadecimal C in register 15. The particular type of physical error is indicated by a code in the RPL FDBK Code field. The possible codes for physical errors are shown in Box 24.3. When physical errors occur, VSAM also stores into a message area a message that

BOX 24.2 Common logical errors

Feedback Code (Hex)	Logical Error
08	Record with duplicate key already exists
0C	Key sequence error
10	Record not found
18	Volume cannot be mounted
1C	Volume cannot be extended
20	Invalid RBA
28	Not enough virtual storage available
2C	Work area not large enough
5C	No previous GET issued for PUT or ERASE

BOX 24.3 Physical errors

Feedback Code (Hex)	Physical Error
04	Read error occurred in data component
08	Read error occurred in index set
0C	Read error occurred in sequence set
10	Write error occurred in data component
14	Write error occurred in index set
18	Write error occurred in sequence set

describes the cause of the error. The contents of the message area can be accessed by issuing a SHOWCB macro that requests the contents of the RPL MSGAREA and MSGLEN fields, as in the following example:

```
SHOWCB RPL=REQRPL,                                      *
       FIELDS=(MSGAREA,MSGLEN),                         *
       AREA=MESSAGE,                                    *
       LENGTH=8
          :
MESSAGE  DS    F
LENGTH   DS    F
```

After a physical error occurs and the above SHOWCB macro is executed, the MESSAGE fullword contains the address of the message that further describes the cause of the physical error, and the LENGTH fullword contains the length of the message. The *VSAM Reference* manual for your operating system version contains detailed information about the format of the message area.

REGISTER CONVENTIONS

The register contents when the LERAD, EODAD, and SYNAD exit routines are entered are similar. The following describes the register contents for all three of the above exits:

- Reg O Unpredictable
- Reg 1 Address of the RPL for the request
- Regs 2–13 Same as when the I/O request was issued
- Reg 14 Address for passing control back to VSAM
- Reg 15 Entry point address of the exit routine

Register 15 contains the exit routine's entry point and can be used to establish initial addressability if desired. If the exit routine passes control back to VSAM via the address contained in register 14, VSAM gives control back to the program at the point at which it was interrupted. However, the exit routine may choose not to return control to VSAM using the return address in register 14. For example, with an EODAD exit, the user may wish to pass control directly to a routine that performs termination processing. A LERAD exit routine might also want to perform termination processing if it is determined that it is not possible to recover from the logical error that occurred. Since registers 2–13 are restored before the exit routine is given control, they will contain the same values they had before the request macro that invoked the exit was issued. If the exit routine is part of the same control section as the main program, these registers can be used in the same way as they are in any other part of the main program. The base registers remain set and all data areas contained in the main program remain addressable. Keep in mind, however, that if any of these registers are changed during the processing of the exit routine, and control is returned to VSAM via register 14, VSAM will again restore the registers before passing control back to the statement following the request macro that caused the exit to be invoked. So the program will not be aware of any changes to the registers that the exit routine might have made. Thus, the exit routine is free to use registers 2 through 13 in any desired way in a LERAD, SYNAD, or EODAD exit, but they cannot be used to pass parameters back to the main program.

If the exit routine intends to pass control back to VSAM via the address in register 14, it is important that the exit routine properly save and restore registers 1, 13, and 14 before issuing any macro or calling any subroutine that modifies these registers. For example, an exit routine may find it necessary to

```
                 :
SYNRTN   DS     0H
         LR     2,15
         USING  SYNRTN,2
         STM    13,14,SAVE1A
         ST     1,SAVE1A+8
         LA     13,SAVE1B
*
         SHOWCB RPL=RPL1,                                              *
                AREA=AREA1,                                            *
                FIELDS=(FDBK),                                         *
                LENGTH=4
                 :
EXIT     LM     13,14,SAVE1A
         L      1,SAVE1A+8
         BR     14
SAVE1A   DS     3F
AREA1    DS     F
SAVE1B   DS     18F
```

Figure 24.2 A SYNAD exit routine.

issue a GENCB, MODCB, SHOWCB, or TESTCB macro in the course of its processing. Since these macros modify registers 1 and 14, and use the save area that register 13 points to, the contents of these registers must be saved before issuing the macro and restored after the macro returns control to the exit routine. The exit routine must also provide a new save area and load its address into register 13 before issuing a macro that requires a save area. The save area that register 13 points to when the exit routine gains control is the same one that is provided by the main program, and it cannot be used by the exit routine. Figure 24.2 shows how registers might be handled in a SYNAD exit routine that issues a SHOWCB macro.

Four exits, in addition to the three discussed above, are available for performing special processing in conjunction with I/O requests. The following sections discuss these special-processing exits and discuss the register contents that apply to these exits.

THE JRNAD EXIT

The JRNAD exit can be used to gain control at various points during the processing of I/O requests that may cause the data set's contents to change. The most common use of the JRNAD exit is to *journalize,* or record the results of processing that may update the records in a data set. Specifically, the JRNAD routine is entered when any of the following events occurs:

- Each time a GET, PUT, or ERASE request is issued for the ACB.
- Each time data are shifted in a control interval or moved to another control interval.
- Each time an I/O event completion occurs, a shared or nonshared request is received, and the buffer contents change.
- Each time a physical I/O error occurs.

THE UPAD EXIT

The UPAD exit can be used to perform any desired user processing in conjunction with VSAM I/O requests. The UPAD exit is entered immediately prior to a WAIT function being executed that waits for the completion of a physical I/O operation. The UPAD exit is also entered when a POST function is executed in conjunction with an asynchronous processing I/O request. The UPAD exit is most often used in applications that share common data sets.

THE EXCEPTION EXIT

The exception exit routine, specified in the DEFINE command for a cluster, can be used to monitor I/O errors that are associated with a data set. When both an exception exit routine and a SYNAD routine are specified for a data set, the exception exit routine is invoked first.

THE USER SECURITY VERIFICATION EXIT

A user security verification exit routine, specified in the DEFINE command for a cluster, can be used to handle any type of security verification functions that the application requires. The user security verification exit is entered whenever the cluster is opened and a correct password, other than the master password, is supplied. The security verification routine can specify that the user be denied access to the data set based on the processing it performs.

REGISTER CONVENTIONS

For the above four exits, the contents of registers 14 and 15 are the same as for the LERAD, EODAD, and SYNAD routines; however, the contents of registers 2 through 13 for these exits are unpredictable. Since base registers for the main program are no longer set, these exits cannot assume that addressability still exists on data areas in the main program. They can, however, use the contents of register 15 to establish initial addressability and can then load their own base registers as required. Register 1 for these exits points to a parameter list that is different for each of the four exits. Detailed descriptions of the pa-

```
MAINPROG CSECT
          :
BEGIN    BALR  12,0
         USING *,12
          :
JRNRTN   DS    0H
         LR    12,15
         USING JRNRTN,12
         STM   13,12,SAVE2A
         LA    13,SAVE2B
          :
         SHOWCB RPL=(8),                                              *
               AREA=AREA2,                                            *
               LENGTH=4,                                              *
               FIELDS=(FDBK)
          :
EXIT     LM    13,12,SAVE2A
         BR    14
SAVE2A   DS    16F
SAVE2B   DS    18F
AREA2    DS    F
         USING BEGIN+2,12
```

Figure 24.3 Saving and restoring registers.

rameter lists that apply to each exit can be found in the *VSAM User's Guide* manual for your operating system version. Figure 24.3 shows techniques that can be used to handle registers in these exits using a JRNAD exit as an example. Notice that we are using register notation in the SHOWCB macro to reference the RPL. This is necessary because the label on the RPL is not addressable to the exit routine whether or not it is part of the same source module as the main program.

ASSEMBLING AND LINKING AN EXIT ROUTINE

Figure 24.4 shows an example of the JCL needed to assemble and link edit an exit routine as a separate load module. An exit routine must be defined as *reusable* by using the REUS linkage editor parameter. REUS is necessary, because without it a new copy of the exit routine will be loaded each time the exit is taken. REUS says that the module is reusable, thereby preventing the loading of multiple copies. The DD statement shown causes the linkage editor to create a PDS named EXLIB and to store the exit routine in it under the member name JROUT. Once the exit routine is stored in this way, it can be invoked by any VSAM program that has access to the EXLIB PDS if SYNAD=(JROUT,A,L) is specified in the EXLST macro.

SAMPLE JRNAD EXIT

Figure 24.5 shows the partial coding for a JRNAD exit that records before and after images of records that are updated. Each time a record is retrieved for update, the contents of the record are written to a journal data set as a *before* image. After any record is updated, deleted, or inserted, an *after* image is written. The exit gains control after each GET, PUT, or ERASE request is issued. When the JRNAD exit routine is entered, register 1 contains a pointer to a list of parameters. The first four bytes in the list contain the address of the RPL. Since we have access to the RPL, we can gain access to the work area or buffer that contains the current record. The twentieth byte of the list contains a code

```
//LINK       EXEC  ASMFCL,PARM=(XREF,LET,LIST,NCAL,REUS)
//ASM.SYSIN DD     *
JROUT     CSECT
            :
       exit routine coding
            :
          END
//LKED.SYSLMOD  DD  DSN=EXLIB(JROUT),DISP=SHR
```

Figure 24.4 Assembling and linking an exit routine.

```
          :
          L       5,0(0,1)
*
          SHOWCB  RPL=(5),
                  AREA=RECADR,
                  LENGTH=4,
                  FIELDS=(AREA)
          LTR     15,15
          BNZ     ERROR
*
          L       7,RECADR
          :
          CLI     20(1),X'00'
          BE      GETRTN
          CLI     20(1),X'04'
          BE      PUTRTN
          CLI     20(1),X'08'
          BE      ERASERTN
          :
```

Figure 24.5 A JRNAD exit routine.

indicating the type of request that was made. Following is what VSAM stores in that byte for the three types of requests that can cause the JRNAD exit routine to be entered.

GET	X'00'
PUT	X'04'
ERASE	X'08'

Notice that there is no direct way to tell if a PUT request was one that updated a record or one that inserted a new record. Figure 24.6 shows how we can use the TESTCB macro for this purpose. The TESTCB macro in the example causes VSAM to compare the OPTCD specified in the RPL with the value UPD.

```
          :
          L       5,0(0,1)
          TESTCB  RPL=(5),
                  OPTCD=UPD
          BE      UPDATERT
*
INSERTRT  DS      0H
          LTR     15,15
          BNZ     ERROR
          :
          (Code to process NUP OPTCD)
          :
UPDATERT  DS      0H
          LTR     15,15
          BNZ     ERROR
          :
          (Code to process UPD OPTCD)
          :
```

Figure 24.6 Using the TESTCB macro.

This concludes our presentation of Assembler Language techniques for working with VSAM data sets. Additional Assembler Language techniques are discussed in two of the appendices that follow. Appendix C discusses additional techniques that can be employed in Assembler Language to implement asynchronous I/O requests; Appendix D discusses programming techniques for implementing reentrant programs.

PART VI APPENDICES

Appendix

A PROCESSING ISAM DATA SETS

VSAM key-sequenced data sets have many features in common with the data sets that are processed by the older indexed-sequential access method (ISAM). In general, ISAM provides a subset of the features supported by VSAM. The first step in converting an application system from ISAM to VSAM is to use the AMS REPRO command to convert the ISAM data sets into their VSAM KSDS equivalents. The following example shows how this can be done:

```
//CONVERT      EXEC  PGM=IDCAMS
//SYSPRINT     DD    SYSOUT=A
//ISAM         DD    DSN=EMPLOYEE.ISAM,DISP=OLD
//VSAM         DD    UNIT=3380,VOL=SER=DSK001,DISP=OLD
//SYSIN        DD    *
  DEFINE CLUSTER
         (NAME           (EMPLOYEE.KSDS)                  -
          KEYS           (0  4)                           -
          VOLUMES        (DSK001)                         -
          CYLINDERS      (10 1)                           -
          RECORDSIZE     (26 26)                          -
          FREESPACE      (25 25))
  REPRO  INFILE          (ISAM)                           -
         ODS             (EMPLOYEE.KSDS)
```

After executing the above job step, the new EMPLOYEE.KSDS data set is an equivalent VSAM version of the old EMPLOYEE.ISAM data set.

ISAM INTERFACE

Two approaches can be used in accessing the new VSAM KSDS cluster. One method is to convert the application programs so they VSAM techniques to access the new VSAM data set. The second method is to use the *ISAM interface* feature to allow existing application programs to access the new VSAM data set. The ISAM interface feature allows a COBOL, PL/I, or Assembler Language program that accesses ISAM data sets to execute correctly when used with equivalent VSAM data sets. The ISAM interface can be used to load a data set, to retrieve data from it, and to update the records stored in it. In most cases, an existing ISAM program needs no changes in order to access an equivalent VSAM data set. The ISAM interface feature is implemented by a load module that intercepts ISAM I/O requests and converts them into their VSAM equivalents. The processing performed by the ISAM interface load module is transparent to the application program, and nothing in the program needs to be changed. When the application program opens the ISAM DCB, VSAM automatically loads the ISAM interface module and uses its services.

Since the purpose of the ISAM interface is to allow existing ISAM programs to access VSAM data sets, the feature does not support any VSAM functions that are not provided by ISAM. To take advantage of unique VSAM features, the ISAM program must be rewritten. The ISAM interface is not designed to allow the user to write *new* ISAM programs that read and write VSAM data sets. As such, the ISAM interface module assumes that the ISAM program is completely debugged and working correctly. It is difficult to debug an ISAM program that accesses a VSAM data set via the interface module. If, for some reason, it is necessary to write a new ISAM program that reads and writes VSAM data sets, the program should be tested and debugged using ISAM data sets. Once it is working properly with the ISAM data sets, the interface module can be used to allow the program to process VSAM data sets.

VSAM JCL CONSIDERATIONS

In most cases, an existing ISAM program can be used without modification when using the ISAM interface. However, the JCL must be rewritten to provide the program access to VSAM data sets rather than ISAM data sets. The following are three considerations that apply to the JCL that is used with the ISAM interface:

- **Compatible Devices.** VSAM does not support certain older direct access storage devices that are supported by ISAM. If the ISAM data set resides on a direct access device that VSAM does not support, the data set must be moved to a supported device for proper execution.
- **Cataloged Data Sets.** ISAM data sets may or may not be cataloged; VSAM data sets *must* be cataloged. If the original ISAM data set was not cataloged, the JCL must be changed to reflect access to a cataloged VSAM data set.
- **Data Set Sharing.** With both VSAM and ISAM, data sets can be shared between multiple concurrently executing jobs. However, because of the extensive data sharing facilities provided by VSAM, coding DISP=SHR in the JCL does not necessarily mean that other jobs will have access to the data set. Chapter 23 discusses VSAM data set sharing.

ISAM INTERFACE EXAMPLE

The following example shows the JCL needed to define and load a VSAM data set using an existing ISAM load program named ISAMLOAD. The input data are contained in a cataloged sequential data set named LOAD.INPUT; the data are being loaded into a new KSDS cluster named EMPLOYEE.KSDS.

```
//DEFINE       EXEC   PGM=IDCAMS
//SYSPRINT     DD     SYSOUT=A
//VSAM         DD     UNIT=3380,VOL=SER=DSK001,DISP=OLD
//SYSIN        DD     *
  DEFINE CLUSTER
           (NAME        (EMPLOYEE.KSDS)                    -
            KEYS        (0   4)                            -
            VOLUMES     (DSK001)                           -
            CYLINDERS   (10  1)                            -
            RECORDSIZE  (26  26)                           -
            FREESPACE   (40  40))
//LOAD         EXEC   PGM=ISAMLOAD
//VSAMOUT      DD     DSN=VSAM.MASTER,DISP=OLD
//DATAIN       DD     DSN=LOAD.INPUT,DISP=OLD
```

The first step in the above job runs the AMS utility program that executes a DEFINE command to create a new KSDS cluster named EMPLOYEE.KSDS. The second step executes the ISAMLOAD program to load the newly defined EMPLOYEE.KSDS cluster. Notice that nothing in the above job stream references the ISAM interface load module. This load module is automatically loaded when VSAM detects the OPEN for an ISAM DCB.

Appendix

B RRDS RANDOMIZING TECHNIQUES

RRDS records are accessed via their *relative record,* or *slot* numbers. VSAM does not provide any assistance in determining the relative record number of a desired record; this is left up to the individual application. In many applications, a *randomizing algorithm,* also called a *hashing function,* is used to determine relative record numbers; in these applications, a subroutine is used that implements a randomizing algorithm to convert a symbolic key value contained in a record into the relative record of the slot in which the record belongs. This appendix describes some commonly used randomizing algorithms that are employed with RRDS clusters.

DIRECT ADDRESSING

In some applications an RRDS cluster can be used without a randomizing algorithm. For example, the application might use a cross-reference table that stores the slot numbers of all records that need to be directly accessed. Other applications may use records that use data fields to contain relative record number or RBA addresses. The cross-reference table technique can be used with either an RRDS or an ESDS. The cross-reference table normally is built at the time the cluster is loaded. The table can then be written into a sequential file for later use by retrieval programs. To retrieve a record, a key value is used as the argument in a table lookup to determine the relative record number or RBA address of the desired record. The cross-reference table technique is well suited to small files, but when it is used with very large files, the time required to search the cross-reference table can become excessive.

When direct addresses can be used, they allow records to be very efficiently retrieved from an RRDS or from an ESDS. However, in many (if not most) RRDS applications, individual data records contain symbolic keys, such as part number or employee number, that have no direct relationship to relative record numbers. For these applications, in which cross-reference tables are not practical, a randomizing algorithm is generally employed to determine the relative record number address of each record.

SYNONYMS AND OVERFLOW RECORDS

A natural side effect of using a randomizing algorithm is that multiple symbolic key values will often produce the same relative record number address. Those records whose symbolic key values all cause the randomizing algorithm to produce the same relative record number address are called *synonyms*. Since only one record fits in each slot, all records, other than the first one that produces a given relative record number, are called overflow records. In some cases, an application may use a randomizing algorithm in conjunction with a particular combination of symbolic key values and relative record numbers such that no synonyms or overflow records occur. Such a randomizing algorithm is often called a *perfect hashing function*. Randomizing algorithms that do produce synonyms are called *standard hashing functions*. Unfortunately, perfect hashing functions are a rarity; however, if one can be found for a given application it is much preferred over a standard hashing function. We will begin our investigation of randomizing algorithms by examining perfect hashing functions.

PERFECT HASHING FUNCTIONS

Some applications use records in which a key actually contains a unique relative record number. If this field is used as the record's key, a perfect hashing function exists. The record's key is simply used directly to determine its relative record number address. When the key is used directly as the relative record number, a slot is reserved in the RRDS for every possible key value. For example, an application might use an employee number field that can contain the possible values 0 through 99. If the RRDS is defined with 100 slots, there will be a slot for every possible employee number.

It is theoretically possible to use a perfect hashing function for any symbolic key. For example, many applications in the United States use a nine-digit *social security number* value as a key. We could use a perfect hashing function on this key simply by allocating 999,999,999 slots to the data set. For 100-byte records, this would require approximately 10^{11} bytes of direct access storage space. This would be practical only if the application were required to store records for a very high percentage of all possible social security numbers—an unlikely situation. If we wished to keep track of, say, a thousand, or even a million, people based on social security numbers, our perfect hashing function would waste far too much direct access storage space.

Using a record's key value directly as a relative record number is an example of one perfect hashing function, but it is not the only one. In some cases, a simple mathematical function can be employed to produce a unique relative record number from a symbolic key. For example, suppose we have fifty records, each of which has a unique key value containing an even number ranging from 100 to 198. By dividing the key value by 2 and subtracting 100, we would produce fifty numbers that range from 0 to 49—perfectly suitable for use as relative record numbers in an RRDS having fifty slots.

STANDARD HASHING FUNCTIONS

There are many possible randomizing algorithms that can be classified as standard hashing functions, and entire books have been written about them. The one that should be used for a given application depends on many factors, including the size of the data set and the nature of the symbolic key that is used. We will next discuss some commonly used standard hashing functions, beginning with most commonly used of all: the division/remainder technique.

DIVISION/ REMAINDER

The division/remainder technique has the advantages of being both simple and also highly effective. When this technique is used, a number of slots is allocated to the data set that is somewhat greater than the number of active records that the data set is expected to contain. To convert a symbolic key value into a relative record number, we simply divide the key value by a number that is one fewer than the total number of slots that have been allocated to the data set. We then use the remainder of the division as a relative record number. The reason that this technique works is that the remainder of the division must result in a number that ranges between 0 and one fewer than the total number of slots, no matter what the values of the symbolic keys are. This technique can be used with alphabetic or alphanumeric key fields simply by treating the key value as a binary number. The division/remainder algorithm results in a more or less *random distribution* of the records throughout the file. The distribution will generally be best, and the synonyms produced will be fewest, if a number of slots is chosen that is one greater than a prime number. This allows us to divide each symbolic key value by a prime number.

The efficiency of the division/remainder technique increases as the number of slots that are allocated to the data set increases. In general, the more slots that are allocated, the fewer synonyms the algorithm produces. This is because the more dummy records that are available when a new record is added, the smaller is the likelihood that the algorithm will produce the relative record number of an occupied slot. The beauty of the division/remainder technique is that it is relatively easy to change the algorithm when the data set is made larger; we simply change the number by which the symbolic key values are divided.

DIGIT EXTRACTION

The digit-extraction technique is an example of another type of randomizing algorithm. To use digit extraction, we look for certain positions in the key field that will produce an acceptably random distribution in the range of relative record numbers that are required. We then use these selected key field positions in calculating a relative record number. We begin by determining how many slots the RRDS will contain. As an example, suppose we will store 2500 records in a data set that contains 30,000 slots, thus giving us relative record numbers that range from 00000 through 29999. Each relative record number consists of four digits that range from 0 through 9 and one digit that ranges from 0 through 2. Suppose the data set has an eight-position symbolic key. If we can find four positions in the symbolic key that have an even distribution of the digits 0 through 9 and one position that has an even distribution of the digits 0 through 2, we can use those digit positions of the key directly as relative record numbers. If we cannot find digit positions with the appropriate characteristics, we can perform some simple calculation to produce a digit having the required range. For example, it will probably not be possible to find a digit that ranges only from 0 through 2, so that digit of the relative record number will probably have to be calculated.

The problem with this method is that it is difficult to find digit positions in the symbolic key that produce only the appropriate values and also produce a suitably even spread. If digit positions without the appropriate characteristics are chosen, a great number of synonyms may result. The only way to determine if the symbolic key values in the data set have the required characteristics is to analyze the actual key values of all the records that will be stored. This can be done visually with a printout for small data sets, or a program could be used to count the occurrences of every value in every digit. Another difficulty with the digit-extraction technique is that it is impossible to change the size of the data set without reworking the entire algorithm; the digit positions that are chosen, and the values they contain, determine the range of relative record numbers that will be produced.

FOLDING

In employing the folding technique, we divide the digit position of a symbolic key value into as many groups as we wish. We then add together the values represented by all the groups in order to produce a relative record number. Suppose the key values range from 0000 to 9999 and five of our records have the following key values: 0167, 1455, 2342, 3036, and 5125. Folding the first key value into two groups gives the value 01 and 67. Adding these two values together produces a relative record number of 68. If our key values range from 0000 to 9999, the relative record numbers that this technique produces range from 000 through 198; so this technique is only of value for this particular symbolic key if we will be storing fewer than 199 records in the RRDS.

Folding the key field in other ways will produce different relative record number ranges. For example, by using one grouping of three digits and one group of a single digit, we can produce relative record numbers that range from 0000 through 1008. With larger key fields, the digits can be divided into more groups than two in order to produce various relative record number ranges. As with the digit-extraction technique, the actual key values of the records that will be stored in the data set must be analyzed to determine if the folding technique will be useful for a particular symbolic key. Also, as with digit extraction, the folding technique that is chosen locks in the size of the data set. In order to change the number of slots that must be allocated, the entire algorithm must be reworked.

HANDLING OVERFLOW RECORDS

Overflow records are a result of all standard hashing functions. We next examine a few common techniques that can be employed to handle overflow records. The simplest way to handle overflow records is to simply store them in the next available slot when synonyms occur. Then, when a retrieval is made that reads a record that does not have the correct symbolic key value, the retrieval program simply begins reading records sequentially until the one with the correct symbolic key value is located.

One problem with this technique is that should the retrieval program request a record that is not in the data set, it could, in the worst case, initiate a sequential search of the entire file to determine that the record does not exist. To prevent this, a limit is generally set, and a program that loads the RRDS or inserts a new record does not store an overflow record in a slot that is farther than a certain number of records beyond its home slot. Then retrieval programs use this same limit in searching for a record. Some alternative technique must be used for handling those (hopefully few) synonym records that cause the limit to be exceeded. The disadvantage of the next available slot technique is that it gives poor retrieval performance when records are stored in slots that are far from their home slots. Retrieval performance can be increased by combining next available lot with a chaining technique.

OVERFLOW CHAINS

To use the chaining technique, we increase the size of each record to provide room for a relative record number chain field. Then, when we add each new overflow record to the RRDS, we store into the chain field in the record contained in the home slot the relative record number of the slot into which we stored the overflow record. An advantage of the chaining technique is that if the chain field contains a null value, the retrieval program knows immediately that no overflow record has been stored for the retrieved slot, and so knows that the desired record does not exist.

A disadvantage to the chaining technique when used in conjunction with the next available slot method is that when *spiraling overflows* occur, chains can sometimes get quite long. Spiraling overflows occur when a program attempts to insert a new record into a slot that contains a record that is itself an overflow record. One way to reduce the occurrence of spiraling overflows is to load the RRDS using two passes. On the first pass, records are loaded only into their home slots. Overflow records are written into a temporary file and then inserted into the RRDS after the first pass has been completed. This process generally results in a greater percentage of records initially being in their home slots and reduces the initial number of synonyms.

Chaining overflow records can be inefficient if the overflow chains become long. To retrieve an overflow record that happens to be at the end of a long chain, all preceding records in the chain must be retrieved first. Overflow chains also increase the complexity of delete operations. Deleting an overflow record requires that all records that precede it in the chain first be retrieved. The chain field in the record that precedes it must then be updated after the overflow record is deleted. Deleting a record that is in its home slot, but that has overflow records chained to it, also requires complex processing. The most commonly used technique for this is to move the first record in the overflow chain into the home slot after the original home record is deleted.

OVERFLOW CROSS-REFERENCE TABLES

One way to reduce the number of retrievals that are required in retrieving overflow records is to use a cross-reference table to keep track of the location of overflow records. It may be impractical to use a cross-reference table for every record in the file, but a table can often be used only to maintain overflow records. The cross-reference table can be created as the RRDS is loaded and can be implemented in any desired way. A sequential file could be used if the table will be short and will be loaded into virtual storage when its associated RRDS is opened. A KSDS might be used if the table is expected to be long and will not be entirely loaded into virtual storage. As each synonym occurs, the overflow record can be placed into any desired slot, possibly using the next available record technique, and its symbolic key value and relative record number can be stored in the cross-reference table. The table can then be used by any program that accesses the RRDS to quickly locate overflow records. When a program retrieves a record and finds that the symbolic key of the record does not match the key of the desired record, the program consults the overflow cross-reference table to determine the relative record address of the slot into which the overflow record has been stored. The table lookup technique that is used is determined by how the table is implemented. If the key value is not in the overflow table, the program knows immediately that the record does not exist. A maximum of two retrievals is required (assuming that the cross-reference table fits in virtual storage) to retrieve any record.

SEPARATE OVERFLOW AREAS

All the techniques discussed above assume that a variation of the next available slot technique is used to locate an available slot for an overflow record. An alternative to this technique is to use a separate part of the RRDS, or even an entirely separate cluster, for overflow records, rather than keeping them with the records that are stored in their home slots. For example, if it is expected that the randomizing routine will produce relative record numbers in the range of from 0000 to 9999, the data set might be created with, say, 12,000 slots. Then slot numbers 10,000 through 11,999 might be used exclusively for the storage of overflow records. A separate overflow area can be used to supplement other techniques in order to reduce the length of overflow chains or to handle records that exceed the limit that has been set for sequential searching when the next available slot method is used.

CHOOSING A RANDOMIZING ALGORITHM

A good randomizing algorithm should spread the records evenly over the available space and should minimize the number of synonyms that occur. When possible, a perfect hashing function should be used, since it will produce no synonyms and thus require no provision for handling overflow records. When it is not practical to use a perfect hashing function, the division/remainder algorithm should be considered next; it usually provides a good distribution of records over any desired number of available slots. Other techniques, such as digit extraction or folding, can be used if the symbolic key values lend themselves to these techniques. A cross-reference table can be effective for small files. However, searching the table for every retrieval can become time-consuming for files of more than a few hundred records.

The most important criterion to be used in selecting a randomizing algorithm and overflow technique is retrieval speed, and the factor that most influences retrieval speed is the percentage of synonyms, and thus overflow records, that occur. As a rule of thumb, 80 percent of the records in an RRDS should ordinarily be stored in their home slots, with 20 percent or fewer being stored in overflow slots. With most randomizing algorithms, increasing the number of available slots has the effect of reducing the percentage of synonyms that occur. If we allocate exactly as many slots as are required to store all of the records, the chances are slim of finding an algorithm that will produce only 20 percent synonyms. But by allocating more space than is required, we can reduce the number of synonyms to any desired level. As another rule of thumb, approximately 20 percent additional slots should be allocated just for the purpose of reducing synonyms, with additional slots added for future growth. In general, if a randomizing algorithm produces fewer than 20 percent synonyms with 20 percent additional space allocated, the algorithm is performing well. If the algorithm produces more synonyms or requires more additional space, a better algorithm should probably be sought.

Appendix

C ASYNCHRONOUS PROCESSING

When a task makes a conventional VSAM request, such as GET or PUT, the task is placed into the wait state until the operation is completed. An RPL option can be specified, however, that allows the task to continue processing asynchronously while the I/O operation is executing. For example, suppose the program uses two RPLs to access records from two different key ranges. If the application requires that both records must be available before continuing, the program might issue both GET requests and allow them to execute concurrently. Figure C.1 shows an example of the control block and request macros that could be used to initiate asynchronous I/O requests. Notice that RPL1 specifies ASY as one of its options. This causes VSAM to initiate the retrieval request and immediately return control to the program. RPL2 has specified the default option SYN, which causes the task to be placed into the wait state until the operation is completed. With this code, both GET requests will execute concurrently. The execution of the second GET causes the task to wait until its record is retrieved; the CHECK macro refers to the first RPL and ensures that the task will wait until the record retrieved by the first GET is available, if that I/O operation is not completed before the second GET request completes.

ERROR CHECKING FOR ASYNCHRONOUS REQUESTS

The error checking carried out immediately after an asynchronous request must be different from that used after a synchronous request. After an asynchronous request, register 15 will be zero if VSAM accepts the request and 4 if the request is not accepted. A 4 indicates that the RPL mentioned in the request is currently in use for a previously issued asynchronous request. One action that is often taken when this error occurs is to issue a CHECK macro for the RPL and then reissue

```
         :
         (Obtain key value)
          MVC    KEY1, key value
          GET    RPL=RPL1
          LTR    15,15
          BNZ    ERROR1
         (Obtain another key value)
          MVC    KEY2, key value
          GET    RPL=RPL2
          LTR    15,15
          BNZ    ERROR2
          CHECK  RPL=RPL1
          BNZ    ERROR3
         :
RPL1      RPL    ACB=ACB1,                                              *
                 OPTCD=(KEY,IN,ASY,DIR),                                *
                 ARG=KEY1,

RPL2      RPL    ACB=ACB2,                                              *
                 OPTCD=(KEY,IN,SYN,DIR),                                *
                 ARG=KEY2,
         :
```

Figure C.1 Asynchronous processing.

the request. It is not ordinarily useful to examine the RPL's feedback field immediately after an asynchronous request is issued because it is likely that the I/O operation has not yet completed. The return code check and examination of feedback field contents should be done *after* a subsequent CHECK macro has been issued.

Instead of issuing a CHECK macro, which causes the task to wait for I/O completion, the program could issue the TESTCB macro to determine if the request is completed or not. The IO=COMPLETE parameter of TESTCB can be issued for this purpose. It tests the specified RPL to see if the most recent I/O request issued for it is complete. An equal condition code setting in the PSW indicates a completed request.

Appendix

D REENTRANT PROGRAMMING

There are several ways that a load module can be executed. For example, it can be named in an EXEC statement or it might be brought into storage explicitly through the use of a LINK, XCTL, LOAD, or ATTACH macro. When a request for a load module is made, a new copy of the module may or may not have to be brought into virtual storage. Before loading the module, the operating system first determines if there is already a copy of the module in virtual storage; if none is found, the module is loaded. However, if there already is a copy of the module in an area of virtual storage that the task has access to, the operating system examines the reusability attribute of the module to determine if that copy can be used. The module can be flagged as either *not reusable, serially reusable,* or *reentrant*.

- **Non-reusable Load Modules.** If the module is flagged as not reusable, the existing copy cannot be used and a new copy of the module is loaded.
- **Serially Reusable Load Modules.** If the module is flagged as serially reusable, the existing copy can be used and no new copy is loaded. However, the task requesting the module is not necessarily given control immediately. If another load module is currently executing the program, the task will be placed in the wait state until the first program is finished.
- **Reentrant Programs.** With a reentrant program, any task requesting a module is given control immediately. With a reentrant program, multiple tasks can concurrently execute the program's instructions.

SPECIFYING REUSABILITY ATTRIBUTES

The reusability attribute of a module is specified when the module is link-edited. If no reusability attribute is specified, the load module is marked as non-reusable. The RENT option in the following linkage editor EXEC statement causes the load module to be marked as reentrant:

```
//LINK   EXEC   PGM=IEWL,PARM=(XREF,LET,LIST,NCAL,RENT)
```

The REUS option in the following EXEC statement causes the load module to be marked serially reusable:

```
//LINK   EXEC   PGM=IEWL,PARM=(XREF,LET,LIST,NCAL,REUS)
```

THE GETMAIN MACRO

The only requirement in designing a serially reusable program is to ensure that all data items that the program modifies are properly initialized upon entry to the program. Designing a reentrant program, however, is more difficult. A reentrant program is one that does not modify any of its own instructions or data areas. Any data areas that are modified by a task that executes a reentrant program must be in an area of virtual storage that is owned by the task. The GETMAIN macro is generally used to assign one or more unique storage areas to each task that enters the program. This technique allows any number of tasks to concurrently execute the same instructions without causing the tasks to interfere with one another. For example, most programs must provide an 18-word save area to be used by routines that it calls. A reentrant program must provide a separate save area for each task that enters it. The following reentrant entry linkage code establishes a save area using the GETMAIN macro:

```
RENT     CSECT
BEGIN    SAVE    (14,12)
         USING   BEGIN,12
         LR      12,15
         GETMAIN R,LV=72
         ST      13,4(0,1)
         ST      1,8(0,13)
         LR      13,1
           :
```

The GETMAIN instruction in the above example acquires a separate save area for each task that executes it. The *R* indicates that the address of the virtual storage area acquired by operating system will be placed into register one. LV indicates a request for 72 bytes of virtual storage.

REENTRANT VSAM PROGRAMS

In writing a reentrant VSAM program, each task that enters the program must generate its own copy of all the VSAM control blocks that it uses. This is required because VSAM modifies many of the fields within the control blocks as it processes I/O requests. In a reentrant program, the ACB, RPL, and EXLST macros are not used to generate control blocks at assembly time. Instead, the GENCB macro is used to generate at execution time a separate set of control blocks for each task that enters the program.

GENERATE, LIST, AND EXECUTE MACRO FORMS

Many VSAM imperative macros generate parameter lists that are modified as the macro executes. The macros that generate such parameter lists include:

- OPEN
- CLOSE
- BLDVRP
- DLVRP
- GENCB
- MODCB
- SHOWCB
- TESTCB

When the above macros are executed in a reentrant program, either the *generate* form of the macro or a combination of the *list* and *execute* forms of the macro must be used to ensure that parameter lists are located in an area of virtual storage that was acquired with GETMAIN and belongs to the task. When the generate form of a macro is executed, the macro's parameter list is generated in the specified virtual storage area and the macro's function is immediately performed. The generate form of the macro is used most often when the macro will be executed only once in the program. When a macro will be executed repeatedly, the list and execute forms of the macro are most useful. The list form of a macro simply generates the parameter list required by the macro and does not execute the macro's function. The generate form of the macro is then issued, as many times as desired, using the parameter list generated previously by the list form of the macro. We will see examples of both the generate form and the list and execute forms of imperative VSAM macros.

THE GENERATE FORM OF GENCB

The following generate form of the GENCB macro generates an RPL that can be used to retrieve records from a KSDS:

```
GENCB    MF=(G,(2),GENLEN)                                   *
         BLK=RPL,                                            *
         ACB=KSDSACB,                                        *
         AREA=RECORD,                                        *
         AREALEN=200,                                        *
         OPTCD=(KEY,SEQ,NUP,MVE)
```

The MF parameter specifies the generate form of the macro and indicates that register 2 contains the address of an area of virtual storage that can be used to contain the GENCB macro's parameter list. GENLEN can be any label; the GENCB macro equates this label to a numeric value that is equal to the length of the GENCB macro parameter list. The BLK parameter specifies that the control block to be generated is an RPL. The four remaining parameters are the same as those that would be included in an RPL macro to generate the RPL at assembly time. When the above GENCB macro is executed, VSAM acquires a block of virtual storage big enough to contain the RPL, constructs the RPL in the acquired virtual storage, and places the address of the generated control block into register 1. Individual GENCB macros can be issued, if desired, for each of the VSAM control blocks the program requires. Each one will be created in a block of virtual storage that is owned by the task that executes the GENCB macros. The program must store the value of register 1 after each execution of GENCB so the generated control blocks can later be accessed. Each generate form of the GENCB macro that is issued can share the same virtual storage area for its parameter list, since the list is generated fresh for each macro execution and is not needed again after the macro completes its processing.

In many cases, it is more desirable to execute a GETMAIN macro to acquire a single block of virtual storage and then to generate the required control blocks in that preacquired virtual storage block. The following GENCB macro shows three additional parameters that are useful for generating control blocks in a preacquired area:

```
GENCB   BLK=RPL,                                              *
        ACB=KSDSACB,                                          *
        AREA=RECORD,                                          *
        AREALEN=200,                                          *
        OPTCD=(KEY,SEQ,NUP,MVE),                              *
        WAREA=(3),                                            *
        LENGTH=200,                                           *
        COPIES=3
```

The WAREA parameter specifies that register 3 contain the address of the virtual storage area into which VSAM should build the RPL, and the LENGTH parameter specifies the length of WAREA. The LENGTH value must specify an amount of virtual storage that is big enough to hold the control block that is being generated. The COPIES parameter can be used to generate multiple copies of the control block.

The SHOWCB macro can be used to determine the length of each control block that is to be generated. Again, in a reentrant program, either a generate form of the macro or a combination of the list and execute forms must be used so that the parameter list is constructed in an area of virtual storage belonging to the task. The following SHOWCB macro determines the length of an RPL and places the length into register 4:

```
SHOWCB   MF=(G,(2)),                                *
         FIELDS=(RPLLEN),                           *
         AREA=(4),                                  *
         LENGTH=4
```

LIST AND EXECUTE MACRO FORMS

As mentioned earlier, the generate form of a macro is most useful for those macros, such as GENCB, that are executed once, possibly during program initialization, and are not executed again. Other macros, such as MODCB or TESTCB, might be executed repeatedly by the program. A combination of the list and execute forms of the macro is more efficient than generate for these types of macros.

The following MODCB macro is an example of the list form of that macro:

```
MODCB MF=(L,(2)),                                        *
      RPL=(3),                                           *
      OPTCD=SEQ
```

The MF parameter specifies the list form of the macro and indicates that register 2 contains the address of the virtual storage area into which the macro's parameter list should be placed.

The following execute form of the MODCB macro executes the function specified in the above list form of the macro:

```
MODCB MF=(E,(2))
```

This time the MF parameter specifies the execute form of the macro and indicates that register 2 contains the address of the parameter list to be used in performing the macro's function. Assuming that register 2 contains the address of the parameter list built by the previous list form of the macro, the OPTCD parameter of the RPL, whose address is contained in register 3, will be changed to OPTCD=SEQ.

REENTRANT VSAM PROGRAM EXAMPLE

Figure D.1 shows some of the storage areas for a reentrant VSAM program. We are using a DSECT to define the storage area that will be acquired with a GETMAIN macro. The DSECT shown defines labels for fields that are modified by tasks that execute this program. A single GETMAIN is executed that acquires all the storage needed. The OPEN macro shows one method for implementing a reentrant OPEN macro. The list form of OPEN generates an OPEN parameter list (one fullword) in storage belonging to the program. Later we will see that the program moves this parameter list to a storage acquired by GETMAIN before executing the execute form of OPEN to

```
                :
*
*        OPEN PARAMETER LIST
*
IOPEN    OPEN     (OPENLIST),MF=L
OPENLIST DS       F
                :
*
*        DSECT TO DESCRIBE ACQUIRED STORAGE
*
SAREA    DSECT
FIRST    EQU      *
ACBADDR  DS       F                     ADDRESS OF ACB
RPLADDR  DS       F                     ADDRESS OF RPL
OPENPARM DS       XL(DUMMY-IOPEN)       OPEN PARAMETER LIST
WORKAREA DS       CL100                 RECORD WORK AREA
RGENCB1  DS       XL(ACBLEN)            ACB AREA
RGENCB2  DS       XL(RPLLEN)            RPL AREA
                :
LAST     DS       0H
         END
```

Figure D.1 Reentrant program storage areas.

actually perform the open processing. The fullwords labeled ACBADDR and RPLADDR are reserved to hold the addresses of the ACB and the RPL that will be generated. The RGENCB1 and RGENCB2 areas will hold the parameter lists used by the generate forms of GENCB that will be used to generate an ACB and an RPL. The ACBLEN and RPLLEN labels will be equated by GENCB to the lengths of those parameter lists. The label LAST is included at the end of the DSECT for the purpose of calculating the total length of the storage area to be acquired.

Figure D.2 shows part of the program's executable code. Notice that a GETMAIN macro is issued that acquires enough virtual storage to contain all of the storage areas defined in the DSECT. After storage is acquired, an LR instruction and a USING statement establish addressability on all the labels in the DSECT. Next come two generate forms of the GENCB macro that generate an ACB and an RPL in the acquired storage area. In this example the addresses of the remote areas that are set aside for the GENCB parameter lists are specified in the form of S-type address constants. The use of S-type address constants is necessary here because the labels RGENCB1 and RGENCB2 are in the DSECT. Notice that the ACB parameter value in the RPL is specified as an *indirect* S-type address constant. This is because the label ACBADDR is in the DSECT, and the ACBADDR fullword contains the address of the ACB; the label does not refer to the ACB itself. Before opening the ACB, the parameter list generated previously by the list form of the OPEN macro is moved to a field in the acquired virtual storage area, and the address of that field is loaded into register 5. The execute form of the OPEN macro is then issued to open the

```
          :
*
*              ACQUIRE STORAGE AREA FOR TASK
*
         LA    8,FIRST-LAST
         GETMAIN R,LV=(8)
         LR    3,1
         USING SAREA,3
*
*              GENERATE ACB AND STORE ADDRESS
*
         GENCB MF=(G,(S,RGENCB1),ACBLEN),                              *
               BLK=ACB,                                                *
               DDNAME=DS1,                                             *
               MACRF=(IN,SEQ)
         LTR     15,15
         BNZ     ERROR
         ST    1,ACBADDR
*
*              GENERATE RPL AND STORE ADDRESS
*
         GENCB MF=(G,(S,RGENCB2),RPLLEN)
               BLK=RPL,
               ACB=(*,ACBADDR),
               AREA=(5,WORKAREA),
               AREALEN=100,
               OPTCD=(SEQ,MVE),
         LTR     15,15
         BNZ     ERROR
         ST    1,RPLADDR
*
*              MOVE OPEN PARMS TO ACQUIRED STORAGE AND ISSUE OPEN
*
         MVC   OPENPARM,OPENLIST
         L     2,ACBADDR
         LA    1,OPENPARM
         OPEN  ((2)),MF=(E,(1))
         LTR   15,15
         BNZ   ERROR
*
*              ISSUE GET REQUEST FOR RECORD RETRIEVAL
*
         L     1,RPLADDR
         GET   RPL=(1)
          :
```

Figure D.2 Reentrant program executable code.

ACB. Notice that no special handling is required for the GET macro, which is always reentrant.

If we include the RENT option when a module is assembled, the assembler checks the program to ensure that we have not inadvertently included any instructions that cause the program to modify itself. This is shown below:

```
//STEP 2  EXEC  ASMFCLG,PARM.ASM=(RENT,NODECK,LOAD)
```

Appendix

E COMMAND AND STATEMENT SYNTAX DESCRIPTIONS

Throughout this book, we have included syntax diagrams and parameter descriptions for commands and statements that are used in working with VSAM. For ease of reference, these syntax diagrams and parameter descriptions are repeated here. This appendix repeats the commands and statements in alphabetical order within the following groupings:

- AMS commands
- COBOL statements
- PL/I statements
- Assembler Language macros

AMS COMMANDS

The ALTER Command

```
ALTER    [NEWNAME(newname)]
         [ADDVOLUMES(volser[ volser...])]
         [REMOVEVOLUMES(volser[ volser...])]
         [INHIBIT|UNINHIBIT]
         [NULLIFY(
             [AUTHORIZATION(MODULE|STRING)]
             [CODE]
             [CONTROLPW]
             [EXCEPTIONEXIT]
             [MASTERPW]
             [OWNER]
             [READPW]
             [RETENTION]
             [UPDATEPW]
         [additional DEFINE command parameters]
```

NEWNAME

The NEWNAME (NEWNM) parameter is the counterpart of the DEFINE command NAME subparameter and is used to change the name of the object being altered.

ADDVOLUMES

The ADDVOLUMES (AVOL) parameter is the counterpart of the DEFINE command VOLUMES subparameter and is used to specify additional volumes that can be used if the object needs additional space.

REMOVEVOLUMES

The REMOVEVOLUMES (RVOL) parameter is used to remove a volume from the list of available volumes. If the volume already contains part of the data set, the volume is not removed from the list.

INHIBIT | UNINHIBIT

The INHIBIT (INH) and UNINHIBIT (UNINH) parameters specify whether or not a data set is to be accessible by read operations.

NULLIFY

The NULLIFY (NULL) parameter is used to remove protection options that are currently in effect for the object. The AUTHORIZATION, CODE, EXCEPTIONEXIT, OWNER, RETENTION, and passwords of a data set can be removed using NULLIFY.

The BLDINDEX Command

```
BLDINDEX {INFILE(ddname[/password])|
            INDATASET(entryname[/password])}
         {OUTFILE(ddame[/password]
            [ ddname[/password]...])|
            OUTDATASET(entryname[/password
              [ entryname[/password]...])}
         [EXTERNALSORT|INTERNALSORT]
         [WORKFILES(ddname ddname)]
         [CATALOG(catname[/password])]
```

INFILE

The INFILE (IFILE) parameter identifies a DD statement that describes the base cluster or a path that points to the base cluster.

INDATASET

The INDATASET (IDS) parameter names the base cluster or a path that points to the base cluster.

OUTFILE

The OUTFILE (OFILE) parameter identifies a DD statement that describes the alternate index being loaded. Multiple alternate indexes can be built using the same base cluster by including a DD statement for each one.

OUTDATASET The OUTDATASET (ODS) parameter names the alternate index being loaded. Multiple alternate indexes can be built by listing all of them in this parameter.

EXTERNALSORT The EXTERNALSORT (ESORT) parameter specifies that two work data sets should be created for the purpose of performing an external sort of alternate key/pointer pairs.

INTERNALSORT The INTERNALSORT (ISORT) parameter (the default) specifies that an internal sort of alternate key/pointer pairs should be performed if possible.

WORKFILES The WORKFILES (WFILE) parameter specifies the names of two DD statements that define work data sets to be used if an external sort is required. This parameter is required only if an external sort is necessary and if the names of the DD statements that define the work data sets are other than IDCUT1 and IDCUT2.

CATALOG The CATALOG (CAT) parameter specifies the name of the user catalog into which the catalog entries for the two sort work data sets are to be placed.

The DEFINE ALTERNATEINDEX Command

```
DEFINE   ALTERNATEINDEX
            (NAME(entryname)
             RELATE(entryname[/password])
             {CYLINDERS(primary[ secondary])|
               RECORDS(primary[ secondary])|
               TRACKS(primary[ secondary])}
             [UNIQUEKEY|NONUNIQUEKEY]
             [UPGRADE|NOUPGRADE]
             [optional DEFINE CLUSTER subparameters]

         [DATA
             [UNIQUEKEY|NONUNIQUEKEY]
             [optional DEFINE DATA subparameters]

         [INDEX
             [optional DEFINE INDEX subparameters]

         [CATALOG(catname[/password])]
```

NAME — The NAME parameter is used to give a name to the alternate index being defined.

RELATE — The RELATE (REL) parameter is required and names the base cluster corresponding to the alternate index. Although an alternate index can be created for any existing key-sequenced or entry-sequenced cluster, one cannot be defined for a relative record cluster, a reusable VSAM data set, a catalog, or another alternate index.

CYLINDERS RECORDS TRACKS — The CYLINDERS (CYL), RECORDS (REC), and TRACKS (TRK) parameters are used to allocate space to the alternate index in the same manner as space is allocated to a KSDS cluster.

UNIQUEKEY — The UNIQUEKEY (UNQK) parameter tells VSAM that there is only one base record corresponding to each alternate key in the alternate index.

NONUNIQUEKEY — The NONUNIQUEKEY (NUNQK) parameter is included if each alternate key value can be included in multiple records in the base cluster.

UPGRADE — The UPGRADE (UPG) parameter makes the alternate index part of the base cluster's upgrade set. The alternate index will then automatically be kept current whether the base cluster is updated by itself or as part of a path.

NOUPGRADE — The NOUPGRADE (NUPG) parameter prevents an automatic upgrade and should be used with caution. In certain applications, it is more efficient for the user to maintain the alternate index. But in most cases, it is better to let VSAM do an automatic index upgrade.

Additional Subparameters — Most of the optional subparameters that can be coded following the CLUSTER, DATA, and INDEX parameters when defining a KSDS cluster can also be coded following the AIX, DATA, and INDEX parameters when defining an alternate index.

The DEFINE CLUSTER Command

```
DEFINE  CLUSTER  (subparameter  [subparameter] ... [subparameter])
        [DATA    (subparameter  [subparameter] ... [subparameter])]
        [INDEX   (subparameter  [subparameter] ... [subparameter])]
        [CATALOG (catname[/password])]
```

CLUSTER The subparameters included in the required CLUSTER (CL) subparameter list assign attributes to the cluster as a whole.

DATA The subparameters included in the optional DATA subparameter list assign attributes to the data component of the cluster. (KSDS clusters only.)

INDEX The subparameters included in the optional INDEX subparameter list assign attributes to the index component of the cluster. (KSDS clusters only.)

CATALOG The optional CATALOG (CAT) parameter specifies the name and optional password of the catalog into which the catalog entries associated with the cluster are to be placed.

DEFINE CLUSTER Subparameters

```
DEFINE   CLUSTER
           (NAME(entryname)
             {CYLINDERS(primary[ secondary])|
               RECORDS(primary[ secondary])|
               TRACKS(primary[ secondary])}
             VOLUMES(volser[ volser...])

             [ATTEMPTS(number|2)]
             [AUTHORIZATION(entrypoint[ string])]
             [BUFFERSPACE(size)]
             [CODE(code)]
             [CONTROLINTERVALSIZE(size)]
             [CONTROLPW(password)]
             [DESTAGEWAIT|NODESTAGEWAIT]
             [ERASE|NOERASE]
             [EXCEPTIONEXIT(entrypoint)]
             [FILE(ddname)]
             [FREESPACE(CI-percent[ CA-percent]|0 0)]
             [IMBED|NOIMBED]
             [INDEXED|NONINDEXED|NUMBERED]
             [KEYRANGES((lowkey highkey)[ (lowkey highkey)...])]
             [KEYS(length offset|64 0)]
             [MASTERPW(password)]
             [MODEL(entryname[/password][ catname[/password]])]
             [ORDERED|UNORDERED]
             [OWNER(ownerid)]
             [READPW(password)]
             [RECORDSIZE(average maximum)]
             [REPLICATE|NOREPLICATE]
             [REUSE|NOREUSE]
             [SHAREOPTIONS(crossregion[ crosssystem]|1 3)]
             [SPANNED|NONSPANNED]
             [SPEED|RECOVERY]
             [STAGE|BIND|CYLINDERFAULT]
             [TO(date)|FOR(days)]
             [UPDATEPW|password)]
             [WRITECHECK|NOWRITECHECK])
```

Optional Parameters for ICF Catalogs Only

```
[UNIQUE | SUBALLOCATION]
```

Optional Parameter for VSAM Catalogs Only

```
[RECATALOG | NORECATALOG]
```

NAME

The NAME subparameter specifies the name of the cluster being defined.

CYLINDERS ¦ RECORDS ¦ TRACKS

The CYLINDERS (CYL), RECORDS (REC), and TRACKS (TRK) subparameters allocate space for the cluster.

VOLUMES

The VOLUMES (VOL) subparameter lists the serial numbers of the volume or volumes on which space for the cluster is to be allocated.

ATTEMPTS

The ATTEMPTS (ATT) subparameter specifies the maximum number of times the operator can enter a password in gaining access to the cluster.

AUTHORIZATION

The AUTHORIZATION (AUTH) subparameter specifies information about a security verification routine to be used in conjunction with this cluster.

BUFFERSPACE

The BUFFERSPACE (BUFSP or BUFSPC) subparameter specifies the minimum amount of space that VSAM should provide for I/O buffers when processing this cluster.

CODE

The CODE subparameter specifies a code name to be used in password prompting messages when a program attempts to gain access to this cluster without supplying a password.

CONTROLINTERVALSIZE

The CONTROLINTERVALSIZE (CISZ or CNVSZ) subparameter specifies the size of the control interval to be used for this cluster.

CONTROLPW	The CONTROLPW (CTLPW) subparameter assigns a control password to the cluster.
DESTAGEWAIT ¦ NODESTAGEWAIT	The DESTAGEWAIT (DSTGW) and NODESTAGEWAIT (NDSTGW) subparameters are used only in conjunction with a Mass Storage System.
ERASE ¦ NOERASE	The ERASE (ERAS) and NOERASE (NERAS) subparameters specify whether or not VSAM should physically erase the cluster by overwriting it with binary zeros when its catalog entry is deleted.
EXCEPTIONEXIT	The EXCEPTIONEXIT (EEXIT) subparameter specifies the name of a routine to be executed when an I/O error occurs while processing the cluster.
FILE	The FILE subparameter identifies the DD statement in the AMS job step that defines UNIT and VOLUME information for the cluster.
FREESPACE	The FREESPACE (FSPC) subparameter specifies the percentage of free space that should be allocated in each control interval and each control area when the cluster is loaded and when control interval and control area splits occur. (KSDS clusters only.)
IMBED ¦ NOIMBED	The IMBED (IMBD) and NOIMBED (NIMBD) subparameters specify whether or not VSAM should write the sequence set records as many times as they will fit on the first track of each control area. (KSDS clusters only.)
INDEXED	The INDEXED (IXD) subparameter (the default) specifies that a KSDS cluster is being defined.
NONINDEXED	The NONINDEXED (NIXD) subparameter specifies that an ESDS cluster is being defined.

NUMBERED	The NUMBERED (NUMD) subparameter specifies that an RRDS cluster is being defined.
KEYRANGES	The KEYRANGES (KRNG) subparameter specifies that a KSDS cluster is to be divided into separate areas called key ranges, some of which can be placed on separate volumes. (KSDS clusters only.)
KEYS	The KEYS subparameter is used to specify the length and the location in the record of the cluster's prime key. (KSDS clusters only.)
MASTERPW	The MASTERPW (MRPW) subparameter assigns a master password to the cluster.
MODEL	The MODEL subparameter specifies the name of an existing cluster to be used as a model in defining this path.
ORDERED ¦ <u>UNORDERED</u>	The ORDERED (ORD) and <u>UNORDERED</u> (<u>UNORD</u>) subparameters specify whether or not VSAM should use the volumes in the order in which they are coded in the VOLUMES parameter.
OWNER	The OWNER subparameter identifies the owner of the cluster.
READPW	The READPW (RDPW) subparameter assigns a read password to the cluster.
RECORDSIZE	The RECORDSIZE (RECSZ) subparameter specifies the average and maximum length of the records to be stored in the data component of the cluster.
REPLICATE ¦ <u>NOREPLICATE</u>	The REPLICATE (REPL) and <u>NOREPLICATE</u> (<u>NREPL</u>) subparameters specify whether or not VSAM should write sequence set records as many times as they will fit on a track. (KSDS clusters only.)
REUSE ¦ <u>NOREUSE</u>	The REUSE (RUS) and <u>NOREUSE</u> (<u>NRUS</u>) subparameters specify whether or not VSAM can reset the cluster's high-used RBA to zero to

make the cluster appear empty when opened.

SHAREOPTIONS

The SHAREOPTIONS (SHR) subparameter specifies how the cluster can be shared between concurrently executing tasks.

SPANNED ¦ NONSPANNED

The SPANNED (SPND) and NONSPANNED (NSPND) subparameters specify whether records are allowed to span across control interval boundaries. (KSDS and ESDS clusters only.)

SPEED ¦ RECOVERY

The SPEED and RECOVERY (RCVY) subparameters specify whether or not VSAM should preformat the space allocated to the data set as part of the define process.

STAGE ¦ BIND ¦ CYLINDERFAULT

The STAGE, BIND, and CYLINDERFAULT (CYLF) subparameters are used only in conjunction with a Mass Storage System.

TO ¦ FOR

The TO and FOR subparameters assign an expiration date to the cluster.

UPDATEPW

The UPDATEPW (UPDPW) subparameter assigns an update password to the cluster.

WRITECHECK ¦ NOWRITECHECK

The WRITECHECK (WCK) and NOWRITECHECK (NWCK) subparameters specify whether VSAM should perform write check verification when writing data into the cluster.

UNIQUE ¦ SUBALLOCATION

The UNIQUE (UNQ) and SUBALLOCATION (SUBAL) subparameters specify whether or not VSAM should assign the cluster to its own unique data space. (VSAM catalogs only; not valid for ICF catalogs.)

RECATALOG ¦ NORECATALOG

The RECATALOG (RCTLG) and NORECATALOG (NRCTLOG) subparameters specify whether or not an entry already exists in the VVDS on the primary volume. (ICF catalogs only; not valid for VSAM catalogs.)

DEFINE DATA Subparameters

```
DEFINE    [DATA
             ([ATTEMPTS(number)]
             [AUTHORIZATION(entrypoint[ string])]
             [BUFFERSPACE(size)]
             [CODE(code)]
             [CONTROLINTERVALSIZE(size)]
             [CONTROLPW(password)]
             [CYLINDERS(primary[ secondary])|
          RECORDS(primary[ secondary])|
          TRACKS(primary[ secondary])]
        [DESTAGEWAIT|NODESTAGEWAIT]
        [ERASE|NOERASE]
        [EXCEPTIONEXIT(entrypoint)]
        [FILE(ddname)]
        [FREESPACE(CI-percent [CA-percent])]
        [KEYRANGES((lowkey highkey)[ (lowkey highkey)...])]
        [KEYS(length offset)]
        [MASTERPW(password)]
        [MODEL(entryname[/password][ catname[/password]])]
        [NAME (entryname)]
        [ORDERED|UNORDERED]
        [OWNER(ownerid)]
        [READPW(password)]
        [RECORDSIZE(average maximum)]
        [REUSE|NOREUSE]
        [SHAREOPTIONS(crossregion[ crosssystem])]
        [SPANNED|NONSPANNED]
        [SPEED|RECOVERY]
        [STAGE|BIND|CYLINDERFAULT]
        [UPDATEPW|password)]
        [VOLUMES(volser[ volser...])]
        [WRITECHECK|NOWRITECHECK])]
```

Optional Subparameter for VSAM Catalogs Only

```
[UNIQUE|SUBALLOCATION]
```

```
DEFINE    [INDEX
          ([ATTEMPTS(number)]
          [AUTHORIZATION(entrypoint[ string])]
          [CODE(code)]
          [CONTROLINTERVALSIZE(size)]
          [CONTROLPW(password)]
          [CYLINDERS(primary[ secondary])|
            RECORDS(primary[ secondary])|
            TRACKS(primary[ secondary])]
          [DESTAGEWAIT|NODESTAGEWAIT]
          [EXCEPTIONEXIT(entrypoint)]
          [FILE(ddname)]
          [IMBED|[NOIMBED]
          [MASTERPW(password)]
          [MODEL(entryname[/password][ catname[/password]])]
          [NAME(entryname]
          [ORDERED|UNORDERED]
          [OWNER(ownerid)]
          [READPW(password)]
          [REPLICATE|NOREPLICATE]
```

```
[REUSE|NOREUSE]
[SHAREOPTIONS(crossregion[ crosssystem]))]
[STAGE|BIND|CYLINDERFAULT]
[UPDATEPW|password)]
[VOLUMES(volser[ volser...]))]
[WRITECHECK|NOWRITECHECK]))]
```

Optional Subparameter for VSAM Catalogs Only

```
[UNIQUE|SUBALLOCATION]
```

The DEFINE NONVSAM Command

```
DEFINE    NONVSAM
            (NAME(entryname)
           DEVICETYPES(devtype[ devtype...])
           VOLUMES(volser[ volser...])

           [FILESEQUENCENUMBERS(number[ number...])
           [OWNER(ownerid)])
           [TO(date)|FOR(days)])

          [CATALOG(catname[/password]))]
```

NAME The NAME parameter specifies the name of the non-VSAM data set being defined.

DEVICETYPES The DEVICETYPES (DEVT) parameter specifies the device types on which the non-VSAM data set resides.

VOLUMES The VOLUMES (VOL) parameter specifies the volume serial numbers of the volumes on which the non-VSAM data set resides.

FILESEQUENCENUMBERS The FILESEQUENCENUMBERS (FSEQN) parameter specifies the file sequence numbers of the non-VSAM data set.

OWNER The OWNER parameter specifies the owner identifier of the non-VSAM data set.

TO | FOR The TO and FOR parameters specify the expiration date to be assigned to the non-VSAM data set.

CATALOG The CATALOG (CAT) parameter specifies the name of the catalog into which the new catalog entry is to be placed.

The DEFINE PATH Command

```
DEFINE   PATH
           (NAME(entryname)
            PATHENTRY(entryname[/password])
            [ATTEMPTS(number|2)]
            [AUTHORIZATION(entrypoint[ string])]
            [CODE(code)]
            [CONTROLPW(password)]
            [MASTERPW(password)]
            [MODEL(entryname[/password][ catname[/password]])]
            [OWNER(ownerid)]
            [READPW(password)]
            [TO(date)|FOR(days)]
            [UPDATEPW|password)]
            [CATALOG(catname[/password])]
```

Optional Parameter for VSAM Recoverable Catalogs Only

```
[FILE(ddname)]
```

Optional Parameter for ICF Catalogs Only

```
[RECATALOG|NORECATALOG]
```

NAME The NAME parameter specifies the name of the path being defined.

PATHENTRY The PATHENTRY (PENT) parameter specifies the name of the alternate index when the path consists of an alternate index and a base cluster. This parameter specifies the name of the base cluster when the path defines an alias for a base cluster.

ATTEMPTS The ATTEMPT (ATT) parameter specifies the maximum number of times the operator can enter a password.

AUTHORIZATION The AUTHORIZATION (AUTH) parameter specifies information about a security verification routine to be used in conjunction with this path.

CODE The CODE parameter specifies a code name to be used in password prompting messages for the path.

CONTROLPW The CONTROLPW (CTLPW) parameter assigns a control password to the path.

MASTERPW The MASTERPW (MRPW) parameter assigns a mater password to the path.

MODEL The MODEL parameter specifies the name of an existing path entry to be used as a model in defining this path.

OWNER The OWNER parameter identifies the owner of the path.

READPW The READPW (RDPW) parameter assigns a read password to the path.

TO ¦ FOR The TO and FOR parameters are used to assign an expiration date to the path.

UPDATEPW The UPDATEPW (UPDPW) parameter assigns an update password to the path.

CATALOG The CATALOG (CAT) parameter identifies the user catalog into which the catalog entry for the path is to be placed.

FILE The FILE parameter specifies the name of a DD statement in the JCL that identifies unit and volume information for the recovery volume associated with the alternate index or path identified in the PATHENTRY parameter. (Used with VSAM recoverable catalogs only.)

RECATALOG
NORECATALOG The RECATALOG (RCTLG) and NORECATALOG (NRCTLG) parameters specify whether or not an entry for the path already exists in the VVDS on the primary volume. (Used with ICF catalogs only.)

The DEFINE SPACE Command

```
DEFINE   SPACE
         ({CANDIDATE|
         {CYLINDERS(primary[ secondary])|
           RECORDS(primary[ secondary])|
             RECORDSIZE(average maximum)|
           TRACKS(primary[ secondary])}
         VOLUMES(volser[ volser...])
         [FILE(ddname)])

    [CATALOG(catname[/password])]
```

CANDIDATE The CANDIDATE (CAN) parameter specifies that the volumes listed in the command are to be reserved for future use by the catalog in effect for this DEFINE SPACE command.

CYLINDERS ¦
RECORDS ¦
TRACKS The CYLINDERS (CYL), RECORDS (REC), and TRACKS (TRK) parameters are used to allocate direct access space to the data space.

RECORDSIZE — The RECORDSIZE (RECSZ) parameter is used when requesting space in terms of records to define the average and maximum record length to be used in allocating space.

VOLUMES — The VOLUMES (VOL) parameter specifies the volume serial numbers of the volumes to reserve or the volumes on which the data space is to be allocated.

FILE — The FILE parameter specifies the name of the DD statement that provides UNIT and VOLUME information for the data space.

CATALOG — The CATALOG (CAT) specifies the name of the user catalog to which ownership of the volume or volumes is to be assigned.

The DEFINE UCAT/MCAT Commands

```
DEFINE   USERCATALOG | MASTERCATALOG
            (subparameter  [subparameter] ... [subparameter])

         [DATA    (subparameter  [subparameter] ... [subparameter])]
         [INDEX   (subparameter  [subparameter] ... [subparameter])]
         [CATALOG (catname[/password])]
```

USERCATALOG | MASTERCATALOG — The subparameters included in the required USERCATALOG (UCAT) or MASTERCATALOG (MCAT) subparameter list assign attributes to the catalog as a whole.

DATA — The subparameters included in the optional DATA subparameter list assign attributes to the data component of the catalog.

INDEX — The subparameters included in the optional INDEX subparameter list assign attributes to the index component of the catalog.

CATALOG — The optional CATALOG (CAT) parameter specifies the name and optional password of the master catalog.

DEFINE UCAT/MCAT Subparameters

```
DEFINE   USERCATALOG|MASTERCATALOG
          (NAME(entryname)
          {CYLINDERS(primary[ secondary])|
            RECORDS(primary[ secondary])|
            TRACKS(primary[ secondary])}
         VOLUME(volser)

          [ATTEMPTS(number|2)]
          [AUTHORIZATION(entrypoint[ string])]
```

```
[BUFFERSPACE(size)|3072]
[CODE(code)]
[CONTROLPW(password)]
[DESTAGEWAIT|NODESTAGEWAIT]
[FILE(ddname)]
[MASTERPW(password)]
[MODEL(entryname[/password][ catname[/password]])]
[OWNER(ownerid)]
[READPW(password)]
[RECORDSIZE(average maximum)]
[TO(date)|FOR(days)]
[UPDATEPW|password)]
[WRITECHECK|NOWRITECHECK])
```

Optional Parameter for VSAM Catalogs Only

```
[RECOVERABLE|NOTRECOVERABLE])
```

Optional Parameters for ICF Catalogs Only

```
[BUFND(number)]
[BUFNI(number)]
[CONTROLINTERVALSIZE(size)]
[FREESPACE(CI-percent[ CA-percent]|0 0)]
[IMBED|NOIMBED]
[REPLICATE|NOREPLICATE]
[SHAREOPTIONS(crossregion[ crosssystem]|3 4)]
[STRNO(number|2)]
[VSAMCATALOG|ICFCATALOG]
```

Parameter for VSAM Catalogs Only

RECOVERABLE | NOTRECOVERABLE — The RECOVERABLE (RVBL) and NOTRECOVERABLE (NRVBL) parameters specify whether or not a catalog recovery area is to be created on each volume owned by the catalog.

Parameters for ICF Catalogs Only

BUFND — The BUFND (BFND) parameter specifies the number of buffers to be used in transferring records between the data component of the catalog and virtual storage.

BUFNI — The BUFNI (BFNI) parameter specifies the number of buffers to be used in transferring records between the data component of the catalog and virtual storage.

STRNO — The STRNO parameter specifies the number of concurrent requests for positioning that can be made.

VSAMCATALOG | ICFCATALOG — The VSAMCATALOG (VSAMCAT) and ICFCATALOG (ICFCAT) parameters specify which type of catalog is to be defined by this command.

DEFINE Catalog DATA and INDEX Subparameters

```
DEFINE DATA
         ([BUFFERSPACE(size)|3072]
         [CYLINDERS(primary[ secondary])|
           RECORDS(primary[ secondary])|
           TRACKS(primary[ secondary])]

         [DESTAGEWAIT|NODESTAGEWAIT]
         [RECORDSIZE(average maximum)]
         [WRITECHECK|NOWRITECHECK]
```

Optional Parameters for ICF Catalogs Only

```
           [BUFND(number)]
           [CONTROLINTERVALSIZE(size)]
           [FREESPACE(CI-percent[ CA-percent]|0 0)])
```

```
DEFINE INDEX
         ([CYLINDERS(primary)|
           RECORDS(primary)|
           TRACKS(primary)]
         [DESTAGEWAIT|NODESTAGEWAIT]
         [WRITECHECK|NOWRITECHECK]
```

Optional Parameters for ICF Catalogs Only

```
         [BUFNI(number)]
         [CONTROLINTERVALSIZE(size)]
         [IMBED|NOIMBED]
         [REPLICATE|NOREPLICATE])
```

The DELETE Command

```
DELETE   (entryname[/password][ entryname[/password]...])

         [ALIAS]
             [ALTERNATEINDEX]
             [CLUSTER]
             [GENERATIONDATAGROUP]
             [NONVSAM]
```

```
        [PAGESPACE]
        [PATH]
        [USERCATALOG]
    [ERASE|NOERASE]
    [FILE(ddname)]
    [FORCE|NOFORCE]
    [PURGE|NOPURGE]
    [SCRATCH|NOSCRATCH]

    [CATALOG(catname[/password])]
```

Optional Parameter for VSAM Catalogs Only

```
[SPACE]
```

Optional Parameter for ICF Catalogs Only

```
[TRUENAME]
[VVR]
[RECOVERY|NORECOVERY]
```

Positional Parameters — The DELETE command can optionally begin with one or more positional parameters that identify the types of objects that AMS is to delete.

ERASE | NOERASE — The ERASE (ERAS) and NOERASE (NERAS) parameters specify whether or not AMS should overwrite the object with binary zeros when it is deleted.

FILE — The FILE parameter specifies the name of a DD statement that describes the unit and volume on which the object being deleted resides.

FORCE | NOFORCE — The FORCE (FRC) and NOFORCE (NFRC) parameters specify whether or not the specified object, such as a generation data group or user catalog, should be deleted whether or not it is currently empty.

PURGE | NOPURGE — The PURGE (PRG) and NOPURGE (NPRG) parameters specify whether or not the specified object should be deleted even if its expiration date has not been reached.

SCRATCH | NOSCRATCH — The SCRATCH (SCR) and NOSCRATCH (NSCR) parameters specify whether or not the associated entry is to be removed from the volume's volume table of contents (VTOC) as well as having its catalog entry removed.

CATALOG — The CATALOG (CAT) parameter specifies the name and optional password of the catalog that contains the catalog entries for the objects being deleted.

SPACE The SPACE (SPC) parameter is an additional positional parameter that specifies that a VSAM data space is to be deleted. (VSAM catalogs only; not valid for ICF catalogs.)

TRUENAME The TRUENAME (TNAME) parameter is an additional positional parameter that specifies that AMS is to delete a truename entry for an object. (ICF catalogs only; not valid for VSAM catalogs.)

VVR The VVR parameter is an additional positional parameter that specifies that AMS is to delete a VVR entry from a VVDS. (ICF catalogs only; not valid for VSAM catalogs.)

RECOVERY | NORECOVERY The RECOVERY (RCVRY) and NORECOVERY (NRCVRY) parameters are used only when replacing ICF catalogs with imported copies. (ICF catalogs only; not valid for VSAM catalogs.)

The EXPORT Command

```
EXPORT   entryname[/password]
         {OUTFILE(ddname)|OUTDATASET(entryname)}

         [ERASE|NOERASE]
         [INFILE(ddname)]
         [INHIBITSOURCE|NOINHIBITSOURCE]
         [INHIBITTARGET|NOINHIBITTARGET]
         [PURGE|NOPURGE]
         [TEMPORARY|PERMANENT]
```

Entryname The required positional parameter gives the name and optional password of the object being exported. EXPORT can be used to create a copy of a cluster, an alternate index, or an ICF catalog.

OUTFILE The OUTFILE (OFILE) parameter specifies the name of the DD statement that describes the data set that will contain the portable copy.

OUTDATASET The OUTDATASET (ODS) parameter specifies the name of the data set that will contain the portable copy. (Either OUTFILE or OUTDATASET must be specified for EXPORT.)

ERASE ¦ NOERASE	The ERASE (ERAS) and NOERASE (NERAS) parameters specify whether or not AMS should overwrite the exported object with binary zeros when it is deleted. (Valid only for clusters and alternate indexes.)
INFILE	The INFILE (IFILE) parameter specifies the name of the DD statement that describes the object being exported.
INHIBITSOURCE ¦ NOINHIBITSOURCE	The INHIBITSOURCE (INHS) and NOINHIBITSOURCE (NINHS) parameters specify whether or not AMS should mark the object being exported as being accessible only for retrieval after the export operation.
INHIBITTARGET ¦ NOINHIBITTARGET	The INHIBITTARGET (INHT) and NOINHIBITTARGET (NINHT) parameters specify whether or not AMS should mark the portable copy of the object being exported as being accessible only for retrieval after the export operation.
PURGE ¦ NOPURGE	The PURGE (PRG) and NOPURGE (NPRG) parameters specify whether or not the object being exported should be deleted, even if its expiration date has not been exceeded. (Applies only when the PERMANENT option is in effect.)
TEMPORARY ¦ PERMANENT	The TEMPORARY (TEMP) and PERMANENT (PERM) parameters specify whether or not the object being exported should be deleted after the EXPORT operation has been completed successfully. (Valid for clusters and alternate indexes only. ICF catalogs must be exported as TEMPORARY, which is the default value for this parameter when an ICF catalog is exported.)

The EXPORT DISCONNECT Command

Usercatname	The required position parameter specifies the name of the user catalog to be disconnected.
DISCONNECT	The DISCONNECT (DCON) parameter causes the specified user catalog entry to be removed from the master catalog.

IF-THEN-ELSE Command Sequence

```
IF   {LASTCC|MAXCC} comparand number
    THEN[ command|
       DO
       command-set
       END]
    [ELSE[ command|
       DO
       command-set
       END]]
```

The IMPORT Command

```
IMPORT    {INFILE(ddname)|INDATASET(entryname)}
          {OUTFILE(ddname[/password])|
             OUTDATASET(entryname[/password])}

          [ERASE|NOERASE]
          [INTOEMPTY]
          [OBJECTS
             ((entryname
                [FILE(ddname)]
                [(KEYRANGES((lowkey highkey)[lowkey highkey)...]))]
                [NEWNAME(newname)]
                [ORDERED|UNORDERED]
                [VOLUME(volser[ volser...])])
             [entryname...)...])]
          [PURGE|NOPURGE]
          [SAVRAC|NOSAVRAC]

          [CATALOG(catname[/password])]
```

INFILE The INFILE (IFILE) parameter specifies the name of the DD statement that describes the portable copy of the object being imported.

INDATASET The INDATASET (IDS) parameter specifies the name of the data set that contains the portable copy of the object being imported.

OUTFILE The OUTFILE (OFILE) parameter specifies the name of the DD statement that describes the object being imported.

OUTDATASET The OUTDATASET (ODS) parameter specifies the name of the object being imported.

ERASE | NOERASE The ERASE (ERAS) and NOERASE (NERAS) parameters specify whether or not AMS should overwrite the original copy of the object being imported with binary zeros. (Valid only when importing an object that was exported previously using the TEMPORARY option.)

INTOEMPTY The INTOEMPTY (IEMPTY) parameter specifies that the object is being imported into an already existing empty data set.

OBJECTS The OBJECTS (OBJ) parameter specifies the original name of the object being imported and assigns a new name and/or selected attributes to the object being imported.

PURGE ¦ NOPURGE The PURGE (PRG) and NOPURGE (NPRG) parameters specify whether or not the original copy of the object being imported should be deleted, even if its expiration date has not been exceeded. (Valid only when importing an object that was previously exported using the TEMPORARY option.)

SAVRAC ¦ NOSAVRAC The SAVRAC and NOSAVRAC parameters specify whether or not the RACF profile that already exists for the object being imported is to be used.

CATALOG The CATALOG (CAT) parameter specifies the name of the catalog into which the catalog entry for the object being imported is to be placed.

The IMPORT CONNECT Command

```
IMPORT    CONNECT
          OBJECTS ((usercatname
             DEVICETYPE(devtype)
             VOLUMES(volser)))

          [CATALOG(catname[/password])]
```

CONNECT The CONNECT (CON) parameter causes the specified user catalog entry to be placed into the master catalog.

OBJECTS The OBJECTS (OBJ) parameter specifies the name, device type, and volume serial number of the user catalog.

CATALOG The CATALOG (CAT) parameter specifies the name and optional password of the catalog into which the user catalog entry is to be placed. (Used to specify a catalog other than the master catalog or to specify the password for a password-protected master catalog.)

The LISTCAT Command

```
LISTCAT  [ALIAS]
            [ALTERNATEINDEX]
            [CLUSTER]
            [DATA]
            [GENERATIONDATAGROUP]
            [INDEX]
            [NONVSAM]
            [PAGESPACE]
            [PATH]
            [USERCATALOG]
         [CREATION](days)
         [ENTRIES(entryname[/password]
            [ entryname[/password]...])|
           LEVEL(level)]
         [EXPIRATION(days)]
         [NAME|HISTORY|VOLUME|ALLOCATION|ALL]
         [OUTFILE(ddname)]

         [CATALOG(catname[/password])]
```

Optional Parameters for VSAM Catalogs Only

```
[SPACE]
[NOTUSABLE]
```

Optional Parameter for ICF Catalogs Only

```
[FILE(ddname)]
```

Positional Parameters The LISTCAT command can optionally begin with one or more positional parameters that identify the types of catalog entries that AMS is to display.

CREATION The CREATION (CREAT) parameter specifies a number of days; entries of the specified type are listed only if they were created the specified number of days ago or earlier.

ENTRIES The ENTRIES (ENT) parameter specifies the names of the catalog entries to display.

LEVEL The LEVEL (LVL) parameter specifies the high-level qualifier or qualifiers of the catalog entries to be listed.

EXPIRATION The EXPIRATION (EXPIR) parameter specifies a number of days; entries of the specified type are listed only if they will expire in the specified number of days or earlier.

NAME The NAME parameter (the default) specifies that AMS should display only the name and entry type for the selected catalog entries.

HISTORY The HISTORY (HIST) parameter specifies that AMS should display the name, entry type, ownerid, creation date, and expiration date for the selected catalog entries.

VOLUME The VOLUME (VOL) parameter specifies that AMS should display HISTORY information plus the volume serial numbers and device type for all selected catalog entries.

ALLOCATION The ALLOCATION parameter (ALLOC) specifies that AMS should display VOLUME information plus detailed information concerning space allocation for the selected catalog entries.

ALL The ALL parameter specifies that AMS should display all the information contained in the catalog for the selected catalog entries.

OUTFILE The OUTFILE (OFILE) parameter specifies the name of the output DD statement when it is other than SYSPRINT.

CATALOG The CATALOG (CAT) parameter specifies the name and optional password of the catalog that contains the selected entries.

SPACE The SPACE (SPC) parameter is an additional positional parameter that specifies that AMS is to display catalog entries for VSAM data spaces. (VSAM catalogs only; not valid for ICF catalogs.)

NOTUSABLE The NOTUSABLE (NUS) parameter specifies that only selected entries that have the "unusable" indicator set should be listed. The unusable indicator is set when a system failure damages the object's catalog entry. (VSAM catalogs only; not valid for ICF catalogs.)

FILE The FILE parameter specifies the name of the DD statement that describes the devices and volumes that contain information in the VVDS. (ICF catalogs only; not valid for VSAM catalogs.)

PARM Command Parameters

```
PARM     [GRAPHICS(CHAIN(chain)|TABLE(mnsame))]
         [MARGINS(left-margin right-margin)]
         [TEST({ [TRACE
                 [AREAS(area-id[ area-id ...])
                 [FULL ((dump-id[ count1[ count2]])
                     [(dump-id ...) ...])]|
                  OFF})]
```

GRAPHICS The GRAPHICS parameter provides information concerning graphics character sets or user-supplied graphics tables that are to be used in special-purpose printing applications.

MARGINS The MARGINS parameter specifies the left and right margins to control which positions of SYSIN input records are to be scanned for AMS commands.

TEST Various keywords can be included following the TEST parameter to control diagnostic aids that are used to help in debugging complex command sequences.

The PRINT Command

```
PRINT    {INFILE(ddname[/password])|
            INDATASET(entryname[/password])}

         [CHARACTER|DUMP|HEX
         [FROMKEY(key)|FROMADDRESS(address)|
            FROMNUMBER(number)|SKIP(count)]
         [OUTFILE(ddname)]
         [TOKEY(key)|TOADDRESS(address)|
            TONUMBER(number)|COUNT(count)]
```

INFILE The INFILE (IFILE) parameter specifies the name of the DD statement that describes the input object.

INDATASET The INDATASET (IDS) parameter specifies the name of the input object.

CHARACTER The CHARACTER (CHAR) parameter specifies that AMS should display the output in character format.

DUMP The DUMP parameter (the default) specifies that AMS should display the output in both hexadecimal and character format, as in a virtual storage dump.

HEX The HEX parameter specifies that AMS should display the output in hexadecimal format.

FROMKEY The FROMKEY (FKEY) parameter specifies the full or generic key value that defines the starting point of the print operation. (KSDS clusters, alternate indexes, catalogs, and ISAM data sets only.)

FROMADDRESS The FROMADDRESS (FADDR) parameter specifies the RBA value that defines the starting point of the print operation. (KSDS and ESDS clusters only.)

FROMNUMBER The FROMNUMBER (FNUM) parameter specifies the relative record number that defines the starting point of the print operation. (RRDS clusters only.)

SKIP The SKIP parameter specifies the number of records to skip before displaying records.

OUTFILE The OUTFILE (OFILE) parameter specifies the name of the output DD statement when it is other than SYSPRINT.

TOKEY The TOKEY parameter specifies the full or generic key value that defines the ending point of the print operation. (KSDS clusters, alternate indexes, catalogs, and ISAM data sets only.)

TOADDRESS The TOADDRESS (TADDR) parameter specifies the RBA value that defines the ending point of the print operation. (KSDS and ESDS clusters only.)

TONUMBER The TONUMBER (TNUM) parameter specifies the relative record number that defines the ending point of the print operation. (RRDS clusters only.)

COUNT The COUNT parameter specifies the number of records to include in the print operation.

The REPRO Command

```
REPRO    {INFILE(ddname[/password] [ ENVIRONMENT(DUMMY)]) |
            INDATASET(entryname[/password] [ ENVIRONMENT(DUMMY)])}
         {OUTFILE(ddname[/password]) |
            OUTDATASET(entryname[/password])}

         [FROMKEY(key) |FROMADDRESS(address) |
            FROMNUMBER(number) |SKIP(count)]
         [REPLACE|NOREPLACE]
         [REUSE|NOREUSE]
         [TOKEY(key) |TOADDRESS(address) |
            TONUMBER(number) |COUNT(count)]
```

Optional Parameters for ICF Catalogs Only

```
[ENTRIES(entryname[/password]
  [entryname[/password]...]) |
  LEVEL(level)]
[FILE(ddname)]
[MERGECAT|NOMERGECAT]
```

INFILE	The INFILE (IFILE) parameter specifies the name of the DD statement that describes the input object.
ENVIRON-MENT	The ENVIRONMENT (DUMMY) or ENV (DUM) parameter is used only when the input object is an ISAM data set and specifies that dummy records are to be copied along with active records.
INDATASET	The INDATASET (IDS) parameter specifies the name of the input object.
OUTFILE	The OUTFILE (OFILE) parameter specifies the name of the DD statement that describes the output object.
OUTDATASET	The OUTDATASET (ODS) parameter specifies the name of the output object.
FROMKEY	The FROMKEY (FKEY) parameter specifies the full or generic key value that defines the starting point of the copy operation. (KSDS clusters, alternate indexes, and ISAM data sets only.)
FROMAD-DRESS	The FROMADDRESS (FADDR) parameter specifies the RBA value that defines the starting point of the copy operation. (KSDS and ESDS clusters only.)
FROMNUM-BER	The FROMNUMBER (FNUM) parameter specifies the relative record number that defines the starting point of the copy operation. (RRDS clusters only.)
SKIP	The SKIP parameter specifies the number of records to skip before copying records.
REPLACE ¦ NOREPLACE	The REPLACE (REP) and NOREPLACE (NREP) parameters specify whether VSAM is to replace records in the output data set with matching records in the input data set.
REUSE ¦ NOREUSE	The REUSE (RUS) and NOREUSE (NRUS) parameters specify whether or not VSAM should open the output data set as a reusable data set.
TOKEY	The TOKEY parameter specifies the full or generic key value that defines the ending point of the copy operation. (KSDS clusters, alternate indexes, and ISAM data sets only.)
TOADDRESS	The TOADDRESS (TADDR) parameter specifies the RBA value that defines the ending point of the copy operation. (KSDS and ESDS clusters only.)

TONUMBER The TONUMBER (TNUM) parameter specifies the relative record number that defines the ending point of the copy operation. (RRDS clusters only.)

COUNT The COUNT parameter specifies the number of records to include in the copy operation.

ENTRIES The ENTRIES (ENT) parameter is valid only when the MERGECAT option is in effect and specifies the names of the objects in the input catalog to be merged. (ICF catalogs only; not valid for VSAM catalogs.)

LEVEL The LEVEL (LVL) parameter specifies the low-level qualifiers that identify the names of the objects to be merged. (ICF catalogs only; not valid for VSAM catalogs.)

FILE The FILE parameter specifies the name of the DD statement that describes the volumes that contain the VVDSs to be updated. (ICF catalogs only; not valid for VSAM catalogs.)

MERGECAT | NOMERGECAT The MERGECAT (MRGC) and NOMERGECAT (NOMRGC) parameters are valid only when copying ICF catalogs and specify whether or not VSAM should merge the entries in the input catalog with the entries already in the output catalog. (ICF catalogs only; not valid for VSAM catalogs.)

The SET Command

```
SET     {MAXCC|LASTCC}=number
```

The VERIFY Command

```
VERIFY    {FILE(ddname[/password])|
             DATASET(entryname[/password])}
```

FILE The FILE parameter specifies the name, and optional password, of the DD statement that describes the cluster or alternate index to be verified.

DATASET The DATASET (DS) parameter specifies the name, and optional password, of the cluster or alternate index to be verified.

COBOL STATEMENT SYNTAX

The CLOSE Statement

```
CLOSE  file-name-1 [WITH LOCK

     [file-name-2 [WITH LOCK]] ...
```

The DELETE Statement

```
DELETE file-name RECORD

   [INVALID KEY imperative-statement].
```

The OPEN Statement

```
OPEN {INPUT    file-name-1 [file-name-2] ...
      OUTPUT   file-name-1 [file-name-2] ...
      I-O      file-name-1 [file-name-2] ...
      EXTEND   file-name-1 [file-name-2] ...} ...
```

READ Statement Syntax for Sequential ESDS Retrieval

```
READ file-name RECORD

    [INTO identifier]
    [AT END imperative-statement].
```

READ Statement Syntax for Direct KSDS

```
READ file-name RECORD

   [INTO identifier]
   [INVALID KEY imperative-statement].
```

READ Statement Syntax for Sequential KSDS Retrieval

```
READ file-name [NEXT] RECORD

   [INTO identifier]
   [AT END imperative-statement].
```

REWRITE Statement Syntax for ESDS

```
REWRITE record-name

    [FROM identifier].
```

REWRITE Statement Syntax for KSDS

```
REWRITE record-name

   [FROM identifier]
   [INVALID KEY imperative-statement].
```

SELECT Statement Syntax for ESDS

```
FILE-CONTROL.
   SELECT OPTIONAL file-name
   ASSIGN TO AS-ddname-1 [AS-ddname-2 ...]

   [RESERVE integer {AREA|AREAS}]
   [ORGANIZATION IS SEQUENTIAL]
   [ACCESS MODE IS SEQUENTIAL]
   [PASSWORD IS data-name-1]
   [FILE STATUS IS data-name-2].
```

SELECT Statement Syntax for KSDS

```
FILE-CONTROL.
  SELECT file-name
  ASSIGN TO ddname-1 [ddname-2 ...]
  ORGANIZATION IS INDEXED
  RECORD KEY IS data-name-3
     [PASSWORD IS data-name-1]

  [RESERVE integer {AREA|AREAS}
  [ACCESS MODE IS {SEQUENTIAL|RANDOM|DYNAMIC}]
  [ALTERNATE RECORD KEY IS data-name-4
     [PASSWORD IS data-name-5]
     [WITH DUPLICATES]]
  [FILE STATUS IS data-name-2].
```

SELECT Statement Syntax for RRDS

```
FILE-CONTROL.
   SELECT file-name
   ASSIGN TO ddname-1 [ddname-2 ...]
   ORGANIZATION IS RELATIVE

   [RESERVE integer {AREA|AREAS}]
   [ACCESS MODE IS {SEQUENTIAL|RANDOM|DYNAMIC}]
   [RELATIVE KEY IS dataname-1]}
   [PASSWORD IS data-name-2]
   [FILE STATUS IS data-name-3].
```

The START Statement

```
START file-name

  [KEY IS {EQUAL TO |
           = |
           GREATER THAN |
           > |
           NOT LESS THAN |
           NOT <          } data-name]

  [INVALID KEY imperative-statement].
```

WRITE Statement Syntax for ESDS

```
WRITE record-name

   [FROM identifier].
```

WRITE Statement Syntax for KSDS

```
WRITE record-name

   [FROM identifier]
   [INVALID KEY imperative-statement].
```

PL/I STATEMENT SYNTAX

The CLOSE Statement

```
CLOSE FILE (file-reference)

      [,FILE (file-reference)]...;
```

DCL Syntax for ESDS

```
DCL   file-name FILE RECORD SEQUENTIAL
      ENV(VSAM [PASSWORD (password-specification)])
      {INPUT|OUTPUT|UPDATE};
```

DCL Syntax for KSDS

```
DCL file-name FILE RECORD
   ENV(VSAM [PASSWORD (password-specification)])
   [KEYED]{SEQUENTIAL|DIRECT}
   {INPUT|OUTPUT|UPDATE};
```

DCL Syntax for RRDS

```
DCL file-name FILE RECORD
   ENV(VSAM [PASSWORD (password-specification)])
   [KEYED]{SEQUENTIAL|DIRECT}
   {INPUT|OUTPUT|UPDATE};
```

The DELETE Statement

```
DELETE FILE (file-reference)

   [KEY (expression)];
```

The OPEN Statement

```
OPEN FILE(file-reference)

   [,FILE (file-reference)]...;
```

The READ Statement

```
READ FILE (file-reference)

   [INTO (reference)]
   [KEY (expression)]
   [KEYTO (reference)];
```

The REWRITE Statement

```
REWRITE FILE (file-reference)

    [FROM (reference)]
    [KEY (RBA-expression)];
```

WRITE Statement Syntax for ESDS

```
WRITE FILE (file-reference)

    [FROM (reference)]
    [KEYTO (RBA-reference)];
```

WRITE Statement Syntax for KSDS

```
WRITE FILE (file-reference)

    [FROM (reference)]
    [KEYFROM (expression)];
```

ASSEMBLER LANGUAGE MACROS

The ACB Macro

```
[label]    ACB    [AM=VSAM]
                  [,BSTRNO=number]
                  [,BUFND=number]
                  [,BUFNI=number]
                  [,BUFSP=number]
                  [,CATALOG=YES|NO]
                  [,CRA=SCRA|UCRA]
                  [,DDNAME=ddname]
                  [,EXLST=address]
                  [,MACRF=(code)]
                  [,MAREA=address]
                  [,MLEN=number]
                  [,PASSWD=address]
                  [,STRNO=number]
```

AM=VSAM Specifies that the access method in use is VSAM. Since this is the only allowable keyword, and it is the default, this parameter is normally not coded.

BSTRNO Specifies the number of strings allocated for access to the base cluster of a path. Typically, one string is required for each concurrent positioning request that is required. Strings are allocated dynamically as required, but specifying a number that is too low or too high may have an effect on performance and/or virtual storage utilization. See the *VSAM Reference* manual for more specific information.

BUFND Specifies the number of I/O buffers that VSAM is to use for data records.

BUFNI Specifies the number of I/O buffers that VSAM is to use for index records.

BUFSP Specifies the total number of bytes of virtual storage space VSAM is to use for both data and index buffers.

CATA-LOG Specifies whether a catalog is being opened as a catalog or as a conventional VSAM data set.

CRA Specifies that a catalog recovery area is to be created either in system storage or in user storage.

DDNAME Gives the name of the DD statement in the JCL that further defines the VSAM object described by this ACB.

EXLST Specifies the address of the EXLST control block to be chained to this ACB.

MACRF Specifies one or more codes that indicate the kinds of processing that will be performed using this ACB. Commonly used MACRF codes are described in the chapters that follow. For a complete list, see Box 18.4.

MAREA Specifies the address of a message area to be used during executions of OPEN and CLOSE macros. This message area can be optionally used to contain information about errors that occur during OPEN and CLOSE processing.

MLEN Specifies the length of the message area referenced by the MAREA parameter.

PASSWD Specifies the address of a field that contains a password. The first byte of the field contains the length of the password field. A zero in the length field indicates no password.

STRNO Specifies the number of requests that will require concurrent data set positioning. VSAM automatically increases this value if required, but specifying a number that is either too low or too high may have an effect on performance and/or virtual storage utilization.

ACB MACRF Subparameter Values

```
MACRF   ([ADR][,CNV][,KEY]
          [,CFX|NFX]
          [,DDN|DSN]
          [,DFR|NDF]
          [,DIR][,SEQ][,SKP]
          [,ICI|NCI]
          [,IN|OUT]
          [,NIS|SIS]
          [,NRM|AIX]
          [,NRS|RST]
          [,NSR|LSR|GSR]
          [,NUB|UBF])
```

ADR ¦ CNV ¦ <u>KEY</u>	These parameters control the way individual records are accessed. ADR indicates addressed access by RBA value, CNV indicates control interval access, and <u>KEY</u> (the default) indicates keyed access by symbolic key or relative record number.
CFX ¦ <u>NFX</u>	CFX specifies that VSAM control blocks and I/O buffers are to be fixed in real storage.
<u>DDN</u> ¦ DSN	DSN specifies that shared control block connection is to be made based on common data set names. With DDN, sharing is based on common ddnames. Chapter 23 discusses sharing of VSAM resources.
DFR ¦ <u>NDF</u>	DFR specifies that the writing of I/O buffers is to be deferred until a WRTBFR request is issued.
DIR ¦ <u>SEQ</u> ¦ SKP	These parameters control the way the data set as a whole is accessed. DIR indicates direct access, <u>SEQ</u> (the default) indicates sequential access, and SKP indicates skip-sequential access.
ICI ¦ <u>NCI</u>	ICI specifies that processing is to be limited to control interval processing for increased performance.
<u>IN</u> ¦ OUT	IN specifies that records will be retrieved from the data set; OUT specifies that records will be written into the data set.
<u>NIS</u> ¦ SIS	SIS specifies that control interval splits are to occur at the insertion point rather than roughly at the midpoint.
<u>NRM</u> ¦ AIX	AIX specifies that the alternate index, rather than the base cluster, is to be processed when the object to which the ACB refers is a path.
<u>NRS</u> ¦ RST	NRS specifies that the data set is not reusable; RST specifies that the data set is reusable.
<u>NSR</u> ¦ LSR ¦ GSR	These parameters are used to control resource sharing. Shared resources are discussed in Chapter 23.

NUB | **UBF** — UBF specifies that the user program, rather than VSAM, is to manage the VSAM I/O buffers. When the UBF option is in effect, the work area specified in the RPL refers to an entire I/O buffer rather than to an individual record work area.

The CLOSE Macro

```
[label]   CLOSE   (address,[(options)],...)
                  [,TYPE=T]
```

The ENDREQ Macro

```
[label] ENDREQ  RPL=address
```

The ERASE Macro

```
[label]   ERASE    RPL=address
```

The EXLST Macro

```
[label]   EXLST    [,AM=VSAM]
                   [,EODAD=address[,A|N][,L])]]
                   [,JRNAD=address[,A|N][,L])]]
                   [,LERAD=address[,A|N][,L])]]
                   [,SYNAD=address[,A|N][,L])]]
                   [,UPAD=address[,A|N][,L])]]
```

AM=VSAM — Specifies that the access method in use is VSAM. Since this is the only allowable keyword, and it is the default, this parameter is normally not coded.

EODAD — Specifies the address of the routine to be executed when VSAM detects the end of the data set while performing sequential access.

JRNAD — Specifies the address of the routine to be executed for journalizing changes that are made to a VSAM data set.

LERAD — Specifies the address of the routine to be executed when VSAM detects a logical error in processing an I/O request.

SYNAD — Specifies the address of the routine to be executed when VSAM detects a physical error in processing an I/O request.

UPAD — Specifies the address of the routine to be executed for user processing during a VSAM request. This routine is given control during the processing of all VSAM executable macros, with the exception of GENCB, MODCB, SHOWCB, and TESTCB.

The GENCB Macro

```
[label]   GENCB   BLK={ACB|RPL|EXLST}
                  [,controlblockparm],...
```

The GET Macro

```
[label]   GET     RPL=address
```

The MODCB Macro

```
[label]   MODCB {ACB=address|RPL=address|EXLST=address}
                [,controlblockparm],...
```

The OPEN Macro

```
[label]   OPEN     (address,[(options)],...)
```

The POINT Macro

```
[label]   POINT    RPL=address
```

The PUT Macro

```
[label]   PUT      RPL=address
```

The RPL Macro

```
[label]   RPL      [ACB=address]
                   [,AM=VSAM]
                   [,AREA=address]
                   [,AREALEN=number]
                   [,ARG=address]
                   [,ECB=address]
                   [,KEYLEN=number]
                   [,MSGAREA=address]
                   [,MSGLEN=number]
                   [,NXTRPL=address]
                   [,OPTCD=(code)]
                   [,RECLEN=number]
                   [,TRANSID=number]
```

ACB Specifies the address of the ACB that controls access to the data set for which the I/O request applies.

AM=VSAM Specifies that the access method in use is VSAM. Since this is the only allowable keyword, and it is the default, this parameter normally is not coded.

AREA Specifies the address of a work area to be used by this I/O request. Depending on the OPTCD value specified, the work area contains either a data record or the address of the data record in a VSAM buffer.

AREALEN Specifies the length of the work area identified in the AREA parameter.

ARG Specifies the address of a field that contains a search argument.

ECB Specifies the address of an event control block (ECB), generally used only for asynchronous processing requests.

KEYLEN Specifies the length of a generic key supplied in the area defined by the ARG parameter.

MSGAREA Specifies the address of an area that VSAM can use to store an error message after a physical error.

MSGLEN Specifies the length of the area defined in the MSGAREA parameters.

NXTRPL Specifies the address of the next RPL in a chain of RPL control blocks.

OPTCD Specifies a code that defines the type of operation requested by the RPL. Commonly used OPTCD codes are described in the chapters that follow. For a complete list, see Box 18.6.

RECLEN Specifies the length of a record being stored as a result of a PUT request.

TRANSID Specifies a number that relates to modified buffers in a shared resource application. The use of shared VSAM resources is introduced in Chapter 23.

RPL OPTCD Parameter Values

```
OPTCD  ([ADR|CNV|KEY]
        [,DIR|SEQ|SKP]
        [,ARD|LRD]
        [,FWD|BWD]
        [,ASY|SYN]
        [,NSP|NUP|UPD]
        [,KEQ|KGE]
        [,FKS|GEN]
        [,NWAITX|WAITX]
        [,LOC|MVE])
```

ADR ¦ CNV ¦ KEY These are the RPL counterparts to the same keywords in the ACB macro and control the way individual records are accessed. If one of these keywords is coded in the RPL, the ACB to which it refers must also have that keyword coded. ADR indicates addressed access by RBA value, CNV indicates control interval access, and KEY (the default) indicates keyed access by symbolic key or relative record number.

DIR ¦ SEQ ¦ SKP — These are the RPL counterparts to the same keywords in the ACB macro and control the way the data set as a whole is accessed. If one of these keywords is coded in the RPL, the ACB to which it refers must also have that keyword coded. DIR indicates direct access, SEQ (the default) indicates sequential access, and SKP indicates skip-sequential access.

ARD ¦ LRD — ARD specifies that an argument supplied in the request determines the record to be located; LRD causes VSAM to establish position on the last record in the data set. Either ARD or LRD, but not both, can be coded. If LRD is specified, BWD must also be specified.

FWD ¦ BWD — FWD specifies that processing is to proceed in a forward direction; BWD indicates that processing is to proceed in a backward direction.

ASY ¦ SYN — ASY specifies asynchronous processing, in which the program continues executing after an I/O request is initiated. Asynchronous processing is discussed in Appendix C.

NSP ¦ NUP ¦ UPD — NSP is valid only when used in conjunction with the DIR access option and causes VSAM to keep track of current position for subsequent sequential access. NUP specifies that a retrieved record will not be later updated or deleted. UPD indicates that a retrieved record can later be updated or deleted.

KEQ ¦ KGE — KEQ specifies that key arguments must equal the symbolic key or relative record number in searching for a record; KGE specifies that when key values do not match, the record having the next higher key value will be accessed.

FKS ¦ GEN — FKS indicates that key arguments contain full key value; GEN indicates that a key argument can contain a generic, or partial, key value.

NWAITX | **WAITX** — WAITX specifies that the UPAD exit routine is to be executed at appropriate times. Exit routines are discussed in Chapter 24.

LOC | **MVE** — LOC specifies that records are to be processed in the I/O buffer; MVE specifies that VSAM is to move records to and from a user work area for I/O requests.

The SHOWCB Macro

```
[label]     SHOWCB {ACB=address|RPL=address|EXLST=address}
                   ,AREA=address
                   ,LENGTH=number
                   ,FIELDS=(parmkeyword[,...])
```

The TESTCB Macro

```
[label]     TESTCB {ACB=address|RPL=address|EXLST=address}
                   [,controlblockparm],...
```

Appendix

F IBM REFERNECE MANUALS

There are a great many IBM reference manuals that are devoted to VSAM and related topics. The specific manuals that should be used depend on the particular operating system version and catalog facility that is in use by the installation. The following manual listings give the titles and order numbers for the reference manuals that are most useful to staff members who develop VSAM applications. The manuals listed are for the latest versions of the following operating systems:

- MVS Extended Architecture (MVS/XA)
- MVS System Product (MVS/SP)
- VSE Advanced Function (VSE/AF)

Since IBM may change manual titles and order numbers from time to time, the current IBM *Bibliography* should be consulted for the most up-to-date list. Also, if your installation uses an older operating system version, other manuals may apply; again the current IBM *Bibliography* should be consulted.

MVS/XA

The following reference manuals are most useful to installations that use the MVS/XA operating system:

GC26–4015 *MVS/XA VSAM Administration Guide*. This reference manual, formerly entitled *VSAM User's Guide,* is intended mainly for Assembler Language programmers and describes how to use VSAM macros in developing VSAM applications.

GC26–4016 *MVS/XA VSAM Administration: Macro Instructions*. This reference manual, formerly entitled *VSAM Reference,* is the main reference manual for VSAM Assembler Language programmers and contains the descriptions of all VSAM macro instructions.

GC26–4019 *MVS/XA AMS Reference for ICF*. This is the main Access Method

Services reference manual for installations that use ICF catalogs. It presents detailed descriptions of all AMS commands that can be issued when ICF catalogs are used.

GC26–4075 *MVS/XA AMS Reference for VSAM Catalogs*. This is the main Access Method Services reference manual for installations that use VSAM catalogs. It presents detailed descriptions of all AMS commands that can be issued when VSAM catalogs are used.

GC26–4041 *MVS/XA Catalog Users Guide*. This reference manual discusses the use of ICF catalogs. It also contains lengthy appendices that discuss the use of VSAM catalogs and OS CVOLs.

GC26–4013 *MVS/XA Data Management Services*. This reference manual discusses MVS data management, concentrating on the concepts and facilities associated with non-VSAM access methods.

GC26–4014 *MVS/XA Data Management Macro Instructions*. This reference manual is intended for Assembler Language programmers and contains descriptions of all non-VSAM data management macro instructions. Descriptions of such macros as GET, PUT, OPEN, and CLOSE are found in this manual.

GC28–1154 *Supervisor Services and Macro Instructions*. This reference manual is intended for Assembler Language programmers and contains descriptions of all macro instructions that are not associated with data management. Descriptions of such macros as ENQ and DEQ are found in this manual.

GC28–1148 *MVS/XA JCL*. This is the main reference manual for the MVS Job Control Language and presents detailed descriptions of all JCL statement parameters.

MVS/SP

The following manuals are most useful to installations that use the MVS operating system with the MVS/370 Data Facility Product:

GC26–4066 *MVS/370 VSAM Users Guide*. This reference manual is intended mainly for Assembler Language programmers and describes how to use VSAM macros in developing VSAM applications. This reference manual is designed to be used in conjunction with *VSAM Reference*.

GC26–4074 *MVS/370 VSAM Reference*. This is the main reference manual for VSAM Assembler programmers and contains the descriptions of all VSAM macro instructions. This reference manual is designed to be used in conjunction with *VSAM Users Guide*.

GC26–4059 *MVS/370 AMS Reference for VSAM catalogs*. This is the main Access Method Services reference manual for installations that use VSAM catalogs. It presents detailed descriptions of all AMS commands that can be issued when ICF catalogs are used.

GC26–4051 *MVS/370 AMS Reference for ICF*. This is the main Access Method Services reference manual for installations that use ICF catalogs. It presents detailed descriptions of all AMS commands that can be issued when ICF catalogs are used.

GC26–4053 *MVS/370 Catalog Users Guide*. This reference manual discusses the use of ICF catalogs. It also contains lengthy appendices that discuss the use of VSAM catalogs and OS CVOLs.

GC26–4058 *MVS/370 Data Management Services*. This reference manual discusses MVS data management, concentrating on the concepts and facilities associated with non-VSAM access methods.

GC26–4057 *MVS/370 Data Management Macro Instructions*. This reference manual is intended for Assembler Language programmers and contains descriptions of all non-VSAM data management macro instructions. Descriptions of such macros as GET, PUT, OPEN, and CLOSE are found in this manual.

GC28–1154 *Supervisor Services and Macro Instructions*. This reference manual is intended for Assembler Language programmers and contains descriptions of all macro instructions that are not associated with data management. Descriptions of such macros as ENQ and DEQ are found in this manual.

GC28–1300 *MVS JCL*. This is the main reference manual for the MVS Job Control Language and presents detailed descriptions of all JCL statement parameters.

VSE/AF

The following manuals are most useful to installations that use the VSE operating system:

SC24–5144 *Using VSE/VSAM Commands and Macros*. This is the main VSE/VSAM reference manual that describes AMS commands and VSAM macro instructions.

SC24–5145 *VSE/VSAM Programmer's Reference*. This is a technically oriented reference manual intended mainly for system programmers who must install and maintain the VSE/VSAM software.

SC24–5210 *VSE/AF Macro User's Guide*. This reference manual is intended for Assembler Language programmers and explains how to use VSE non-VSAM data management and supervisor macro instructions.

SC24–5211 *VSE/AF Macro Reference*. This reference manual is intended for Assembler Language programmers and contains detailed descriptions of non-VSAM VSE data management and supervisor macro instructions.

SC33–6095 *VSE/AF System Control Statements*. This is the main reference manual for the VSE Job Control Language and presents detailed descriptions of all VSE JCL statement parameters.

Appendix

G VSE DIFFERENCES

Many of the examples in this book use MVS JCL statements. However, to application developers, the version of VSAM that operates in the VSE environment is almost identical to the version of VSAM used with MVS. Almost all AMS commands are the same, and the same programming techniques are used in COBOL, PL/I, and Assembler Language to process VSAM data sets. VSAM data sets are also easily passed back and forth between an MVS or MVS/XA computing system and a VSE computing system. This is done by producing a portable copy of any VSAM object on one computing system using EXPORT and then reloading the VSAM object on the other computing system using IMPORT.

With VSE systems, parameters such as INFILE and OUTFILE specify the name of a DLBL statement that describes an input or output file. When these parameters refer to non-VSAM files, they can contain additional information that describes the attributes of the non-VSAM file. The following VSE job step defines a new KSDS cluster and loads it. It uses the INFILE parameter to identify a sequential file and to provide information about the file's attributes:

```
// JOB    DEFINE AND REPRO
// ASSGN  SYS006,X'153'
// DLBL   INPUT,'SEQ INPUT',,SD
// EXTENT SYS006,DSK001,1,0,380,570
// ASSGN  SYS007,X'154'
// DLBL   OUT1,'EMPLOYEE.KSDS',,VSAM
// EXTENT SYS007,DSK002
// EXEC   IDCAMS
   DEFINE CLUSTER
            (NAME        (EMPLOYEE.KSDS)            -
             KEYS        (0 4)                      -
             VOLUMES     (DSK002)                   -
             CYLINDERS   (10 1)                     -
             RECORDSIZE  (26 26)                    -
             FREESPACE   (33 33))
```

```
REPRO   INFILE  (INPUT  ENV (RECFM (FB)        -
                             BLKSZ (300)       -
                             RECSZ (75)        -
                             PDEV  (3380)))    -
        OUTFILE (OUT1)
```

The only difference between a COBOL program that runs in the MVS environment and one that operates in the VSE environment is in the SELECT statement. For VSE, the SELECT statement identifies the symbolic unit that is used in the JCL to define the data set, as in the following VSE SELECT statement:

```
SELECT ESDS-FILE
       ASSIGN TO AS-SYS003
       ORGANIZATION IS SEQUENTIAL
       ACCESS IS SEQUENTIAL
       FILE STATUS IS STATUS-KEY.
```

In an ASSIGN clause for an ESDS, the symbolic unit name must be preceded by the characters ''AS-''; for a KSDS or RRDS, the ''AS-'' characters must be omitted. All other statements are coded in the same way for a VSE COBOL program as for an MVS program.

INDEX

A

B

C

D

E

F

G

H

I

M

N

O

P

Q

R

S

T

U

V

W

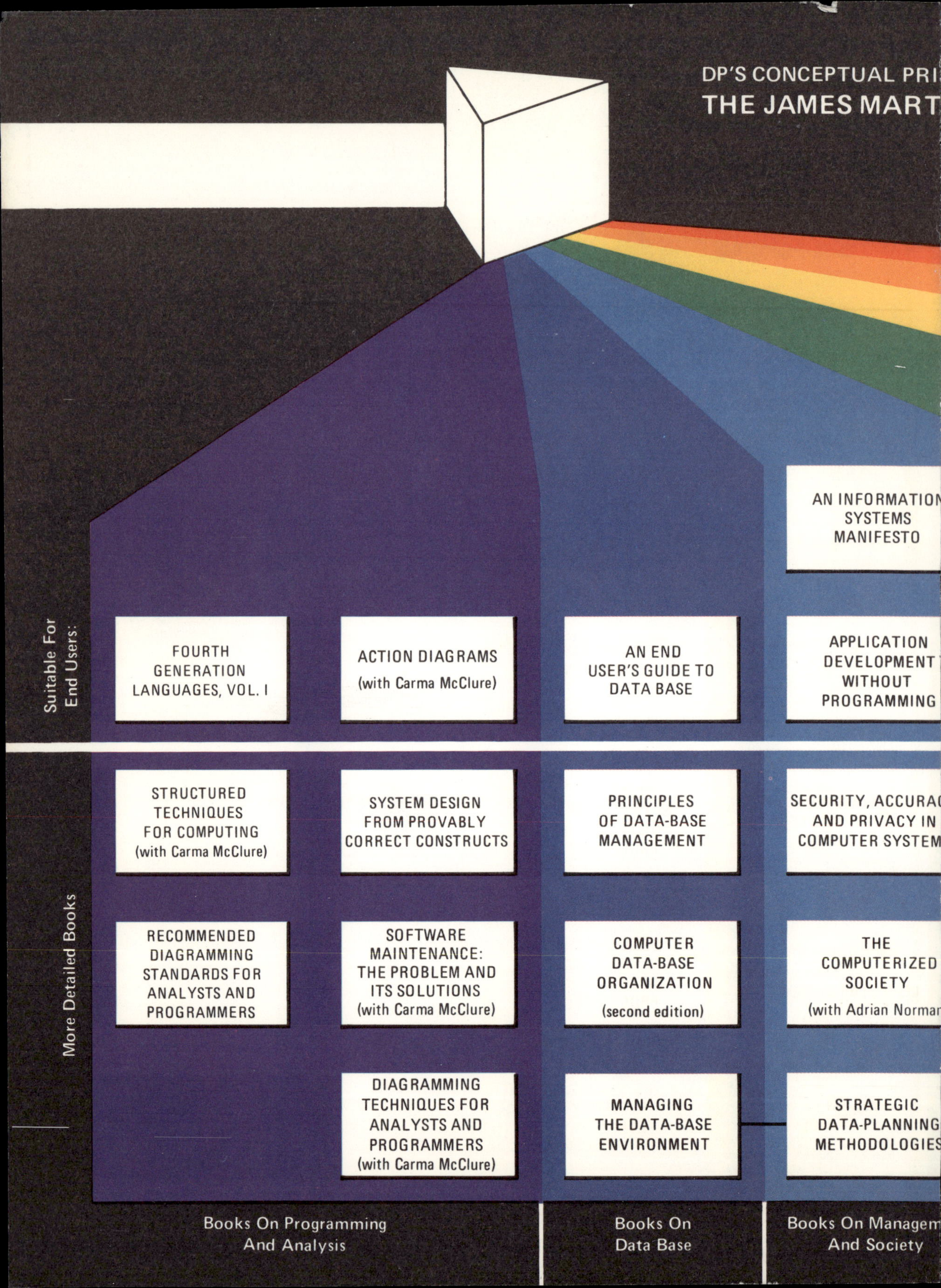

DP'S CONCEPTUAL PRI
THE JAMES MART
AN INFORMATION SYSTEMS MANIFESTO
Suitable For End Users:
FOURTH GENERATION LANGUAGES, VOL. I
ACTION DIAGRAMS (with Carma McClure)
AN END USER'S GUIDE TO DATA BASE
APPLICATION DEVELOPMENT WITHOUT PROGRAMMING
More Detailed Books
STRUCTURED TECHNIQUES FOR COMPUTING (with Carma McClure)
SYSTEM DESIGN FROM PROVABLY CORRECT CONSTRUCTS
PRINCIPLES OF DATA-BASE MANAGEMENT
SECURITY, ACCURA AND PRIVACY IN COMPUTER SYSTEM
RECOMMENDED DIAGRAMMING STANDARDS FOR ANALYSTS AND PROGRAMMERS
SOFTWARE MAINTENANCE: THE PROBLEM AND ITS SOLUTIONS (with Carma McClure)
COMPUTER DATA-BASE ORGANIZATION (second edition)
THE COMPUTERIZED SOCIETY (with Adrian Norma
DIAGRAMMING TECHNIQUES FOR ANALYSTS AND PROGRAMMERS (with Carma McClure)
MANAGING THE DATA-BASE ENVIRONMENT
STRATEGIC DATA-PLANNING METHODOLOGIE
Books On Programming And Analysis
Books On Data Base
Books On Managem And Society